Builder's Essentials

Estimating Building Costs

Wayne J. DelPico

RSMeans

Builder's Essentials

Estimating Building Costs

For the Residential & Light Commercial Contractor

Wayne J. DelPico

Reed Construction Data.

Copyright ©2004
Reed Construction Data, Inc.
Construction Publishers & Consultants
63 Smiths Lane
Kingston, MA 02364-0800
(781) 422-5000
www.rsmeans.com
RSMeans is a product line of Reed Construction Data

The editor for this book was Andrea St. Ours. The managing editor was Mary Greene. The production manager was Michael Kokernak. The production coordinator was Marion Schofield. The electronic publishing specialist was Jonathan Forgit. The proofreader was Robin Richardson. The book and cover were designed by Norman R. Forgit.

Printed in the United States of America

10 9 8 7 6 5 4 3

Library of Congress Catalog Number Pending

ISBN 0-87629-741-6

Dedication
To Krisanne, Maria-Laina, and Kristina.

Table of Contents

Foreword

"Estimate" may be one of the most misunderstood words in the construction industry, and the job description of an estimator is also up for debate. Consider this: a contractor submits a price to perform a project based on the estimates of a variety of subcontractors and suppliers, and the assessment of the company's own ability to perform in relationship to its *actual* ability to perform. An estimate at the time the price is submitted cannot be considered a "best guess" or an approximation of anticipated cost. It must be an actual, real number arrived at by a competent estimator, someone who is knowledgeable in estimating. When costs begin to go over, or budgets are blown, then the estimate was just a "guess," and the person responsible really was not as competent or properly trained as an estimator should be. Interestingly enough, if the same project makes money or stays on budget, then that estimate and the estimator are hailed as genius.

The truth of the matter is that in both scenarios, the estimator started out with the intent to produce an estimate that would create revenue and ultimately produce a profit. How can the results be so different? It is not hard to see why the word "estimate" and the job of the estimator are open to interpretation.

Estimating takes on a whole new significance in today's competitive construction marketplace. If you consider the number of start-up companies, the maturing workforce, and new technology in both the field and the office, estimating becomes perhaps the most important function of the successful building company.

The key to producing an accurate estimate lies in the organization of the information that will be used to determine the amount of material, labor, and equipment required for the project. Based on this information, the estimator can apply prices, contingencies, and profit. The estimating process does not end here. Once the project is awarded and the work begins, the original estimate will be revisited over and over again. It will be reviewed, referred to, praised, criticized, second-guessed, and, yes, even cursed as the project progresses. And in the end, it will be put to the final test of profitable or not.

It is in the best interest of the construction industry that we develop competent estimators and accurate estimates. Successful builders are not afraid of competition. What they *are* afraid of is the ever-present "low ball" estimate that only serves to put legitimate pricing in question. Following the logical estimating sequence and organization of information outlined in this text will greatly improve an estimator's chances of producing sound estimates. Students learning estimating will benefit from the author's experience and advice on how to approach estimating. And, finally, no matter how you are currently doing your estimating, this text will either prove that you are doing it right or provide you with a system that will increase your accuracy and, in the end, make you more profitable.

— Howard Chandler, Executive Officer, Builders Association of
    Greater Boston

About the Author & Contributors

Wayne J. DelPico is Vice President of The Mulligan Company, Inc., where he currently oversees residential and commercial development and building projects in southeastern Massachusetts. He has more than 25 years' experience in construction management, and has been involved in projects throughout most of the United States. Mr. DelPico holds a degree in Civil Engineering from Northeastern University in Boston, where he now teaches construction estimating and project management. He is the author of *Plan Reading & Material Takeoff*, also published by RSMeans, and is a lecturer on construction estimating topics in programs presented throughout the U.S.

About the Reviewers

Howard Chandler, reviewer of this book and author of the "Foreword," is the Executive Officer of the Builders Association of Greater Boston, where he represents residential and light commercial builders throughout the region. He has spent more than 30 years in many aspects of the construction industry—as the owner of a residential construction company; manager of field operations for a firm specializing in commercial, industrial, and institutional construction; and as a consultant, educator, and estimator. Mr. Chandler is a lecturer at Wentworth Institute of Technology, where he currently teaches estimating and scheduling.

Robert W. Mewis, CCC, reviewer of this publication and author of the "Estimating Resources" section, is a Senior Engineer/Editor at RSMeans. He is responsible for overseeing several components of the Means cost database, in addition to teaching estimating seminars throughout the country. Prior to his tenure at Means, Mr. Mewis served as construction cost estimator for Hanscomb Associates and Chief Estimator for Franny's Landscape and Construction, where he was responsible for all bidding, takeoff, and development of material databases.

Introduction

Estimating has always been one of the weakest links in the construction process. Most contractors can recall one or two craftsmen whose talents have been enviable, but who have ultimately failed miserably in business. Many of these failures have been a result of poor estimating practices. As common a problem as estimating appears to be, a systematic approach is clearly needed.

This book was created as a reference for contractors—in both the new and remodeling markets—who want to master organized, efficient industry standards for estimating residential and light commercial projects. It is designed and presented for use by the professional contractor or homebuilder who has some experience in the industry and is familiar with the materials and tasks typical to building projects. The chapters provide step-by-step guidelines—ideal for learning estimating.

For novices, *Estimating Building Costs* explains the fundamentals of the estimating process, which will become an essential part of their work. Experienced estimators will find the book useful for reviewing their own methods and enhancing their expertise. Regardless of whether the "estimating staff" is a dedicated person among a company's many employees, or the same individual who performs the work, the principles are the same. The text is written in what is referred to as *general knowledge estimating practice*, from the point of view of the general contractor's estimator, yet it is equally helpful as a foundation for subcontractors' estimators.

Chapters 1 and 2 explain what estimators can expect to find on the drawings and in the specifications—the information and details necessary to create an accurate estimate. These documents are complementary tools that must be reviewed and understood before attempting to prepare a project estimate. Chapter 3 presents the mathematical principles needed to accurately take off material quantities, by calculating area and volume.

Chapter 4 reviews the accepted rules for quantity survey, or *takeoff*, and the mechanics of the takeoff process. Chapter 5 explains in detail how material costs are derived, how to determine allowances for waste, and how to assign markups typical to material and labor. These are essential to understanding how a unit price estimate is built. The chapter also covers labor productivity, crew and individual tasks, and budgeting for subcontractor work.

The next group of chapters is organized according to the Construction Specifications Institute's (CSI) MasterFormat—the most widely recognized and used system for organizing construction information in specifications and estimates. Learning estimating techniques for each building system in this format helps estimators understand and apply them according to the industry's most professional standards. Each chapter describes specific estimating tasks for that particular trade—including special cost considerations, and standard quantity takeoff guidelines for each building system and material. The examples and easy-to-follow steps can be referred to time and again. These chapters include all of the work you might encounter on a typical residential or light commercial project—from site construction and concrete and masonry, to windows and doors, siding, roofing, mechanical and electrical systems, and finish work.

Chapter 19 explains computerized estimating, including benefits and cautions. It includes tips for developing and customizing simple spreadsheet estimating applications, rather than relying on "canned" software alone.

Chapter 20 introduces two topics crucial to finalizing a reliable estimate, yet rarely addressed by books or courses on estimating: profit and contingencies. The chapter addresses both the tangible and intangible aspects of residential and light commercial projects that must be evaluated before assigning a suitable profit or adding a contingency amount to cover unknowns. Some of the factors to evaluate are risk, scheduling impacts, and contractual obligations.

The "Estimating Resources" section at the end of this book provides an overview of professional construction cost databases. This published data can be a useful tool for those who lack reliable historical costs of their own. It allows you to check pricing on thousands of items and tasks, both common and specialized, in residential and light commercial construction.

Accurate construction estimating is an essential skill of every successful contractor. *Estimating Building Costs* gives you a course you can rely on—whether for review or first-time learning—to establish your estimating skills at a truly professional level.

—Wayne J. DelPico

Chapter One

The Working Drawings

Estimating projects requires fluency in the language and symbols used in construction plans. This chapter provides an overview of a project's working drawings and plans. It does not offer detailed instruction in plan reading, but will review the organization of the plans and the information necessary for estimating.*

The Role of the Drawings

The three terms most often used to refer to the graphic portion of the documents for a building project are:

- Plans
- Drawings
- Blueprints

For the purpose of this text, these terms are synonymous and can be used interchangeably. They are the graphic representation or illustration of the project, and comprise the lines, symbols, and abbreviations printed on paper that represent the owner's wishes, as interpreted by the architect. The plans and specifications (discussed further in Chapter 2) together make up the contract documents and form the basis of the contract for construction.

Design Development

Most drawings develop over several generations of review and modification as a result of owner input, coordination with other design disciplines, building code compliance, and general fine-tuning. This process is referred to as *design development* and occurs before the release of the final version of drawings, called the *working drawings*. Working drawings are the completed design—a code-compliant representation of the project, ready for bidding and, ultimately, construction. They will be the focus of this chapter and are the prerequisite for preparing a detailed unit price estimate. (Note: "Preliminary" drawings created early in the design development process may be used as a basis for budget estimates,

For more than the basic review here, consult Plan Reading & Material Takeoff, *published by RSMeans.*

but budget estimating requires specific skills of seasoned professional estimators who have years of experience developing unit price estimates.)

The completed drawings become a "set," which incorporates all adjustments, changes, and refinements made by the architect or engineer as the final step in design development. Working drawings should comply with all applicable building codes, including any local ordinances having jurisdiction. Drawings should include all the information you will need to prepare a detailed estimate and eventually build the project. The set of working drawings consists of various disciplines of design, including the architectural or *core drawings* design, structural engineering to ensure that the structure will support the imposed loads, and mechanical and electrical engineering to make the space habitable and functional.

All buildings are constructed with a definitive purpose and require professionals skilled in specific areas to make the design suitable. Just as most contractors develop an expertise in one market type of construction (residential, light commercial, etc.), design professionals focus on one general area of expertise. A good example is a commercial kitchen designer for restaurant kitchens. Specialty drawings, included as part of the set, often require considerable coordination with the mechanical and electrical systems, as well as with the core drawings.

Other drawings in the set include designs that are less concerned with the structure itself than with support services, such as utilities, that will be provided to the structure. These *civil* or *site drawings* include grading and drainage plans, which indicate how surface precipitation will be channeled away from the structure; landscaping and irrigation design; paving; and curbing layout. Ordinary site improvements, such as fencing, patios, walks, flagpoles, and the like, are shown on a kind of "catch-all" *site improvements drawing*.

Some drawings are cross-overs and show items of work or systems that may also be found in another set. For example, site electrical drawings indicating site lighting, power distribution, and low-voltage wiring (cable TV, telephone, and data) may also be shown on the electrical drawings.

Organization of the Working Drawings

There is a distinct organizational structure to the working drawings, which is almost universally accepted, and is as follows.

- **Architectural drawings:** Core drawings showing the layout of the building and its use of space. They convey the aesthetic value of the structure and show the dimensions and placement of all key features. The first architectural drawings in a set generally show large areas in less detail. As one progresses through the architectural set, the level of detail increases. These drawings are prefixed by the letter "A" and sequentially numbered.
- **Structural drawings:** Illustrate how the various load-carrying systems will transmit live and dead loads of the structure to the earth. Structural design is based on the architectural features, and is

designed around the core drawings. (For example, columns and beams are designed to avoid interrupting a space.) Structural drawings are prefixed by the letter "S" and are sequentially numbered.

- **Mechanical drawings:** Illustrate the physical systems of a structure, such as plumbing, fire suppression/protection, and HVAC (heating, ventilating, and air conditioning) systems. These drawings may be prefixed by the letter "M" for mechanical, or "H" for heating. Plumbing drawings use the letter "P," and fire suppression drawings use "FP" (fire protection), "SP" (sprinkler system), or "F" (fire). The drawings are all sequentially numbered and shown mainly in plan view.

- **Electrical drawings:** Illustrate the electrical requirements of the project, including power distribution, lighting, and low-voltage specialty wiring, such as for fire alarms, telephone/data, and technology wiring. They often show the provision for power wiring of equipment illustrated on other types of drawings. They are prefixed by the letter "E" and are sequentially numbered.

- **Specialty drawings:** Illustrate the unique requirements of various spaces' special uses (such as kitchens, libraries, retail spaces, and home theatre systems). They define the coordination among other building systems, most commonly the mechanical and electrical systems. The drawings are sequentially numbered, and named according to the type of drawings. For example, "K" might be used for kitchen drawings, "F" for fixture drawings, and so forth.

- **Site drawings:** Illustrate the structure's relationship to the property, including various engineering improvements to the site, such as the sanitary system, utilities, paving, walks, curbing, and so forth. They are sequentially numbered, but have a less formal naming convention, open to the interpretation of the design engineer. They are easily recognized from the core drawings, since they only deal with the site.

Drawings for each of the above categories will show only the work of the particular discipline. All lines and symbols that are not specifically related to that discipline are shown in a lighter line weight, or "grayed-out." This helps coordinate or locate the work of a specific drawing with other drawings that indicate adjacent, but unrelated work.

There are some common, basic elements in a set of contract drawings, which will be discussed in the following sections. These include a cover sheet, title block, and revisions. (Some revisions will be encountered on every drawing.)

The Cover Sheet

The cover sheet, although very basic in nature, is one of the most important pages in a set of drawings. It lists information, such as the name of the project; the location; and the names of the architects, engineers, owners, and other consultants involved in the design. The cover sheet also lists the drawings that comprise the set in the order they will appear. The drawing list is organized by the number of each drawing and the title of the page on which it appears. The cover sheet may also list information specifically required by the building code having jurisdiction over the design of the project, including the total square foot area of the structure, the building code use group the structure will fall under, and the type of construction.

Another important element on the cover sheet is a list of abbreviations or graphic symbols used in the drawing set. There is often a section that contains "general notes," such as, "All dimensions shall be verified in the field," or "All dimensions are to face of masonry." These notes help set the standards for background information that you will encounter throughout the drawings. In the absence of a separate set of bound specifications (most common in the residential market, where separate specs are not often written), the cover sheet may list the general technical specifications that will govern the quality of materials used in the work. Optional information, such as a locus plan locating the project with respect to local landmarks or roadways or an architectural rendering of the structure, may be included in the cover sheet.

Title Block

The title block is located in the lower right-hand corner of the drawing and should include the following information:

- The prefixed number of the sheet (so you can identify the discipline and order in which it belongs)
- The name of the drawing (e.g., "First Floor Plan")
- The date of the drawing
- The initials of the draftsperson
- Any revisions to the final set of drawings

The date and scope of the revisions should be noted within the title block. If there is not enough space available, the revisions should be noted close to it. The title block should specify whether the entire drawing is one scale, or whether the scale varies per detail, as in the case of a sheet of details. Sets of drawings for commercial projects require a stamp (and usually a signature) of the architect or engineer responsible for the design.

Revisions

Often, after the set of working drawings has been completed, recommendations are made for correction or clarification of a particular detail, plan, or elevation. While major changes may require redrafting an entire sheet, smaller changes are shown as a revision of the original. All changes must be clearly recognizable. They are indicated with a *revision marker*, which encloses the revised detail within a scalloped line that resembles a cloud. Tied to the revision marker is a triangle that encloses the number of the revision. Revisions are noted in the title block, or close to it, by date and number. This procedure provides a mechanism for identifying the latest version of drawings.

Graphic Formats Used in Drawings

There are accepted standards or methods that architects and engineers use to present graphic information. Different views ensure that all required information is available on the drawings. There are six main graphic formats:

- Plan views
- Elevations
- Sections
- Details
- Schedules
- Diagrams

Each method illustrates the various aspects of a project from a different viewpoint. The information is most effectively presented when multiple views are used together. Showing the same item in different views helps confirm and add to the information that can be seen in a single view.

Plan Views

The most common graphic view, the plan view, is presented as if looking down on the space. Plan views form the basis of the project, and often provide the most complete view. The most common plan view is the *architectural floor plan*, which shows doors, windows, walls, and partitions.

Variations of plan views include *structural, fire suppression, plumbing, HVAC,* and *electrical plans*. Each shows the work of the respective trades in plan view as they fit into the architectural floor plan. Other types of plan views include *reflected ceiling plans* and *partial plan views*, which illustrate a particular area and enlarge it for clarity. Partial views are most often used in areas of high congestion or detail. *Demolition plans* show proposed changes to the existing floor plan. *Roof plans* show the roof layout as would be seen from overhead.

Plan views provide dimensions, which help you to calculate areas. Dimensions should be accurate, clear, and complete, showing both exterior and interior measurements of the space. Plan views are also a starting point from which the architect directs the reader to other drawings for more information.

Elevations

Elevations provide a pictorial view of the walls of the structure, similar to a photograph of a wall taken perpendicular to both the vertical and horizontal planes. Exterior elevations may be titled based on their location with respect to the headings of a compass (north, south, east, or west elevation), or their physical location (front, rear, right side, or left side elevation). The scale of the elevation should be noted either in the title block or under the title of the elevation.

Interior elevations provide views of the walls of the inside of a room. They illustrate architectural features, such as casework, standing and running trims, fixtures, doors, and windows. Exterior elevations provide a clear depiction of doors and windows, often using numbers or letters in circles to show types that correspond to information provided in the door and window schedule. In addition, elevations show the surface materials of walls, and any changes within the plane of the elevation or facade. While the floor plan shows measurements in a horizontal plane, elevations provide measurements in a vertical plane with respect to a horizontal plane. These dimensions provide a vertical measure of floor-to-floor heights, windowsill or head heights, floor-to-plate heights, roof heights, ceiling heights, or a variety of dimensions from a fixed horizontal surface. You can use these measurements to calculate quantities of materials needed.

Building Sections

The building section, commonly referred to as the *section*, is a "vertical slice" or cut-through of a particular part of the building. It offers a view through a part of the structure not found on other drawings. Several different sections may be incorporated into the drawings. Sections taken from a plan view are called *cross-sections*; those taken from an elevation are referred to as *longitudinal sections*, or simply *wall sections*. Wall sections provide an exposed view of the building components and their arrangement within the wall itself. By referring to sections, in conjunction with floor plans and elevations, you can see the composition of the building component.

Details

For greater clarification and understanding, certain areas of a floor plan, elevation, or a particular part of the drawing may need to be enlarged. This enlargement provides information that is critical to a part of the building item that may otherwise not be available in another view. Enlargements are drawn to a larger scale and are referred to as *details*. Details can be found either on the sheet where they are first referenced, or grouped together on a separate detail sheet included in the various disciplines they reference. The detail is shown in larger scale to provide additional space for dimensions and notes. Details are not limited to architectural drawings, but can be used in structural and site plans and, to a lesser extent, in mechanical or electrical plans.

Schedules

In an effort to keep drawings from becoming cluttered with too much printed information or too many details, architects have devised a system to organize all types of repetitive information in an easy-to-read table, known as a *schedule*. Schedules list information pertaining to a similar group of items, such as doors, windows, room finishes, columns, trusses, and light or plumbing fixtures. The most common schedules are door, window, and room finish schedules. However, information on any repetitive type of item can be assembled into a table and incorporated in a set of drawings.

Schedules are not limited to architectural drawings, but can be found in any discipline included within the set. A typical door schedule lists each door by number, or *mark*, and provides information on size and type, thickness, frame material, composition, and hardware. In addition, the door schedule will provide specific instructions or requirements for an individual door, such as fire ratings, undercutting, weatherstripping, or vision panels. In the "remarks" portion of the schedule, the architect lists any non-standard requirements or special notes to the installer.

Diagrams

Some of the information presented in the set of drawings is more diagrammatical than pictorial. A *diagram* illustrates how the various components of a system are configured, and is often provided for purposes of coordination. Diagrams are commonly used for mechanical and electrical drawings, because of the complex nature of the work. Common examples include diagrams for fire alarm risers, waste and vent piping risers, and fire protection.

Drawing Conventions

Certain conventions have been adopted to provide a standard for drawings—from one design firm to another. The most common graphic features are lines, in-fill techniques, and shading, which can often contain subtle, but very important information relative to the detail shown. While most of these conventions are widely accepted and practiced, there will always be minor deviations based on local practices. This is most apparent in the use of abbreviations and symbols. In many cases, any unfamiliar symbols and abbreviations will usually become clear by studying the drawings.

Lines

Drawings must convey a great deal of information in a relatively small space, where there is no room for a lot of wording. Consequently, different types of lines are used to communicate information. The most common ones are discussed below.

- **Main object line:** A thick, heavy, unbroken line that defines the outline of the structure or object. Used for the main outlines of walls, floors, elevations, details, or sections.
- **Dimension line:** A light, fine line with arrowheads or "tic" marks at each end, used to show the measurements of the main object lines. The arrowheads fall between extension lines that extend from the

main object lines to show the limits of the item drawn. The number that appears within the break in the dimension line is the required measurement between extension lines.

- **Extension line:** A light line that extends from the edge or end of the main object line, touching the arrowheads. Used together with dimension lines to help you determine the limits of a particular feature.
- **Hidden or invisible line:** A light dashed line of equal segments that indicates the outlines of an object hidden from view, under or behind some other part of the structure, such as a foundation shown in elevation that would be below grade.
- **Center line:** A light line of alternating long and short segments that indicates the center of a particular object. Frequently labeled with the letter "C" superimposed over the letter "L."

Material Indication Symbols and Shading

In-filling certain graphic features on a drawing helps convey their content or composition. In-filling can indicate whether the feature is solid, as in the case of cast-in-place concrete, or hollow, as with concrete masonry block. In-fills are called *material indication symbols*. Because of the different views used on drawings, various materials must be recognizable at each view, from plan to section to elevation. As with abbreviations, material indications symbols are subject to change based on specific materials used in various parts of the country.

Shading

Architects and engineers can convey information in a subtler manner by changing the intensity of a particular feature. This effect, called *shading*, increases or decreases the focus on the item, merely by its intensity. Items in the foreground or focus are often drawn darker or thicker. Objects in the background are lighter in color, and drawn less sharply. Shading is often used to differentiate between proposed and existing work on renovation projects.

Graphic Symbols

Graphic symbols are another means of providing a standardized way to recognize information and depict repetitive information on drawings. *Section markers* indicate where a section is cut through an object, and can be directional or non-directional. *Elevation symbols* direct the reader to the drawing that contains a noted elevation. They indicate differences in vertical height, such as the distance between floors, and provide a reference point to use in calculating the height of components in walls or partitions.

Frequently, the design professional draws a feature, and, to save space on the page, uses a *break in a continuous line*. This symbol conveys that the feature is not drawn to scale. Geometric shapes with letters, numbers, or dimensions within the shape define certain features or main objects. This graphic symbol is frequently used to name windows, doors, rooms, partition types, and ceiling heights. The important information is within the shape, not the shape itself. The shape used will often be based on the preference of the individual design professional or the local accepted practice.

Trade-Specific Symbols

Like graphic symbols, trade-specific symbols depict items that are common to the various trades. Because of the highly diagrammatic nature of mechanical and electrical drawings, there is an abundance of unique, trade-specific symbols used on these drawings. Engineers typically provide legends that define the symbols used. Some, such as for a water closet or toilet, are highly recognizable because they mirror the feature in real life.

Abbreviations

Abbreviations are used to save design professionals time, as well as space, on drawings. There is a wide and varied selection of abbreviations used in daily practice. It is not neccesary to memorize each abbreviation. Standard practice is to list the abbreviations on the cover sheet of the set of drawings. This compilation of abbreviations saves time by locating the meaning of each abbreviation in a central location.

Scale

Since there are various physical limitations to drawing a building's actual size on a piece of paper, the drawings retain their relationship to the actual size of the building using a ratio, or *scale*, between full size and what is seen on the drawings. There are two major types of scales: the *architect's scale* and the *engineer's scale*.

Architect's Scale

The architect's scale is used for building drawings, as well as the engineering disciplines. The actual architect's scale may be flat, like a ruler, or three-sided. The three-sided architect's scale has ten separate scales: 1/8" and 1/4", 1" and 1/2", 3/4" and 3/8", 3/16" and 3/32", and 1-1/12" and 3". The one remaining side is in inches, similar to a ruler. For example, when used on a floor plan that is 1/4" scale, each 1/4" delineation represents one foot. The same rules apply for 1/8" scale, in that each 1/8" segment on the drawing represents 1'-0" of actual size. The same approach applies to each of the other scales. There is no strict convention that states which scale should be used on which drawings. In general, as the area of detail being drawn becomes smaller, the scale often increases. For example, a floor plan may be fine at 1/4" = 1'-0", yet the detail of an element within that floor plan would be better illustrated in 1/2" or 3/4" = 1'-0" for clarity.

Engineer's Scales

The engineer's scale is similar to the architect's scale and is typically (though not exclusively) used to prepare civil drawings. The difference is the size of the increments on the sides of the scale. The engineer's scale has six scales: 10, 20, 30, 40, 50, and 60. For example, the 10 scale refers to 10 feet per inch; the 20 scale is 20 feet per inch, and so on. Other specialty scales are divided into even smaller increments, such as 100.

The engineer's scale is used to measure distance on site plans, when it is greater than would be encountered in the plans of the building. Occasionally, architects and engineers include a detail strictly for visual clarification. These details are labeled "NTS," meaning "Not to Scale." This lets the reader know that the details are not for determining quantities and measurements, but for illustrating a feature that would otherwise be unclear. Diagrams are also typically not drawn to scale.

Civil Drawings

Commercial and custom residential projects typically include a *site plan*, which illustrates the relationship of the proposed structure to the building's lot, as well as the various site improvements needed to accommodate the new building. The grouping of different types of site drawings, such as utility and drainage, grading, site improvement, and landscaping plans, are known under the general classification of *civil drawings*. Civil drawings encompass all work that pertains to projects other than the structure itself. They have some unique conventions and nomenclature that merit a separate review. The most obvious difference between civil drawings and architectural drawings is the use of the engineer's scale. (As mentioned earlier, smaller scales are used on site drawings to indicate much larger areas.) It is important to note the scale in order to avoid errors in measuring during the takeoff. To avoid confusion, it is best to use the title block to clarify the type of drawing and scale.

The following sections review the most common terms and symbols associated with the various civil drawings.

Site Plan

The main purpose of the site plan is to locate the structure within the confines of the building lot. Even the most basic site plans clearly establish the building's dimensions, usually by the foundation's size and the distance to property lines. The latter, called the *setback* dimensions, are shown in feet and hundredths of a foot, versus feet and inches on architectural drawings. For example, the architectural dimension of 22'-6" would be 22.50' on a site plan. This decimal system is used because it is the basis of measurement for the land surveyor, the predominant engineer responsible for laying out the site.

As a starting point for the site design, a site survey is performed by a registered land surveyor, who also records special conditions. These may include existing natural features, such as trees or water, as well as man-made improvements, such as walks, paving, fences, or other structures. The new site plan shows how the existing features will be maintained, modified, or removed to accommodate the new design.

Another chief purpose of the site plan is to show the unique surface conditions, or *topography*, of the lot. Changes in the elevation of the lot, such as slopes, hills, valleys, and other variations in the surface, are shown on a site plan by means of a *contour*, which is a line connecting points of equal elevation. An *elevation* is a distance above or below a known point of reference, called a *datum*. The datum could be sea level, or an arbitrary plane of reference established for the particular building. For projects in which the topography must be shown separately for clarity, a *grading plan* is used.

A known elevation on the site for use as a reference point during construction is called a *benchmark*. The benchmark is established in reference to the datum, and is commonly noted on the site drawing with a physical description and its elevation relative to the datum. For example: *"Northeast corner of catch basin rim—Elev. 102.34"* might be a typical benchmark found on a site plan. When individual elevations, or *spot grades*, are required for other site features, they are noted with a "+" and then the grade. For example: *"+123.45"* would designate a spot grade for a particular feature. (Grades are accurate to two decimal places, whereas contours are expressed as whole numbers.) Some site plans include a small map, called a *locus*, showing the general location of the property in respect to local highways, roads, and adjacent pieces of property.

Drainage and Utility Plans

Larger projects will have several site plans showing different scopes of related or similar work, such as drainage and utility plans. Utility drawings show locations of water, gas, sanitary sewer, and electric utilities that will service the building. Drainage plans detail how surface water will be collected, channeled, and dispersed on or off site. Both plans illustrate, in plan view, the size, length, and type of pipes and special connections or terminations of the various piping. Because the effluent in certain types of pipe moves by gravity, the elevation of each end of the pipe must be different.

Certain site plans require clarification in the form of a detail, similar to the architectural detail. Classic examples are sections through paving, pre-cast structures, pipe trenches, and curbing. Details are not limited to scaled drafting, but occasionally appear in the form of perspective drawings, which are not drawn to scale and are used as a means of clarification only.

Landscaping Plans

Landscaping plans show the location of various species of plantings, as well as lawns and garden areas. The plantings are noted with an abbreviation, typically three letters, along with the quantity of the particular species. This designation corresponds to a planting schedule, which is a complete listing of plantings by common name, Latin or species name, and quantity and size. Notes describing planting procedures or handling specifications accompany the schedule. Irrigation drawings may be included, which illustrate how the landscaping elements should be watered.

Paving/Curbing Layout Drawings

To accurately show the layout of parking lots and driveways, a *paving/curbing layout drawing* is needed. This plan shows the various types of bituminous, concrete, and brick paving and curbing, and the limits of each—helpful for calculating areas and measurements. Again, it is important to review the legend symbols in order to clearly delineate where one material ends and another begins. Details showing sections through the surface are used to differentiate between thickness and the substrate below.

Site Improvement Drawings

When the project warrants, separate drawings may be needed to clarify various site improvements, such as walks, retaining walls, patio paving, fences, steps, benches, play areas, and flagpoles. Site improvement drawings are often used as a "catch-all" to show the miscellaneous items that do not fall neatly into one of the above classifications of work.

Existing Conditions Site Drawings

For projects with existing drainage, utilities, and structures, an *existing conditions plan* is provided, which is invaluable for understanding and calculating the difference between actual conditions and proposed work. The existing conditions are shown in the background "grayed out" or lightly shaded, and the new work is shown darker in the foreground. Other methods include showing existing conditions as dotted or broken lines and proposed conditions as solid, darker lines. Sometimes test boring logs are provided, which document engineering tests to determine the load-bearing and general quality of the subsurface at the site.

Conclusion

This chapter reviewed the different types of plans and drawing elements that together comprise a full set of working drawings. It is essential to become familiar with the drawings prior to the site inspection and quantity takeoff. A thorough review of the drawings will reveal discrepancies or omissions and will help determine whether to proceed with the next step in bidding the job. It should also be noted that the various views should be used together. Information located on one drawing can often be corroborated on another. This checks and balances process is fundamental in estimating.

Chapter Two

Understanding the Specifications

As owners become more informed and technically savvy, they are no longer satisfied by the term, "industry standard" when defining the quality of materials or workmanship to be included in a project. As a result, many contractors, especially in the high-end residential market, use technical specifications to establish the quality level for owners and as a guideline for subcontractors. Over the last decade, in fact, specifications have become increasingly popular as *the* standard of measurement for quality.

The Role of the Specifications

The specifications, or *specs*, as they are commonly referred to, are part of the contract documents, along with the working set of drawings (discussed in Chapter 1), and define in detail the processes and materials for the project. Technical information about the quality of materials and workmanship is not always incorporated on the drawings themselves, due to lack of space and the need to maintain clarity. For most light commercial and many upscale residential projects, working drawings are issued with a separate set of specifications. Even the simplest projects have some specifications, whether incorporated on the drawings or issued as a separate document to guide the contractor and subcontractors.

The specs perform a variety of functions, including:

- Serving as the legal basis for the Contract for Construction
- Defining the quality or grade of materials to be used in the project
- Defining the acceptable workmanship or providing standards to judge workmanship
- Providing guidelines for resolving disputes between parties to the contract
- Providing a basis for accurately estimating cost
- Complementing the graphic portion of the project, the drawings

The specs are intended to be used in conjunction with the drawings. If the drawings are the *quantitative* representation of the project shown in a graphic format, then the specs are the *qualitative* requirements of the project described in a written document.

Technologies, processes, and products are continually evolving in the construction industry, and architects and engineers incorporate these advancements more frequently into their designs. As a result, highly specific information is needed in the specifications. The materials and processes are described in such detail that the intent of the designer, as well as the product or system, can be upheld in case of a dispute or if products are installed incorrectly.

The specifications serve as a basis for bidding and performing the work. The person preparing the specifications, sometimes called a *specification* or *technical writer*, makes every effort to cover all of the items or segments of work shown on the working drawings. In the past, if there was a discrepancy between the specifications and the drawings, the specifications generally took precedence. This is no longer always the case. Many specifications now state that when there is a discrepancy between the plans and specifications, whichever results in the greater quantity, is more expensive, or is of greater benefit to the project will supersede.

Organizing Specifications by CSI MasterFormat

Throughout this book, we will refer to the CSI MasterFormat, which is the most widely accepted system for arranging construction specifications and estimates. Developed by the Construction Specifications Institute, the MasterFormat system is also used for classifying data and organizing manufacturers' literature for construction products and services. CSI has allocated a five-digit code and topic descriptions to all components of the specifications. MasterFormat groups the information into four major categories:

- Bidding Requirements
- Contract Forms
- General Conditions
- Specifications (Technical)

MasterFormat also consists of 16 construction divisions, each of which is a grouping of similar or related work numerically organized into subsections. Figure 2.1 shows the four major categories, the 16 divisions, and the relationship of the specs to the overall project documents. *(Note: The plans and specifications are of equal importance to the contract documents, although not illustrated as such in Figure 2.1.)*

The 16 MasterFormat divisions were determined based on relationships of activities in the actual construction process, and roughly follow the natural order of the construction of a building. The specification divisions and a general summary of their contents are as follows:

Division 1—General Requirements: A summary of the work, as well as the definitions and standards for the project and project coordination, meetings, schedules, reports, testing, samples, submittals, shop

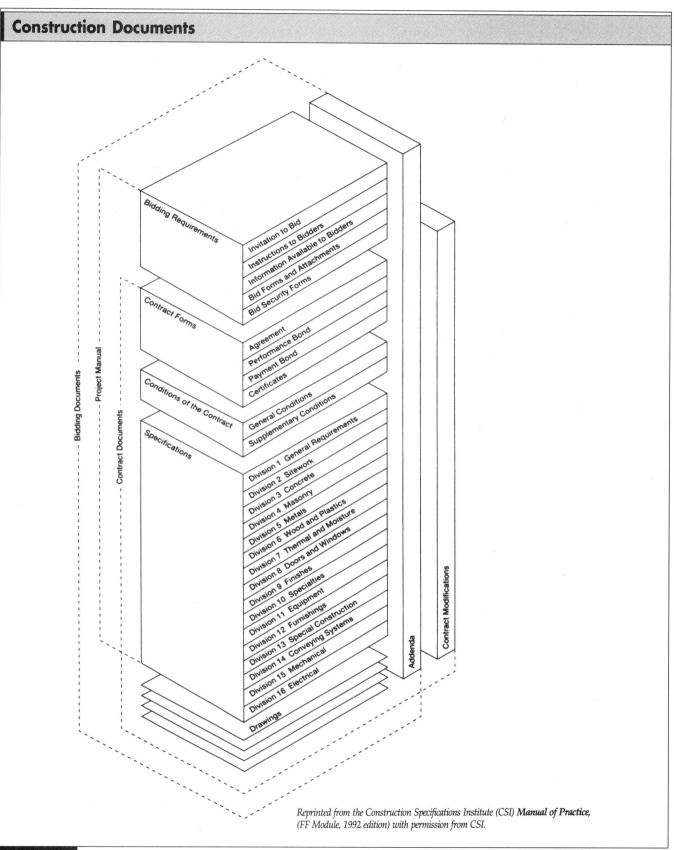

*Reprinted from the Construction Specifications Institute (CSI) **Manual of Practice,**
(FF Module, 1992 edition) with permission from CSI.*

Figure 2.1

drawings, close-out, cleanup, quality control, and temporary facilities. In addition, addresses pricing issues, such as unit prices, alternates, and allowances.

Division 2—Site Construction: Clearing of the site, earthwork, site drainage, utilities, roads, walks, paving, curbing, general site improvements, subsurface investigations, landscaping, and heavy site work, such as shoring, pile driving, and caissons.

Division 3—Concrete: Formwork, reinforcing, pre-cast and cast-in-place concrete, and cementitious decks.

Division 4—Masonry: Brick, block, stone, mortar, anchors, reinforcement, and masonry restoration and cleaning.

Division 5—Metals: Structural steel, metal joists, metal decking, light-gauge framing, and ornamental and miscellaneous metals.

Division 6—Wood and Plastics: Rough and finish carpentry, millwork, casework, and plastic fabrications.

Division 7—Thermal and Moisture Protection: Waterproofing, dampproofing, insulation, roofing, siding, caulking, and sealants.

Division 8—Doors and Windows: Metal and wood doors and frames, windows, glass and glazing, and finish hardware.

Division 9—Finishes: Gypsum wallboard systems, board and plaster systems, painting and wallcoverings, flooring, carpeting, acoustical ceiling systems, and ceramic and quarry tile.

Division 10—Specialties: Items such as demountable partitions, toilet partitions and accessories, fire extinguishers, postal specialties, flagpoles, lockers, signage, and retractable partitions.

Division 11—Equipment: Specialized equipment for homes, as well as banks, gymnasiums, schools, churches, laboratories, prisons, libraries, and hospitals.

Division 12—Furnishings: Cabinetry, rugs, tables, seating, artwork, and window treatments.

Division 13—Special Construction: Greenhouses, swimming pools, integrated ceilings, incinerators, and sound vibration controls, and clean rooms.

Division 14—Conveying Systems: Elevators, lifts, dumbwaiters, escalators, cranes, and hoists.

Division 15—Mechanical: Fire protection systems, plumbing, heating, air-conditioning, ventilating, gas piping, special piping, refrigeration, and controls.

Division 16—Electrical: Electrical service and distribution, wiring devices, fixtures, communications, and power.

The group of tasks included within each of the 16 divisions of CSI MasterFormat is numerically organized with a five-digit code. The first two numbers of the code identify the division. The next three digits further define the type of work within the division. The contractor should be familiar with major division codes by number. Figure 2.2 is a detailed listing of the MasterFormat divisions and subdivisions.

MasterFormat Classification with Subcategories

Division 1—General Requirements
01100 Summary
01200 Price and Payment Procedures
01300 Administrative Requirements
01400 Quality Requirements
01500 Temporary Facilities and Controls
01600 Product Requirements
01700 Execution Requirements
01800 Facility Operation
01900 Facility Decommissioning

Division 2—Site Construction
02050 Basic Site Materials and Methods
02100 Site Remediation
02200 Site Preparation
02300 Earthwork
02400 Tunneling, Boring, and Jacking
02450 Foundation and Load-bearing
    Elements
02500 Utility Services
02600 Drainage and Containment
02700 Bases, Ballasts, Pavements, and
    Appurtenances
02800 Site Improvements and Amenities
02900 Planting
02950 Site Restoration and Rehabilitation

Division 3—Concrete
03050 Basic Concrete Materials and
    Methods
03100 Concrete Forms and Accessories
03200 Concrete Reinforcement
03300 Cast-in-Place Concrete
03400 Precast Concrete
03500 Cementitious Decks and
    Underlayment
03600 Grouts
03700 Mass Concrete
03900 Concrete Restoration and
    Cleaning

Division 4—Masonry
04050 Basic Masonry Materials and
    Methods
04200 Masonry Units
04400 Stone
04500 Refractories
04600 Corrosion-Resistant Masonry
04700 Simulated Masonry
04800 Masonry Assemblies
04900 Masonry Restoration and Cleaning

Division 5—Metals
05050 Basic Metal Materials
    and Methods
05100 Structural Metal Framing
05200 Metal Joists
05300 Metal Deck
05400 Cold-Formed Metal Framing
05500 Metal Fabrications
05600 Hydraulic Fabrications
05650 Railroad Track and Accessories
05700 Ornamental Metal
05800 Expansion Control
05900 Metal Restoration and Cleaning

Division 6—Wood and Plastics
06050 Basic Wood and Plastic Materials
    and Methods
06100 Rough Carpentry
06200 Finish Carpentry
06400 Architectural Woodwork
06500 Structural Plastics
06600 Plastic Fabrications
06900 Wood and Plastic Restoration
    and Cleaning

Division 7—Thermal and Moisture Protection
07050 Basic Thermal and Moisture
    Protection Materials and Methods
07100 Dampproofing and Waterproofing
07200 Thermal Protection
07300 Shingles, Roof Tiles, and Roof
    Coverings
07400 Roofing and Siding Panels
07500 Membrane Roofing
07600 Flashing and Sheet Metal
07700 Roof Specialties and Accessories
07800 Fire and Smoke Protection
07900 Joint Sealers

Division 8—Doors and Windows
08050 Basic Door and Window Materials
    and Methods
08100 Metal Doors and Frames
08200 Wood and Plastic Doors
08300 Specialty Doors
08400 Entrances and Storefronts
08500 Windows
08600 Skylights
08700 Hardware
08800 Glazing
08900 Glazed Curtain Wall

Division 9—Finishes
09050 Basic Finish Materials and
    Methods
09100 Metal Support Assemblies
09200 Plaster and Gypsum Board
09300 Tile
09400 Terrazzo
09500 Ceilings
09600 Flooring
09700 Wall Finishes
09800 Acoustical Treatment
09900 Paints and Coatings

Division 10—Specialties
10100 Visual Display Boards
10150 Compartments and Cubicles
10200 Louvers and Vents
10240 Grilles and Screens
10250 Service Walls
10260 Wall and Corner Guards
10270 Access Flooring
10290 Pest Control
10300 Fireplaces and Stoves
10340 Manufactured Exterior
    Specialties
10350 Flagpoles
10400 Identification Devices
10450 Pedestrian Control Devices
10500 Lockers
10520 Fire Protection Specialties
10530 Protective Covers
10550 Postal Specialties
10600 Partitions
10670 Storage Shelving
10700 Exterior Protection
10750 Telephone Specialties
10800 Toilet, Bath, and
    Laundry Accessories
10880 Scales
10900 Wardrobe and Closet
    Specialties

Figure 2.2a

MasterFormat Classification with Subcategories

Division 11—Equipment
11010 Maintenance Equipment
11020 Security and Vault Equipment
11030 Teller and Service Equipment
11040 Ecclesiastical Equipment
11050 Library Equipment
11060 Theater and Stage Equipment
11070 Instrumental Equipment
11080 Registration Equipment
11090 Checkroom Equipment
11100 Mercantile Equipment
11110 Commercial Laundry and
      Dry Cleaning Equipment
11120 Vending Equipment
11130 Audio-Visual Equipment
11140 Vehicle Service Equipment
11150 Parking Control Equipment
11160 Loading Dock Equipment
11170 Solid Waste Handling
      Equipment
11190 Detention Equipment
11200 Water Supply and Treatment
      Equipment
11280 Hydraulic Gates and Valves
11300 Fluid Waste Treatment and
      Disposal Equipment
11400 Food Service Equipment
11450 Residential Equipment
11460 Unit Kitchens
11470 Darkroom Equipment
11480 Athletic, Recreational,
      and Therapeutic Equipment
11500 Industrial and Process
      Equipment
11600 Laboratory Equipment
11650 Planetarium Equipment
11660 Observatory Equipment
11680 Office Equipment
11700 Medical Equipment
11780 Mortuary Equipment
11850 Navigation Equipment
11870 Agricultural Equipment
11900 Exhibit Equipment

Division 12—Furnishing
12050 Fabrics
12100 Art
12300 Manufactured Casework
12400 Furnishings and Accessories
12500 Furniture
12600 Multiple Seating
12700 Systems Furniture
12800 Interior Plants and Planters
12900 Furnishings Repair
      and Restoration

Division 13—Special Construction
13010 Air-Supported Structures
13020 Building Modules
13030 Special Purpose Rooms
13080 Sound, Vibration, and Seismic
      Control
13090 Radiation Protection
13100 Lightning Protection
13110 Cathodic Protection
13120 Pre-Engineered Structures
13150 Swimming Pools
13160 Aquariums
13165 Aquatic Park Facilities
13170 Tubs and Pools
13175 Ice Rinks
13185 Kennels and Animal Shelters
13190 Site-Constructed Incinerators
13200 Storage Tanks
13220 Filter Underdrains and Media
13230 Digester Covers and Appurtenances
13240 Oxygenation Systems
13260 Sludge Conditioning Systems
13280 Hazardous Material Remediation
13400 Measurement and Control
      Instrumentation
13500 Recording Instrumentation
13550 Transportation Control
      Instrumentation
13600 Solar and Wind Energy
      Equipment
13700 Security Access and Surveillance
13800 Building Automation and Control
13850 Detection and Alarm
13900 Fire Suppression

Division 14—Conveying Systems
14100 Dumbwaiters
14200 Elevators
14300 Escalators and Moving
      Walks
14400 Lifts
14500 Material Handling
14600 Hoists and Cranes
14700 Turntables
14800 Scaffolding
14900 Transportation

Division 15—Mechanical
15050 Basic Mechanical
      Materials and Methods
15100 Building Services Piping
15200 Process Piping
15300 Fire Protection Piping
15400 Plumbing Fixtures and
      Equipment
15500 Heat-Generation
      Equipment
15600 Refrigeration Equipment
15700 Heating, Ventilating, and
      Air Conditioning
      Equipment
15800 Air Distribution
15900 HVAC Instrumentation
      and Controls
15950 Testing, Adjusting, and
      Balancing

Division 16—Electrical
16050 Basic Electrical Materials
      and Methods
16100 Wiring Methods
16200 Electrical Power
16300 Transmission and
      Distribution
16400 Low-Voltage Distribution
16500 Lighting
16700 Communications
16800 Sound and Video

Figure 2.2b

The Project Manual

Successful communication of the architect's/engineer's design intent to the contractor depends heavily on how well the *Project Manual* is written and organized. The project manual is the bound document that contains all of the four major categories of CSI MasterFormat. Information in the manual must be written clearly and presented logically. It should be easy to follow and comprehensive in order to prevent delays as a result of constant clarification.

Preparation of the project manual is a substantial task, primarily the responsibility of the architect. Individual disciplines, such as mechanical, electrical, and structural engineers, review, edit, and contribute to their individual sections of the technical specifications. Problems tend to occur when the various disciplines fail to coordinate their part of the work with each other and with the core language of the General and Supplemental Conditions, as well as with the drawings. The technical writer must create a complete document using very specific language that will guide the contractor in the bidding and building processes, and will also serve as a powerful tool to enforce the contract. It takes a skillful use of language, a high level of proficiency in understanding and coordinating technical information, and the ability to process that data into usable information. Over the next several pages, we will review the structure of the project manual and its four main components.

> Over time, the term "specifications" has come to be synonymous with the project manual. In actuality, the specifications most often refer to the technical specifications contained in Divisions 1-16, whereas the project manual is the entire bound document that includes:
> - Bidding Requirements
> - Contract Forms
> - General Conditions
> - Technical Specifications

Bidding Requirements

The Bidding Requirements are composed of the following items:
- Bid Solicitation
- Instructions to Bidders
- Information Available to Bidders
- Bid Forms and Supplements

Bid Solicitation

The bidding requirements begin with a solicitation for bids or proposals. This solicitation can be in the form of an *Invitation for Bid, Request for Proposals (RFP)*, or, in the case of public work, an *Advertisement for Bid*. In the private sector, bid solicitations can also be offered as an Invitation to Bid to selected firms only. All are similar in that they request bids from contractors. The RFP invites qualified general contractors and subcontractors to submit proposals for a particular project. It identifies the name and location of the project, along with a brief summary of the work involved. It clearly defines the date, time, and location for bids to be submitted. The RFP should name the owner or authority responsible for the bid award, whether the bids will be publicly or privately opened, and even (in some cases) the lender responsible for the funding. In the case of taxpayer-funded projects, the bids are usually opened publicly and made available for the inspection of the general public. The RFP typically identifies the architect and key engineering firms contributing to the design. For publicly funded projects, the statute governing such considerations as bidding and payments is also identified, along with any established budget for the work.

Some publicly funded projects require that certain subcontractors submit their proposals separately prior to the general contractor's bid date. This practice is called *filed sub-bidding* and is the law in one form or another in many states. The trades required to be filed sub-bidders are listed according to their MasterFormat section numbers. The RFP states the date, time, and location for the submission of filed sub-bids.

Instructions to Bidders

The Instructions to Bidders contain any required pre-qualification or eligibility criteria to eliminate bidders who could later be considered unacceptable. In the case of private bidding, the Invitation to Bid may be all that is required. In some states, publicly bid projects require formal qualification forms and a summary of the contractor's performance record. If a pre-bid conference or site inspection is scheduled, the date, time, and location are also stated. Additionally, the Instructions to Bidders defines the various forms and amount of bid security or bid bond that will be required. It states any liquidated damages that may be part of the contract, times for the commencement and completion of the work, and addenda or rules governing interpretation of the documents.

The Instructions to Bidders portion of the Bidding Requirements indicate the date, time, and location for procuring a set of contract documents and the cost, if any, to bidders. Other pertinent information, such as the time frame for award or rejection, special wage rates, tax-exempt status, or legal rights of the awarding authority to accept or reject proposals, is also provided.

Information Available to Bidders

The Information Available to Bidders provides locations where bidders can obtain copies of additional documents helpful in the bidding process. These documents could include geotechnical reports or subsurface investigation, property surveys and record drawings, conservation commission reports or directives, and hazardous materials management reports.

Bid Forms and Supplements

This section contains the forms developed by the architect for use by the contractors submitting bids, as well as bid security forms. Bid forms are used to keep proposals uniform in appearance and content. They provide the owner and architect with a mechanism for comparing "apples to apples." Bid forms provide the language of the proposal with blanks for the contractor to fill in. Space is provided to acknowledge addenda; add or deduct alternates; unit prices; the name, address, and signatory party of the bidding contractor; and, naturally, the dollar amount. "Non-responsive" is the term applied to a bidder who has incorrectly filled out or inadvertently left out information on the bid form, thereby rendering that bidder ineligible for award.

Supplements, or supplemental forms, include a certificate of compliance with tax laws form that requires bidders to certify under the penalties of perjury that they have complied with the tax laws regulating the state in which the work is to be done. A *Non-Collusion Affidavit* attests that bidders have not colluded or conspired with any entity, including other bidders, to defraud the owner or awarding authority. Other forms, although less common, include *Conflict of Interest* and *Power of Attorney* statements.

The Bidding Requirements often contain sufficient information for contractors to decide whether the project is right for their firm and, essentially, worth bidding.

Contract Forms

The most important contract form is the agreement between the owner and contractor, more commonly referred to as the *Contract for Construction*. This is a legal instrument supported by all of the contract documents. The Contract for Construction must contain the following basic items in order for it to be considered a functional document:

- Clear identification of the parties to the agreement
- Clear identification of the project
- Rights and responsibilities of each party
- Basis and terms of compensation

This agreement is incorporated within the project manual so that prospective bidders can carefully review the contract that will be executed when the project is awarded. Review the proposed contract immediately to ensure that items such as terms for payment, penalty or damage assessments, and any unfavorable clauses are acceptable. It may also be advisable to seek legal counsel for terms and conditions that may not be fully understood.

The American Institute of Architects (AIA) publishes a series of contract documents that are frequently used by owners and architects and have become the recognized standard. It should come as no surprise that contracts written by architects and/or owners tend to favor those parties. Some of these contracts are written in such a manner as to impose an unfair majority of the risk on the contractor. If the risks greatly outweigh the chance for success or profit, the contract should be analyzed carefully. Bidders should be aware of this and make every effort to understand the contract and any related information prior to making a commitment of company resources to bid. In fact, bidders should either accept the contract language as written or decline to bid the project. Changes to unfavorable contract language after the contract has been awarded (or the bidder selected) are unlikely.

Performance and Payment Bonds

Other contract forms include Performance and Payment Bond forms. Many owners issue a standardized form to prevent the surety from including exculpatory language of their own. The issuing of a Performance and Payment bond on a project has serious financial implications to the company as well as its principals. Default and/or termination while under the protection of a Performance and Payments bond can be devastating. It is important to review the terms and conditions of the contract carefully with the surety's representative, and even legal counsel. Securing a reputable surety to provide bonding to a contractor can be a long and detailed process. It is important to understand all of the liabilities that can be associated with bonding; do not venture into this process uninformed.

Certificates

The last section in the contract forms section of the specifications contains forms for insurance required for the project. This document defines the dollar limits for the various policies required. Most contractors understand basic insurance requirements included with policies, such as General Liability and Workers' Compensation. However, many projects today are required to carry more unusual forms of insurance, such as *Owner's Protective* and *Completed Operations* policies, that have potential impact long after the project has been completed. Again, seek professional guidance from your insurance agents when new policies or limits are required.

General Conditions of the Contract

Although the Contract for Construction is the primary legal instrument in the project manual, it is insufficient on its own. Because of its complexity, a separate set of guidelines is necessary, called the *General Conditions of the Contract for Construction*. The General Conditions are meant to complement the Contract for Construction, defining the complex relationships between the owner, architect, and contractor and the mutual responsibilities and rights of the signatory parties. The General Conditions include the definitions of key terms and provide procedures and mechanisms for resolving disputes or clarifying information provided on the drawings or specifications.

Owners in both the private and public sector have elected the AIA General Conditions of the Contract as the document of choice. Some owners have drafted versions of their own General Conditions using the AIA A201 as a model. In short, the General Conditions of the Contract are the administrative ground rules for executing the contract and the work. All are similar in content and address the 14 basic articles found in AIA A201, which address specific relationships made as a result of the agreement, and the unique situations that are created during the construction process. The basic articles of AIA A201 are:

1. General Provisions
2. Owner
3. Contractor
4. Administration of the Contract
5. Subcontractors
6. Construction by Owner/Separate Contractors
7. Changes in the Work
8. Time
9. Payments and Completion
10. Protection of Persons and Property
11. Insurance and Bonds
12. Uncovering and Correction of Work
13. Miscellaneous Provisions
14. Termination or Suspension of the Contract

The General Conditions establish the legal requirements of the project in general terms:

- **Articles 1-6**: Provide definitions of terms and relationships and define the responsibilities of the various parties to the contract. They also establish procedures for resolving disputes during the construction process. Article 6 covers the owner's right to contract separately with other independent contractors to perform work concurrently with the prime contractor.

- **Article 7**: Defines procedures for handling changes to the work, including when there is disagreement.

- **Article 8**: Explains time and its impact on the schedule and defines the remedies for delay, as well as the procedure for requesting an extension of time.

- **Articles 9-12**: Set forth terms for payment and justification for withholding funds. Article 9 defines the project's completion in contractual terms. Article 10 assigns responsibility for the protection of persons and property, as well as safety programs and responsibilities governing hazardous materials. Article 11 deals with loss and insurance required to make the owner "whole" (or fully reimbursed by the contractor's insurance carrier). Article 12 assigns responsibility for the correction of defective and non-conforming work.

- **Articles 13 and 14**: Explain the legal provisions for assignment or termination of the contract by either signatory party.

Supplements to the General Conditions of the Contract

As noted previously, the General Conditions of the Contract address specific issues (in a general format) that could be considered applicable to the industry as a whole. Often projects have specific needs or unique conditions that require an amendment to the General Conditions. Because the AIA A201 is intended to interface with a whole series of other AIA documents, any modifications to this document itself can have serious legal ramifications. For this reason, it is best to leave the General Conditions intact as written and modify them by adding a separate document, called the *Supplemental Conditions of the Contract*, frequently referred to as the *Supplementary General Conditions*. This custom-tailoring process allows the author of the project manual great flexibility in meeting the specific needs of the individual client or project without risking the loss of continuity that the General Conditions provide.

Review and analyze the specific impact that the Supplementary General Conditions have on the General Conditions and the project as a whole. The importance of this review cannot be overstated. The Supplementary General Conditions often are used to modify already stringent contract language aimed at the contractor. They are often presented in a way that a dollar value can be established against its impact. A classic example is insurance requirements. While the General Conditions describe the type and extent of insurance coverage, the Supplementary Conditions establish its limits. Using this information, you can establish the increased insurance policy dollars and thereby include the difference in the appropriate category of the estimate.

Technical Specifications

The last of the four categories is called the *Technical Specifications*, or *Technical Sections*, which define the scope, products, and execution of the work. This is the "meat and potatoes" section, providing the estimator with the necessary information (in a highly organized and industry-accepted format) to accurately price and build the structure. The technical sections provide the following information for each activity:

> *The three-part format of the technical sections provides a consistent organizational system for locating pertinent information quickly and efficiently:*
>
> *Part 1 – General*
> *Part 2 – Products*
> *Part 3 – Execution*

- Administrative requirements
- Quality or governing industry standards
- Products and accessories
- Installation or application procedures
- Workmanship requirements

Part 1, General

Part 1, the general section of the specifications, provides a summary of the work included within that particular section. It ties the technical section to the General Conditions and Supplementary General Conditions of the Contract, an essential feature in maintaining continuity between the general contractor and subcontractors. Part 1 identifies the applicable agencies or organizations by which quality assurance will be measured. It defines the scope of work that will be governed by this technical section, including, but not limited to items to be furnished by this section only, or furnished by others and installed under this section. It also identifies other technical sections that have potential coordination requirements with this section, and defines the required submittals or shop drawings for the scope of work described in this section. Part 1 also establishes critical procedures for the care, handling, and protection of work within this section, including such ambient conditions as temperature and humidity. If applicable, it addresses inspection or testing services required for this scope of work.

Part 2, Products

Part 2 deals exclusively with the products and materials to be incorporated within this technical section of the work. For products that are directly purchased by the contractor from a manufacturer or supplier, the items can be identified using one of three methods:

- Proprietary Specification
- Performance Specification
- Descriptive Specification

Proprietary Specifications: These specifications spell out a product by name and model number. Proprietary specifications have the unique advantage of allowing the architect or owner to select a product they desire or have used successfully on prior projects. The advantage of requiring specific products is the level of reliability they provide. The disadvantage is that they eliminate open competition. To help reduce the exclusivity of the proprietary spec, the architect often adds phrasing called the "or equal" clause, that allows limited competition. While the "or equal" clause opens the door to some competition, it can be risky, as it puts the burden of equality on the party (the contractor or the subcontractor, or even the vendor) who proposes the substitution. If you are pricing alternate products that are not specifically listed, research substitutions carefully. What may appear as a comparable product might not pass muster under closer scrutiny by the architect during review of the submittals or shop drawings. If the proposed substitution is not acceptable, you are responsible for providing the specified product originally named in the specification, even if the bid was based on the proposed substitution.

Performance Specifications: An alternate method of specifying products and materials is based less on makes and models and more on the ability to satisfy a design requirement or perform a specific function. This type of specifying is called a *performance specification*. In lieu of specifying a particular product by name, the architect opens competition to all products or materials that can perform the specific functions required to complete the design. This approach allows healthy competition among various manufacturers that have a similar line of products. It ensures competitive pricing and more aggressive delivery schedules.

Performance specs can identify products by characteristics, such as size, shape, color, durability, longevity, resistivity, and an entire host of other requirements. Some products that are not specified by name can be identified generically by reference to a particular ASTM testing number or a Federal Specification number. Use caution when pricing materials or products by their conformance with an ASTM number, however, as there could be several different grades of one product with vastly different prices. Also, remember that the architect makes the final decision as to whether a product has satisfied the performance criteria. You should be able to prove performance compliance with comprehensive facts and evidence, such as copies of pertinent tests and their results, and manufacturers' data. For a specification section that involves custom-fabricated work, the language might be a mixture of proprietary and performance specifications.

Descriptive Specifications: The last method of specifying a product or process is by using *descriptive specifications*, which are written instructions or details for assembling various components to comprise a system or assembly. Most often, descriptive specifying is used for generic products such as mortar or concrete. Frequently, no manufacturers' or proprietary names are mentioned or needed.

Part 3, Execution

Part 3, called the *Execution*, deals exclusively with the method, techniques, and quality of the workmanship. This section makes clear the allowable tolerances of the workmanship. The term "tolerances" refers to plumb, straight, level, or true. The Execution section should also describe any required preparation to the existing surfaces in order to accommodate the new work, as well as a particular technique or method for executing the work. Take this method or technique into account while deriving the quantities of the task, as other methods may render the work unacceptable during review by the architect. In addition, verify the conditions as a precursor to performing the work. Part 3 also addresses issues such as fine-tuning or adjustments to the work after initial installation, general cleanup of the debris generated, final cleaning, and protection of the work once it is in place. Some sections of Part 3 may identify any ancillary equipment or special tools required to perform the work, such as staging or scaffolding.

Conflicts Between Drawings & Specifications

Discrepancies between the contract drawings and the specifications should be addressed, in writing, to the architect or owner immediately. When the drawings and specifications differ as to the quality of a particular product, a correction or clarification needs to be issued by the architect. One of the main objectives of the specifications is to equalize the bidding process. Clarifying any discrepancies helps to maintain a fair and equal process.

Each page of a particular section within the specifications should be sequentially numbered, including the MasterFormat code number. This helps you verify that all the pages are intact, and the complete information for each section is included.

Modifications to the Contract Documents

Addenda

The bidding process often produces questions that require answers or clarification from the architect or engineer. Any changes to the contract documents made during the bidding period (the time period beginning on the date the drawings are issued and ending on bid day) in the form of modifications, clarifications, or revisions, for any reason, are called *addenda*. Addenda, or an addendum (singular), can be issued only by the architect. Addenda must be issued in writing and will automatically become part of the contract documents, complete with all of the benefits of the Contract for Construction and the General Conditions of the Contract. Addenda should, at a minimum, contain the following information:

- Number of the addendum and date of issue
- Name and address of the architect and/or engineer
- Project name and location
- Bidders' names to whom the addendum is addressed
- Contract documents that are to be modified
- Explanation of the addendum's purpose

Bid forms include an area for bidders to acknowledge addenda, and failure to do so could render the bid non-responsive. Be sure to evaluate how each addendum will affect the bid price. As addenda can affect the bids of all parties involved, subcontractors and materials suppliers should be made aware of any addenda, so they can adjust their bids accordingly.

Alternates

Often, owners want to see how a change in materials, method of construction, or addition or subtraction of work will affect the project's price. This information is presented in the form of additions or deletions to the base price, called *alternates*. Typically, the alternate is listed at the end of the specification section that is affected by it, and also in Division 1 under the section, "Alternates." Be sure to include the increase or decrease in cost for all work, including all taxes, labor burden, and overhead—both direct and indirect costs and profit. *(See Chapter 20 for more on calculating direct and indirect costs and profit.)*

For example, the total consequence of an alternate might look like:

> *Alternate 1: Delete door frame and hardware for Door #3 in its entirety. DELETE $500*

In this example, you would not only delete the cost of the door, frame, and hardware, but must also include the additional wall materials, wood, gypsum board, paint, etc., to fill in the area Door #3 originally occupied in the base bid. The actual price of the alternate is the difference between the two. In some cases, the addition or deletion of large scopes of work by alternates can have a tremendous effect on the project's duration, thereby increasing or decreasing overhead and other time-sensitive costs of the project. Projects with limited budgets often include a series of alternates as a way of choosing how to most effectively use the budget.

Allowances

Occasionally, as the contract documents are ready to be issued, certain items have yet to be finalized and are not ready for inclusion in the bid set. Rather than leaving the item out altogether, the designer includes a cash allowance. The allowance is a fixed lump sum, such as "$10,000 for the purchase and delivery of sod and plantings." The allowance can also be in the form of a unit price, such as, "an allowance of $450 per M (thousand) for brick, including delivery to the job site." Typically, it is clearly stated what the allowance is for: materials, furnished and delivered only; materials and labor; or the entire scope of work. If there is any doubt, request clarification. At the completion of the project, the actual cost is computed for items included as allowances, savings are returned to the owner, and overages are added to the contract price.

Unit Prices

In the course of design for some projects, architects or engineers are sometimes unable to provide sufficient detail to the drawings so that the estimator can determine an exact quantity of a certain task or activity. An example of this is excavation of rock or unsuitable fill materials. The architect or engineer may be aware of what needs to be done and the techniques or quality required, but is unable to determine the exact amount of rock or materials to be removed. In an effort to at least establish the cost of this work for post-bid purposes, unit prices are requested and submitted as part of the bid form or proposal. Unit prices are included on the bid for each item by a unit of measure, such as excavation of unsuitable materials at $45 per CY. The unit price should always include markups for taxes, insurance, overhead, and profit.

Always try to calculate the approximate quantity of the task, as unit prices tend to decrease as the quantity increases, a concept referred to as economy of scale. Frequently, the unit price may be tiered based on stipulated quantities. For example:

Excavation of unsuitable materials $75 per CY for 1 to 50 CY quantities

Excavation of unsuitable materials $65 per CY for 51 to 200 CY quantities

Excavation of unsuitable materials $45 per CY for 201 and over quantities

Conclusion   Once you have reviewed and studied the plans, specifications, and any addenda, and if appropriate, conducted a site visit, then the quantity survey or takeoff can begin. (This process will be discussed in Chapter 4.) Prior to beginning the takeoff, it may be helpful to review basic area and volume calculations, covered in Chapter 3.

Chapter Three

Calculating Linear Measure, Area, & Volume

To perform even the most basic quantity takeoff, contractors should be well-versed in the calculations of linear measurements, area, and volume. This chapter will review the basic formulas and relationships needed to perform these calculations. The formulas are fairly simple, and it is not necessary to memorize them. However, it is essential to know which formula to use in the proper application, and where it can be found.

Units of Measure

The most fundamental rule is to use the correct units of measure for area and volume. Area is always expressed in square units, most often square feet (SF) or square yards (SY). Volume is always in cubic units, the most common of which are cubic feet (CF) or cubic yards (CY). Another important point to remember is to be consistent and keep the units the same. For example, feet multiplied by feet results in square feet, yards multiplied by yards results in square yards, and so on. Multiplying a dimension in feet by a dimension in inches leads to an erroneous value. It is common to find different dimensions used in various parts of the drawings. Be sure to convert the dimensions given into the same units. Often, a dimension on the drawings is given in both feet and inches.

Decimal Equivalents

To calculate the area of a space that is 24'-6" x 20'-3", the dimensions must be converted to their decimal equivalents. The feet-and-inches dimensions are changed to feet in order to arrive at a measurement in square feet for the area. This is a fairly simple process to convert the inches portion of the dimension to its decimal form and then add it to the whole number. Once this has been done, the values can be easily entered into a calculator. Following are the decimal equivalents of the twelve inches in a foot:

1" = 0.08 feet	7" = 0.58 feet
2" = 0.17 feet	8" = 0.67 feet
3" = 0.25 feet	9" = 0.75 feet
4" = 0.33 feet	10" = 0.83 feet
5" = 0.42 feet	11" = 0.92 feet
6" = 0.50 feet	12" = 1.00 feet

Note that the decimal equivalent of 2" in the table above is not precisely two times the decimal equivalent of 1". This is because two-place accuracy after the decimal point is sufficient for estimating purposes in most cases. (While the actual value of 2" in decimal form is .0166666 of a foot, the value is rounded up to 0.17.) The decimal value is limited to two places after the decimal and is always rounded up. For example:

If the total quantity of concrete in a takeoff is 34.22 CY, round to 35 CY for use in the cost analysis portion of the estimate.

According to the table above, it should hold true that if:

1" = 0.08 feet, then 1/8" = 0.01 feet.

Using this simple mathematical analogy, it is easy to covert any feet-and-inches dimension to decimals to an accuracy of 1/8". For example:

To convert a dimension of 20'-3-5/8" to its decimal equivalent, start by converting the 3" to 0.25', then 5/8" to 0.05'. When these two are added together, 0.25' + 0.05', the result is 0.30'. This can be added to the 20', with the result of 20.30'.

To calculate the area of a room that is 24'-6" x 20'-3-5/8", first determine that the decimal equivalent is 20.5' x 20.30', which equals 497.35 SF.

Decimal equivalents can be found using a calculator. Decimal equivalents of fractions of an inch are as easy as pushing a few buttons. For example:

3-1/2" = 3.5"; 3.5" divided by 12"/ft. = 0.29'.

The remainder of this chapter will be divided into three sections:

- Linear Measurement: the measurement of lines in a single dimension.
- Area: the measurement of surfaces in two dimensions—length by width.
- Volume: the measurement in three dimensions—length, width, and height or thickness.

Linear Measurement

Perimeter

If, for a moment, we imagine the floor of a building as a simple planar surface with no depth, the sum of the sides of that planar surface is called its *perimeter*. Since perimeter is a linear measurement and the dimensions of the sides are added, its units are also linear, most often LF. The perimeter of a surface can be found by adding the length to the width and multiplying it by 2, or by adding the length and width of all the sides.

Knowing how to find the perimeter is helpful in determining the length of various items you would find in a building, such as baseboard and other running trims within various rooms.

Angles

If a rectangle with four 90° corners was divided in half by a line connecting two opposite corners, the resulting shape would be a *right triangle*. A triangle has three angles that total 180°. It also has three sides: a base, an altitude, and a *hypotenuse*, the diagonal line connecting the end point of the base to the end point of the altitude.

Calculating the length of the hypotenuse is helpful in determining the length of rafters, stair stringers, and the like. To do so, the Pythagorean Theorem or the Right Triangle Law is used. The Right Triangle Law is the same as the "3-4-5 triangle" that framers and contractors use to "square up" work in the field. It states:

> *The square of the hypotenuse of a right triangle is equal to the sum of the squares of the other two sides. (See Figure 3.1.)*

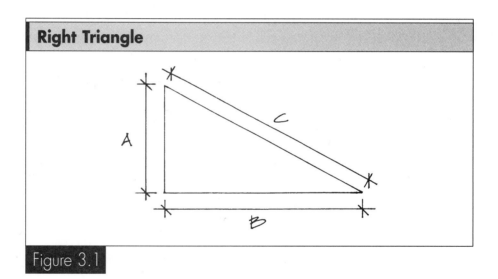

Right Triangle

Figure 3.1

Converting this to a formula:

$C^2 = A^2 + B^2$, *where C = length of the hypotenuse, A = length of the altitude, and B = length of the base.*

Using this formula, we can determine the length of a side of a right triangle, provided the lengths of the other two sides are known.

There are three types of triangles that frequently occur in a set of construction drawings. An *equilateral* triangle has three sides that are equal in length. An *isosceles* triangle has two sides that are of equal length. In a *scalene* triangle, none of the sides are equal in length. *(See Figure 3.2.)*

Equilateral, Isosceles, and Scalene Triangles

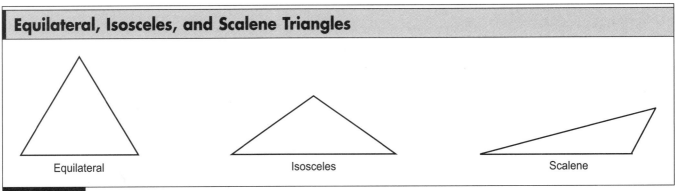

Equilateral   Isosceles   Scalene

Figure 3.2

Area & Square Measure

Possibly the most common calculation performed by estimators is determining the area of a shape. The most common shape in the construction business is some variation of the rectangle. A rectangle, by definition, has four sides, with all angles equal at 90°. If all four sides are equal in length, it is a *square*. A rectangle with opposite sides only that are equal in length and parallel is a *parallelogram* (the angles are not 90°). A *trapezoid* has two opposing sides that are parellel, but not of equal length. When no sides are equal in length, and none are parallel, the shape is a *trapezium. (See Figure 3.3.)*

Area calculations take into account only the surface, not the depth. Areas are expressed in square units—most commonly square feet, square yards, or square inches. The area of a rectangle or square is defined as the product of its length and width. The formula for area is:

$A_R = L \times W$, *where A_R = area of a rectangle, L = length, and W = width.*

Since a triangle is essentially a bisected rectangle, the formula for the area of a rectangle could be modified for a triangle:

$A_T = (\frac{1}{2} B) \times A$, *where A_T = area of a triangle, B = length of the base, and A = length of the altitude. This formula requires that the angle between the base and the altitude be 90°.*

Rectangle, Parallelogram, Trapezoid, and Trapezium

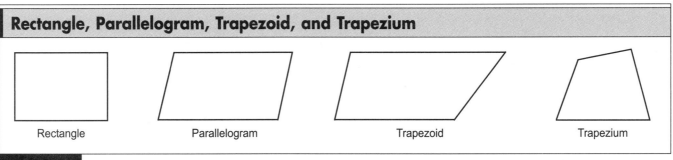

Rectangle   Parallelogram   Trapezoid   Trapezium

Figure 3.3

Irregular Shapes

Contractors may be required to calculate the areas of more complex polygons and other irregular shapes. Determining the area of a construction feature is not always one simple area calculation, and sometimes it requires additional calculations. Frequently, the area to be quantified is calculated by dividing it into several smaller areas, calculating each, then adding the results back together to arrive at the total area. (Remember to break odd-shaped features into recognizable rectangles and triangles.) The same holds true when determining a smaller portion of the whole. In this case, deduct all unwanted areas until the desired area is achieved. For most construction applications, a close approximation of the area of an irregular shape is sufficient.

Area of a Circular Shape

Many construction elements are circular, such as brick patios and concrete-filled sonotubes. Before reviewing the formula for the area of a circle, it will be helpful to define various parts and some constant relationships.

The *circumference* is the perimeter of the circle. The *diameter* is a line drawn through the center of the circle, beginning and ending on the circumference. Any number of possible diameters drawn on a circle should render the two halves of that circle equal. All diameters of the same circle are also equal.

The *radius* of a circle is a line from the center point within a circle to a point on the circumference. All radii of the same circle are equal in length. The radius, by definition, is equal to one-half of the diameter. Knowing this relationship, we can establish the following formulas:

$D = 2 \times R$ *or* $R = 1/2 \times D$, *where D = diameter and R = radius.*

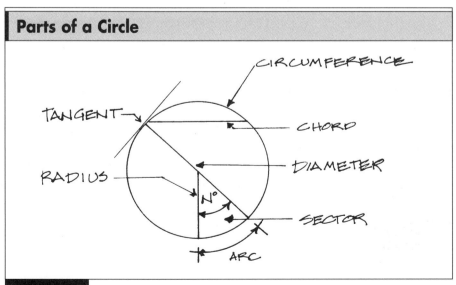

Parts of a Circle

Figure 3.4

A *constant* is a unitless number that expresses a relationship in a mathematical formula. The circumference of a circle has a constant relationship to the diameter of the same circle. That constant is the number 3.1416, *pi*, which has a corresponding symbol, π. For most calculations in construction, π can be truncated at two places after the decimal point, or 3.14. If the area to be calculated is very large, π can be extended to a third decimal place, 3.142. The formula for the relationship between the circumference and the diameter is as follows:

$C = \pi \times D$ or $C = 2 \times \pi \times R$, where C = circumference, π = 3.14, D = diameter and R = radius.

A *chord* is a straight line connecting two points on the circumference, without passing through the center of the circle. An *arc* is any portion of the circumference of the circle. A circle has 360°. Therefore, if the radius and the interior angle between two radii are known, the length of the arc between them can be calculated using the formula:

$L_A = N/360 \times 2 \times \pi \times R$, where N is the central angle, π = 3.14, and R = radius.

The *tangent* of a circle is a straight line touching only one point on the circumference. A radius drawn to this point is at 90° to the tangent.

The area of a circle is the radius multiplied by the radius, then multiplied by π. As a formula:

$A_c = \pi \times (R \times R)$, or $A_c = \pi \times R^2$

An alternative method for calculating the area of a circle is to multiply the diameter by itself, then multiply the resultant area by the constant 0.7854. Expressed as a formula:

$A_c = (D \times D) \times 0.7854$, or $A_c = D^2 \times 0.7854$, where D = diameter and 0.7854 is a constant.

It is also possible to calculate the area of a portion of a circle. If we cut a pie-shaped piece out of a circle—two radii with an angle in between, with a known radius and known angle between—we can calculate that area, which is called a *sector*. The length of the arc is a fraction of the total circumference. A similar deduction can be used to devise a formula for the area of the sector:

$A_s = N/360 \times \pi \times R^2$, where A_s = area of a sector, N = angle between the radii in degrees, π = 3.14, and R = radius.

Surface Area of Cylinder, Pyramid, and Cone Shapes

Estimators often need to calculate the surface area of a three-dimensional shape, such as a cylinder, pyramid, or cone. A good example would be when estimating painting for one of these shapes. The outside surface area of a three-dimensional shape is referred to as its *lateral area*.

The formula for calculating the lateral area of a cylinder is:

$A_L = C \times H$, where C = circumference of the cylinder base and H = height of the cylinder.

The lateral area of a pyramid can be expressed as:

$A_L = p \times \frac{1}{2} \times h_s$, where *p = perimeter of the base of the pyramid where the base is a regular polygon and h_s = slant height of the pyramid.*

The slant height of the pyramid is a line drawn from the vertex, or converging point at the top of the pyramid, to the center of any one side of the base. The lateral area of a cone is the area of its tapering side. It can be expressed as:

$A_L = C_b \times \frac{1}{2} \times h_s$, where *$C_b$ = circumference of the base of the cone and h_s = slant height of the cone.*

The slant height of the cone is a straight line drawn from the vertex of the cone to the circumference. It can be calculated by solving for the hypotenuse in the Pythagorean Theorem, where the altitude of the cone is its height perpendicular to the base, and the radius of the base of the cone is its base.

Volume & Cubic Measure

In contrast to area, which has only two dimensions, volume has a third dimension, depth. The depth of a shape can also be called its *thickness* or *height*. Once a shape takes on this third dimension, it is no longer planar, but becomes a solid. The term *cubic* refers to the volume of a solid, whereas *square* accounts only for its area. The standard units of cubic measure are cubic inches, cubic feet, and cubic yards, with the abbreviations CI, CF, and CY, respectively. There are numerous tasks encountered in construction estimating that require volume calculations. A few examples include excavation, backfill, and concrete for a form.

Volume of a Prism

If we visualize a rectangle as a surface area with a height, it would be called a *prism*. Prisms in construction are virtually everywhere. Examples of volume calculations of prisms that might be required include pilecaps, footings, and excavations. If a prism's dimensions of length, width, and height are the same, it is a *cube*. This is defined in the conversion of CF to cubic yards CY, where 1 CY = 27 CF (3' × 3' × 3').

If we modify the formula for the area of the planar surface by adding the new dimension, the result is the formula for the volume of a prism.

$V = A \times h$, *where V = volume of the prism, A = area of the base, and h = height.*

This formula applies only to shapes whose ends and opposite sides are parallel. To further expand this formula:

$V = l \times w \times h$, *where l = length, w = width, and h = height.*

Contractors may encounter an endless number of shapes that are variations of a prism. A triangular prism has a triangular surface area and a height. The rule of base area multiplied by height still applies:

$V = \frac{1}{2} \times l \times w \times h$, *where again l = length, w = width, and h = height.*

In short, it shares the same relationship that the area of a triangle has with the area of a rectangle. The volume of a triangular shape is one-half of the volume of a prism.

Volume of a Cylinder

A common, yet more sophisticated, shape is the *cylinder*. The formula for its volume is essential in calculating the amount of concrete to fill a sonotube, or a round column form. The volume is the area of its circular base multiplied by its height. Expressed as a formula:

$V_c = \pi \times R^2 \times h$, *where* V_c = *volume of a cylinder,* π = *3.14, R = radius, and h = height.*

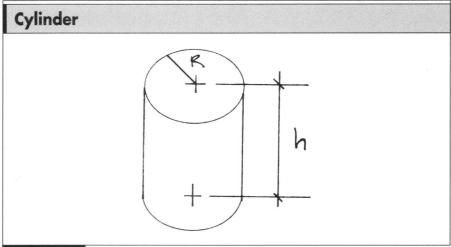

Cylinder

Figure 3.5

Volume of a Pyramid

The volume of a pyramid is calculated as:

$V_p = 1/3 \times A_b \times a$, *where* A_b = *area of the base of the pyramid provided that the base is a regular polygon, and a = the altitude of the pyramid as defined by a line drawn at 90° to the base to the vertex of the pyramid.*

Volume of a Cone

Volume of a cone is very similar to that of a pyramid. It is:

$V_c = 1/3 \times A_c \times a$, *where* A_c = *area of the round base of the cone and a = the altitude of the cone as defined by a line drawn at 90° to the base to the vertex of the cone.*

Conclusion The shapes in this chapter are by no means all the shapes that may be encountered in a quantity takeoff, but they are the most common ones. The table in Figure 3.6 lists additional formulas for less common shapes. Figure 3.7 is a table of conversions for linear, square, and cubic measure. Calculating quantities accurately is essential to a solid base from which to start the estimate. Now that linear, area, and volume calculations have been reviewed, we can begin the takeoff.

Formulas for Less Common Shapes

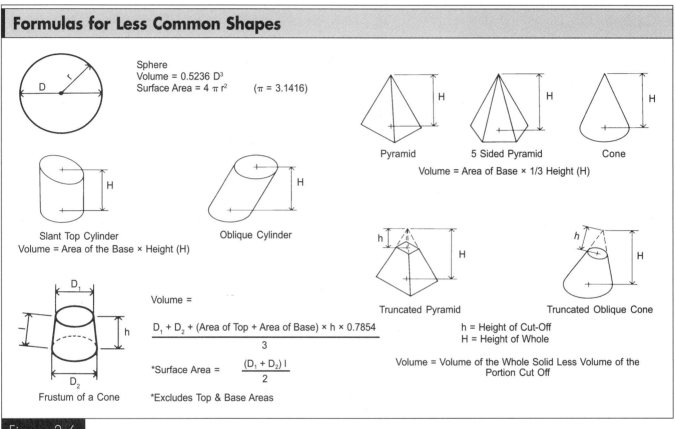

Sphere
Volume = 0.5236 D^3
Surface Area = $4 \pi r^2$ (π = 3.1416)

Pyramid

5 Sided Pyramid

Cone

Volume = Area of Base × 1/3 Height (H)

Slant Top Cylinder
Volume = Area of the Base × Height (H)

Oblique Cylinder

Truncated Pyramid

Truncated Oblique Cone

Volume =

$$\frac{D_1 + D_2 + (\text{Area of Top} + \text{Area of Base}) \times h \times 0.7854}{3}$$

*Surface Area = $\dfrac{(D_1 + D_2)\, l}{2}$

Frustum of a Cone   *Excludes Top & Base Areas

h = Height of Cut-Off
H = Height of Whole

Volume = Volume of the Whole Solid Less Volume of the Portion Cut Off

Figure 3.6

Standard Weights and Measures

Volume and Capacity

Units and Equivalents	
1 cu. ft. of water at 39.1° F	= 62.425 lbs.
1 United States gallon	= 231 cu. in.
1 imperial gallon	= 277.274 cu. in.
1 cubic foot of water	= 1728 cu. in.
	= 7.480519 U.S. gallons
	= 6.232103 imperial gallons
1 cubic yard	= 27 cu. ft. = 46,656 cu. in.
1 quart	= 2 pints
1 gallon	= 4 quarts
1 U.S. gallon	= 231 cu. in.
	= 0.133681 cu. ft.
	= 0.83311 imperial gallons
	= 8.345 lbs.
1 barrel	= 31.5 gallons = 4.21 cu. ft.
1 U.S. bushel	= 1.2445 cu. ft.
1 fluid ounce	= 1.8047 cu. in.
1 acre-foot	= 43,560 cu. ft.
	= 1,613.3 cu. yds.
1 acre-inch	= 3,630 cu. ft.
1 million U.S. gallons	= 133,681 cu. ft.
	= 3.0689 acre-ft.
1 ft. depth on 1 sq. mi.	= 27,878,400 cu. ft.
	= 640 acre-ft.
1 cord	= 128 cu. ft.

Standard Weights and Measures

Linear Measure		Square Measure	
1000 mils =	1 inch	144 square inches =	1 square foot
12 inches =	1 foot	9 square feet =	1 square yard
3 feet =	1 yard		
2 yards =	{ 1 fathom / 6 feet	30-1/4 square yds. =	{ 1 square rod / 272-1/4 square feet
5-1/2 yards =	{ 1 rod / 16-1/2 feet	160 square rods =	{ 1 acre / 43,560 square feet
40 rods =	{ 1 furlong / 660 feet	640 acres =	{ 1 square mile / 27,878,400 / square feet
8 furlongs =	{ 1 mile / 5280 feet	A circular mil is the area of a circle 1 mil, or 0.001 inch in diameter.	
1.15156 miles =	{ 1 nautical mile, / or knot / 6080.26 feet	1 square inch =	1,273,239 circular mils
3 nautical miles =	{ 1 league / 18,240.78 feet	A circular inch is the area of a circle 1 inch in diameter	= 0.7854 square inches.
		1 square inch =	1.2732 circular inches

Dry Measure		Weight—Avoirdupois or Commercial	
2 pints =	1 quart	437.5 grains =	1 ounce
8 quarts =	1 peck	16 ounces =	1 pound
4 pecks =	{ 1 bushel / 2150.42 cubic in. / 1.2445 cubic feet	112 pounds =	1 hundredweight
		20 hundredweight =	{ 1 gross, or long ton / 2240 pounds
		2000 pounds =	1 net, or short ton
		2204.6 pounds =	1 metric ton
		1 lb. of water (39.1°F) =	27.681217 cu. in.
		=	0.016019 cu. ft.
		=	0.119832 U.S. gallon
		=	0.453617 liter

Figure 3.7

Chapter Four

The Quantity Takeoff

A precise and thorough quantity takeoff is the basis for a sound estimate. Errors or inaccuracies in this portion of the estimate can be compounded during the pricing phase, regardless of how reliable the unit prices are. In this chapter, we will explore the most common practices of taking off quantities for a construction project and offer suggestions for developing routine procedures that will help ensure accuracy.

Reviewing the Documents

Before beginning an estimate, it is important to thoroughly review the contract documents, which usually include:

- A set of plans
- A set of specifications
- Any related addenda or bulletins
- Additional relevant documents, such as geotechnical reports and any special documentation or unique requirements from local authorities. Examples include conservation commission directives or conditions and/or amendments made by local inspection officials during the review of the plans.

In the absence of a formal set of specifications (bound and separate from the plans), the plans should contain, at the least, a minimal amount of general information to be used as guidelines by the individual estimating the work. As discussed in Chapters 1 and 2, the plans and specifications each contain equally important, but distinctly different, kinds of information. Both are necessary to prepare an estimate. Information illustrated on the plans should be supported by the written language in the specifications. For example, if the plans depict a reinforced concrete footing, the specifications should define the strength and any special requirements of the concrete material and reinforcing, in such a way that the estimator is able to price the material and labor necessary to complete the task.

Reviewing the documents is essential not only to understand the structure that will be estimated, but also to become familiar with where various information is located within the documents. This preliminary review often raises questions due to insufficient, missing, or contradictory information.

A reasonable amount of missing or contradictory information, however, is normal. The best architects, engineers, and designers are subject to human error, just as builders are. Even a constructibility review by a third party, such as a peer review or a hired consultant, does not always reveal conflicts. A responsible estimator will document any discrepancies and, through a formal written process, will ask the architect, engineer, designer, or owner to clarify conflicts or provide missing information. If you do not seek clarification in writing, you may have to bear the financial responsibility for any problems that arise as a result of unclear, missing, or erroneous information. It is recommended that you make notes of any questions or problems while reviewing the documents, many of which will be answered as the review process proceeds and the documents become more familiar.

The estimating process can be broken down into two phases: *takeoff* and *pricing*. After initial review of the contract documents, and when all questions have been answered, the takeoff can begin.

Beginning the Quantity Takeoff

The quantity takeoff, sometimes called the *quantity survey*, breaks the project down into its elemental parts, called *tasks* or *activities*. (For the purpose of estimating, these terms are interchangeable.) Tasks are actual units of work to be performed, such as *"place and finish concrete slab," "form footings," "frame exterior walls,"* or *"paint interior doors and frames."* They are quantified by details and dimensions provided on the drawings. Tasks are also identified in terms of the quality of materials and labor required. This information is provided in the specifications. Establishing the quantity and quality of a task is an essential part of accurate estimating. Without them, the estimate is nothing more than a guess, which could cause conflict if different methods or materials are required by the architect or owner when the construction work is performed.

Tasks or activities are made up of various components, including material, labor, tools and/or equipment, subcontractors, and occasionally non-production-related expenses, such as building permits, bond costs, and direct overhead costs. Not every task includes all of these components. For example, painting interior doors and frames would have a material and a labor component if you did the work yourself. If the work is performed by a subcontractor, the sub's cost may be the only component in the task. If the work is self-performed using spray equipment, the task would have material, labor, and equipment components. Determining which components apply is a combination of what the documents call for, along with judgment and experience.

Rules to Follow for Accurate Takeoffs

The following takeoff rules are based on common sense practices that will help prevent, or at least minimize, errors. They can help make the takeoff better organized, more efficient, and more accurate.

Rule 1: Write Clear Task Descriptions

Descriptions should be clear and legible and should indicate the work needed and the part of the structure involved—or the location on the drawing where the quantity originates. When taking off quantities, descriptions should be written according to the guidelines of the individual who will apply the unit prices. In smaller companies, one individual may do both. The following is an example of a thorough task description:

Form 24" x 12" footing including keyway along B-line as per Detail 5 on drawing S-2.

Rule 2: Use Industry-Accepted Units

A takeoff is not a list of materials for use in placing an order, but rather a descriptive list of activities with quantities derived from the dimensions on the documents. These quantities must then be extended into accepted units for pricing. For example, concrete is estimated in CY, because that is how it is sold. CY is also the accepted industry standard unit.

Rule 3: Follow a Logical Order

The takeoff should be logical and organized. The best approach is to proceed in roughly the same order as the structure is built—from the ground up. This allows you to visualize it while performing the takeoff. The logical thought process is to consider "what is the next step?" and organize the takeoff according to the CSI MasterFormat classification system. *(See Chapter 2 for more on the MasterFormat.)* For example, all of the work in Division 3—Concrete, should be complete before moving on to Division 4—Masonry.

Occasionally, the MasterFormat divisions may present a problem in that items that would naturally be included as part of a construction task may have components in different divisions, and one element of work may be omitted or forgotten about by the time you reach the later division where the element should be listed. For example, although the vapor barrier under a slab-on-grade is placed during concrete work (Division 3), it is classified as part of Division 7—Thermal and Moisture Protection. As with every rule, there are exceptions. Place the task in the estimate where it makes the most sense. In this example, it might best to include the vapor barrier under Division 3 work, with a simple note in Division 7 that it has been accounted for in Division 3.

Rule 4: Review Scales, Notes, Abbreviations, and Definitions

Review drawings and details carefully for notes and scale. Scale can change from drawing to drawing, and a general rule of thumb is that as the detail becomes smaller in focus, the scale becomes larger.

It is necessary to become familiar with symbols and abbreviations that typically appear on the drawings. Frequently, drawings contain legends that define material and graphic symbols, as discussed in Chapter 1. Abbreviations, such as NTS (not to scale) and TYP (typical), may be used throughout the entire set of plans. Some words in the construction industry have unique meanings, such as *provide*, which is defined as *"to furnish and install."* Carefully review any specification sections that include references or definitions.

Rule 5: Verify Dimensions

Wherever possible, use the dimensions exactly as they appear on the drawings. Add intermediate dimensions to arrive at total dimensions. Scale dimensions should be used only as a last resort. Develop the habit of checking printed dimensions against scaled dimensions. Discrepancies should be brought to the attention of the design team or the owner.

Always express dimensions in the same order, such as length x width x depth. This method avoids errors when referring to the size of certain features, such as windows or doors (which are typically dimensioned as width x height).

Convert dimensions to the same units for calculation purposes: feet x feet x feet. For example, when calculating the volume of concrete in a slab with the dimensions of 10' long x 10' wide x 4" thick, convert the 4" to .33 feet so that all units are the same. Converting all dimensions to the same unit avoids arriving at erroneous values.

Rule 6: Be Consistent

Develop a systematic approach when working with the drawings. For instance, take measurements in a clockwise direction around a floor plan. Begin counting similar features, such as light fixtures, from the left to right and top to bottom. Whatever the procedure, it should become a standard, systematic approach.

Rule 7: Number Takeoff Sheets

Always number each takeoff sheet and keep them in order. Whenever possible, tasks, groups of similar tasks, or entire sheets should be identified by their location on the drawings. For example:

Phase 2-B–Building Foundation Footings.

Rule 8: Define Units for Material, Work, and Assembly Items

Items or tasks that have no labor component are called *material items*. These are furnished only and will be installed under another scope of work. Good examples are lintels for masonry openings. Typically, steel lintels are furnished under Division 5—Metals and installed by a masonry contractor as the brick or block is laid up.

Items that have no material component and require labor only are referred to as *work items*. Examples include fine grading gravel or finishing of concrete. All tasks or items should be labeled with a unit of measure, which will be extended to the final price. For example:

Calculating the volume of concrete in a footing that is 27' long x 3' wide x 2' deep will result in 162 CF. However, concrete is priced in CY, so the calculated quantity of 162 CF must be converted to 6 CY by dividing 162 by 27. (1 CY equals 27 CF.) (Refer to Chapter 3 for more on calculations.)

Calculating the area of a rectangular shape results is a square area unit, most often SF or SY. Even the area of a circle is expressed in SF or SY. For example:

The area of a room 12' long by 17' wide is 204 SF.

When calculating the volume of a shape, the results should be expressed in cubic units, most often CY. For example:

The volume of a prism that is 12' long x 13' wide x 14' deep is 2,184 CF, or 80.88 CY.

All items that have a cost value in the estimate should be assigned a unit of measure. Most items or tasks have defined units of measure. Others are less clear and sometimes assigned a more arbitrary unit of measure, called a *lump sum* (LS), most often applied to work items that are not measured or expressed in more conventional terms. A good example is cutting an opening in a masonry wall. The actual work item includes four separate tasks:

1. Cut the opening with a masonry saw.
2. Cleanup and disposal of debris.
3. Patch in of the masonry at the jambs.
4. Install the lintel at the head.

A compilation or *assembly* of work items often uses a lump sum unit. When tasks are repetitive, sometimes it is easier to group them into one lump sum item. If you use the lump sum unit to incorporate multiple tasks into one item, it is important to accurately and adequately define what tasks are included, so there is no confusion.

Rule 9: Use Decimals

Decimals are preferable in the quantity takeoff in lieu of fractions, because they are faster, more precise, and easier to use with a calculator. Dimensions on drawings should be converted to their decimal equivalent. For example:

A dimension of 24'-6" should be converted to 24.5'.

In calculating the area of a room that is 24'-6" x 24'-6", coverting both dimensions to decimals and performing the multiplication results in an area of 600.25 SF. Always check the final units of the dimension. Adding linear dimensions results in LF or linear yards (LY). For example:

The perimeter of a rectangle that is 12' long x 13' wide is 50 LF.

Rule 10: Verify Appropriate Level of Accuracy

While accuracy is important, over-accuracy wastes time. There is an old adage in the construction business that warns, "Don't spend ten dollars of estimating time figuring a one-dollar item . . . unless there are hundreds of them." Accuracy is relative to the task being taken off or estimated. Rarely is it necessary for a number to be calculated to more than two places after the decimal.

There are acceptable parameters for rounding, depending on the particular task being calculated. Most items can be rounded to the nearest full unit. In some cases, it is necessary to round to the nearest sales unit, if the balance of the sales unit has no inventory or future value. *(Waste factors will be discussed in Rule 11 and in its own section following these rules.)* Rounding quantities should be done when appropriate. For example:

If the volume of concrete for each of 10 footings is 34.56 CF, then the total would be 345.60 CF, or 12.80 CY for all of the footings. The total concrete yardage would be rounded to 13 CY for the total amount of concrete, rather than rounding each individual footing to the nearest CY.

Rule 11: Calculate Net Versus Gross Quantities

Some materials require an added allowance for waste. Waste is applicable to materials only, and should not be applied to labor or confused with productivity. Before waste is added, quantities are referred to as *net quantities*. After an allowance for waste has been added, quantities are referred to as *gross quantities*. *(See the "Accounting for Waste" section later in this chapter.)*

Rule 12: Check the Takeoff

The quantity takeoff should be checked by another individual for accuracy. Ideally, it would be best to have another completely separate takeoff and estimate done as a means of checking the first. However, this may not be practical or cost-effective. Quantities derived by hand (without the use of a digitizer or computer) should be randomly checked. Select several work items or tasks throughout the estimate and recalculate their quantities. Extensions from the takeoff quantities to the final pricing units can even be checked by a reliable clerical staff person who has minimal background in estimating. The extension of quantities involves calculations that can be checked by anyone with an understanding of simple mathematics and a calculator.

Rule 13: Mark up the Drawings as Bid Documents

Mark the drawings using check marks, colored pencils, or highlighters to indicate the work that has already been taken off. These serve as the estimator's work papers and should be kept as a record of how quantities were derived. If original drawings must be returned, make copies and file them as records. This aspect of the takeoff is critical for projects that are bid and then go to contract. Once the project has been awarded, it will be turned over to the project manager, and the bid documents become crucial for relaying information as to how the project was bid.

Rule 14: Focus on the Task at Hand

Those who perform the takeoff and pricing require a high level of concentration in order to accurately do the job, and should not be subject to interruptions from all the normal distractions of the construction office. Phone calls, frequent drop-ins by co-workers, and any type of concentration-breaker are detrimental to accurate performance. Distractions or attempts to multi-task are often the greatest source of error. When the takeoff must be interrupted, select a natural stopping point and mark it clearly so that when work is resumed, there is no doubt as to where you left off.

Rule 15: Organize the Documentation

Careful organization and neatness of work papers and takeoff sheets are crucial. If supporting work papers are needed (including sketches or details as to how unusual features were estimated), they should be retained and attached to the pertinent quantity sheet. Even if the takeoff is performed using a digitizer and the estimate is done on a computer, there will still be work papers and notes.

All calculations should follow a logical and sequential process. Preprinted takeoff sheets and forms, such as shown in Figure 4.1, should be used whenever possible. Erasures should be neat and clean. Work papers, quantity sheets, and all components of the estimate should be maintained for a minimum of one year. Projects are sometimes abandoned for a number of reasons. Often, those same projects are re-started at a later point in time, due to changes in the economy, ownership, or need. Retaining the estimate and its various components is a reliable way to check for what has changed or remained the same over time.

Accounting for Waste

Quantities derived during the takeoff process are often not the same quantities that are purchased when the work is actually in process. For example, it may be determined that the area of a floor to be covered with plywood is 300 SF. However, plywood is sold in full sheets, which are each 32 SF. When the 300 SF required to cover the floor deck is divided by 32 SF per sheet, the result is 9.375 sheets. Since only full sheets are sold, 10 sheets must be included in the takeoff. The difference between what to include in the takeoff and estimate and what is actually installed is called *waste*. As mentioned earlier, the material quantities before waste is added are called *net* quantities, and *gross* quantities after waste has been added. Pricing is done at the gross quantities level, not on net quantities.

Quantity Sheet

SHEET NO.

PROJECT _____

ESTIMATE NO. _____

LOCATION _____ ARCHITECT _____ DATE _____

TAKEOFF BY _____ EXTENSIONS BY _____ CHECKED BY _____

DESCRIPTION	NO.	DIMENSIONS				UNIT				UNIT				UNIT	

Figure 4.1

48

Waste may need to be added for any of three primary reasons:
- To adjust to the standard sales unit
- As anticipated waste resulting from handling
- To achieve a specific assembly lap, as in shingles

Adjusting for Standard Sales Units

Materials often go through some on-site modification. The classic example is wood framing. Framing lumber is purchased in standard lengths, usually in 2' increments, delivered to the site and then cut to exact lengths for the specific component of the frame. It is purchased in lengths as close to the in-place length as possible to minimize waste. For example, if a partition has a single top and bottom plate with a plate-to-plate height of 8', the estimator would include studs to be purchased at 8' long in the takeoff. The studs would then be cut down to 7'-9" for installation between the plates. The remaining 3", sometimes referred to as *"fall-off,"* is the waste. It has no real value, but still needs to be accounted for in the estimate, because it is paid for.

It is important to be attentive to other types of materials with similar waste requirements. Any material with a standard sales unit larger than needed for the task qualifies as having a waste component. Construction materials sold in lengths, rolls, bundles, boxes, and sheets, and fluids sold in gallons, drums, or barrels, should be reviewed for waste.

Waste Resulting from Handling

Waste can occur as a result of handling or placement, which is fairly common. Even with careful planning and execution of a task, waste will occur. One example is concrete with specific types of placement. Concrete placed by a chute has minimal waste, as the concrete slides directly into its final resting place, the form. There is no real handling of the concrete using this method. Concrete placed by pump, however, allows significant loss of the total amount, which needs to be accounted for in the estimate as waste.

Other examples of common materials with waste include soil, gravel, and stone delivered by the truckload. Often these materials are distributed by equipment and, due to the inaccurate nature of placing earthen materials, waste can be significant. Generally, the more the materials are handled, the more waste can be expected.

Waste Required for Lap

Often, additional materials are required to satisfy a specific *lap* in order to maintain continuity of a particular feature. Examples include concrete reinforcement, siding materials such as clapboard and shingles, and roofing underlayments such as bituthene membranes and felt paper. Allowing for lap does not meet the strict definition of waste, since the material is actually used in the project, but lap requires additional materials, so the same principle applies.

Consider the placement of welded wire fabric (WWF) for reinforcement in a slab, which is required to be continuous by design. For the WWF to be effective, there must be no break in the continuity. It is sold in specific sales units, most commonly as a sheet measuring 5' x 10', or 50 SF. The specifications define the amount of lap required based on the design. In this particular example, Section 03300 of MasterFormat, Cast-in-Place Concrete, might define the lap as a minimum of 12" on side laps and 12" on end laps. If the *effective area,* or the net area that one sheet will cover, is compared with the individual sales unit, a significant loss for lap is evident. If a 12" lap is maintained on the end and side of a single sheet, the effective area is reduced from 50 SF to 36 SF, or 72% of its original area. This represents a 28% waste as a result of the lap required.

Other Factors that Affect Quantities

Economy of Scale

In addition to the specific examples noted above, there are other considerations that, while not specifically considered waste, have an impact of the amount of materials included within the takeoff. Price breaks based on total quantities should also be taken into account, referred to as *economy of scale.* This is a simple economic principle that can be defined for our purposes as securing a better unit price for a large quantity of a material purchased.

Suppliers may be able to provide price break points for certain materials. Brick, for instance, is sold by the pallet, varying in quantity based on the size and type. For example, assume that there are 500 bricks per pallet. If it is determined that 63,485 bricks, including normal waste, are needed for a particular project, it might be more economical to order a full pallet rather than having loose bricks. This would mean ordering 63,500 bricks, or 127 full pallets.

Compaction

Other types of tasks require additional materials, though they do not fit the standard definition of waste. Take, for example, soil placement. When soils are imported to a site, placed, and compacted, there is a portion of the *in-truck* or loose volume that is "lost" due to compaction. This is expected and must be accounted for in the takeoff process.

Many of the leftovers from waste not only have no real value to the project, but add a further expense for disposal. Consider the fall-off from the earlier framing example. It has no appreciable value to the project that can be acknowledged in the estimate, and will cost money to dispose of. Most wood frame projects, when completed, have a pile of lumber scraps that need to be disposed of. Associated costs might include dumpster and disposal fees, along with the labor to put the scraps in a dumpster.

Pricing the Estimate

Once the takeoff has been completed, the next step is to start the pricing portion of the estimate. In order to accurately apply unit prices to quantities, one must understand the different types of costs associated with the unit price system.

There are two main types of costs associated with the unit price estimate:
- Production costs
- Non-production costs

Production Costs

Production costs are part of the actual physical project, including materials, labor, tools, equipment, and subcontractor costs for each task or activity incorporated in the final structure. If we analyze the unit price of an individual task, such as a concrete slab that is placed by a contractor's own employees, the individual components are: concrete material itself, labor to place and finish it, and equipment rental/ownership costs for the power trowels. If the slab was placed and finished by a subcontractor, the costs might be estimated as a single cost (lump sum) that includes all of the above components.

Non-Production Costs

Non-production costs are *overhead,* or the cost of supporting the production activities. Overhead costs are divided into two categories:
- Direct overhead costs
- Indirect overhead costs

Direct Overhead Costs

Direct overhead costs, sometimes referred to as *project overhead,* are directly related to one individual project. These include a wide variety of costs such as temporary facilities, trailer rental, supervision, telephone usage, dumpsters, and electrical power usage. All are costs that are directly related to the specific project. They can be broken down further for estimating purposes into:
- Time-sensitive costs
- Fixed costs

Time-Sensitive Costs: Time-sensitive costs are items whose price is driven by time. The longer the particular item is on site, the higher the cost. A good example would be a project trailer. Most contractors rent trailers, and since there is a monthly fee for rental, the cost is a function of time, or time-sensitive. The longer the project goes on, the higher the accrued cost for the trailer rental. There are numerous other examples of time-sensitive costs that can be found in project overhead, such as telephone and fax line costs and the superintendent's wages. To accurately assign a dollar value to these costs, a schedule should be developed to determine how and when they apply during the term of the project. Initial schedules for determining time-sensitive costs tend to be rudimentary and develop with more information as the estimate proceeds. It is not uncommon for a project schedule to evolve through three generations before it is considered sufficient for use. (The development and evolution of schedules for estimating purposes will be discussed in detail in Chapter 6.)

Fixed Overhead Costs: Direct overhead costs that are not affected by time are classified as *fixed* project overhead costs. Examples include building permit fees, registered site layout, engineering design fees, access roads or ramps, and so forth. In most circumstances, there is a single occurrence for each of these costs, independent of the project schedule.

Indirect Overhead Costs

Indirect overhead costs are referred to as *main office overhead,* which is any cost of a general nature that is not unique to a specific project. Indirect overhead costs are associated with being in business. Some examples include main office rent or mortgage, salaries and benefits of staff, base insurance policies, company vehicle costs, and so forth. The costs associated with indirect overhead are accumulated while work is being performed and must be recovered in each estimate when bidding on future work. These costs are recovered by assigning an incremental piece of the indirect overhead to each project that is bid. The most common method is by a percentage of the estimated cost of the work.

All costs associated with indirect overhead are tabulated for a specific review period, most often quarterly (covering three-month periods) for the established company. (Companies experiencing rapid growth or new companies might review indirect overhead costs as frequently as once a month.) Indirect overhead costs are compared to the dollar amount of work completed in the same review period. The idea is that there is a relationship between the dollars spent and the dollars of revenue generated. For example:

> *If the total indirect overhead costs for one calendar year were $500,000, during which time $5,000,000 in construction work was completed, the percentage of indirect overhead could be calculated as 10% of the work completed.*

$$\frac{\text{Indirect Overhead Costs}}{\text{Construction Work Completed}} \times 100 = \text{Indirect Overhead Percentage}$$

$$\frac{\$500,000}{\$5,000,000} \times 100 = 10\%$$

This is a very simple example of the method used to calculate indirect overhead costs for estimating purposes. It shows that the indirect overhead costs are about 10%, or $1 in indirect overhead costs for every $10 of construction costs.

There are alternate methods used to determine indirect overhead costs. Certain types of contractors (such as wood framing contractors) provide labor as their primary product. They allocate indirect overhead using a different method. Their overhead costs are still tracked and reviewed periodically, and adjustments are made based on sound financial practices. The difference is that overhead costs are allocated by *billable hours of work,* sometimes referred to as *service billing allocation.* A framing contractor may have ten billable employees, each working an average of

2,000 hours per year (50 weeks at 40 hours per week), less adjustments for vacations, sicktime, and downtime for weather and other potential lost hours. This translates to 20,000 billable hours per year. If the same company's indirect overhead costs for the same period were $200,000, it would make sense that each billable hour would need to support that $10-per-hour overhead expense. In mathematical terms:

$200,000/20,000 hours = $10.00 per hour

In addition to the hourly wage of the employee, the labor burden, and any direct benefit program costs, such as medical, dental, or retirement, the contractor would have to add $10.00 per hour to cover the cost of the company's indirect overhead expenses. The sum of all these costs, plus an additional markup for profit, would be the billable rate for the individual employee of the framing contractor.

While each method has distinct advantages depending on the type of work, each also has potential flaws. The downside is the risk associated with the difficulty predicting future business. As long as business is as good as predicted or better, both formulas are successful. Any downward trend in the business plan or reduced volume of work under contract will require adjustments, such as cutting back on unnecessary overhead costs. Failure to make adjustments in a timely manner results in lost profits, or worse, burdens that put the company's financial health in jeopardy.

"Gray Areas" of Overhead Costs

Some non-production costs are less clear in terms of whether they should be classified as direct or indirect, and can vary depending on the accounting practices of the contractor, or even the individual project. A classic example is project management costs. If the project manager is assigned to one project and only one project, the project management costs would be considered a direct cost. If that same project manager's time was split between several projects, it might be better considered an indirect overhead cost.

Other unique considerations include insurance premiums. Some premiums have an annual base cost for the policy that fluctuates in conjunction with the volume of work under contract. In this circumstance, the base policy is considered an indirect overhead cost, and the incremental increases relative to specific projects would be classified as direct overhead costs.

A simple, reliable way to determine if a cost is part of direct overhead or indirect overhead is to ask the following question:

If the contractor did not have the project under contract, would the cost still exist?

If the answer is yes, then the item is considered an indirect cost. If the answer is no, it is a direct cost. If the answer is both yes and no, then the cost can be shared as both an indirect and direct overhead cost.

Predicting Overhead Costs

Contractors with a history of success have a distinct advantage over new, growing companies. Over time and with the completion of multiple projects, experienced contractors have the ability to regulate and establish indirect overhead costs through a series of review and adjustments until they have determined their typical overhead costs. This allows them the opportunity to predict future indirect costs based on a business plan for future revenues. While the formula is not always exact and can change as personnel and resources come and go, it is a fairly good indicator of what a company's overhead will be and the volume of work the company needs to maintain to be financially sound. The need to predict and control costs explains why so many contractors develop a market niche and tend to establish a reputation in one type of construction. Few contractors can compete in a wide variety of construction markets. Successful contractors quickly learn the limitations and capabilities of their companies.

The Unit Price Estimate

While there are various reasons for business failures in the construction industry, a major contributor is the inability to produce an accurate, profitable, and defendable estimate. At the root of this chronic problem is poor or unprofessional practices on the part of the estimator.

Estimating is a labor-intensive and costly operation that, at best, only *approximates* the cost of a construction project as seen through the experience and judgment of the professional estimator. Every element within the estimate, ranging from quantities to unit prices, must be substantiated in factual terms in order to be considered professional work. This is the basis for a defendable, detailed estimate.

The work product of the professional estimator is the detailed, or unit price estimate. By definition, the unit price estimate consists of breaking the project down into tasks, quantifying those tasks, and then applying a price based on the units of each task. As mentioned previously, each task can have various and multiple components, e.g., materials, labor, tools, equipment, and subcontractors that make up the unit price. For example:

> In order to be successful, the professional estimator must:
> - Be highly organized and efficient
> - Understand the construction process and its materials
> - Read and fully understand plans and specifications
> - Be able to visualize the project being built
> - Have a working knowlege of basic mathematics

Task Description	Quantity	Unit		Unit Price	Total
Place and finish concrete slab	10,000	SF	@	$1.00	= $10,000

The unit price of $1.00 per SF in this example consists of the labor and equipment used in the placing and finishing of the concrete slab. The example illustrates that the $1.00 unit cost is based on the SF unit. Once the unit price has been multiplied by the quantity, the resultant cost is called the *extended cost,* or total cost for the item.

Other types of estimates, such as conceptual and square foot estimates, are acceptable under certain circumstances, but are the realm of the seasoned professional estimator. Both are less accurate than the unit price estimate and are used as tools for budgeting and feasibility studies during various phases of the design development.

A correct unit price estimate has a quantity and a price for each item of work or expense identified in the bid documents. When the estimate is summarized, and profit is added, it is submitted as the offer, or the *bid.* Should the contractor be successful in attaining the contract, this same estimate now becomes the basis for the cost control system that will determine whether the work has been performed and the costs incurred as estimated—in short, if the project made or lost money.

The unit price estimate serves as the guideline for awarding subcontracts and purchasing materials and standard for judging productivity. It is valuable in assigning a dollar value to each category in the schedule of values that will become the basis for requisitioning payment. In essence, the estimate becomes the foundation of the project. This is why it is of such importance—it is part of virtually every aspect of the construction process. The most proficient contracting firm cannot overcome flawed estimates that represent work taken below cost, or that do not allow for an appropriate profit.

At the heart of the successful estimate is the unit price. The term *unit price* can be defined as the incremental cost per unit of work.

$$\frac{\text{Cost}}{\text{Unit of Work}} = \text{Unit Price}$$

The following are parameters that define the unit price:
- Unit prices are based on dollars, or portions of a dollar, per unit.
- The pricing unit or unit cost should match the extended unit of each task quantity.
- Most unit prices are based on a specific time frame as a means of measuring productivity.
- Labor unit prices can be based on an individual's production or on the production of a crew.
- Unit prices can be based on historical cost data or published cost data.
- Unit prices can include all, one, or a combination of cost types (material, labor, equipment, subcontractors, etc.).

Sources of Unit Price Data

Collecting, organizing, and analyzing the data for the estimate can be a daunting task. Being able to use this data efficiently is a result of how well it has been organized. There are several sources for pricing data, but most fall into these five categories:

1. Written quotations or published prices from suppliers and vendors.
2. Written quotations from subcontractors, including materials and labor.
3. Written quotations from equipment suppliers or rental agencies.
4. Historical cost data from your company's own previously completed projects (similar to the one currently being estimated).
5. Cost data from published sources, such as RSMeans.

Categories 1 through 3 are referred to as *contemporaneous* pricing. They are based on a review of the project documents, with full understanding of the project's unique or special conditions. These prices can usually be assumed to be an offer or bid from a source looking to do business. Pricing by interested parties doesn't just happen. It is typically the result of time (and money) invested in soliciting pricing from various sources. Failure to establish contacts, gain the interest of the bidder, and follow up as bid day approaches can often result in gaps in the estimate on bid day. Quotes from bidders, reviewed and qualified, are usually the best source of costs.

Current pricing should be accepted only from individuals or firms that will provide prices in writing. Frequently, pricing may be verbal, with written confirmation to follow. Such quotations should be written by the person receiving the quotation on a standardized form, called a *telephone quotation sheet*. At the time the quotation is received, it should be *qualified*. This involves asking the person providing the quote what is included. An intimate knowledge of the work involved in each task is necessary in order to ask the right questions. Sometimes all that is required is to confirm that the quoting party has included what was required or requested. The qualification process can also help avoid duplication errors. For example, if a material quote includes sales tax, this should be noted so that tax is not added a second time.

Any notes or pertinent information discussed during the qualification process should be written down on the telephone quotation sheet, so that they can be compared against the written follow-up quote. At a minimum, the telephone quote must document the name of the individual delivering the quote, the date and time, and how long the price is valid. In the absence of a written quote, follow up after the bid with a "confimation of price" fax or letter. This procedure has the benefit of documenting the price while it is fresh in both parties' minds. While most people in the construction business know that the quote is only as valid as the integrity of the firm or individual that makes it, a written quote goes a long way to ensuring compliance. A well-defined price is a big help when comparing various competing numbers.

Category 4 sources are records of actual costs of similar work previously performed by your own company. Historical costs are recorded—actual costs to perform a quantified, specific task. That means that the costs can be analyzed and compared with the project now being bid to obtain unit prices. If the total cost is divided by the total quantity, the result is the unit price. Historical data shows not only actual project costs for previously completed projects, but also the accuracy of those projects' estimates.

Historical costs are typically taken from the company's records for self-performed work. However, it is not uncommon for some general contractors to study and record the time spent and methods employed by other contractors or subcontractors to perform a defined quantity of a specific task in the hopes of gaining better estimating insight for their own future projects.

While historical costs are actual, it is rare that the unit price can be applied without making at least minor modifications to allow for different circumstances between the previously completed project and the project currently being bid. At the very least, there are considerations for cost escalations of wages and materials over time. There may be differing site or weather conditions, varying productivities and supervision, learning curves, and the degree of difficulty that might not be readily apparent from empirical data alone.

Historical data must be analyzed carefully, with some understanding of the unique set of circumstances under which the work was performed. All work papers from mathematical computations from the analysis should be retained for the record. Whenever possible, another individual should check the accuracy of the computations to uncover possible errors before they are incorporated into the estimate, and a bid is offered.

Category 5 costs are from published sources, such as the numerous RSMeans cost data books and software. As with any published construction cost data, there is an applied set of parameters. It is essential to understand all of the conditions that have been applied to the data (normally averages), so that you can make your own adjustments for factors such as location, skill of the crew, climate, availability of resources, and supervision.

Published costs must be adjusted for these considerations. Cost data can be presented in two ways: as *bare costs* without overhead and profit, and *total costs,* which include a markup for overhead and profit. It is important to understand whether the work will be self-performed or subcontracted. If it is self-performed, bare costs are preferable so that the markup can be applied at the end of the estimate. If the work is to be subcontracted, make sure that an allowance for the overhead and profit of the *installing contractor* is carried in the estimate before recapitulation.

Published data is based on normal working conditions, during regular business hours, and under average conditions. There is no accounting for unpredictable costs associated with labor resource shortages, supply and demand cycles, or travel and per diem costs. It is also important to understand price and crew size in published cost data to make adjustments based on experience and judgment.

Pricing the Quantities

After the quantity takeoff for each individual task or activity has been assembled, organized, extended into its final units, and checked, prices must be applied. As discussed previously, unit prices can be obtained from a variety of sources and should be noted within the estimate. In the case of published cost data, such as the RSMeans cost data books and software, a twelve-digit (MasterFormat) line item can be cited. In the case of historical or contemporaneous prices, the specific source should be noted and documented within the estimate. This helps establish the credibility of the unit price.

Cost Analysis Sheets and the Estimate Summary

The cost analysis portion of the estimate can be recorded on preprinted forms or in estimating software applications such as *CostWorks* (cost data software by RSMeans). *(See Figure 19.1 for a sample Cost Analysis sheet.)*

Cost Analysis sheets are different from quantity takeoff sheets in that they provide space for unit prices. Unit prices can be broken into component parts, such as materials, labor, and equipment. Since each component has a different modifier, each component must be calculated and summarized separately. The format of the form allows you to apply unit prices for each component in a columnar sequence.

As each task or activity is priced, its total estimated cost is tabulated at the right of the sheet. Once each task line has been priced and totaled, then the columns are totaled from the top to the bottom of the sheet. Finally, they are totaled for each CSI MasterFormat section number or grouping of tasks.

Tasks can be grouped together for work of a similar nature. For example, the estimator might summarize and total all of the carpentry framing tasks or the entire masonry scope of work for a project. This is done so that the totals for each MasterFormat division can be brought to an *Estimate Summary* sheet. This represents an entire scope of work that might be subcontracted if the project bid is won. Totaling the cost of work by CSI MasterFormat division is an easy and logical way to organize the estimate. The total cost for materials, labor, and equipment can be summarized and brought to the Estimate Summary sheet so that you can view a single number that represents a well-defined scope of work. This allows for comparing a price generated for a division or segment of work to a price that was submitted by a subcontractor bidding the work.

The format of the Estimate Summary sheet is straightforward. The description of the tasks is in column format along the left side of the page, with parallel columns for materials, labor, equipment, and subcontractor costs that start adjacent to the description and move from left to right. At the far right is the total column, which contains the total value of the various components of each grouping of tasks or CSI MasterFormat division. The values of each component are added along the individual rows, which, when totaled, represent the total value for that scope of work.

As a check and balance system each column is totaled. Then the total of each column is added and compared with the last number in the lower right-hand corner of the sheet. Totals for each column are carried over to the reverse of the sheet and entered into a *Totals Brought Forward* row, which again allows checking for accuracy. When all costs have been transposed from the Cost Analysis sheets to the Estimate Summary sheet, costs for project overhead are added. At this level of costs, the totals are referred to as *raw costs*, or *unburdened costs*. Modifiers are added to each category, and the indirect overhead is applied to the subtotals. This is referred to as the *burdened* or "real cost." In theory, if each task was performed and the costs realized exactly as detailed in the estimate, the real cost would be the break-even point with no profit being realized. The last steps would be to add any contingencies deemed justified, profit, and, finally, any costs related to performance and payment bonds, if required. *(See Chapter 20 for more on contingencies and profit.)* This final number rounded to the whole dollar represents the bid amount for a lump sum bid.

Submitting a Bid

The bid is a by-product of the estimate—a proposal to do the work estimated. In short, a bid is an offer to perform work for a certain price. It is the natural progression of the estimate. In simple terms, a bid is composed of:

- An offer to perform a defined scope of work.
- A stipulated compensation for performing the work.
- Name of the party making the offer.
- Name of the party to which the offer is made.

Some bids or proposals are submitted from a firm on letterhead, while some are on generic preprinted proposal forms, and others are on bid forms provided by the architect or owner. In the absense of a bid form, the party making the offer has to quantify, and sometimes qualify, the exact scope of work being provided within the proposal. The bidder must identify the documents used in preparing the bid by listing the plans and specifications, the date of the documents, and any addenda issued that modified the documents. The offer should include any assumptions or qualifications on which the proposal is based. The bid should be executed by a responsible individual having the authority to do so, assigned by the company making the offer. The person who signs the bid should include his or her title. The offer should have an expiration date, and should provide a space for the receiving party to sign, date, and accept the offer.

Using letterhead or preprinted forms in lieu of a bid form has some distinct advantages to the contractor and disadvantages to the owner or architect. The contractor can include or exclude any item or scope of work chosen and can qualify or quantify any item of work within the scope without rendering the proposal null and void. The disadvantage to the owner is that it becomes difficult to compare multiple proposals from different contractors if each has noted some qualifications that affect the price.

When a bid form is provided, it alleviates some of the problems encountered with bids that are submitted on letterhead. Bid forms are printed forms specific to the project with the language of the proposal already typed in the body of the form. They are provided by the architect or owner as part of the documents and contain blank spaces for the contractor to fill in only the information required and offer no space for the contractor to qualify a bid. Using a standard bid form ensures a level of conformity so that each bidder's proposal includes the same scope, where the only difference is in the offered amount. The advantage to the architect and owner is an immediate acknowledgement of where each contractor's price lies in comparison to the prices of the other bidders.

Conclusion

A reliable and comprehensive estimate is a combination of quantities derived during the takeoff and the application of correct unit prices. Unit prices can be categorized into materials, labor, and equipment costs for self-performed work, or subcontractor costs for work performed by those individuals who are not direct employees. There are also overhead or non-production costs that must be applied. When all costs are summarized, profit added, and the price is offered in the hope of securing work, we have a bid.

Chapter Five

Understanding Material & Labor Costs

Before finalizing materials, labor, and equipment costs as unit prices within an estimate, they must first be modified. Some of the modifications, such as for materials, are rather simple. Others are more complex, such as modifiers to labor or depreciation of equipment. We will explore the process of modifying these costs in this chapter. While modifiers vary from state to state and city to city, the process is the same.

Materials

Two modifiers are added to the costs of materials to arrive at an accurate unit price: sales tax and waste. Some taxpayer- and government-funded projects are exempt from sales tax, so there may be no need to add it. However, most residential and commercial projects are subject to a sales tax on materials. Some states also apply sales tax to labor.

Waste is applicable to most materials for several different reasons. *(See Chapter 4, "Waste Net & Gross Quantities.")* Properly accounting for waste is often a matter of judgment based on experience. For example, if you were to prepare a detailed materials list for all lumber and sheathing materials needed on a project, you would then solicit pricing from local lumber suppliers and receive quotations for materials and delivery. Often, the quote is a lump sum derived by multiplying a series of quantities by unit prices. Based on experience, you would know that these are net quantities and must be adjusted for waste.

> *There are some unpredictable and uncontrollable reasons to add waste, including theft, damage from weather, damage by other trades, and human error. This waste can be accounted for by adding a percentage to the lump sum quote provided by the supplier.*

It would be impossible to predict which materials will incur more waste, so the most practical approach is to add a percentage in dollars to the lump sum quote. For example:

The quote from a lumber supplier is $76,890. It was determined based on experience and/or historical cost data that an appropriate waste factor for the particular project is 8%. This translates to an approximate added cost of $6,152, which must be included in the estimate. The two costs added together now equal $83,042. Since the state in which the project is being built has a 5% sales tax, the gross amount of the subquote for the lumber will need to be increased by 5%: $83,042 x .05 = $4,152. When combined and rounded, the total is $91,348.

Waste can be added as an additional quantity of materials, or it can be calculated as an increase in the unit price. The following example illustrates the calculation of carpet material costs for an office space based on a waste factor incorporated into the unit price. To determine a unit price cost per SY of carpet to cover an office floor, the necessary quantities should first be reviewed.

The net area to be covered with carpet is 2,000 SY. However, the carpet is sold in 15'-0" wide rolls, and, when layout is considered, the actual quantity needed is 2,160 SY, or an additional 8%. Applicable sales tax must be added (in this example, 5%). These factors are then reviewed and their impact assessed in the calculation below.

Carpet (as specified)	*$ 38.00 per SY*
Waste factor of 8% applied	*3.04 per SY*
Subtotal	*$ 41.04 per SY*
Sales tax of 5% applied	*2.05 per SY*
Total	*$ 43.09 per SY*

If the $43.09 is extended over the 2,000 SY of the net area, the cost is $86,180. Since the actual quantity to be installed is 2,000 SY, it would be incorrect to use the 2,160 SY to represent the quantity to be installed, since this would add an 8% error in the amount to be installed to the labor portion of the estimate. In addition to the costs, profit would be added to the unit price of $43.09 per SY. If a 10% profit were added, the billing unit price would be $47.40 per SY.

Labor
Calculating the cost of labor unit prices is more difficult than for material unit prices. First, the correct wage rate must be calculated. There are several modifiers that must be added to the cost of the actual wage rate. These include state and federal taxes on wages, insurances, and benefits.

Billing Rate

We should start by defining some basic terms. The term *wage rate* for this discussion refers to the "in the envelope pay," or the agreed upon wage between the employee and employer. Once the wage rate has been modified by all taxes, insurance, and overhead components, the rate is referred to as the *burdened labor cost*. After profit has been added, the result is the full value of the labor-hour, referred to as the *billing rate*. This is the rate that would be charged for labor in a time and material application. The following is a review of the components that make up the billing rate and how those costs are calculated.

Wage Rate

The wage rate, or the hourly rate of pay on which the employee's paycheck is calculated, is regulated by the agreement between the employee and the employer, a collective bargaining agreement, or by a prevailing wage rate. For example, a carpenter hired at $25 per hour would "gross" $1,000 in wages for a 40-hour work week. From this amount, taxes would be deducted, and the employee would receive a "net" paycheck.

Benefits

Many employers provide benefits in the form of medical and dental policies, vacation pay, paid sick days, retirement package contributions, annuities, or a variety of other compensatory benefits. The costs of these benefits are typically included within the calculation of the burdened rate. These benefits represent a cost to the employer that must be recovered, which can be broken down into a percentage of the hourly rate and then extended to a dollar amount per hour. This dollar amount is then added to the wage rate.

State and Federal Taxes/Insurance

All states and the federal government apply a tax to wages to provide a source for unemployment benefits. The Federal Unemployment Tax Act (FUTA) and State Unemployment Tax Act (SUTA) are taxes paid by the employer based on the dollars earned by the employee. They are levied on the employee's gross taxable wages. As of the printing of this book, FUTA is at 0.8% with a cap on the first $7,000 of the employee's gross wages. Once the employee earns more than the cap, the tax stops. The SUTA tax varies from state to state and will fluctuate depending on the employer's experience, which is measured by the number of employees that the employer has laid off. The fewer employees claiming benefits, the less the employer's contribution. As the number of employees claiming benefits increases, the amount of the employer's contribution also increases. The SUTA tax can vary with a number of factors based on the employer's experience in the work force, number of workers, and the type of work. There is typically a cap on the wages, as with the FUTA tax.

The Federal Insurance Corporation of America (FICA), or Social Security, and Medicaid taxes are provided by the federal government, though more appropriately considered insurances than taxes. The employee is taxed at the rate of 7.65% of gross taxable wages, deducted from the employee's paycheck. Additionally, the employer makes a matching contribution of the same percentage. It is this percentage that is recouped in the wage calculation.

Workers' Compensation Insurance: Another type of insurance that protects employees is Workers' Compensation, provided by the employer in the event of injury, disability, or death occurring in the workplace. In most states, this is a compulsory insurance. Workers' Comp, as it is commonly referred to, is different for each classification of worker or trade, and is based on a percentage of the gross non-premium wages of the employee. (In other words, overtime or premium wages do not affect the insurance premium.) Insurance premiums for individual companies performing the same work will vary by experience. Premium rates are based on the employer's number of days without a serious accident on the job site. A safe work environment translates to lower Workers' Compensation premiums based on the experience modifier. Thus, the insurer rewards the employer for promoting a safe work environment with reduced insurance premiums. Lower premiums are reflected in lower labor costs, thereby enabling the contractor to be more competitive in bidding.

General Liability Insurance

General liability insurance protects the project and any adjacent property from damage. This insurance compensates the contractor and, ultimately, the owner for damage by parties under the control of the general contractor, including employees and subcontractors. General liability premiums are again rated on the contractor's success in reducing risk. They are calculated based on two factors: employee wages and subcontracted work. For most general contractors who subcontract more than 70% of their contract work, the largest portion of the premium is based on the costs incurred by those parties under subcontract. However, there is still a portion of the premiums that is based on gross employee wages. Percentages will vary with the limits of the policy, size of the work, performance history of the contractor, and any regulations mandated by the state or insurer.

Labor Productivity

Productivity can best be described as the rate at which work is produced by an individual or crew per unit of time. The unit of time most often used is the day. (The hour is too short of a period to provide an accurate measurement.) A day is considered an eight-hour period, over which productivity will fluctuate up or down, depending on breaks, learning curves, starts and stops, and material handling. Productivity on the same task can vary when performed by two different crews, or during different times of the day. It can also vary with extremes in weather or temperature. When the work produced is measured at the end of the day, it represents a reasonable average for all of the normal fluctuations. It is fairly easy to take a "snapshot" at the beginning of the day and again at the end of the day and compare the difference.

There are also many factors to consider when determining the expected productivity of a task. For example, consider two separate roofs with the same number of units (squares), height from the ground, asphalt shingles, and configuration (style). The only difference is the pitch of the roof; one is a 6:12 pitch, and the other 12:12. Most construction professionals, even novices, would agree that the steeper-pitched roof reduces mobility, thereby making the roofing process slower and more difficult. This is translated into a reduced productivity, and a higher unit cost for labor.

The best measure of a crew's productivity is its own historical data. Job records for payroll and labor-hours to complete a specific task offer the best guidelines for predicting future performance. Experienced estimators know that while this is no guarantee of future performance, it provides a logical model. Specific adjustments can be made based on the needs of the individual project.

Individual and Crew Tasks

All tasks can be categorized for estimating purposes into either an individual task or a crew task. An *individual task* is one performed by a single individual. Performance and productivity is measured by the single output of the individual performing the work. As an example, consider a carpenter trimming a modestly sized interior window with wood casing. This is clearly an individual task. The performance of the individual carpenter can be easily measured by counting the quantity of windows trimmed in a single day, provided the windows are of similar size. After several days of trimming windows, an average productivity could be established, and a model could be created for future window trimming work. The cost of the carpenter per day could then be divided by the number of windows trimmed to establish a baseline cost model per window. Adjustments could be made to this cost model to predict the productivity for trimming windows of sizes different than the one used to create the cost model.

> *An example of a cost model for the carpenter trimming the windows is: 8 carpenter hours x $48.88 per hour = $391.04. For multiple days, the carpenter will trim 10.5 windows per day. The cost per window will be $37.24. It could also be concluded that approximately 0.76 carpenter-hours are needed to trim a window.*

Crew tasks are more challenging to estimate in terms of productivity. They combine the performance of multiple individuals, each of whom performs a specific function to complete the overall task. The measurement of productivity is a by-product of how well the team performs together. Crew tasks have a different dynamic—efficiency as a team. For example, a crew installing brick work might consist of two mason tenders and three bricklayers, one of whom is a foreman. Each member of the crew has a specific function that contributes to the overall performance of the crew. The foreman directs the crew, lays out the work, and aspires to a steady, predictable productivity. The bricklayers, including the foreman, lay up the brick. The foreman produces less as a result of other duties, but still contributes. The mason tenders, or laborers tending the bricklayers, mix mortar, stock the staging with materials, and provide support services. While they do not install the brick, their duties are essential to successful production.

Each crew member's performance relies on the other members to perform their work efficiently. Adding or removing a single individual changes the crew and the productivity. Selecting the most efficient crew is critical to successfully estimating. This is where skill and experience play a major role. Consult historical data for determining the most effective crew size to maximize efficiency.

Subcontractors

Subcontractors are, by definition, independent contractors. They are an indispensable part of the construction process and perform an increasingly larger percentage of work on construction projects. Subcontractors "hire and fire" their own labor, purchase their own materials, run their own equipment, and, quite often, define their success entirely on their own performance. Subcontractors provide their own insurances: both general liability and Workers' Compensation. They are held responsible for their actions and are required to pay their own taxes.

By virtually every test, subcontractors are considered independent of the general or prime contractor, yet why are general or prime contractors held contractually responsible for the errors, losses, and overall performance of their subcontractors? This can be explained in two ways. As a result of ever-advancing technology in the construction industry, projects are becoming more complex. Construction requires a higher level of subcontractor specialization, which in turn demands more training and brings more risk for error or loss to the general/prime contractor.

Subcontractors are bound by agreement to general or prime contractors to execute a "portion of the work." This portion of work is most often well-defined, but of limited scope, with a stipulated sum as the basis of compensation. This sum is a piece of the overall or total amount that comprises the contract value between the general/prime contractor and the owner.

Typical agreements between owners and general contractors do not explicitly recognize subcontractors. The agreement assigns responsibility for subcontractors to the general or prime contractor, who is the only signatory party with the owner. General or prime contractors realize that their firms must be compensated for the coordination, supervision, and risk assumed when hiring subcontractors.

Since subcontractors are separate entities, there is no need to apply markups for taxes and insurance on wages, or taxes and waste on materials. These are implied to be included by the subcontractor, as is the subcontractor's own markup for indirect overhead costs and profit. In order to apply markup to prices received from subcontractors, the general contractor should consider these factors:

- Dollar value of subcontractor quote. How large of a percentage of the overall total contract is the work of this subcontract?
- How often has your company done business with this subcontractor, and how successful has the relationship been?
- How financially stable is the subcontractor? Does he or she require more frequent payments than the terms of your contract with the owner?
- Can the subcontractor provide a performance and payment bond?
- Will the subcontractor require more "management time" than other subcontractors?
- What is the project duration?

The above are all criteria for determining the markup that should be applied to the subcontractor's price. There is no standard or acceptable range; it depends on what the market will bear. If the general contractor adds too much, however, the bid will not be competitive. If the amount is too little, the bid could be too low, which would result in substandard return or worse—performing the work for free. Neither of these is the hallmark of a successful contractor.

One final note concerning subcontractors. The Internal Revenue Service (IRS) has very specific criteria for defining a subcontractor. These criteria have survived many a challenge. All parties should be aware of applying the term "subcontractors" to what otherwise could be considered a thinly veiled attempt at avoiding the payment of insurance and taxes on wages. The common practice in the residential industry of hiring individuals, paying them as subcontractors by issuing a "1099" at the end of the year, and not insuring them with Workers' Compensation and liability insurance will not survive the challenge and could result in fines or penalties being assessed to both parties.

Indirect Overhead

Costs related to the operation of the main office and its staff are indirect overhead expenses. These costs, discussed in greater detail in Chapter 6, are associated with maintaining a business, but not directly attributable to a specific project. Indirect overhead includes, but is not limited to expenses such as:

- Corporate officers' salaries and benefits
- Rent or mortgage for the main office
- Monthly telephone, fax, or Internet charges
- Clerical and office associates' salaries, insurance, and taxes
- Corporate vehicles, insurance, and maintenance/operating costs
- Estimator's salary and benefits
- Legal, accounting, and technology service fees outside the firm
- Heating, electricity, and maintenance of the main office

To recover these costs, a small amount of each is added to the bids as a percentage of the cost of the work. These costs are tracked weekly or bi-weekly and adjusted as dictated by the financial health of the company. Adjustments can include the downsizing of the cost, or the outright elimination of the cost.

Profit

Profit is the reason for doing business. It is the end result of a project done right, and/or the reward for risks taken. While profit is not specifically a cost, it does need to be captured in the calculation of the billing rate. Without it, the project would be considered a failure. Profit is most often assigned as a percentage of all costs of the work. However, it can be assigned as a lump sum or stipulated fee. Calculating profit is based on careful consideration of a host of factors—some less tangible than others. A complete discussion of the assignment of profit will be covered in Chapter 20, "Profit & Contingencies."

Below is a sample calculation to illustrate the billing rate for a carpenter from the wage rate, using hypothetical rates for insurance, taxes, and other markups.

Carpenter Wage Rate	*$25.00*	*per hour*
Benefit Package	*8.55*	
FICA (7.65% on wage)	*1.92*	
FUTA (0.8% on wage)	*.20*	
SUTA (7% on wage)	*1.75*	
Workers' Comp at carpenter rate of 11.05% (on wage)	*2.77*	
General Liability insurance at a rate of 0.82% (on wage)	*.21*	
Subtotal	*$40.40*	
Indirect Overhead at 10% of all costs	*4.04*	
Subtotal	*$44.44*	*Burdened labor cost*
Profit at 10% of all costs	*4.44*	
Billing rate	**$48.88**	*per hour*

Conclusion

Understanding the various modifiers that apply to the material and labor component of the unit price is essential to good estimating practice. It is also a prerequisite for understanding the direct overhead costs that are discussed in Chapter 6.

Chapter Six

General Requirements

As discussed in Chapter 2, the technical portion of the specifications is based on the 16 divisions of the CSI MasterFormat. The first division is appropriately named Division 1—General Requirements and deals primarily with:

- Project overhead requirements
- The basis for administering the project, as defined by the General Conditions of the Contract for Construction

While the General Conditions of the Contract and the General Requirements of Division 1 stand alone as two separate documents, they are related. The General Requirements are important to the estimating process because they provide the information needed to assign a monetary value to the project overhead items.

General Requirements include items such as:

- Temporary facilities and controls
- Project meetings
- Reference standards and definitions
- Submittals
- Testing requirements
- Project closeout
- Construction phasing
- Quality control

Division 1 also identifies the contractor's special contractual obligations that have an associated cost and must be accounted for in the bidding process. This category includes development and provision of:

- Unit prices
- Alternates
- Allowances

While the General Requirements are the first division of the CSI MasterFormat, they are often the last to be priced. This is because most

General Requirements items require a complete understanding of the entire project, which is not possible until after you have become familiar with the contract documents, performed the takeoff of each division, and estimated the majority of the project.

Fixed & Variable Costs

Most items in the General Requirements can be classified for pricing purposes into two main categories: fixed costs and variable costs.

Fixed Costs

Fixed costs are associated with one-time project requirements. Building permit fees are a good example, and may be calculated by a formula that is cost-driven (e.g., $10 per $1,000 of building cost) or by some other fixed means, such as the square footage of the floor plan. Either way, you can determine a fixed cost for these fees to incorporate into the estimated price. Other examples of fixed costs include street opening or water tap permits, water and sewer betterment fees, trailer furnishings, prepaid insurance premiums, and project mobilization costs.

Variable, or Time-Sensitive, Costs

Variable costs are schedule-driven and are determined based on the length of time the items or services are needed on the project. Examples of time-sensitive costs include trailer rental, telephone and electrical power usage, supervision costs, and temporary toilets. Variable costs can also be thought of as more subjective in the sense that they are usually defined based on experience and judgment. Variable, or time-sensitive, costs frequently require that a "means and method" technique be used to develop the estimate. For example:

If scaffolding is required along the exterior façade of a building, the estimator will need to develop a method for staging the structure to perform the work. The options may be numerous and vary greatly in cost. Staging could be included for only one portion of the building at a time and then dismantled, relocated, and re-erected as many times as necessary to complete the work. Each move would have specific costs relative to how long the staging is required on site. Another alternative might be to use a power lift, which may improve mobility, but might limit the number of workers that can be carried. A third option might be a roof-based swing platform, which is less mobile than a lift, yet can provide more work area for personnel. Although all three methods satisfy the requirements for scaffolding, one approach must be selected. Once a strategy is selected, the duration and cost implications can be determined.

Other time-sensitive costs that are less subjective but still require experience and judgment include supervision, temporary utilities (such as job site electricity and water usage), and construction controls (such as barricades or temporary fencing). All of these costs are clearly tied to a specific length of time, or duration, that they are needed for the project.

To accurately determine the duration, first draft a schedule. The estimator, being most familiar with the project, is the likely candidate to develop the schedule. This should be done to estimate any project—residential or commercial—regardless of size, in order to accurately predict time-sensitive costs.

Schedules for Time-Sensitive Costs

Depending on the complexity of the project, several generations of schedules may be required as you become more familiar with the project or as input is added from other members of the project teams, such as the superintendent or the project manager. It should be noted that the schedule used for estimating purposes is not the same version that might be required after the job is awarded. The schedule used to estimate general requirements is a timeline showing where an activity occurs in the project and its duration. This estimate schedule should be comprehensive, but it should be noted that it is for use only as a tool for preliminary estimating.

Bar Graph or Gantt Chart: The most common form of schedule used for residential and light commercial projects is the bar graph, or Gantt chart. (For more complex projects, the Critical Path Method or CPM schedule is recommended.) The bar graph or Gantt chart is a simple graphic of the project schedule. It is easy to understand for the professional, novice, and non-construction personnel. The bar graph roughly follows CSI MasterFormat as an organizational method, with some modifications to follow the way the work will actually progress. Each activity or major activity group is represented graphically. Each has a start date, a duration, and a finish date. The bar graph implies a sequencing of activities with one activity following another. However, each activity is shown independent of its succeeding or preceding activity. This implies that each activity is not affected by other activities, which, of course, is not the case. There is, in fact, interdependence between activities on a construction project. If one task is delayed, it can have a "downstream effect" of disrupting future tasks, and ultimately delaying the project as a whole.

For estimating time-sensitive cost items on simple projects, a bar graph is usually sufficient. It shows the overall duration of the project, as well as the duration of each task, and allows the estimator to locate specific activities, such as weather-sensitive tasks, relative to calendar dates. This can be important in parts of the country where construction activities slow down, or close down altogether, in the winter months due to the cost of enclosing and heating activities. For projects that continue through the winter months in cold-weather climates, a schedule provides start and stop dates to calculate the cost of enclosure, temporary heat, and reduced productivity.

Critical Path Method (CPM) Scheduling: The CPM schedule is useful for larger, more complex construction projects that require a more dynamic and sophisticated scheduling procedure. The CPM format enables the scheduler to identify potential problems and develop plans for corrective action in advance. CPM schedules are more detailed, and the activities are shown as interdependent. If one task on the critical path is delayed, it will cause the delay of all succeeding critical path tasks, and the project as a whole, if corrective action is not taken. The CPM schedule illustrates the fact that on a real construction project, multiple tasks can occur independently at the same time, while other tasks must occur in a certain order and are highly dependent on completion of the preceding task. While developing a CPM schedule for bidding purposes is far more costly and time-consuming than a bar chart schedule, it is also far more reliable for predicting the project schedule.

Schedule Limitations in the Contract

Frequently, projects have a prescribed project duration or set "available time." Statements such as, *"The Contractor will have 270 calendar days from the Notice to Proceed to achieve Substantial Completion,"* are fairly common. As a result, many contractors believe this to be the schedule. It is highly recommended that the project schedule be determined independently of any such statements within the documents. The initial schedule should be developed with normal working times in mind. If the critical path needs to be compressed in order to achieve substantial completion on the required date, then the costs associated with the acceleration must be included as part of the bid. Acceleration options may include:

- Working extended hours
- Working weekends and holidays
- Adding labor resources
- Using multiple work shifts and crews
- Other, more creative options

The costs of acceleration that may be required to meet an "available time" requirement in the contract are sometimes overlooked. The contract-specified project duration may also tend to influence you to shorten the schedule to match.

Collecting General Requirements Cost Items

As noted earlier in this chapter, the costs for the General Requirements of the project are often left to the end of the estimate, when you are familiar with the overall project. A common practice for developing a thorough and realistic cost for Division 1 involves maintaining a checklist or even a handwritten list of reminders as each section of work is estimated. As a particular task is taken off, related General Requirements activities are noted. These may include such items as overtime supervision, cranes or other such equipment, temporary protection, or electrical needs. When it is time to determine the Division 1 costs, you can go through and note the General Requirements items that were checked off or listed while estimating the other divisions. Another option is to develop a checklist of all possible General Requirements items to use for each project, selecting the items that apply. In any case, a system of checks and balances is necessary to ensure that all General Requirements costs are addressed.

Applying Prices to General Requirements Items

Applying prices to fixed-cost items is fairly straightforward. Prices for time-sensitive, or variable, cost items can be determined using the list of needed items, together with the schedule. General Requirements costs, such as supervision, are reasonably clear. The General Conditions will stipulate that the project is required to have "adequate" supervision by the general contractor, defined as supervision licensed by the authority having jurisdiction, with a particular education and experience level in the type of project. The General Requirements might mandate that the supervisor be on site during all times that the work is in progress, including weekends and holidays. These statements help to determine what level of supervision is required, and the associated salary and benefit costs. At that point, it becomes a simple unit price multiplied by the duration.

Other time-sensitive costs may be required only intermittently or for specific periods within the overall project duration. For example, the General Requirements may stipulate that the general contractor provide an office trailer on-site until the building is closed in, and the office can be relocated inside. You would then calculate by the schedule how many weeks or months until the building will be closed-in, and an indoor office can be set up. The period (in weeks or months) from the start of the project until the date the building could house an office would be determined, and then multiplied by the appropriate rate (per week or month).

Costs for General Requirements categories such as project meetings and project closeout are judgment calls and almost exclusively experienced-based. It is difficult to predict accurately how long site meetings will take before the project starts. Any prediction is based purely on past experience, and that is still no guarantee. Possible considerations in determining costs for meetings include level of architect involvement (the more involved, the longer the meetings), level of document development (the more complete, the shorter the meeting time), and contractual requirements. Many contracts mandate a weekly meeting.

Conclusion

In summary, the General Requirements are the administrative costs associated with the execution of the contract and the project. Determining these costs is often a matter of experience, based on past projects and performance. Some costs are time-sensitive and require a schedule to accurately predict.

Chapter Seven

Site Construction

The second division of CSI MasterFormat is Site Construction, which deals primarily with engineering improvements at ground level or below. It includes tasks such as excavation and backfill, compaction, clearing and grubbing, underground utilities and drainage, paving and curbing, site improvements, and landscaping. Site construction takeoff is often the most difficult part of an estimate due to the number of unpredictable factors. Even with subsurface investigation and a careful site inspection, it is not always possible to predict with accuracy what lies beneath the surface. The site contractor must carefully study all available contract documents, as well as any supplemental information provided. A site inspection should be conducted only after becoming familiar with the documents. (Division 2 also includes demolition, which will be addressed at the end of this chapter.)

Civil Drawings Most site construction is shown on a special set of drawings that pertain exclusively to the site, called *civil drawings* or *site drawings*. They are designed under the direction and approval of a civil engineer and focus on the land's changes to accommodate a new structure. The most common drawings in the civil set of drawings are:
- Existing Conditions Drawings (Existing Site Survey)
- Site Demolition or Preparation Plan
- Site Grading and Drainage Plan
- Utilities Plan
- Paving and Curbing Plan
- Septic System or Sanitary Sewer Plan
- Site Lighting and Electrical Plan
- Site Improvements Plan
- Landscape and Irrigation Plan
- Site Details

The quantity of drawings and level of detail will vary from project to project and depend, to a large extent, on the owner's budget. Residential site plans can range from a single drawing to a full set. Commercial projects most often require a comprehensive set of civil drawings as a condition of permit approval. Each drawing in a civil set has special conventions and nomenclature unique to its discipline and provides a specific contribution to the overall civil set. Some drawings are self-explanatory by their title, such as the building drawing set. However, no drawing is used in a vacuum. Each is meant to be complementary and used with the others to help determine accurate quantities for pricing.

How Drawings Correlate

- The Existing Conditions drawing must be used in conjunction with the Site Grading drawing to determine the quantity of bulk cut or fill required to achieve the final grade.
- The Site Grading plan should be consulted along with the Utilities or Site Lighting plan to calculate the trench excavation and backfill required for site features, such as domestic water piping, gas service, electrical power and lighting conduits, and similar utilities.
- Drainage drawings provide information for taking off precast structures, such as tanks, manholes, catch basins, and reinforced concrete pipe. Additional information on the details sheets helps verify accurate pricing.
- Site Demolition or Preparation plans provide information on the removal or relocation of existing site features, such as trees or benches, or subsurface structures like abandoned foundations or rock.
- Architectural and Structural drawings should also be reviewed for details that would be shown in section (such as foundation drains, bottom of foundation footings, and excavations for basement areas).
- Foundation plans and details show the limits of the excavation for the foundation. They also show interior details, such as footings or depressed areas in the slab that will require excavation, backfill, and compaction.
- Mechanical and Electrical drawings must be reviewed for details that show trenching for piping or conduits in the basement or under the slab-on-grade. This work is often overlooked because it is not shown in the civil drawings.

Finally, the specifications must be reviewed for the type and quality of the product and installation. The specifications may offer additional information, such as subsurface investigation reports, general or supplemental conditions that affect site work, and even Division 1 unit prices that are part of the contract. This chapter will review the more common elements of site takeoff and estimating.

Subsurface Investigation Reports

Architects often retain the services of geotechnical engineers, when the budget allows, to investigate the conditions below the surface of the soil before designing foundations on commercial and high-end residential structures. The purpose of the investigation is to define the conditions of the soil that will support the structure, and to provide bidding contractors with an idea of the conditions that may be encountered during excavation.

Several methods can be used to sample the soil beneath the surface. The simplest is the *test pit*, which allows a visual inspection of the soil. Information such as soil content, stratification (layering of soil), water table height, and cohesiveness of the soil can be obtained through visual inspection. Unfortunately, the test pit is restricted by the reach of the excavating equipment, and most structures require analysis of soils at far greater depths.

A fairly common method for reaching greater depths is *test boring*, which provides an actual sample of the materials as they occur in place and identifies the location of the water table. The soil samples are analyzed, and the results are interpreted by a geotechnical engineer and distributed in the form of a report. The report typically provides a plan that locates each boring with respect to the proposed structure. The actual report contained in the specifications is in the form of a simple chart providing the physical description of the soil sample as it occurs vertically, and the corresponding depth. The location of water, if any, should be clearly noted, as should any major obstructions. The subsurface investigation is frequently accompanied by a narrative from the geotechnical engineer that interprets the information contained in the analysis.

When available and interpreted correctly, the subsurface investigation is a valuable tool. Make careful note of the disclaimer that accompanies each report. It will explicitly state that the information contained in the boring reports is for the convenience of the contractor, and that the geotechnical firm assumes no responsibility for the representation of the soil conditions of the site as a whole.

Site Preparation

Clearing of the site refers to the removal of brush, trees, topsoil, and other structures on the surface. *Grubbing* refers to the removal of tree stumps. Most site clearing is done with power equipment, although some smaller sites are still cleared with hand-held chainsaws. Occasionally, clearing and grubbing requires the use of specialized cutting equipment attached to excavating equipment. Carefully inspect the site to identify work that can be done by equipment versus work that must be done by hand.

Part of the process includes stripping and stockpiling topsoil. *Topsoil* is classified as the top layer of soil consisting of non-structural soils high in organic content. The depth of the topsoil can be determined from the test boring report or a visual inspection. Topsoil is typically screened for reuse in planting and lawn areas.

Taking off Quantities

Stripping of topsoil is calculated and listed in the takeoff as an area multiplied by the depth and extended to cubic yards. When calculating the area of topsoil to be removed, it should be enlarged to accommodate any clearance needed. Clearing and grubbing can be taken off and priced by the acre (or partial acre). Takeoff quantities should account for trucking and fees for disposal off site. These should be listed by the truckload in the takeoff.

Excavation & Backfill

In simple terms, *excavation* refers to digging a hole to accommodate a specific engineering improvement. *Backfilling* is placing soil in a controlled method to fill an excavation, again for the purpose of an engineering improvement, such as foundations, piping for utilities, and precast structures. To a lesser degree, excavation and backfill are also required to place pavement, walks, and curbs. Excavation and backfill can be classified into two main categories for estimating purposes:

- Bulk excavation
- Trench or general excavation

Excavation, and earthwork in general, is a volume calculation that is extended for pricing to CY. (1 CY equals 27 CF.)

Bulk Excavation

Moving large masses of earth to establish new grades for parking lots, roads, or building pads is referred to as *bulk excavation*. The most common method for determining the quantities of soil to be moved is the *cross-section method*, which involves tabulating cuts and fills for small increments of the total parcel. *Cutting* refers to removing earth in order to achieve the desired grade. *Filling* is the addition of earth to raise the existing conditions to meet the desired grade. Examine the site closely to determine the amount of earth that will have to be handled in order to transform the existing grades to the proposed grades. *(See Figure 7.1.)*

The cross-section method divides the area into a series of smaller, equal areas. This is done with a grid drawn on the grading plan. It is helpful if both existing and new proposed grades are shown in the form of *contours*, or lines that indicate the same horizontal elevation. Contours are one of the unique conventions of the civil drawings set, which allow you to see the site in three dimensions on two dimensional media—paper. Existing contours are shown on the grading or site plan as dashed lines, with the new or proposed grades shown as solid lines. Figure 7.2 illustrates the cross-section grid in place over the existing grade plan.

The dimensions of the grid should be uniform throughout the plan, and the grids should be square for ease of calculation. The grid spacing depends on the area to be cross-sectioned. If the lot slopes gradually, the spacing can be spread out (larger grid dimensions), but if the lot has

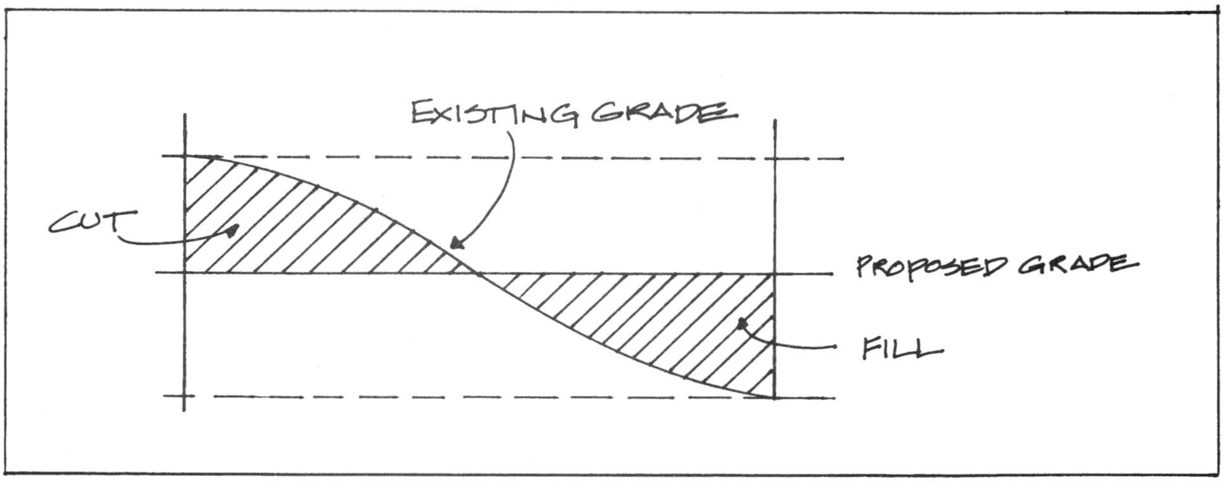

Figure 7.1

dramatic changes in elevation illustrated by a concentration of contours, closer spacing (smaller grid dimensions) may result in a more accurate takeoff.

Each of the smaller areas is identified by a number. The horizontal lines are numbered, and the vertical lines lettered so that each grid intersection can be referenced. Be sure to calculate the elevation of the intersection of each of these lines by interpolating between the contours. (*Interpolation* is an approximation of the elevation of a particular point between two known points.) The existing grade is placed in the upper right-hand quadrant and the proposed grade in the upper left-hand quadrant. The difference in feet between the two is noted as either a cut (signified by a negative sign) or a fill (a positive sign) in the lower right or left quadrant. Each grid area is examined to see if it changes from fill to cut or vice versa within the grid. These grids must be calculated separately. For grids that are all cut or all fill, calculate the average cut or fill for the grid, and multiply it by the area of the grid (using a consistent unit of measure, such as feet). The product will be a quantity of volume in CF. Then divide by 27 to convert CF to CY. The total of each numbered grid is recorded in a separate column on a cut/fill sheet, as shown in Figure 7.3. *(Note: The cut and fill sheet calculations shown in Figure 7.3 are independent of Figure 7.2.)*

For grids that change from cut to fill, you will have to determine which portion of the area is cut and which is fill. The same principles are applied to arrive at the cut and fill portion for each. Once all the grids have been calculated, the total cut and fill for each column is tabulated. From this information, you can determine quantities of earth to be exported or imported to the site, along with the total CY of material to be handled. Figure 7.4 is an example of Grid #5 and the resulting calculations.

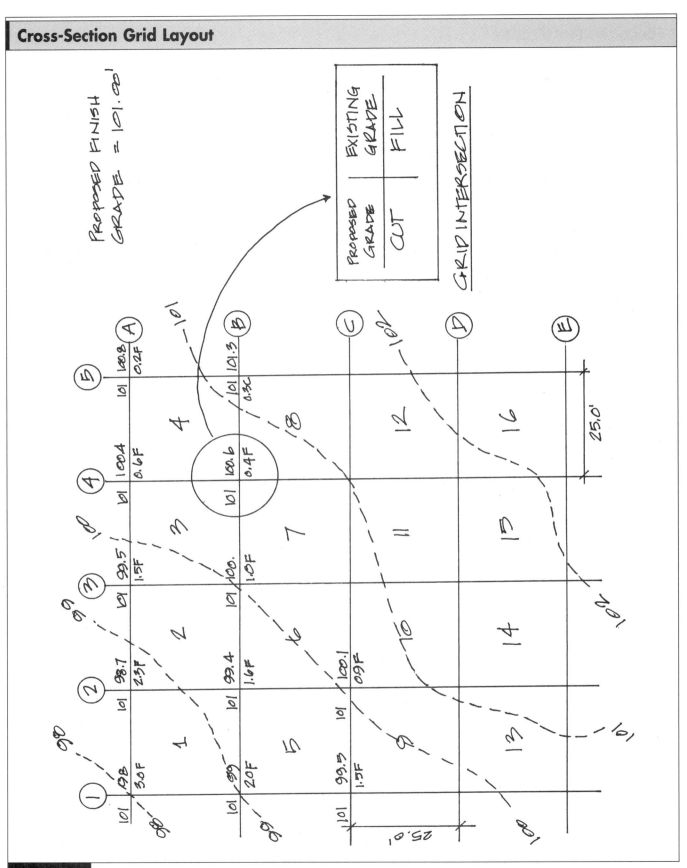

PROPOSED FINISH GRADE = 101.00'

PROPOSED GRADE	EXISTING GRADE
CUT	FILL

GRID INTERSECTION

Figure 7.2

Sample Cut and Fill Tally Sheet

	CUT				FILL		
Grid No.	Area (SF)	Ave. Cut Depth (Ft.)	Cut (CF)	Grid No.	Area (SF)	Ave. Fill Depth (Ft.)	Fill (CF)
1	625	1.54	962.50				
2	625	2.11	1318.75				
3	625	3.25	2031.25				
4	625	2.90	1812.50				
				5	625	2.07	1293.75
				6	625	1.85	1156.25
				7	625	1.66	1037.50
8	625	1.22	762.50				
9	625	1.23	768.75				
				10	625	0.92	575.00
11	625	1.81	1131.25				
12	625	2.03	1268.75				
				13	625	0.88	550.00
				14	625	0.78	487.50
				15	625	1.07	668.75
16	625	0.09	56.25				
		Total Cut (CF)	**10,112.50**			**Total Fill (CF)**	**5,768.75**
		Total Cut (CY)	**374.54**			**Total Fill (CY)**	**213.66**

Figure 7.3

Trench or General Excavation

A major portion of earthwork takeoff and estimating includes calculating trench or general excavation. Most of this work is done with excavating equipment, such as backhoes and excavators, although some of the dressing of the excavated area is performed by hand. It is a good idea to keep the quantities for machine and hand excavation separate, as there is a considerable difference in pricing.

When determining the limits of excavation, take into account the actual size of the basement foundation, pipe trench, or buried structure, then add a sufficient buffer to provide access for workers and materials. Also include overdigging to stabilize the slope, which allows the soils to stabilize naturally and prevents earth from sliding into the excavated area. Different soil compositions tend to stabilize at different angles, as measured from the horizontal plane at the bottom of the excavation. This is called the *angle of repose*. The more cohesive the soil, the steeper the angle of repose. The less cohesive the soil, the shallower the angle of repose. The term *cohesive* refers to soils with a large clay content. *Non-cohesive soils* consist of sand or gravel materials, such as finely-graded beach sand. Regardless of the care taken in digging sand, it always caves right back in. In contrast, excavated trenches in extremely cohesive soils can stabilize vertically (90° angle) at the limits of the bucket on the excavator. While the exact angle of repose is not critical for estimating,

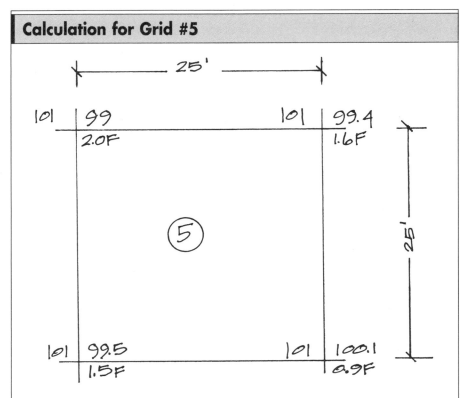

Calculation for Grid #5

In analyzing Grid #5 from the Cross-Section Grid in Figure 7.2, it is determined that the grid is a "fill" grid, because all four intersections show that fill is required to reach the Proposed Grade. The total amount of fill required is the average depth of fill multiplied by the area to be filled. In this case the area to be filled is the area of Grid #5–25' × 25' or 625 square feet.

To find the average fill required; add the fill required for each intersection and divide by 4 to find the average.

$$\frac{2.0 + 1.6 + 0.9 + 1.5}{4} = 1.5 \text{ ft. (average depth of fill)}$$

1.5 ft. × 625 SF = 937.5 CF divided by 27 CF per CY = 34.7 CY

Figure 7.4

a general classification of the soil helps determine the slope of the excavation. Figure 7.5 illustrates the angle of repose for various soil types.

Once the angle of repose and the required size of the excavation have been determined, it is fairly easy to calculate the cross-sectional area of the trench and, subsequently, its volume. Figure 7.6 shows the cross-sectional area of a sample trench. Its corresponding calculations follow.

Calculate the volume of earth to be excavated for a trench 4' deep x 100' long. The bottom of the trench is 4' wide at its widest point. The angle of repose is 45°, a ratio of 1:1. For every foot of depth, the excavation is 1' wide, as measured from the vertical plane.

Angle of Repose

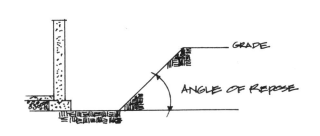

SOIL TYPE	ANGLE OF REPOSE (DEGREES)	
	DRY	DAMP
SAND	25-45	30-50
GRAVEL	25-40	20-30
CLAY	45-90 *	30-45

* IT SHOULD BE NOTED THAT SOME CLAYS OR COHESIVE SOIL WILL MAINTAIN A VERTICAL ANGLE OF REPOSE WHEN EXCAVATED.

Figure 7.5

Sample Trench

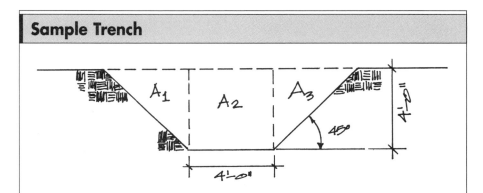

Figure 7.6

The area of A1 = 4' x 4' / 2 = 8 SF. Since A3 is symmetrical to A1, A3 = 8 SF.

The area of A2 = 4' x 4' = 16 SF.

Adding the three areas: A1 + A2 + A3 = 32 SF

If the total cross-sectional area of the trench is 32 SF and the length of the trench is 100 LF, apply the formula for volume:

V = A x L

V = 32 SF x 100 LF = 3,200 CF / 27 CF per CY = 118.51 CY or approximately 119 CY

When stabilizing a slope, be sure to address OSHA regulations for worker safety and the actual requirements of the specifications. Some earthwork specs require that a minimum slope of 1:1 (45°) be maintained. While this may be a required minimum, it is not always the best answer for the particular situation. In some instances, the excavated trench must be stabilized by artificial means, as discussed in the next section.

Shoring & Bracing

Shoring and bracing are mechanical means of stabilizing a slope, and may be required either because of safety considerations or if there is insufficient space to stabilize the slope naturally. Shoring can be in the form of wood, steel, or concrete sheet piling. Other similar artificial means, such as trench boxes, are frequently employed. Be sure to calculate the area to be retained or held back. The shored area will require overdigging to provide sufficient access. Shoring and bracing are taken off and priced by the SF of surface area of the trench retained. The area is calculated by multiplying the perimeter of the area to be shored by the height of the shoring from the bottom of the trench to the top of the excavation. The vertical dimension should include additional length to embed the shoring below the bottom of the trench level. In addition to the actual unit price for installation of the shoring, a separate line item in the estimate should include the materials, labor, and equipment to remove the shoring. The estimated cost for shoring and bracing should be separate from the work it is meant to protect.

Backfill

As stated previously, the process of filling in an excavated area under controlled methods is called *backfilling*. Note that where there is excavation, there is usually a backfill component to be considered.

Soil naturally expands once it has been excavated, which increases the volume the fill will occupy. This is called the *swell* of the material. Swell is expressed as a percentage over and above the original volume. The inverse is also true; when the volume of a material is compacted, it tends to shrink or lose volume, called *compaction*. The actual percentage of swell or compaction will depend on the conditions and type of material being excavated. Compaction is also a characteristic of the soil itself. Finely-graded soils of a uniform size, such as fine sand, have less volume change. Soils with varying gradations of particle size have more voids, or spaces, between individual particles, and more swell and compaction can be expected. Figure 7.7 lists soil characteristics and factors for calculating soil volume in various conditions.

It is a good idea to become familiar with the requirements for backfilling and compaction as mandated in the specifications. Pay special attention to the allowable thickness of the layers of backfill, the materials required, and their density after compaction. In the absence of written specifications on backfill placement and compaction, refer to sections on the architectural drawings that show the thickness of compacted materials under the slab. Trench excavation for utilities or drainage, as well as general excavation for foundations, requires backfill and compaction in some capacity.

When backfilling at any engineering improvement, remember to deduct the volume displaced by the feature. For example, once a precast tank is placed in an open excavation, deduct the tank's volume when calculating

Soil Characteristics

Weights and Characteristics of Materials

Approximate Material Characteristics*				
Material	Loose (Lbs./C.Y.)	Bank (Lbs./C.Y.)	Swell (%)	Load Factor
Clay, dry	2,100	2,650	26	0.79
Clay, wet	2,700	3,575	32	0.76
Clay and gravel, dry	2,400	2,800	17	0.85
Clay and gravel, wet	2,600	3,100	17	0.85
Earth, dry	2,215	2,850	29	0.78
Earth, moist	2,410	3,080	28	0.78
Earth, wet	2,750	3,380	23	0.81
Gravel, dry	2,780	3,140	13	0.88
Gravel, wet	3,090	3,620	17	0.85
Sand, dry	2,600	2,920	12	0.89
Sand, wet	3,100	3,520	13	0.88
Sand and gravel, dry	2,900	3,250	12	0.89
Sand and gravel, wet	3,400	3,750	10	0.91

*Exact values will vary with grain size, moisture content, compaction, etc. Test to determine exact values for specific soils.

Typical Soil Volume Conversion Factors				
Soil Type	Initial Soil Condition	Bank	Converted to: Loose	Compacted
Clay	Bank	1.00	1.27	0.90
	Loose	0.79	1.00	0.71
	Compacted	1.11	1.41	1.00
Common earth	Bank	1.00	1.25	0.90
	Loose	0.80	1.00	0.72
	Compacted	1.11	1.39	1.00
Rock (blasted)	Bank	1.00	1.50	1.30
	Loose	0.67	1.00	0.87
	Compacted	0.77	1.15	1.00
Sand	Bank	1.00	1.12	0.95
	Loose	0.89	1.00	0.85
	Compacted	1.05	1.18	1.00

$$\text{Swell (\%)} = \left(\frac{\text{Wt./bank C.Y.}}{\text{Wt./loose C.Y.}} - 1 \right) \times 100$$

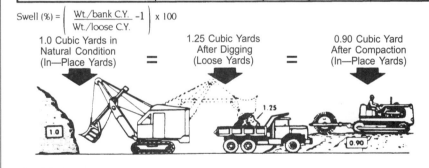

| 1.0 Cubic Yards in Natural Condition (In—Place Yards) | = | 1.25 Cubic Yards After Digging (Loose Yards) | = | 0.90 Cubic Yard After Compaction (In—Place Yards) |

Figure 7.7

the amount of backfill. It should also be noted that this calculation occurs only when the amount of material displaced by the engineering improvement is significant. (For example, it would not be necessary to deduct the volume of soil displaced by a 4" diameter pipe placed within a trench.) A good rule of thumb is to consider deducting the volume of displaced soil when it exceeds 8%–10% of the volume of the excavation.

Taking off Quantities

Backfill and compaction can be estimated by the CY, although some estimators prefer to separate backfill from compaction, because backfill is placed by machine and compaction is done by hand with the aid of a plate compactor or roller. Backfill should still be quantified by CY, and compaction by SF per layer or *lift*. It may be necessary to add the cost of delays for testing the compacted soils between layers. Although not usually a major factor, some on-site testing can be time-consuming, especially for tests required to comply with governmental regulations.

Grading

The task of altering the ground surface to a designed elevation or contour is called *grading*. Grading can be accomplished by equipment, by hand, or a combination of the two. Grading done by equipment should be priced separately from grading done by hand. Movement of large quantities of earth should not be mistakenly priced as grading, but as excavation. Grading should be restricted to dressing previously filled or cut areas. You can determine the area to be graded as shown on the site grading and drainage plan, as well as architectural drawings showing preparation for slabs-on-grade. Areas paved with bituminous concrete, brick walkways, and concrete walks or pads require a graded subbase as preparation for the work.

Taking off Quantities

Hand grading is taken off by the SF. Machine grading is performed by bulldozer or similar equipment and supplemented by hand grading in areas close to structures. Typically, machine grading is taken off and priced by the SF and converted to a larger unit, such as SY or acres (if the site is large).

The cost of grading varies according to the degree of accuracy required. Use caution in selecting the appropriate equipment for the task. Be sure to consider maneuverability and the proximity of buildings or other site improvements. You may want to include costs for additional equipment to "spot" fill in low areas, or remove excess materials in "high" areas.

Hauling

As part of the excavation process, materials frequently need to be moved greater distances than would be economically feasible using the excavating equipment. Moving materials to an alternate location must be done by truck. The quantity of soil to be transported is calculated by the CY. Factors for increased volume from swell must be added in the form of additional truckloads. Be sure to calculate the distance to be traveled and the approximate time needed to load and dump the material must be calculated to determine the number of truckloads per day. This information will allow you to calculate the unit price cost per CY. Additional costs for dumping excess material and handling at the dump site may have to be included.

Rock Removal

Rock can be removed by several methods, although drilling and splitting or blasting are the most common. Take off of rock is calculated by its in-ground size, expressed in CY. Most contracts and specifications have specific language and obligations in the event that rock is encountered and must be removed. Carefully review this section of the specifications in case a separate unit price is required. Once the rock has been excavated, it is usually removed from the site. Unearthed rock can exceed its in-ground volume by as much as 60%, which must be considered when determining the number of trucks required. Rock excavation is affected by a variety of factors. Price rock excavation only after careful review of the contract documents and consideration of the following factors:

- Classification of rock—hard, medium, or soft
- Proximity of adjacent structures (affected by blasting)
- Depth of drilling
- Quantity of rock to be drilled/blasted
- Type of explosive required
- Special permits, insurance, and safety requirements

Minor rock drilling may be done by a jackhammer with carbide bits. Because each situation is different, the price of drilling and blasting should be secured from a contractor specializing in this work. The unit price of rock removal should be based on the anticipated quantity to be removed and typically decreases as the quantity increases.

Piping & Precast Structures

Drainage and utilities require piping and related fittings to carry services to and from the building and site. Frequently, this work includes precast concrete structures, such as catch basins, manholes, and tanks. Check the site plans to determine the limits of the drainage and utility work. Site drainage and utility plans will show the location of the various types of piping and any changes in direction or elevation. Sections of the piping and trench are typically shown on site detail plans. Refer to the specifications for particulars on the type of materials used and the method of installation. This information is essential for accurately taking off and pricing the work. Additional details on precast structures are also shown on the site detail plans, with elevations for inverts of piping and rims of the cover. Sections or details for these items are referred to in order to clarify the construction and materials to be included in the takeoff.

Taking off Quantities

All pipe is taken off and priced by the LF. Depending on the material and size of the pipe, costs for cutting it to specific lengths in the field must be included. The cost for cutting a thin-wall PVC pipe with a handsaw is negligible. The cost for cutting larger-diameter pipe that requires special cutting tools, such as reinforced concrete pipe (RCP) or ductile iron (CLDI), however, is significant. The quantity of cuts for such pipe should be taken off by each piece (EA). Quantities for different types and sizes of pipe should be kept separate. The connection of pipe lengths should also be kept separate, especially if it involves labor-intensive tasks such as welding, fusion, or installing mechanical-type fittings. Typical bell-and-spigot or glued PVC couplings are not classified as a separate labor task. Special fittings, such as valves, bends, tees, or wyes, should be taken off separately and listed according to type and size, with the unit of each. Any other tasks for the connection of various pipe, such as the mortaring of joints in reinforced concrete pipe, should be noted separately, taking into account the pipe's diameter and accessibility.

Many types of piping can be installed by hand, as in the case of smaller-diameter PVC pipe. Larger-diameter pipe, such as ductile iron, corrugated drain pipe, or reinforced concrete pipe, requires equipment for lifting and placing. The cost of this equipment and additional labor should be included as part of the unit cost for installation.

Certain types of utility work require precast concrete structures, such as manholes, handholes, catch basins, and tanks. These should be taken off individually, separated by type, size, capacity, or use. Similar items whose sizes are constant should be quantified as each (EA, e.g., 1,000 gallon septic tanks or 4' catch basins). Items that vary in size, such as the vertical heights of manholes, must be separated and quantified by each or vertical linear foot (VLF). Additional pieces to complete the structure, such as manhole frames and covers, catch basin frames and grates, metal steps, and special swales or inverts, should be quantified and priced separately or combined as part of the completed unit. When possible, always solicit pricing from manufacturers of precast structures to confirm the estimated value. Be sure to note that many precast structures are large and cumbersome to handle and may require a crane and additional crew to set in place. This is an added cost that should be accounted for in the estimate.

Testing and Additional Information

Many project specifications include comprehensive testing of piping and structures after the work has been completed as a means of confirming compliance. These tests require the services of a certified laboratory or testing agency. Be sure to secure quotes for testing installed piping and structures. The cost should be carried as an independent contractor price. Typically, the cost of testing the pipe should be included in Division 2, because it is considered part of the actual installation work.

Piping-Related Work

Related work, such as concrete thrust blocks (concrete restraints) for water piping, should be calculated on an individual basis, including the CY of concrete needed and any required formwork. Special work for the support of existing pipe should be taken off and priced separately, and may be quantified as a lump sum (LS). Takeoff and pricing for excavation and backfill for site drainage and utilities should be kept separate from the actual piping and appurtenances.

Use caution when estimating piping on plans of large engineering scale (1" = 50' or greater), as the chance for error increases dramatically. Piping is sold in specific lengths, and the takeoff should be rounded to the nearest full length required.

Special bedding materials, such as sand and stone, may also be required as part of the installation. The quantities should be kept separate and should be included as part of the backfill work. In most jurisdictions, pipe within the confines of the foundation itself, such as underground waste lines for sanitary sewer services or conduit piping for underground electrical work, is the responsibility of the respective trade and not the work of the site contractor. Similarly, piping for underground gas services or site lighting may be the responsibility of the gas utility company or licensed electrician. These items may not always be apparent on the drawings, but should be researched and, if necessary, qualified in the bid.

Underpinning

When the excavation for new work comes too close to, or goes below, the foundation of an existing structure, that structure must be *underpinned*. While underpinning is not always required in the specifications, it is a matter of safety and responsibility. Most contracts hold the contractor liable for damage to adjacent structures. Underpinning requires the existing foundation support footings to be extended or brought to the depth of the proposed structure. This is often an expensive task and may require the services of a specialized contractor if there is a considerable quantity of underpinning. Small quantities or localized underpinning applications limited to specific areas can often be handled by the site contractor.

Taking off Quantities

Underpinning can be quantified and priced by a variety of units, depending on the application. Common units include CY, CF, LF, and LS. Although much of the work can be done by machine, remember that there is always handwork required for final dressing of the area. Sometimes the hand portion of the work is best quantified and priced per labor-hour, since the work is slow and detailed.

Paving & Subbase Preparation

Paving refers to surfacing a subbase, typically compacted gravel or stone, with a course of materials, such as bituminous concrete, brick, or concrete, to provide a wearing surface for vehicular or pedestrian traffic. The subbase is often estimated under the excavation and backfill portion of the work, because the work is performed by the site contractor. The rough grading or preparation of the subbase is categorized under the grading scope of work. Fine grading and rolling of the subbase just prior to installation is typically done by the paving contractor. The most common examples are parking areas, driveways, walks, and patios.

Taking off Quantities

Paving is taken off by the SF and extended to the SY for pricing. The cost of paving can vary dramatically, depending on the type of mix specified, the thickness required, and the number of placement layers. Paving walks and smaller areas should be taken off and estimated separately from larger areas, such as driveways and parking areas. While both are considered paving, they are frequently performed by separate crews with different pricing structures.

Bituminous concrete or asphaltic paving is usually applied in two courses. The first course is called the *binder* or base course. The top course is called the *wearing* course. Each course should be taken off and priced separately. It is not uncommon for the binder to be placed early in the project, with the wearing surface applied just prior to project turnover.

Paving large areas is typically done by multiple pieces of equipment with a full crew. This work often has an associated mobilization charge. Small areas have a more modest crew size and require less and smaller equipment. Additional work for tying in new surfaces to existing surfaces may be required and should be listed separately, taken off and priced by the linear foot of abutting surfaces. More time-consuming work, such as leveling of existing low spots prior to the top course, applying a tack course, and blending new and existing work, should all be taken off and priced separately after careful consideration of the specific application and site conditions. Trenches that require patching should be taken off and priced by the SY, but this information should be kept separate from the larger production quantities. Paving contractors often have a minimum charge for work such as patches. Include the cost of sweeping between courses, if the binder has been down a long time, before applying the wearing surface.

Other types of paving include cast-in-place concrete and brick or masonry pavers. Placing concrete for walkways or aprons involves calculating the cubic yards of concrete necessary. Include a small percentage for waste resulting from spillage of concrete while handling. The quality and strength of the concrete, including additives or hot water, should be noted, as it will affect the unit cost.

Concrete should be quantified and priced by the CY. Placement and finishing of the surface should be taken off and priced by the SF of surface area finished. The pricing will vary depending on the type of finish required.

Also, remember that cast-in-place concrete requires some type of formwork, which will be specified along with the composition of the concrete in Division 3—Concrete of the specifications. Formwork at the perimeter of the pour is usually called *edge forms*, and is quantified by the LF. Pricing should include the cost of stripping the forms. Materials for edge forms can often be used on multiple jobs, and costs may be divided by the number of expected uses. Reinforcing for concrete walkways in the form of welded-wire fabric is calculated by the square foot, with allowances for overlap determined by the details on the drawings. *(Formwork, concrete materials, finishing, and reinforcing will be discussed in depth in Chapter 8.)*

Special curing compounds or protection from rapid evaporation of water should be listed separately and priced by the square foot of surface area. In the case of liquid compounds, the SF can be converted to coverage of gal./SF and to the manufacturer's units, such as 5-gallon containers. Polyethylene sheeting material to retain moisture can be calculated similarly by the SF and converted to the convenient size roll. Additional labor may be required to manually ensure proper hydration of the concrete.

Brick paved walks and patios are quantified by the SF of paved area, converted to the total quantity of bricks needed based on the number of bricks per square foot. This will vary from manufacturer to manufacturer, based on the size of the paver. The associated labor is often calculated based on the number of pavers an installer can lay in a day. A reasonable allowance for waste should be included for breakage and cuts.

Curbing

The perimeters of parking areas and walkways are often surrounded by curbing. Curbing is available in many types and compositions, each type taken off and priced separately. Curbing manufactured off site, such as granite or precast concrete, often requires mortaring the joints between each section once it has been set. This step should be included as part of the installation cost. Radii for curved precast concrete or granite curbs are listed separately. These are more expensive than straight pieces. The cost of materials should include delivery charges, if needed. Because of its weight, manufactured curbing requires special equipment for setting, as well as poured concrete to hold the curb in place. These items should be included in the cost. Ready-mix concrete for holding the precast curb in place should be taken off and priced by the CY.

Other types of curbing include cast-in-place concrete, bituminous, and extruded concrete (for curbing and gutter). The concrete for these types of curbing should be calculated in CY. You may include waiting time for ready-mix concrete trucks, as curbing tends to pour more slowly. Cast-in-place curbing requires the use of forms. The unit cost should include forming, placing, stripping, and rubbing of the exposed surfaces.

Taking off Quantities

Cast-in-place curbing is taken off and priced by the LF. The cost for bituminous concrete curbing extruded by machine is based on the production (quantity) rate and type of material used and is taken off by the LF. All extruded curbing, concrete or bituminous, is based on the production (quantity) rate, setup and moves, small quantities, and the accessibility of the work, all of which affect unit costs.

Dewatering

High levels of groundwater during excavation may require pumping or dewatering equipment. Simple dewatering may require the use of a localized pump, in which case the cost would include fuel, pump rental, and labor to operate the pump. The cost of dewatering could be calculated based on the time required to dewater the excavation, estimated as an allowance or lump sum, and listed in the takeoff by the day, week, or month. Some projects require a more elaborate means of dewatering, such as a wellpoint system, used to dewater large areas.

Factors that can affect the cost of dewatering are location, season, and the amount of precipitation. Dewatering large areas requires a contractor specializing in this type of work. Secure a price from an independent contractor for this work.

Landscaping & Irrigation

Landscaping includes a variety of components to improve the appearance of the site. Projects of a more sophisticated nature often include a landscaping plan as part of the site plans. A landscaping drawing is created in plan view, and often includes sections or details for plant material installation, decorative stone walls, or general improvements of an ornamental nature. As part of the landscaping drawings, a planting schedule lists the plantings by species, size, and variety. Landscaping work requires spreading, raking, and grading topsoil as a base for sod or grass seed. The installation of plantings, seed or sod, and bark mulch are frequently part of the landscaping scope of work.

Taking off Quantities

Plantings should be taken off by counting each and listing it according to species, size, and variety (EA). Check the quantities with the planting schedule as a means of verification. These quantities should then be submitted to a nursery for up-to-date pricing of stock. The cost of plantings is affected by availability, season, species, and size.

Sod and seeded areas are taken off by the SF, and can be extended to SY. Convert the SF area of seed to the rate required in the specifications. Rate refers to pounds per 100 SF. Spreading, fine grading, and raking topsoil is taken off by the SF. The quantity of topsoil needed is calculated by multiplying the area by the required depth and extending the amount to the cubic yard. Placement and rough grading of topsoil is often included in the excavation and backfill section of the specifications.

Grading and distribution of topsoil can be accomplished with small equipment, such as a bobcat or backhoe. Areas that are inaccessible by machine are graded by hand and should be listed separately. Grading, raking, and rolling topsoil is quantified by the square foot. Additional topsoil may be needed for raised areas in planting beds and is calculated by the CY.

Other landscaping tasks may involve placing stone or timbers for a focal point. Such tasks should be taken off and estimated separately. Units will vary according to the task.

Additional costs for landscaping work include fertilizers converted from lbs./SF to lbs. and wood stakes and wire for staking trees, taken off by the piece (EA). Spreading of bark mulch, wood chips, or similar materials is taken off by the SF or SY. The materials are calculated in cubic yards, based on the depth of the material. Allowances should be made for compaction resulting from rolling of the topsoil. When calculating the cost of labor for planting trees and shrubs, the contractor may want to include equipment for placing items too big to be handled by hand.

Maintenance Requirements

Always read the specifications carefully for landscape maintenance clauses. Frequently, the specifications call for a maintenance period that includes watering until growth has been established. This often requires that lawns be mowed on specific schedules. The cost for such work depends on the frequency and season.

Irrigation Systems

The landscape plan may be accompanied by an irrigation plan for maintaining lawns and plantings. An irrigation plan indicates the placement of sprinkler heads for watering. It may show pipe runs, manifolds with zone valves, and a backflow preventer connected to the source. The quantity of pipe is calculated by the LF and priced according to size (diameter). Valves, heads, fittings, and miscellaneous components are taken off and priced by the piece (EA). Special equipment for laying the pipe below grade is often needed. Special connections to potable water systems include devices such as vacuum breakers and backflow preventers.

Site Improvements

Site improvements include a wide range of miscellaneous items and tasks. These can be shown on the site plan, or on a separate plan called a *site improvement plan*. The site improvement drawing is known as a "catch-all" drawing. It is provided in plan view and shows items such as fencing, playground equipment, trash receptacles, benches, decorative water fountains, planters, outdoor furniture, bicycle racks, flag poles, and so forth. Each item has its own takeoff and pricing units. Be sure to secure quotes on specialty equipment typically found on this drawing. Some site improvement items may require assembly or shipping costs. This should be noted in the takeoff for accurate pricing.

Miscellaneous Considerations

There are several miscellaneous items to consider that may be required in the site work takeoff and estimate. These include but are not limited to:
- Special fees or permits for street openings or water taps
- Charges for transporting equipment (mobilization)
- Temporary protection for open excavations
- Engineering (layout and grades)
- Police details for street work (traffic control)
- Storage or trailer charges for large items

- Registered engineering layout by a surveyor
- As-built or record drawings
- Assessments or betterment fees
- Barricades or access roads
- Snow plowing and removal (if applicable)
- Securing the services of a licensed arborist to oversee all tree planting, pruning, and care

Demolition

Demolition refers to dismantling, removing, and disposing of unwanted existing work. It can be classified into two major groups for estimating purposes. The first is *full* or *total demolition*, which includes the removal of entire structures, both above and below grade, in preparation for a new structure. The second classification is called *selective demolition*, which involves the careful and coordinated removal of specific items as part of a renovation project. Both groups can include a wide variety of tasks and are usually labor- and equipment-intensive. Selective demolition would include such tasks as the removing and disposing of doors and frames, windows, partitions, and a variety of finishes. It also includes cutting and patching portions of the structure to accommodate new features, such as stairs, doors, windows, elevators, and below-slab improvements.

The work of selective demolition is detailed and often requires coordination between other drawings within the set. The scope of the demolition work, both total and selective, includes removing, hauling, and legally disposing of debris off site. Be sure to view the site conditions prior to submitting a bid to collect additional information that may not be discernible from the drawings. For example, if the drawings call for removing and disposing of VCT flooring, it is important to know whether the floor tile is in good condition and therefore difficult to remove, or in poor condition and potentially easier to remove.

Taking off Quantities

Frequently, units of demolition are difficult to label. Demolition tasks can be quantified by the LF, SF, CF, CY, or each. There are some tasks or segments of work that contain more than one operation, but are better left as a whole for the purposes of estimating. This work is sometimes classified as a lump sum. An example might be removing a metal window and frame from an existing concrete block wall, cutting the jambs to the floor, and removing debris. It might be wise to consider a lump sum because of the variety of tasks to be performed. Calculate the number of labor-hours necessary to perform each segment of the lump sum task. The hours would be summarized, priced, and added to the cost of any other items required to perform the work, such as special tools or protection. The total cost would then be entered into the estimate as a lump sum amount.

Sometimes demolition work requires erecting barriers, ramps, chutes, staging, and work platforms, or protecting surrounding work. Protection can be as simple as a polyethylene dust barrier, or as complex as building temporary partitions to protect existing features. Be sure to include these costs. In addition to protection, the cost of disposal by means of a dumpster or trucking to a landfill must be included. The cost for disposal should be a separate item so that you can analyze various options.

Carefully review the documents for any special considerations about working within an occupied building. Certain portions of the work may have to be performed after normal business hours, thereby requiring shift work. Other costly means of protection may include stringent air quality provisions and monitoring. Review these carefully, as the cost can be significant.

Conclusion

Costs for site work can vary from project to project, as well as from season to season. Estimating site work costs accurately require a complete understanding of both the existing and proposed conditions. The site work estimator should evaluate all information available before applying pricing.

Chapter Eight

Concrete

Concrete is a composite material consisting of sand, coarse aggregate, cement, and water. It forms a stone-like material when mixed and allowed to harden. Because of its high compressive strength, durability, ability to withstand the weather, and relative ease in handling and shaping, concrete is a versatile material in widespread use in the construction industry. When used with steel reinforcing, it takes on the ability to withstand elongation, called *tensile strength*, along with its own compressive strength, making it an ideal product for use as a structural component. Because of its versatility, concrete is used in many parts of most construction projects.

To prepare an accurate takeoff for pricing, first review all drawings in the set for concrete work. CSI Division 3 work, Concrete, is found in the structural drawings, specifically the foundation plan and sections showing details of footings, walls, piers, slabs-on-grade, and elevated slabs. Site drawings should also be reviewed for items such as concrete walks, pads, and miscellaneous site concrete. Note that in some circumstances, the site concrete is included in Division 2—Site Construction.

Other drawings, such as mechanical and electrical, should be studied for items like boxouts for piping and conduits, or "housekeeping" pads for specific pieces of equipment, such as furnaces and hot water heaters. Architectural drawings may include indications of surface finish treatments or architectural concrete with exposed surfaces. The specifications and drawings should be reviewed to determine the strength of the mix or the particular additives specified, in order to properly separate the different mixes for accurate pricing.

Concrete work can be organized into the following categories for takeoff and estimating:

- Concrete materials
- Formwork/placement of concrete
- Concrete finishing
- Concrete curing
- Concrete reinforcement
- Precast concrete
- Embedded items

Concrete Materials

While concrete has many applications in construction, its main function is as a structural component. Concrete has an extremely high ability to resist a crushing force, usually imposed by the weight of the structure it supports. Concrete materials are rated by their compressive strength. Once thoroughly mixed, the ingredients undergo a chemical process called *hydration*, which produces heat as a by-product and results in a cured, rock-hard building material. With water as a main ingredient, mixed concrete is greatly affected by temperature and weather extremes. In cold weather, cast-in-place concrete must be protected against freezing. Concrete that freezes prior to curing will never achieve its full strength. Similarly, placing concrete on hot, dry days may cause evaporation of essential water used for hydration before it has a chance to set. Both conditions must be avoided if the concrete is to perform as designed. Evaluating the requirements for placing and curing concrete is covered later in this chapter.

Taking off Quantities

Concrete is taken off by the CF and converted to CY, the accepted units for both estimating and purchasing. One CY of concrete contains 27 CF. The quantities of different types and strengths of concrete should be listed separately in the takeoff and estimate, because a variety of factors will affect pricing. Concrete components should also be segregated by application. For example, concrete for foundations should be separated from concrete for *flatwork*, concrete placed as a slab, pad, or walkway. Study the specifications carefully for type and strength, as well as any additives to the mix.

The following factors affect the price of concrete and should be acknowledged in the takeoff description so that pricing is accurate:

- The strength of the mix specified as the concrete's compressive strength per square inch after curing (e.g., 3,000 psi, 3,500 psi, or 4,000 psi).
- The use of additives that accelerate or retard the curing process, such as calcium chloride.
- The size and type of the coarse aggregate used in the batching, such as gravel, peastone, stone, and/or local aggregates, such as slag.

- The percentage of air incorporated into the mix in the form of tiny air bubbles, known as air entrainment, which adds to workability.
- Special cements, such as High Early Strength Portland Cement, that will achieve the same strength in 72 hours that other types normally achieve in seven days.
- Plasticizer for pump mixes, which increases workability and flow through a concrete pump, frequently used where normal access is not available.
- Hot water or ice chips to control the water temperature (offsetting the effect of high or low ambient temperature on the concrete mix). This is common practice in areas with extreme climatic changes.
- Fibers for reinforcement.

Calculating a waste factor for concrete is often a matter of experience. A reasonable waste factor of approximately 3% can be applied for an average concrete placement. Excessive handling or transporting of concrete after it has left the mixer may require a 5% waste factor, but this is more the exception than the rule.

Ready-Mixed Concrete

Other factors affecting the price may be more closely related to local batching practices and should be reviewed on an individual basis. As a result of significantly better quality control, the use of ready-mixed concrete has all but eliminated the job-site batching of concrete in any large quantity. *Ready-mixed concrete* refers to concrete that is batched at an off-site location, then transported to the site in mixers.

When calculating the unit price of ready-mixed concrete, consider any small quantities, typically under 5 CY, as "short loads." Most ready-mixed concrete companies have a 3 to 5 CY minimum charge for short loads, unless prior arrangements have been made. Difficulty in placing concrete may also affect the unit price in the form of a charge for "waiting time" accrued by a mixer that is delayed while unloading the concrete. Be sure to separately list the cost of concrete for short loads and placements that take extra time.

Formwork

Because of its fluid-like consistency during placement, all cast-in-place concrete must be contained in some type of formwork. Formwork varies in size and composition, but is most often constructed from a wood facing applied over a steel or wood frame. Simpler forms, such as those used in forming a footing, may be no more than a plank anchored by stakes and straps. The cost of formwork should include the erection and bracing of forms until the concrete has hardened, and stripping and cleaning the forms. Separate the cost of each of these tasks for pricing, or price the work as a single process. Contractors performing the work themselves may prefer to list the cost items separately. For developing a budget for work that will later be subcontracted, a single, overall cost may be sufficient. Formwork is typically listed in separate categories based on each application. Some of the more common types of formwork and their respective takeoff units are described in the following section.

Footing Forms

There are two main types of footings: *continuous strip footings*, on which walls will be erected, and *isolated spread footings*, which are used for supporting interior columns. Figure 8.1 illustrates both types.

Strip Footings

Continuous strip footings are designed to support a uniformly distributed load, such as would be applied at the perimeter of a structure. Strip footings are wider than the walls they support to evenly distribute the dead and live loads. They are typically formed on both sides and braced on the top with temporary wood braces at 2' – 4' intervals. The bottom of the footing is braced with a perforated metal strap at approximately 2' – 4' intervals. The forms used for footings are rough planking, similar to staging planks, approximately 2" x 12" in varying lengths. Common sizes for footings are 20" to 36" in width by 12" to 18" in depth. The materials, with the exception of the perforated straps, are reusable. *(See Figure 8.2.)*

Continuous and Isolated Footings

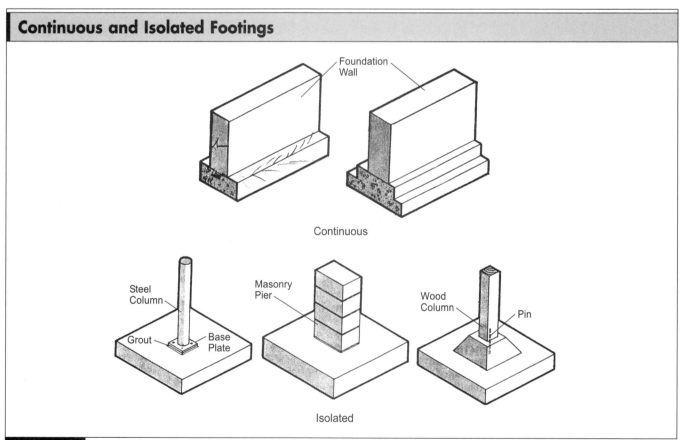

Continuous

Isolated

Figure 8.1

Strip Footings

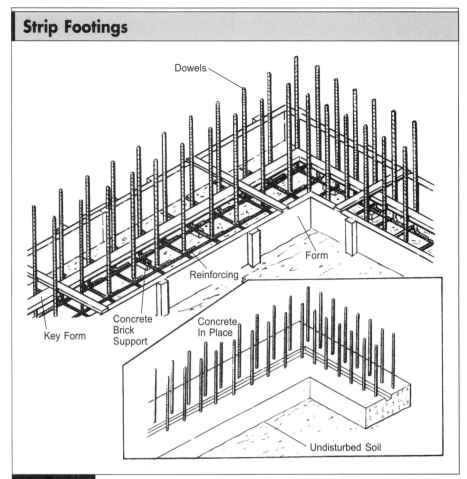

Figure 8.2

Continuous strip footings are taken off and priced by the LF, because most strip footings remain constant in height. Changes in elevation at the bottom of the footings may be required, based on the design criteria. When this occurs, the footing bottom is *stepped*. Note any changes in elevation that may require stepping the footings. Figure 8.3 illustrates a stepped footing.

Productivity is reduced for stepped footings, so an additional cost is typically calculated per occurrence. To reduce the lateral movement of the wall to be placed on the continuous strip footing, a small trough, called a *keyway*, is formed by using a tapered 2" x 4" embedded in the top surface of the wet concrete in the footing. Takeoff and pricing of the keyway can be separate or part of the completed formwork unit. If priced separately, it is taken off and priced by the LF. Figure 8.4 illustrates the keyway form and the resulting trough after the forms have been stripped.

101

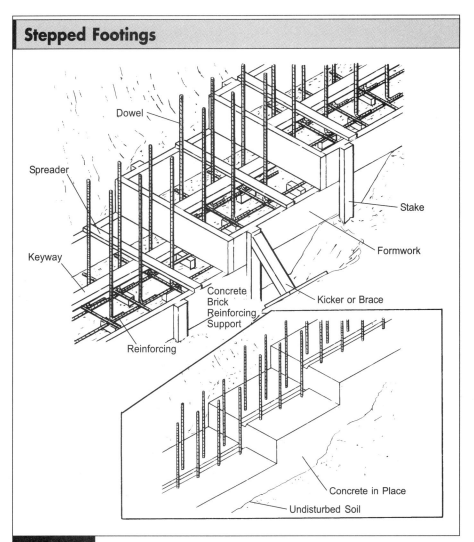

Stepped Footings

Dowel

Spreader

Keyway

Stake

Formwork

Concrete
Brick
Reinforcing
Support

Kicker or Brace

Reinforcing

Concrete in Place

Undisturbed Soil

Figure 8.3

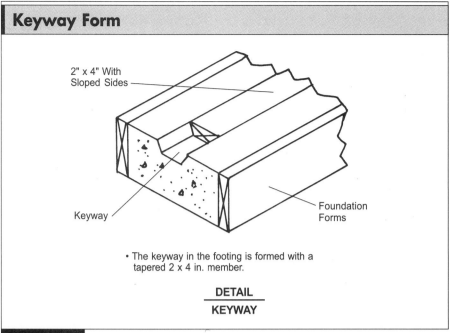

Keyway Form

2" x 4" With Sloped Sides

Keyway

Foundation Forms

• The keyway in the footing is formed with a tapered 2 x 4 in. member.

DETAIL
KEYWAY

Figure 8.4

Spread Footings

Spread footings, also known as *isolated footings*, are isolated masses of concrete, often square or rectangular in shape, with thicknesses varying from 12" – 24". Their main purpose is to support point loads of columns that rest on them. Their actual size can vary, depending on the load carried and the soil's bearing capacity. A typical spread footing is shown in Figure 8.5.

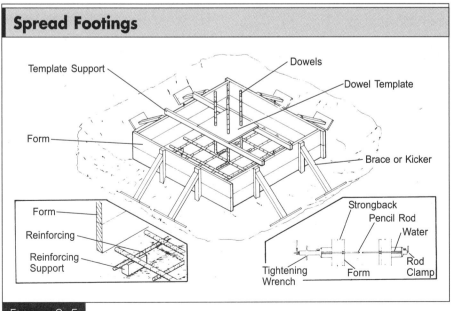

Spread Footings

Template Support

Dowels

Dowel Template

Form

Brace or Kicker

Form
Reinforcing
Reinforcing Support

Strongback
Pencil Rod
Water
Rod Clamp
Tightening Wrench
Form

Figure 8.5

Taking off Quantities

The form material may be planks or panels, depending on the thickness of the footing. Footing forms are erected and braced in a manner similar to that used for strip footings.

Spread footings are typically taken off and priced by the piece, and labeled each (EA) for those of a repetitive size. Foundations with various sized footings are typically listed in a footing schedule shown on the structural drawings. Spread footings may require a template for embedded anchor bolts to attach the column, which can be listed separately from the formwork, as it requires precise layout and, often, the services of a site engineer. (This topic is discussed in more detail at the end of this chapter.)

Foundation Walls and Piers

Concrete foundation walls are cast-in-place below grade to support the structure above. They can be cast in a variety of heights and are supported by footings. In a structure with a basement, foundation walls act to retain or hold back the soil. A *pier* is a short column of plain or reinforced concrete used to support a concentrated load. Piers are used as components in foundation walls or as isolated, separate members.

Formwork for foundation walls is constructed of smooth wood sheathing applied to a 2" x 4" wood or steel frame. Formwork is built in modular sizes starting at approximately 8" in width and increasing to 16" widths in 2" increments. Larger panels for longer straight runs are in 24" and 48" widths. Standard panel heights are 48", 72", and 96". Foundation walls are formed by erecting and fastening modular panels side-by-side on top of the strip footing. Foundation wall formwork requires "doubling up" panels to create a narrow box to hold the concrete until it has hardened. The panels are held apart at a predetermined space using metal ties. This space is ultimately the thickness of the wall. Figure 8.6 illustrates formwork for a typical wall.

Ties are usually spaced at 24" on center, both horizontally and vertically, though they may require closer spacing for greater loads imposed by the wet cast-in-place concrete. In addition, the panels are braced on the exterior (against the hydrostatic pressure caused by the wet concrete) by a series of horizontal wood or metal braces known as *walers*.

Taking off Quantities

Formwork for foundation walls can be quantified and priced using one of two separate units. The first unit is the area of the form that comes in contact with the concrete. It is listed as square foot of contact area (SFCA). While this is the most accepted and long-standing method, it does not always represent the pricing structure in some segments of the industry.

Another unit that can be used in the takeoff of foundation walls is the LF, most often used by residential contractors. This method is best where contact area is less critical than the size of the form panels used. For

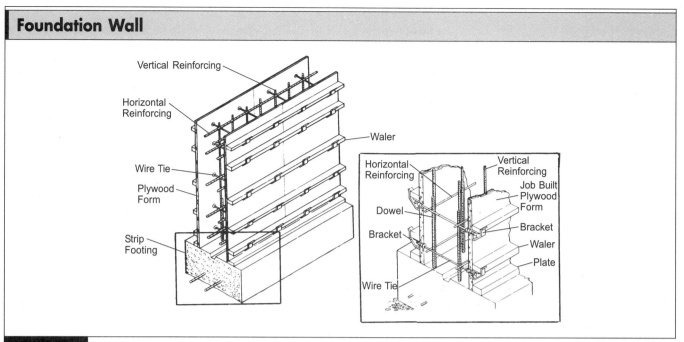

Figure 8.6

example, pricing formwork for a foundation wall that has concrete to 3'-10" versus 3'-6" in height is irrelevant since both would require a 4'-0" panel. In this application, the cost of one LF of formwork actually reflects two completed sides. Once the concrete placement exceeds the 4'-0" height of the panel, there is an added cost because larger panels are needed.

Because the price of forming a wall is affected more by the size (height) of the panel than the amount of concrete that will later be placed in it (and estimated separately), separately list formwork of different sizes (heights)—specifically 4', 6', and 8' heights. Walls to be formed in excess of 8' in height should be listed separately in vertical increments of 2', because of the premium cost for such formwork. Odd-shaped, custom-built, "one-of-a-kind," or round forms should also be listed separately for pricing. The pricing of formwork based on SFCA still is used in one-of-a-kind applications, where the materials are used once, and the formwork is custom-fabricated versus assembled.

As part of the cost of the formwork, be sure to include costs for coating the forms with a release agent to break the bond between the wood and the concrete, the ties that remain in the wall, and for stripping, cleaning, and reloading the forms on trucks after the work has been completed. Releasing agents are liquid and are converted from SF of area to gallons per SF, and, finally to actual gallons needed, including 10%–15% waste. Wall ties are by the piece (EA), converted to the common method of purchase—per hundred count. Study the specifications thoroughly for incidentals such as breaking off ties, patching holes, or "honeycombing." These can be time-consuming and costly if not estimated correctly or missed altogether.

Other costs that may be necessary include the rubbing of "green" concrete. Exposed concrete walls, such as retaining walls may, in some cases, require a rubbed finish to make the work more visually appealing. In this process, the forms are stripped before the concrete has fully cured and then rubbed with a special abrasive float that gives the appearance of smoother finish. The labor-intensive work is done by hand and may require mixing small quantities of mortar to patch holes or voids in the rubbed surface area. This process is taken off and priced by the square foot of surface area.

Grade Beams and Elevated Slabs

Grade Beams

These are horizontal beams supported at the ends, as opposed to foundation walls, which are supported by footings on the ground. The structure's load is carried along the grade beam and transmitted through the end supports (piers) to the soil below. Formwork for grade beams is taken off and priced by the SFCA. Grade beams differ from wall formwork in that they sometimes require forming the bottom of the grade beam as well as its sides. *(See Figure 8.7.)* If custom-made or one-time-use forms are required for certain applications, list and price this work separately.

Grade Beams

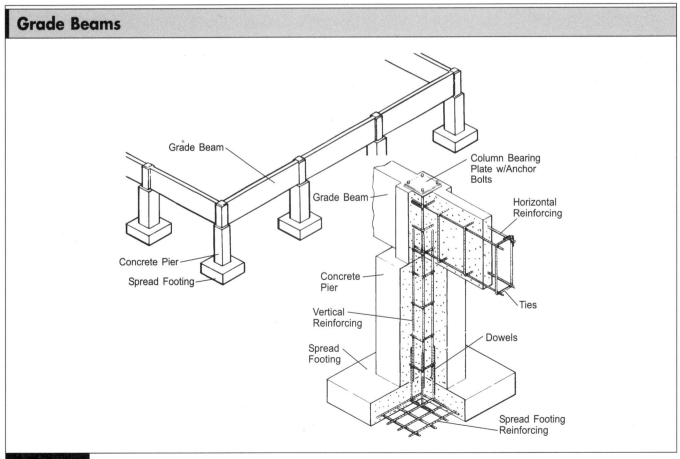

Figure 8.7

106

Elevated Slabs

Elevated cast-in-place slabs are often integrated with concrete beams, similar to grade beams. Again, the unit of takeoff and pricing is SFCA. Formed horizontal areas should be listed separately, because they require considerably more bracing to support the weight of the concrete they contain. Figure 8.8 illustrates an elevated cast-in-place slab.

Elevated Slab

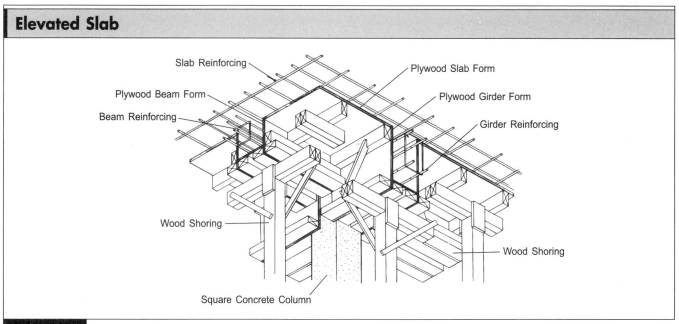

Figure 8.8

Edge Forms

The simplest type of form, called the *edge form*, is most commonly used to contain shallow pours of concrete for slab-on-grade, walks, or pads. Edge form materials are typically rough-grade lumber in the dimension required by the depth of the pour, such as 2" x 4", 2" x 6", and 2" x 8". Other types of edge forms include those more flexible to allow for bending to achieve radii on walks or patios. The process is the same. The actual edge form is held in place by wood or metal stakes, driven into the ground at spacing needed to support the work and prevent bowing.

Taking off Quantities

Edge forms are taken off and priced by the linear foot. Quantities of straight edge forms should be listed separately from curved edge forms. Also note any vertical surfaces that may be used as edge forms. For example, using a foundation wall as an edge when placing a basement slab may eliminate most of the edge form requirement.

Labor

The labor for formwork, with very few exceptions, is based on the productivity of a multi-person crew. Crews are typically composed of carpenters and labors. Carpenters erect, brace, and eventually disassemble formwork, while laborers distribute panels, bracing, and other related components of the system. The total labor cost for the crew per day is then divided by the production quantity in LF (or SF, if applicable) to arrive at the unit cost.

Placement of Concrete

Concrete placement into forms is most often calculated separately from formwork. The placement of wet concrete in erected formwork (as opposed to flatwork) is taken off and priced by the CY. Concrete is ordered, sold, delivered, and handled by the CY. The cost of placement is determined by the number of yards, calculated in the concrete materials takeoff. Placement is most often done by a crew of two or more, depending on the size of the task.

Other considerations when pricing concrete placement include pumps, buckets, cranes, and provisions such as additional chutes. Small equipment, such as a hand-held-vibrator for concrete, is part of the normal hand tools of the trade. Again, the method of placement will affect the cost. Concrete placed directly from a chute off a ready-mix truck yields the lowest placement cost. To direct-chute concrete, the truck must have sufficient access to pour, and the formwork must be lower than the lowest point on the chute, as this method relies on gravity. Some specifications require the use of a vibrator to evenly distribute the mix within the form and to fill voids caused by air pockets. This is included as part of the placement cost.

Flatwork   Concrete is frequently used as a flat surface, such as a slab-on-grade, composite slab, or a walkway. This type of concrete placement is called *flatwork*. The costs for placement of flatwork concrete are substantially different from those in walls and footings. The only exception to this occurs when placing concrete flatwork or slab work requires leveling and smoothing the surface of fresh concrete, commonly referred to as *finishing*. Concrete flatwork surfaces are finished using a hand or power trowel, a float, or even a broom.

Placement of concrete for flatwork can be by the same methods as concrete in formwork. Direct-chute is the least expensive. Concrete pumps are also common, but add substantially to the cost. For any application of concrete where access is limited, or height above the ground makes direct-chute or wheeled placement impractical, concrete pumping equipment may be necessary. Concrete pumping involves depositing fresh concrete into a truck-mounted pump, which uses a piston-type action to push the mix. The cost of placement per unit by such means is typically expensive.

Another placement method involves the use of a bucket and crane. Concrete is deposited directly from the mixer to a bucket hoisted by a crane to the forms, thereby minimizing the amount of handling. This method is often more economical than the concrete pump, but it does require that the pour be free from overhead obstructions. Analyze the pour to determine whether there is sufficient quantity to justify the use of a bucket and crane. A fourth method of placement, mainly for ground-level flatwork, is the use of a power buggy or even a wheelbarrow. This method is less productive than the direct chute method, but may be the most economical for inaccessible areas and small quantities. The use of equipment of any type in the placement of concrete may warrant the separation of CY placement units from SF finishing units so that different options can be evaluated.

It is important to determine whether the quantity of concrete required warrants the use of pumping equipment. Most concrete pumping companies charge by the day or a minimum of one-half day, regardless of the quantity pumped. Concrete pumping is often used for difficult access situations, such as when the formwork takes up the entire excavated area and the access area, making it difficult to place by chute, power buggy, or crane and bucket. The cost of erecting, maintaining, and dismantling riser piping (temporarily attached vertically to the structure) should be listed and estimated separately.

Be sure to coordinate the sequence of concrete placement in such a way as to maximize cost-effectiveness. This means placing concrete only when sufficient forms are available, or using concrete pumps or the bucket-and-crane method when there is a sufficient quantity to keep the equipment busy for the entire day. Frequently, concrete slab placement requires materials to separate flatwork from other surfaces. This separation is achieved by the use of an expansion joint.

Taking off Quantities

Concrete slab placement is taken off and estimated by the SF of surface area, as SF units more closely define the scope of work than do CY, because slabs generally have a larger SF area than CY volume. Be sure to calculate the SF area of the slab to be finished based on areas shown on plan view drawings. These are simple length by width calculations of the surface area. "Cement finishing," as this task is referred to in the trade, requires more than one tradesperson, except when finishing small slabs or pads. The productivity rate is based on the individual production of each cement finisher combined to represent the output of the crew.

Expansion Joints

Concrete, like other construction materials, expands and contracts with temperature changes. To allow for safe expansion and contraction without defects to the work, certain precautions must be taken during construction. A premolded joint filler (which compresses as the concrete expands) allows space for expansion. These asphalt-impregnated fibrous boards come in a variety of widths, the most common of which are 4" and 6". Thicknesses range from 1/2" to 1". Expansion joints typically occur at the perimeter of a concrete slab, where it terminates at a masonry or concrete wall. Figure 8.9 shows the use of a premolded joint filler at the perimeter of a slab that meets a foundation wall.

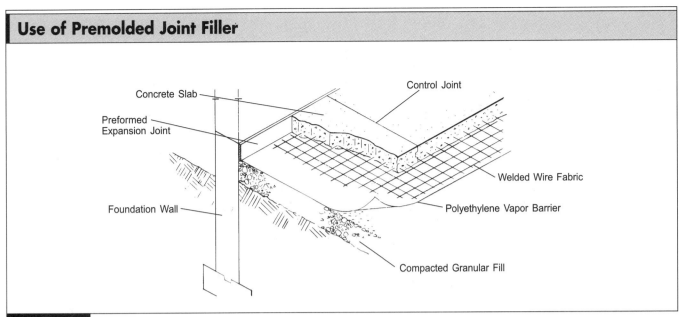

Concrete Slab

Preformed Expansion Joint

Foundation Wall

Control Joint

Welded Wire Fabric

Polyethylene Vapor Barrier

Compacted Granular Fill

Figure 8.9

Taking off Quantities

Expansion joints are taken off and priced by the linear foot. List each quantity separately by size and thickness. A modest allowance for waste should be included.

Control Joints

It is not uncommon for concrete to crack, even when placed correctly. As noted earlier, concrete expands and contracts with temperature. Containing or controlling the cracking by predicting where it will occur is the function of the control joint. A control joint is a formed, sawed, or tooled groove in a concrete surface. Its purpose is to create a weakened plane to regulate the location of cracking that results from the dimensional changes in large volumes of poured concrete. Each method of providing control joints—formed, sawed, or tooled—involves taking off and pricing quantities by the LF. It is not uncommon to have a combination of all three methods on the same project.

Tooled joints are accomplished by the use of a hand-held tool, and are typically used for exterior walkways. The grooves are cut perpendicular to the length of the walk at intervals of approximately 5' during the finishing process. *Saw cutting* is done after the surface is hardened, but before the final strength of the concrete has been achieved. Saw cutting is done with a diamond blade set to a specific depth, commonly 1/4" to 1/2". Saw-cut control joints occur at column lines in large slabs. *Formed control joints* are created by edge-forming areas to be placed at different times. (The slab is edge-formed in a checkerboard fashion, and alternate squares are placed.) Formed joints are typically created at the intersection of a column's base and the surrounding slab. Figure 8.10 shows a control joint at the base of a column.

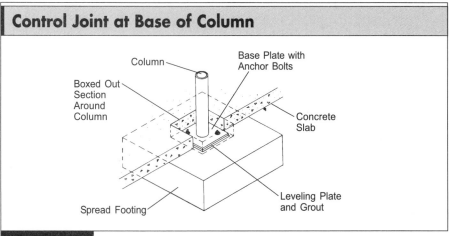

Control Joint at Base of Column

Column

Base Plate with Anchor Bolts

Boxed Out Section Around Column

Concrete Slab

Spread Footing

Leveling Plate and Grout

Figure 8.10

Curing

Concrete curing involves maintaining the proper moisture and temperature in the environment where concrete has been placed to ensure the proper hydration (chemical reaction) and hardening. Curing can be as simple as spraying water on the concrete surface after it has initially hardened and protecting it from evaporation. It can also be accomplished by spraying chemicals on freshly-finished concrete to create a membrane on the slab surface. This membrane prevents the premature evaporation of water in the mix before the concrete has had adequate time to cure properly. Repeated applications may be required in dry or hot weather conditions. The area to be sprayed for curing is calculated in SF. This figure is converted to gallons, based on the individual product's coverage per manufacturer recommendations. For example, if the product has a coverage of 400 SF per gallon and the area to be covered is 4,000 SF, 10 gallons would be required. Quantities should be rounded up to the nearest gallon and may need to be rounded to the nearest common sales unit.

Another curing method requires spraying water with a hose after the initial setting of the surface. Applications are as required based on weather conditions. The unit of takeoff and pricing for this method is also SF, and is regarded mainly as a labor cost, since most projects have an ample supply of water. The duration of curing may be as long as 24 hours, requiring overtime or shift work.

A similar method calls for covering the moistened surface of the finished slab with a vapor barrier, such as polyethylene, to prevent evaporation of the surface moisture. This is also calculated and priced by the SF. The area is then converted to the required size roll. Sufficient allowances for overlap and waste are necessary for full coverage. A maximum of 10% waste and overlap is usually adequate.

During winter, in cold weather climates, additional protection, such as temporary portable heaters and insulating materials, may be required to ensure proper curing. Sometimes, the heat produced during the chemical reaction of hydration is sufficient to maintain a temperature above freezing, and covering the work with straw and polyethylene or insulating blankets is adequate.

Portable kerosene heaters, called *salamanders*, or similar heaters fueled by propane, are also used. Both require supervision while in use, because of the danger of fire and the continued requirement for adequate ventilation. Constant supervision and the consumption of fuel can be costly. Therefore, portable heaters are employed only when no other means will suffice. The cost for temporary heat is computed based on the time required, usually by the day, and the fuel consumption of the individual heating apparatus.

Allow for the set-up and dismantling of any necessary enclosures to contain the heat, including both materials and labor-hours. The cost of this work is often based on historical data. This is a difficult cost to accurately predict, since it involves predicting future weather conditions and the fuel commodities market. The experienced estimator uses available historical data to predict this cost and carefully checks the specifications for any language preventing the use of portable heaters.

Reinforcement

Concrete reinforcement refers to placing steel bars or wire within the formwork prior to placing concrete. The concrete and steel reinforcing are designed to act as a single unit, providing both compression and tensile strength in resisting the forces caused by the weight and mass of the structure. There are two basic types of reinforcing: welded wire fabric and steel reinforcing bars.

Welded Wire Fabric

Welded wire fabric (WWF), also called *welded wire mesh*, is a series of longitudinal and transverse wires of various gauges arranged at right angles to each other and welded at all points of intersection. Welded wire fabric is used in concrete slabs, both to provide reinforcement against thermal expansion and contraction and to reduce cracking.

Taking off Quantities

WWF is taken off and priced by the square foot. It is manufactured in sheets and rolls, and is sold based on the price per SF. Rolls are 250' x 5' wide, and flat sheets are 5' x 10'. Figure 8.11 is a table of specifications for common styles of WWF and an illustration of its parts.

Be sure to list the different sizes of WWF separately. While waste is minimal, overlap can be substantial. *(See Chapter 4.)* Review the specifications of structural drawing details for specified lap at the sides and ends of the sheet. In the absence of a specified overlap, add a minimum 15% for overlap.

The specifications should also be consulted for specified coatings, which can have a dramatic effect on the cost of the material. The most common

Welded Wire Fabric

New Designation	Old Designation	Steel Area per Foot				Approximate Weight per 100 S.F.	
Spacing – Cross Sectional Area (in.) – (Sq. In. 100)	Spacing Wire Gauge (in.) – (AS & W)	Longitudinal		Transverse			
		in.	cm	in.	cm	Lbs.	kg
Rolls							
6 x 6 – W1.4 x W1.4	6 x 6 – 10 x 10	0.028	0.071	0.028	0.071	21	9.53
6 x 6 – W2.0 x W2.0	6 x 6 – 8 x 8 (1)	0.040	0.102	0.040	0.102	29	13.15
6 x 6 – W2.9 x W2.9	6 x 6 – 6 x 6	0.058	0.147	0.053	0.147	42	19.05
6 x 6 – W4.0 x W4.0	6 x 6 – 4 x 4	0.080	0.203	0.080	0.203	58	26.31
4 x 4 – W1.4 x W1.4	4 x 4 – 10 x 10	0.042	0.107	0.042	0.107	31	14.06
4 x 4 – W2.0 x W2.0	4 x 4 – 8 x 8 (1)	0.060	0.152	0.060	0.152	43	19.50
4 x 4 – W2.9 x W2.9	4 x 4 – 6 x 6	0.087	0.221	0.087	0.221	62	28.12
4 x 4 – W4.0 x W4.0	4 x 4 – 4 x 4	0.120	0.305	0.120	0.305	85	38.56
Sheets							
6 x 6 – W2.9 x W2.9	6 x 6 – 6 x 6	0.058	0.147	0.058	0.147	42	19.05
6 x 6 – W4.0 x W4.0	6 x 6 – 4 x 4	0.080	0.203	0.080	0.203	58	26.31
6 x 6 – W5.5 x W5.5	6 x 6 – 2 x 2 (2)	0.110	0.279	0.110	0.279	80	36.29
6 x 6 – W4.0 x W4.0	4 x 4 – 4 x 4	0.120	0.305	0.120	0.305	85	38.56

Notes:
1. Exact W-number size for 8 gauge is W2.1
2. Exact W-number size for 2 gauge is W5.4

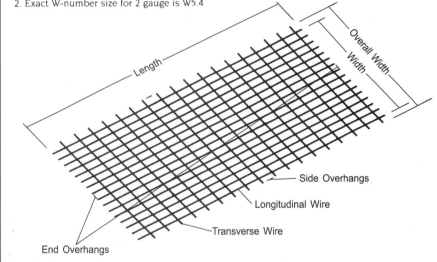

Figure 8.11

coating is epoxy, which reduces the deterioration caused by alkalines in the concrete mix or salts from ambient conditions, thereby extending the life of the WWF.

Reinforcing Bars

Steel reinforcing bars, commonly referred to as *rebar,* are deformed or knurled round bars of high-grade steel used to provide tensile strength. Rebar is available in stock lengths of 20', or can be cut, formed, or bent into any required shape. Bars are designated by a number that refers to the nominal diameter of the bar in eighths of an inch. Standard bar designation numbers are 3, 4, 5, 6, 7, 8, 9, 10, 11, 14, and 18. Therefore, the diameter of a #3 bar is 3/8". Figure 8.12 is a table of standard rebar weights and measures. Rebar placement in walls or footings is horizontal and/or vertical.

Taking off Quantities

Horizontal bars are taken off by total length, multiplied by the number of bars shown. Vertical bars are taken off by dividing the total length of wall or footing by the spacing, and multiplying by their height or length. All rebar is converted from LF to weight. *(See Figure 8.12.)* Rebar is priced by weight, both for material cost and installation cost. For total weights in excess of 2,000 lbs., the quantity is reported in tons, tns. For quantities less than 2,000 lbs., the quantity is reported in pounds, lbs.

Reinforcing Steel Weights and Measures

Bar Designation No.**	Nominal Weight, Lb./Ft.	U.S. Customary Units Nominal Dimensions*			Nominal Weight kg/m	SI Units Nominal Dimensions*		
		Diameter in.	Cross Sectional Area, in.²	Perimeter in.		Diameter, mm	Cross Sectional Area, cm²	Perimeter mm
3	0.376	0.375	0.11	1.178	0.560	9.52	0.71	29.9
4	0.668	0.500	0.20	1.571	0.994	12.70	1.29	39.9
5	1.043	0.625	0.31	1.963	1.552	15.88	2.00	49.9
6	1.502	0.750	0.44	2.356	2.235	19.05	2.84	59.8
7	2.044	0.875	0.60	2.749	3.042	22.22	3.87	69.8
8	2.670	1.000	0.79	3.142	3.973	25.40	5.10	79.8
9	3.400	1.128	1.00	3.544	5.059	28.65	6.45	90.0
10	4.303	1.270	1.27	3.990	6.403	32.26	8.19	101.4
11	5.313	1.410	1.56	4.430	7.906	35.81	10.06	112.5
14	7.65	1.693	2.25	5.32	11.384	43.00	14.52	135.1
18	13.60	2.257	4.00	7.09	20.238	57.33	25.81	180.1

*The nominal dimensions of a deformed bar are equivalent to those of a plain round bar having the same weight per foot as the deformed bar.
**Bar numbers are based on the number of eighths of an inch included in the nominal diameter of the bars.

Figure 8.12

Figure 8.13 lists symbols and abbreviations commonly found on structural drawings referring to reinforcing steel.

List each size separately (by bar designation) and shape in order to calculate weights for correct pricing of rebar. When the length of continuous reinforcing exceeds the length of stock bars (20'-0"), overlap becomes necessary to maintain the structural integrity of the member. Most specifications or structural drawings indicate the amount of overlap as a multiple of the bar diameter.

For example:

#4 bars will be overlapped by 20d", where 20d refers to 20 times the bar diameter (in inches).

In the case of #4 bar: 20 x 1/2" = 10"

To determine the amount of overlap required for continuous horizontal bars, calculate the overlap as a function of the maximum length of the continuous bar being used. This could be converted to a percentage added to the total length. For example:

Calculate the total amount of #5 rebar required, including the specified overlap of 20d", if the footing is 1,000 LF with 3 continuous bars.

Start by calculating the amount of overlap required on one bar assuming the maximum bar length is 20'-0";

20 x 5/8" = 12-1/2" or approximately one foot for every 20-foot length of rebar. This translates to 1 divided by 20, or .05. This can be converted to 5%. Therefore, the overlap can be calculated at 5% of the total length of horizontal bar.

1,000 LF x 3 pieces x 1.043 lbs./LF = 3,129 lbs. If this number is now increased by 5%, the overlap can be included: 3,129 x 1.05 = 3,285.45 lbs.

Rebar may have additional costs associated with the production, submittal, and review of rebar shop drawings, required by most commercial projects. Also, be sure to include costs associated with the transportation, delivery, unloading, storage, and protection of rebar. Accessories, such as chair bolsters for the support of the WWF, should be included in the cost. Specifications should identify any required accessories.

> *To calculate quantities of rebar in slabs, the length and width of the slab are divided by the longitudinal and transverse spacing, respectively. Multiply the quantity in pieces by the length of each piece to determine a total linear footage. For example:*
>
> *Calculate the LF of #4 bar in a 20' x 25' slab where the bars are spaced at 12" OC each way.*
>
> *Longitudinal (length): 25' / 12" OC = 26* pcs x 20' = 520 LF*
>
> *Transverse (width): 20' / 12" OC = 21* pcs x 25' = 525 LF*
>
> *Total of #4 bar = 1,045 LF*
>
> ** Note that the final quantity of pieces includes one to start.*
>
> *Using Figure 8.12, the total linear footage of 1,045 can be extended to pounds (lbs.) by multiplying the 1,045 LF x 0.668 lbs. per LF, which equals 698 lbs.*

Labor

Labor costs for setting rebar are calculated per ton. Productivity is based on one ironworker for smaller diameter bars (#3 up to and including #6). For bar designations #7 or higher, productivity will be reduced due to higher bar weight per LF. A multi-person crew is needed to set the long length bars. In some instances, cranes will be needed for setting larger rebar configurations, such as spiral reinforcement used in round columns or mats in pile caps. Equipment costs are typically included in the per ton setting price.

#	Indicates size of deformed bar number	
$\emptyset$	Round, used mainly for plain round bars	
@	Spacing, center to center	
$\longleftrightarrow$	Direction in which bars extend	
$\longleftrightarrow$	Limits of area covered by bars	

Pl	Plain bar	Of	Outside face
Bt	Bent	Nf	**Near face**
Str	Straight	Ff	Far face
Stir	Stirrup	Ef	Each face
Sp	Spiral	Bot	Bottom
Ct	Column tie	Ew	Each way
If	Inside face	T	Top

Figure 8.13

Precast Concrete

Precast concrete includes structural concrete components formed, poured, and finished in a location other than their final position in the structure. Precast components are fabricated off site and must be transported to the site. Items such as bulkhead enclosures, precast steps, wheel stops, lintels, wall panels, and concrete planking (also known as hollow-core planking) are common examples of precast concrete members.

Taking off Quantities

Precast items are typically shown and identified on structural drawings in plan and sectional views, but can also be noted on site drawings, in the form of items such as precast steps or wheel stops. The units for estimating precast concrete items vary. Quantities should be listed according to size, length, or any other characteristics that would allow accurate pricing. Most are priced by the individual piece, or each, EA. Other products, such as wall panels and concrete planking, are priced by the SF. Lintels are priced by the LF, and precast steps can be priced by the riser. As most precast items require equipment for handling and installation, include sufficient equipment and labor-hours based on standard production rates for the individual items. On-site cutting of precast plank or caulking of joints between the planks should be included as part of the installation cost. Both are quantified and priced by the LF. Other costs associated with the installation of precast wall panels, such as welding or bolting, are taken off and priced by the piece, EA. It should be noted that precast concrete structures for use in sewer and drainage work and precast concrete curbs are specified under Division 2—Site Construction.

Cementitious Decks

Cementitious decks are lightweight, noncombustible panels used in floor and roof construction with steel framing. In place of concrete, a gypsum core is used, as it offers a lightweight, fire-resistant construction. Cementitious decks are taken off by either the individual piece (EA) or by the square foot. It should be noted that cementitious deck materials are available in varying thicknesses, with varying prices. Hoisting the panels to the roof or floor is usually accomplished with a crane, but the precise placement and attachment are done manually. Installation costs should include the welding of clips or metal edging to the steel support framing, and is typically calculated per labor-hour of a specific crew. Costs for welding are also based on labor-hours per individual welder.

Embedded Items

Embedded items are encased or cast within the formwork for connecting future work or supporting reinforcing within the formwork. The most common embedded items are described below.

Sleeves

Sleeves are block-outs within the formwork that hold back concrete, so that when the formwork is stripped, there is a hole in the concrete wall or slab. Sleeves are specifically located to facilitate the passage of piping through the wall at a later date. When the sleeve is removed, it should allow clear passage of the piping. Sleeves can be made of PVC pipe, wood, or rigid insulation. A sleeve is fitted between formwork panels and fastened by nails or other means. Sleeves are taken off and priced by the individual piece and listed according to size. Included in the price should be the cost of patching around the piping with mortar or concrete after the pipe or conduit has been inserted through the sleeve.

Sleeves are not always shown on the drawings, but may be required where utility piping passes through the foundation wall. Coordinate with the mechanical and electrical drawings for the locations, size, and quantity of sleeves. The specifications typically require that the formwork contractor provide and install sleeves, if needed.

Anchor Bolts

An *anchor bolt* is a threaded rod or bolt with a right-angle bend that is embedded in cast-in-place concrete. Anchor bolts are used to connect steel columns, beams, or wood sill plates to the concrete structure. The size, quantity, spacing, and location of anchor bolts are noted on the structural drawings. Anchor bolts are taken off by the piece and are priced as each, EA. A template (usually made from wood) may be needed to hold the bolts in position during the hardening. The template is stripped along with the formwork. Figure 8.14 illustrates a template supporting anchor bolts on an isolated footing.

Other Embedded Items

Steel window frames for basement window sashes and doors in residential construction are installed in a manner similar to sleeves. They are taken off and priced by the piece and separated according to size. After the forms are stripped, the steel frames remain, and the wood or steel sash is installed within the frame. The locations are noted in both plan and elevation views on the architectural drawings.

Labor

Labor to install all embedded items including anchor bolts is calculated by the individual piece, EA, or by the labor-hour for tasks that include a multi-person crew.

Vapor Barriers

Polyethylene is sometimes specified as a vapor barrier between the compacted sub-base and the cast-in-place slab-on-grade. A vapor barrier prevents the transmission of moisture from the ground through the slab. Although part of Division 7—Thermal and Moisture Protection, vapor barriers are sometimes included in Division 3—Concrete. The thickness of the poly vapor barrier is noted on the drawings in mils (with one mil equal to .001 inch). Polyethylene is commonly specified in 4 or 6 mil thicknesses. The vapor barrier is installed by spreading the polyethylene on the sub-base just prior to pouring the concrete. An allowance of 7%–10% is usually sufficient for the overlapping of seams and waste. Vapor barrier is taken off by the SF and listed separately by thickness. The contractor should allow additional time for setting and finishing concrete slabs with vapor barriers, as water is retained longer as a result of the inability of the water to pass directly to the sub-base.

Conclusion

Accurately estimating the cost of concrete work is critical to a successful overall project estimate. Concrete work is not limited to foundation and slab work alone. There are numerous other applications in which concrete is used separately or as part of a multi-trade system. In any application, a thorough understanding of concrete installation practices, as well as the particular job site conditions, are essential to a reliable estimate.

Installation Time in Labor-Hours for Spread Footings

Description	Labor-Hours	Unit
Formwork	.105	S.F.C.A.
Reinforcing		
#4 to #7	15.239	ton
#8 to #14	8.889	ton
Placing Concrete under 1 C.Y.		
Direct Chute	.873	C.Y.
Pumped	1.280	C.Y.
Crane and Bucket	1.422	C.Y.
Over 5 C.Y.		
Direct Chute	.436	C.Y.
Pumped	.610	C.Y.
Crane and Bucket	.640	C.Y.
Anchor bolt or dowel templates	1.000	Ea.

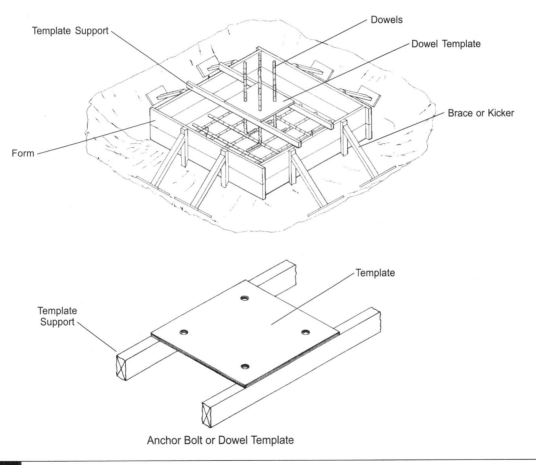

Anchor Bolt or Dowel Template

Figure 8.14

Chapter Nine

Masonry

The use of masonry in construction is appealing for a number of reasons. It is fireproof, durable, requires little or no maintenance, and can be configured to satisfy most structural requirements. Masonry units are available in an enormous selection of colors, shapes, textures, and sizes that can be installed for an aesthetically pleasing appearance. CSI Division 4, Masonry, includes brick, block (CMU), glazed block, glass block, fieldstone, and cut stone, as well as the labor, tools, and equipment required to install these materials.

Brick and block are the two most common types of masonry units, and the process of installing them is referred to as *unit masonry*. Brick is modular and adaptable, and can be installed in a variety of patterns, called *bonds*. Concrete masonry units, commonly referred to as *CMU*, consist of concrete block. CMU is primarily used for walls and partitions that will support a structural load or as the backup for a face brick veneer. It is used extensively in commercial and industrial building applications, and as a foundation material in residential construction. All masonry work is installed with *mortar*, the "adhesive" that holds the units together. Mortar is spread between the joints of individual masonry units and allowed to harden, which bonds the units together.

In reviewing the contract documents, there are several factors that will affect the cost of masonry work to consider:

- What type of unit masonry will be used? Are there multiple types?
- What is the bonding pattern of the masonry and the size of the mortar joint?
- Is the masonry reinforced vertically and laterally?
- Will scaffolding be required?
- What are the seasonal conditions that will affect productivity when the work is ongoing?

- Will enclosures or temporary heat be required?
- Are there incidentals that need to be considered, such as precast lintels or sills, through-wall flashings, steel lintels, embedded items, chimney components, etc.?

Mortar

Mortar is a composition of water, fine aggregates (such as sand), cement (Portland, hydraulic, or masonry), and lime. Mortar requirements are specified in the products section of the masonry specifications. The mortar, or its components, is often listed as complying with American Society for Testing and Materials (ASTM), one of the primary agencies that sets standards for masonry products and procedures.

Types of Mortar

The compressive strength of mortar varies with the proportions of the ingredients. The four basic types of mortar and their uses are based on mixing proportions and strengths. They are as follows:

- *Type M*: A high-strength mortar used primarily in foundation masonry, retaining walls, walkways, sewers, and manholes. In general, Type M mortar is used when maximum compressive strength is required.
- *Type S*: A relatively high-strength mortar that develops maximum bonding strength between masonry units. It is recommended for use where lateral and flexural strength are required.
- *Type N*: Medium-strength, general-use mortar for above-grade exposed applications.
- *Type O*: A low-strength mortar for interior non-load-bearing applications.

Figure 9.1 lists the mixing proportions and strengths of the four basic types of mortar that are most commonly used.

Taking off Quantities

Since the mortar quantity required is directly related to the number of bricks or blocks, first calculate the quantity of masonry units in order to determine the quantity of mortar needed. The size of the joints must also be specified or determined in the absence of a specified size. Mortar quantities are typically in CF or can be converted to CY (27 CF = 1 CY). Quantities are frequently determined from established tables, such as in Figure 9.2.

> *Calculate the quantity of mortar required for laying up 50,000 standard bricks with a 1/2" joint thickness:*
>
> *50,000 brick/1,000 brick = 50 bricks.*
>
> *50 bricks x 11.7 CF per 1,000 brick = 585 CF of mortar.*
>
> *If 585 CF is increased by 15% for waste: 585 CF x .15 = + 585 CF = 672.75 CF, rounded to 673 CF.*
>
> *To convert to CY, divide by 27: 673 CF/27 = 24.93, or 25 CY.*

Brick Mortar Mix Proportions and Compressive Strengths

Brick Mortar Mix Proportions

This chart shows some common mortar types, the mixing proportions and their general uses.

Brick Mortar Mixes*					
Type	Portland Cement	Hydrated Lime	Sand (maximum)**	Strength	Use
M	1	1/4	3-3/4	High	General use where high strength is required, especially good compressive strength; work that is below grade and in contact with earth.
S	1	1/2	4-1/2	High	Okay for general use, especially good where high lateral strength is desired.
N	1	1	6	Medium	General use when masonry is exposed above grade; best to use when high compressive and lateral strengths are not required.
O	1	2	9	Low	Do not use when masonry is exposed to severe weathering; acceptable for non-loadbearing walls of solid units and interior non-loadbearing partitions of hollow units.

*The water used should be of the quality of drinking water. Use as much as is needed to bring the mix to a suitably plastic and workable state.

**The sand should be damp and loose. A general rule for sand content is that it should not be less than 2-1/4 or more than 3 times the sum of the cement and lime volumes.

Compressive Strengths

This table lists the expected 28 day compressive strengths for some common types of mortar mixes.

Mortar Type	Average Compressive Strength at 28 Days
M	2500 p.s.i.
S	1800 p.s.i.
N	750 p.s.i.
O	350 p.s.i.

Masonry and Concrete Construction, Ken Nolan, Craftsman Book Co.

Figure 9.1

Mortar Quantities for Brick and Concrete Block Masonry

Mortar Quantities for Brick Masonry

This table can be used to determine the amounts of mortar needed for brick masonry walls for various joint thicknesses and types of common brick.

Brickwork	Joint Thickness (in inches)	Actual Requirement (in C.F. per 1,000)	Requirement with 15% Waste (in C.Y. per 1,000)
Standard	3/8	8.6	0.4
Standard	1/2	11.7	0.5
Modular	3/8	7.6	0.3
Modular	1/2	10.4	0.4
Roman	3/8	10.7	0.5
Roman	1/2	14.4	0.6
Norman	3/8	11.2	0.5
Norman	1/2	15.1	0.6

Type	Thickness (in inches)	Actual Requirement (in C.F. per S.F.)	Requirement with 15% Waste (in C.Y. per 1,000 S.F.)
Parging or Backplastering	3/8	0.03	1.3
	1/2	0.04	1.7

Note: Quantities are based on 4" thick brickwork. For each additional 4" brickwork, or where masonry units are used in backup, add parging or backplastering.

Modular dimensions are measured from center to center of masonry joints. To fit into the system, the unit or number of units must be the size of the module, less the thickness of the joint. A standard face brick with a 1/2" joint would measure 8-1/2" long, whereas a modular brick with the same joint would measure 8".

Mortar Quantities for Concrete Block Masonry

This table can be used to determine the amounts of mortar needed for concrete block masonry walls for joint thicknesses for various types of masonry units.

Type	Joint Thickness (in inches)	Actual Requirement (in C.Y. per 1,000)	Requirement with 15% Waste (in C.Y. per 1,000)
Concrete Block			
Shell Bedding			
All thicknesses	3/8	0.6	0.7
Full Bedding			
12 x 8 x 16, 3-Core	3/8	0.9	1.0
12 x 8 x 16, 2-Core	3/8	0.8	0.9
8 x 8 x 16, 3-Core	3/8	0.7	0.8
8 x 8 x 16, 2-Core	3/8	0.7	0.8
6 x 8 x 16, 3-Core	3/8	0.7	0.8
6 x 8 x 16, 2-Core	3/8	0.7	0.8
4 x 8 x 16, 3-Core	3/8	0.7	0.8
4 x 8 x 16, Solid	3/8	0.8	0.9

Type	Joint Thickness (in inches)	Actual Requirement (in C.F. per 1,000)	Requirement with 15% Waste (in C.Y. per 1,000)
4S Glazed Structural Units			
(nominal 2-1/2" x 8")			
4 SA (2" thick)	1/4	2.6	0.1
4 S (4" thick)	1/4	5.6	0.2
4D Glazed Structural Units			
(nominal 5" x 8")			
4 DCA (2" thick)	1/4	3.3	0.1
4 DC (4" thick)	1/4	7.1	0.3
4 DC 60 (6" thick)	1/4	10.9	0.5
4 DC 80 (8" thick)	1/4	13.7	0.6
6T Glazed Structural Units			
(nominal 5" x 12")			
6 TCA (2" thick)	1/4	4.2	0.2
6 TC (4" thick)	1/4	9.3	0.4
6 TC 60 (6" thick)	1/4	14.2	0.6
6 TC 80 (8" thick)	1/4	19.1	0.8
6P Glazed Structural Units –			
1/4" Joints (nominal 4" x 12")			
6 PCA (2" thick)		4.0	0.2
6 PC (4" thick)		8.6	0.4
6 PC 60 (6" thick)		13.1	0.6
6 PC 80 (8" thick)		17.7	0.8

Figure 9.2a

Mortar Quantities for Concrete Block Masonry (continued)

This table can be used to determine the amounts of mortar needed for concrete block masonry walls for joint thicknesses for various types of masonry units.

Type	Joint Thickness (in inches)	Actual Requirement (in C.F. per 1,000)	Requirement with 15% Waste (in C.Y. per 1,000)
8W Glazed Structural Units (nominal 8" x 16")			
8 WCA (2" thick) (6")	1/4	6.0	0.3
8 WCA (2" thick)	3/8	9.1	0.4
8 WC (4" thick)	1/4	12.9	0.6
8 WC (4" thick)	3/8	19.4	0.8
Spectra-Glaze® Units – 3/8" Joints (nominal 4" x 16")			
44S (4" thick)		16.0	0.7
64S (6" thick)		24.5	1.0
84S (8" thick)		33.0	1.4
Spectra-Glaze® Units – 3/8" Joints (nominal 8" x 16")			
2S (2" thick)		9.0	0.4
4S (4" thick)		19.2	0.8
6S (6" thick)		29.5	1.3
8S (8" thick)		39.7	1.7
10S (10" thick)		50.0	2.1
12S (12" thick)		60.2	2.6
Structural Clay Backup and Wall Tile			
5 x 12 (4" thick)	1/2	20.0	0.9
5 x 12 (6" thick)	1/2	30.4	1.3
5 x 12 (8" thick)	1/2	40.5	1.7
8 x 12 (6" thick)	1/2	35.6	1.5
8 x 12 (8" thick)	1/2	47.5	2.0
8 x 12 (12" thick)	1/2	71.2	3.0
Structural Clay Partition Tile			
12 x 12 (4" thick)	1/2	28.4	1.2
12 x 12 (6" thick)	1/2	42.5	1.8
12 x 12 (8" thick)	1/2	56.7	2.4
12 x 12 (10" thick)	1/2	70.9	3.0
12 x 12 (12" thick)	1/2	85.1	3.6
Gypsum Block (all 12" x 30")*			
2" thick	1/4	12.2	0.5
	3/8	18.4	0.8
	1/2	24.6	1.0
3" thick	1/4	18.3	0.8
	3/8	27.6	1.2
	1/2	36.9	1.6
4" thick	1/4	24.5	1.0
	3/8	36.8	1.6
	1/2	49.2	2.1
6" thick	1/4	36.7	1.6
	3/8	55.2	2.4
	1/2	73.8	3.1
Glass Block (all 3-7/8" thick)			
5-3/4 x 5-3/4	1/4		
7-3/4 x 7-3/4	1/4		
11-3/4 x 11-3/4	1/4		
Firebrick Thin joints, including waste 300 lbs. fireclay per 1,000.			

*Note: Gypsum partition tile cement should be used. 900 lbs. are required per cubic yard, plus 1 cubic yard of sand. 1,000 units equals 2,610 square feet.

Figure 9.2b

The quantity of mortar for setting stone varies with the size of the stone and the joint. However, a general rule is that 4-5 CF of mortar will be required per 100 CF of stone. Quantities for various strengths of mortar should be listed separately for accurate pricing. Mortar that requires special coloring should also be listed separately, as the pigment required to color mortar will affect the cost. Review the specifications carefully for additives that will affect the price of the mortar or its longevity after it has been batched. Labor costs may vary for preparing mortar in the proper strength and color, as each mixture requires some experimentation. There are many additives that can be specified in the mix. Mortar is mixed on site by labor and machine. Only in the rarest of circumstances is the mortar mixed by hand. This is reserved for small repairs when machine set-up is not practical. The labor cost of batching the mortar is frequently included as part of the labor costs for setting the brick or CMU.

Brick

Brick is a solid masonry unit made of clay or shale and formed into a rectangular prism while soft, then burned or fired in an oven, called a kiln, until hard. There is a wide and ever-changing variety of bricks available to the industry. For estimating purposes, most brick can be classified into one of the following groups.

Types of Brick

- *Face brick* is used where appearance is important (e.g., veneer walls). Its manufacture is closely controlled so that color, size, hardness, strength, and texture are uniform.
- *Common brick* is used in applications where performance is more important than appearance (e.g., below-grade masonry, as a backup for face brick, or in manholes).
- *Glazed brick* is fired with a ceramic or other type of glazing material on the exposed surfaces. It is typically used in applications where durability and cleanliness are essential (e.g., restrooms, kitchens, and hospitals).
- *Fire brick* is used in areas of high temperatures, such as furnaces and fireplaces.
- *Brick pavers* are used as a wearing surface for floors, walks, and patios. Pavers are typically hard and durable, with a high resistance to damage from both freeze-thaw cycles and the corrosive salts used to melt snow.
- *SCR brick* is a patented type of brick developed by the Structural Clay Products Institute (SCR). SCR brick has a nominal width of 6" in contrast to the nominal 4" associated with modular brick. It can therefore be used structurally in a single width. It is most commonly used in the residential market for single-story applications.

To thoroughly understand the plans and specifications for masonry work and create an accurate takeoff, it is important to become familiar with brick nomenclature. *(See Figure 9.3.)*

Brick Nomenclature

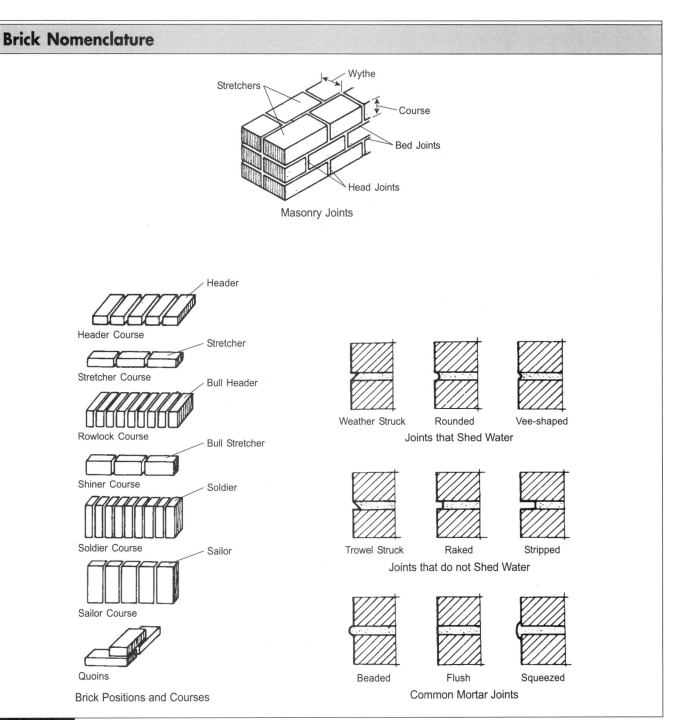

Masonry Joints

Brick Positions and Courses

Header Course — Header

Stretcher Course — Stretcher

Rowlock Course — Bull Header

Shiner Course — Bull Stretcher

Soldier Course — Soldier

Sailor Course — Sailor

Quoins

Joints that Shed Water — Weather Struck, Rounded, Vee-shaped

Joints that do not Shed Water — Trowel Struck, Raked, Stripped

Common Mortar Joints — Beaded, Flush, Squeezed

Figure 9.3

Most brick are modular in design, and either the width, length, or coursing height is a multiple of 4". Brick sizes are designated as nominal, versus actual size. The difference between the actual and nominal is made up by the thickness of the mortar joint. Figure 9.4 provides the nominal and actual sizes, as well as the modular coursing of various modular brick in use today.

Since brickwork is modular, be sure to determine the width of brick for each application. Face bricks in veneer walls are one brick width, while other construction may be two, three, or four bricks in width. While the

Sizes of Modular Brick

Unit Designation	Nominal Dimensions (in inches)			Joint Thickness (in inches)	Manufactured Dimensions (in inches)			Modular Coursing (in inches)
	t	h	l		t	h	l	
Standard Modular	4	2-2/3	8	3/8	3-5/8	2-1/4	7-5/8	3C = 8
				1/2	3-1/2	2-1/4	7-1/2	
Engineer	4	3-1/5	8	3/8	3-5/8	2-13/16	7-5/8	5C = 16
				1/2	3-1/2	2-11/16	7-1/2	
Economy 8 or Jumbo Closure	4	4	8	3/8	3-5/8	3-5/8	7-5/8	1C = 4
				1/2	3-1/2	3-1/2	7-1/2	
Double	4	5-1/3	8	3/8	3-5/8	4-15/16	7-5/8	3C = 16
				1/2	3-1/2	4-13/16	7-1/2	
Roman	4	2	12	3/8	3-5/8	1-5/8	11-5/8	2C = 4
				1/2	3-1/2	1-1/2	11-1/2	
Norman	4	2-2/3	12	3/8	3-5/8	2-1/4	11-5/8	3C = 8
				1/2	3-1/2	2-1/4	11-1/2	
Norwegian	4	3-1/5	12	3/8	3-5/8	2-13/16	11-5/8	5C = 16
				1/2	3-1/2	2-11/16	11-1/2	
Economy 12 or Jumbo Utility	4	4	12	3/8	3-5/8	3-5/8	11-5/8	1C = 4
				1/2	3-1/2	3-1/2	11-1/2	
Triple	4	5-1/3	12	3/8	3-5/8	4-15/16	11-5/8	3C = 16
				1/2	3-1/2	4-13/16	11-1/2	
SCR brick	6	2-2/3	12	3/8	5-5/8	2-1/4	11-5/8	3C = 8
				1/2	5-1/2	2-1/4	11-1/2	
6-in. Norwegian	6	3-1/5	12	3/8	5-5/8	2-13/16	11-5/8	5C = 16
				1/2	5-1/2	2-11/16	11-1/2	
6-in. Jumbo	6	4	12	3/8	5-5/8	3-5/8	11-5/8	1C = 4
				1/2	5-1/2	3-1/2	11-1/2	
8-in. Jumbo	8	4	12	3/8	7-5/8	3-5/8	11-5/8	1C = 4
				1/2	7-1/2	3-1/2	11-1/2	

(courtesy Masonry and Concrete Construction, Ken Nolan, Craftsman Book Company)

Figure 9.4

popularity of this type of multi-width masonry construction has declined in recent years, it still does occur in unique circumstances. To accurately determine the quantity of brick in the takeoff, list the work separately by width of wall.

Taking off Quantities

Brick masonry units are taken off by the SF of wall in the case of single-width walls such as veneers. Multiple-width walls are taken off by the CF. In either case, the final conversion for pricing is to the quantity of brick. Determine the number of bricks per SF or CF based on the size of the brick, the size of the mortar joint, and the brick bond. The *brick bond* is the pattern of overlapping of one brick on another, either along the length of the wall or through its thickness. Bricks are shifted so that the vertical mortar joints of successive courses do not line up, except in the case of stack bond. There are two basic arrangements of bricks in a bond. The frequency of these arrangements determines the bond. The first is the *stretcher*, where bricks are laid parallel to the face of the wall. The other arrangement, *header*, features bricks laid perpendicular to the face of the wall. In addition, there are ornamental courses, such as rowlock, soldier, sailor, and shiner, examples of which are illustrated in Figure 9.3.

The most common types of bonds and their respective coursing are illustrated in Figure 9.5. Running bond is the continuous use of stretcher courses, where each alternating course overlaps the preceding course by 1/2 brick. Modifications of the standard running bond are also used, such as 1/3 running bond.

Other bonds illustrated in Figure 9.5 are defined as follows:

- *Common*, or *American, bond* is similar to running bond, but has a course of headers at every 5th, 6th, or 7th course.
- *Stack bond* is created by stretchers laid up directly over one another, where all vertical joints line up. The bond is a pattern for appearances only, and has relatively little structural value.
- *English bond* consists of alternating courses of stretchers and headers where the vertical joints of alternating courses align.
- *Dutch bond,* or *English Cross bond*, is similar to English bond except that the stretcher courses do not align, but alternate by 1/2 brick.
- *Flemish bond* consists of alternating headers and stretchers in each course. The header is centered over the stretcher in each consecutive course.

There are other types of bonds, but they are variations of the preceding types.

To calculate SF for veneer walls, multiply the length by the height. Always make deductions in full for areas greater than 2 SF. Show, as closely as possible, the actual number of brick needed to do the work.

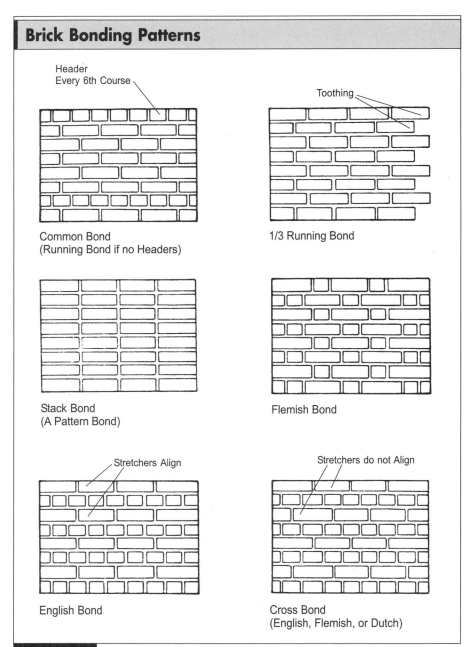

Brick Bonding Patterns

Header
Every 6th Course

Common Bond
(Running Bond if no Headers)

Toothing

1/3 Running Bond

Stack Bond
(A Pattern Bond)

Flemish Bond

Stretchers Align

English Bond

Stretchers do not Align

Cross Bond
(English, Flemish, or Dutch)

Figure 9.5

When deducting window or door openings from the wall, consider the depth of the jambs or returns, commonly called *reveals*. If the reveal is only the width of brick (approximately 4" for most brick), the entire opening must be deducted. If the depth of the reveal varies, subtract the additional brick in the reveal from the opening size to be deducted.

For example, if the opening is 5'-4" x 6'-8" with a 16" reveal on either jamb, the calculation would be:

2 sides x 16" = 32" or 2'-8".

Subtract 2'-8" from 5'-4", which equals 2'-8".

Therefore, the actual deduction for the opening will be 2'-8" x 6'-8", or 17.81 SF.

Quantities for waste for brickwork vary with the application, type of brick, bond, and quality of workmanship. Determine an appropriate waste factor for each project. On face brick veneers set in a running bond with no header courses, a standard acceptable waste would be between 3% and 5%. For more complex bonds, Figure 9.6 lists the most common brick bonds and the associated wastes.

Waste Allowances for Various Brick Bonding Patterns

Type of Pattern	% of Waste
Running or Stretcher Bond	The face brick are all stretchers and are tied to the backing by metal or reinforcing. Waste — 5%
Common or American Bond	Every sixth course of stretcher bond is usually a header course. Waste — 4%.
Flemish Bond	Each course has alternate headers and stretchers with the alternate headers centered over the stretcher. Waste — 3 to 5 %.
English Bond	Consists of alternate headers and stretchers with the vertical joints in the header and stretcher aligning or breaking over each other. Waste — 8 to 15%
Stack Bond	Has no overlapping of units since all vertical joints are aligned. Usually this pattern is bonded to the backing with rigid steel ties. Waste — 3%.
English Cross or Dutch Bond	Built up on interlocking crosses. This wall consists of two headers and a stretcher forming a cross. Waste — 8%.

Figure 9.6

Once the SF area of brick, the size of the mortar joint, and the brick bond are known, consult the tables in Figures 9.7 and 9.8 to determine the quantity of brick per SF and, finally, the total number of bricks. Figure 9.7 refers to brick laid in a running bond pattern with various size joints. Figure 9.8 shows factors in determining the accurate quantity of brick materials in a particular bond.

Labor

The bond also has a direct effect on productivity as well. Generally speaking, as the quantity of brick per square foot increases, the labor-hours per square foot to install the brick also increases. Figure 9.9 shows the labor-hours required per square foot, vertical linear foot, or linear foot of brick in various bonds.

There are many factors that affect the amount of brick a bricklayer will set in a day. If ten bricklayers work side-by-side under identical conditions,

Brick Quantities per SF

Number of bricks per SF based on brick type and size of joints.

Brick Type & Size	Size of Joint (in inches)					
	1/4	1/3	3/8	1/2	5/8	3/4
Standard face brick (8" x 2-1/4")	6.98	6.70	6.55	6.16	5.81	5.49
Standard common brick (8" x 2-1/4")	6.98	6.70	6.55	6.16	5.81	5.49
Concrete brick (7-5/8" x 2-1/4")	7.31	7.00	6.86	6.45	6.07	5.73
Modular brick (7-1/2" x 2-1/6")	7.68	7.35	7.19	6.73	6.35	5.98
Modular Roman brick (11-5/8" x 1-5/8")	6.47	6.15	6.00	5.59	5.22	4.90
Modular Norman brick (11-5/8" x 2-1/4")	4.85	4.66	4.57	4.32	4.09	3.88

Note: Above constants are net, i.e., no waste is included.

Figure 9.7

Adjustments to Brick Quantity Factors

This table provides factors for determining the additional quantities of brick needed when specific bonding patterns are used.

For Other Bonds Standard Size Add to SF Quantities				
Bond Type	Description	Factor	Description	Factor
Common	Full header every fifth course Full header every sixth course	+20% +16.7%	Header = W x H exposed Rowlock = H x W exposed	+100% +100%
English	Full header every second course	+50%	Rowlock stretcher = L x W exposed Soldier = H x L exposed	+33.3% —
Flemish	Alternate headers every course every sixth course	+33.3% +5.6%	Sailor = W x L exposed	-33.3%

(See "Brick Quantities per SF" table above for basic quantities of brick per SF).

Figure 9.8

producing the same class of workmanship, no two would lay the same number of brick in a day. For this reason, averages are established. Extenuating circumstances, such as weather, temperature, access, mobility, and the specific application, all affect productivity. Long, straight walls with little or no interruptions proceed more quickly than those with numerous window or door openings that require layout calculations or cutting jamb brick. The actual conditions must be studied carefully to ascertain an average productivity. It is not uncommon for productivity to change depending on the different applications around the building. The class of workmanship required will also affect productivity.

Since most brickwork—and masonry in general—has an aesthetic value, the class of workmanship expected is normally considered first rate. This is referred to as *first-class workmanship*, and is sometimes defined as such in the Execution portion of the specifications. However, there are times in which first-class workmanship is not required. The next acceptable classification of workmanship is called *ordinary*. Both classifications are

Labor-Hours Required for the Installation of Brick Masonry

Description	Labor-Hours	Unit
Brick Wall		
Veneer		
4" Thick		
Running Bond		
Standard Brick (6.75/S.F.)	.182	S.F.
Engineer Brick (5.63/S.F.)	.154	S.F.
Economy Brick (4.50/S.F.)	.129	S.F.
Roman Brick (6.00/S.F.)	.160	S.F.
Norman Brick (4.50/S.F.)	.125	S.F.
Norwegian Brick (3.75/S.F.)	.107	S.F.
Utility Brick (3.00/S.F.)	.089	S.F.
Common Bond, Standard Brick (7.88/S.F.)	.216	S.F.
Flemish Bond, Standard Brick (9.00/S.F.)	.267	S.F.
English Bond, Standard Brick (10.13/S.F.)	.286	S.F.
Stack Bond, Standard Brick (6.75/S.F.)	.200	S.F.
6" Thick		
Running Bond		
S.C.R. Brick (4.50/S.F.)	.129	S.F.
Jumbo Brick (3.00/S.F.)	.092	S.F.
Backup		
4" Thick		
Running Bond		
Standard Brick (6.75/S.F.)	.167	S.F.
Solid, Unreinforced		
8" Thick Running Bond (13.50/S.F.)	.296	S.F.
12" Thick, Running Bond (20.25/S.F.)	.421	S.F.
Solid, Rod Reinforced		
8" Thick, Running Bond	.308	S.F.
12" Thick, Running Bond	.444	S.F.
Cavity		
4" Thick		
4" Backup	.242	S.F.
6" Backup	.276	S.F.
Brick Chimney		
16" x 16", Standard Brick w/8" x 8" Flue	.889	V.L.F.
16" x 16", Standard Brick w/8" x 12" Flue	1.000	V.L.F.
20" x 20", Standard Brick w/12" x 12" Flue	1.140	V.L.F.
Brick Column		
8" x 8", Standard Brick 9.0 V.L.F.	.286	V.L.F.
12" x 12", Standard Brick 20.3 V.L.F.	.640	V.L.F.
20" x 20", Standard Brick 56.3 V.L.F.	1.780	V.L.F.
Brick Coping		
Precast, 10" Wide, or Limestone, 4" Wide	.178	L.F.
Precast 14" Wide, or Limestone, 6" Wide	.200	L.F.

Figure 9.9a

Labor-Hours Required for the Installation of Brick Masonry

Description	Labor-Hours	Unit
Brick Fireplace		
30" x 24" Opening, Plain Brickwork	40.000	Ea.
Firebox Only, Fire Brick (110/Ea.)	8.000	Ea.
Brick Prefabricated Wall Panels, 4" Thick		
Minimum	.093	S.F.
Maximum	.144	S.F.
Brick Steps	53.330	M
Window Sill		
Brick on Edge	.200	L.F.
Precast, 6" Wide	.229	L.F.
Needle Brick and Shore, Solid Brick		
8" Thick	6.450	Ea.
12" Thick	8.160	Ea.
Repoint Brick		
Hard Mortar		
Running Bond	.100	S.F.
English Bond	.123	S.F.
Soft Mortar		
Running Bond	.080	S.F.
English Bond	.098	S.F.
Toothing Brick		
Hard Mortar	.267	V.L.F.
Soft Mortar	.200	V.L.F.
Sandblast Brick		
Wet System		
Minimum	.024	S.F.
Maximum	.057	S.F.
Dry System		
Minimum	.013	S.F.
Maximum	.027	S.F.
Sawing Brick, Per Inch of Depth	.027	L.F.
Steam Clean, Face Brick	.033	S.F.
Wash Brick, Smooth	.014	S.F.

Figure 9.9b

produced by skilled workers, trained and experienced in the craft, and are not differentiated by experience (unlike the difference between a mechanic and an apprentice, for example). The difference lies in the average productivity that can be expected. To illustrate the difference between first-class workmanship and ordinary workmanship, consider the two different applications of brick. Assume that the cost of the materials, labor rate, and individuals laying up the brick are identical in both applications.

An interior partition 50' long x 10' high will feature a 4" brick veneer in a running bond. It will be a major focal point in the main corridor of the building, and must be done as first-class workmanship.

Application #1—First-Class Workmanship

The masonry crew, consisting of two bricklayers and a tender, will take eight days to complete the work as first-class workmanship. This represents a productivity of approximately 410 bricks per day.

If this major focal point wall was suddenly changed by addendum to be furred and drywalled over, the masonry crew could perform this work as ordinary workmanship.

Application #2—Ordinary Workmanship

The same masonry crew from Application #1 could install the same wall in six days as ordinary workmanship. This now represents an approximate productivity of 546 brick per day, or a 33% increase in production.

Productivity is also affected by the type of mortar joint. A flush mortar joint is the most economical, because it does not require a separate operation to "tool" the joint. It is struck flush by the bricklayer in the normal setting process. For rounded, beaded, vee-shaped, or weathered joints, the process requires the additional operation after the joint has been struck flush and has had a short time to cure. The bricklayer uses a trowel or a joint tool to achieve the final joint. Raked or stripped joints are even more labor intensive, and require a limit on the height of the brick courses until the work has cured.

Excessive heights also reduce productivity because of the effort and time required for the handling or hoisting of mortar and brick to the elevated work areas. Scaffolding and the cutting of masonry units are other factors in estimating masonry work. They are discussed in detail later in this chapter, along with cleaning of new masonry work.

Concrete Masonry Units (CMU)

Concrete masonry units (CMU) have, over the years, come to be known as *concrete block* and *concrete brick*. They are used extensively as interior or exterior load-bearing walls, or as the backup for brick veneer walls. Because of their larger size, fewer units are required, and the setting labor is less than if the same backup wall was constructed from brick. CMUs are composed of Portland cement, water, and a variety of fine aggregates (sand, crushed stone, and shale) or lightweight aggregates (perlite, vermiculite, or pumice).

Concrete Brick

Concrete bricks are solid, modular units of concrete used in much the same way as regular brick. They are typically manufactured to 2-1/4" x 3-5/8" x 7-5/8", although additional sizes may be available in some locations. They are also used as infill material in concrete block walls, where cut block is impractical. Concrete brick are taken off the same way as regular brick. The quantity of brick required is a function of the number of brick per square foot multiplied by the number of square feet to arrive at the total quantity. (Refer to Figure 9.7 for the quantity of concrete brick per SF.) Include a 3%–5% waste factor for exposed concrete brick. Labor to lay out concrete brick is much the same as regular brick. However, concrete brick is rarely laid up in bonds other than running bonds.

Concrete Block

Concrete block consists of hollow-core, load-bearing masonry units. The standard nominal dimensions of concrete block are 8" high x 16" long x 4", 6", 8", 10", or 12" wide. The actual size is 3/8" smaller in length and height so that the addition of a 3/8" mortar joint will produce an 8" x 16" finished unit. Solid versions of the hollow units are available, as well as half-block for corners, and specialty block such as bond beam and bull nose block. Concrete block is manufactured using two basic weights of concrete: heavyweight concrete (weighing approximately 145 lbs. per CF) and lightweight concrete (approximately 100 lbs. per CF). This translates to heavyweight units that range from 40 to 50 lbs. each, and lightweight units that vary in weight from 25 to 35 lbs. each. Concrete block is manufactured and sold in a variety of designs, colors, shapes, and surface textures.

The most common types of CMU are:

- *Scored block*: Units scored across the face to give the appearance of smaller units.
- *Split face block*: Units split lengthwise and installed with the split face exposed.
- *Split rib block*: Units with a corrugated look achieved by molding the block with coarse, vertical ribbing.
- *Deep groove block*: Units with deep vertical grooves scored at intervals along the face of the block.
- *Slump block*: Units manufactured so that the face of the block sags, giving a unique appearance.
- *Glazed concrete block*: Units with factory-applied glazing on one or more faces. These are used for applications that require a durable, washable surface.
- *Ground face block*: Units that have been ground on the face to give a coarse, textured surface.

Taking off Quantities

The standard procedure for taking off concrete block is similar to that used for brick. Calculate the areas of walls and partitions by multiplying the length by the height of the various walls and partitions, and computing a total area in SF. Separate the different types of block by size, weight, surface textures, shapes, and color, as each affects pricing. Convert the SF area to the actual number of blocks by dividing the total area by the area of an individual block, based on its nominal 8" x 16" size (when using a standard 3/8" mortar joint). For example:

A standard hollow concrete block with the nominal dimensions of 8" x 16" has an individual area of 128 square inches, or .89 SF. If this calculation is applied to 100 SF, the result is approximately 112.5 block per 100 SF, or 1.125 block per SF.

It is important to accurately calculate the actual quantity of CMU required. Make deductions for all openings over 2 SF to get an accurate count on the block. Corners should not be counted twice. Because concrete block are typically installed in a running bond pattern, include half-block at vertical terminations of the wall such as control joints and door or window jambs. These are taken off by counting the half-block at alternating courses at each location. For example:

Both sides of the control joint are 20 courses high. Therefore, 20 courses divided by 2 (for alternating courses) equals 10 pieces of half-block. Since there are two sides to the control joint, multiply the 10 pieces by 2. The result, 20, is the total half-block needed.

In addition, specialty blocks, such as *bond beam* blocks, must be included as part of the takeoff. Bond beam blocks are trough-shaped concrete blocks typically installed at the top course (or a story height) to provide horizontal reinforcing. Steel rebar are laid laterally within the trough and grouted solid to provide a continual lateral reinforced beam. (Both grout and reinforcing will be discussed later in this chapter.) Bond beams are taken off by the LF and converted to the number of blocks by dividing the length by the nominal length of the block (16"). Figure 9.10 illustrates a bond beam and its use.

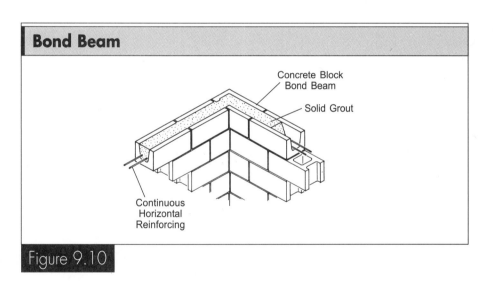

Bond Beam

Concrete Block Bond Beam

Solid Grout

Continuous Horizontal Reinforcing

Figure 9.10

Include an allowance for waste on all CMU. Under normal circumstances, an average of 3% and a maximum of 5% is adequate. If considerable cutting is required for top of wall courses of CMU, the waste should be increased an additional 1%–2%.

Labor

The labor cost of installing CMU is based on the crew's productivity, which varies depending on whether the CMU is lightweight or heavyweight block, the number of openings in the wall or how "cut-up" the wall is, and the finishing of the joint. Most CMU is finished with a rounded or v-shaped tool. CMU below grade, as in the case of foundation work, proceeds faster than above grade. If the CMU is meant as the final finished surface on both or either side of the wall, calculate the costs for a tooled finish on one or both surfaces. Because of the size and weight of concrete block, some union regulations require that two masons set a block. This has a direct effect on productivity, and should be reviewed. Figure 9.11 is a table of productivity for the installation of various types of CMU.

Other Cost Considerations

Other cost considerations include the cost of hoisting CMU to staging or above grade. Mechanical means of transporting CMU to and from the staging area are often required while the work is in progress. Cleaning of completed CMU is typically figured separately. Reinforcement, both lateral and vertical, and the masonry grout to fill the cells solid are typically estimated separately. Reinforcement will be discussed in detail later in this chapter.

Stone

Because it is a product of nature, stone varies dramatically in type, size, shape, and weight with each different species and geographic location. In general, stone for construction purposes can be classified in one of the following groups:

- *Rubble*: Irregularly-shaped pieces broken from larger masses of rock, installed or "laid up" with little or no cutting or trimming.
- *Fieldstone*: Irregularly-shaped rocks used as they are found in nature. Most commonly used in fireplaces and stone walls in landscaping.
- *Cut stone*: Stone that has been cut to specific shapes and sizes, with a uniform texture. Most commonly used for veneers.
- *Ashlar*: Characterized by saw-cut beds and joints, usually rectangular in shape, with flat or textured facing.

Taking off Quantities

Stone work prices will vary by location and species of stone. In general, the following rules apply.

Most stone used in landscaping walls is taken off by the CF. This is done by multiplying length by height by width (or thickness) of the wall. Then the CF volume is converted to tons based on the individual stone's volume per ton. The stone materials are priced by the ton both for purchase and setting. The volume in CF per ton of stone is often available from the distributor for each type of stone. Each species of stone will vary depending on the size, shape, and density of the wall. Stone in veneer wall and fireplace applications is taken off by the SF and converted to tons in much the same manner.

It is recommended that you obtain a direct quote for each species of stone delivered to the job site. Prices will vary with availability and popularity. Because most stone is extremely heavy, costs for shipping and handling can

Installation Time in Labor-Hours for Block Walls, Partitions, and Accessories

Description	Labor-Hours	Unit
Foundation Walls, Trowel Cut Joints, Parged 1/2" Thick, 1 Side, 8" x 16" Face		
Hollow		
8" Thick	.093	S.F.
12" Thick	.122	S.F.
Solid		
8" Thick	.096	S.F.
12" Thick	.126	S.F.
Backup Walls, Tooled Joint 1 Side, 8" x 16" Face		
4" Thick	.091	S.F.
8" Thick	.100	S.F.
Partition Walls, Tooled Joint 2 Sides 8" x 16" Face		
Hollow		
4" Thick	.093	S.F.
8" Thick	.107	S.F.
12" Thick	.141	S.F.
Solid		
4" Thick	.096	S.F.
8" Thick	.111	S.F.
12" Thick	.148	S.F.
Stud Block Walls, Tooled Joints 2 Sides 8" x 16" Face		
6" Thick and 2", Plain	.098	S.F.
Embossed	.103	S.F.
10" Thick and 2", Plain	.108	S.F.
Embossed	.114	S.F.
6" Thick and 2" Each Side, Plain	.114	S.F.
Acoustical Slotted Block Walls Tooled 2 Sides		
4" Thick	.127	S.F.
8" Thick	.151	S.F.
Glazed Block Walls, Tooled Joint 2 Sides 8" x 16", Glazed 1 Face		
4" Thick	.116	S.F.
8" Thick	.129	S.F.
12" Thick	.171	S.F.
8" x 16", Glazed 2 Faces		
4" Thick	.129	S.F.
8" Thick	.148	S.F.
8" x 16", Corner		
4" Thick	.140	Ea.

Figure 9.11a

Installation Time in Labor-Hours for Block Walls, Partitions, and Accessories

Description	Labor-Hours	Unit
Structural Facing Tile, Tooled 2 Sides		
5" x 12", Glazed 1 Face		
4" Thick	.182	S.F.
8" Thick	.222	S.F.
5" x 12", Glazed 2 Faces		
4" Thick	.205	S.F.
8" Thick	.246	S.F.
8" x 16", Glazed 1 Face		
4" Thick	.116	S.F.
8" Thick	.129	S.F.
8" x 16", Glazed 2 Faces		
4" Thick	.123	S.F.
8" Thick	.137	S.F.
Exterior Walls, Tooled Joint 2 Sides, Insulated		
8" x 16" Face, Regular Weight		
8" Thick	.110	S.F.
12" Thick	.145	S.F.
Lightweight		
8" Thick	.104	S.F.
12" Thick	.137	S.F.
Architectural Block Walls, Tooled Joint 2 Sides		
8" x 16" Face		
4" Thick	.116	S.F.
8" Thick	.138	S.F.
12" Thick	.181	S.F.
Interlocking Block Walls, Fully Grouted		
Vertical Reinforcing		
8" Thick	.131	S.F.
12" Thick	.145	S.F.
16" Thick	.173	S.F.
Bond Beam, Grouted, 2 Horizontal Rebars		
8" x 16" Face, Regular Weight		
8" Thick	.133	L.F.
12" Thick	.192	L.F.
Lightweight		
8" Thick	.131	L.F.
12" Thick	.188	L.F.
Lintels, Grouted, 2 Horizontal Rebars		
8" x 16" Face, 8" Thick	.119	L.F.
16" x 16" Face, 8" Thick	.131	L.F.
Control Joint 4" Wall	.013	L.F.
8" Wall	.020	L.F.
Grouting Bond Beams and Lintels		
8" Deep Pumped, 8" Thick	.018	L.F.
12" Thick	.025	L.F.
Concrete Block Cores Solid		
4" Thick By Hand	.035	S.F.
8" Thick Pumped	.038	S.F.
Cavity Walls 2" Space Pumped	.016	S.F.
6" Space	.034	S.F.

Figure 9.11b

Installation Time in Labor-Hours for Block Walls, Partitions, and Accessories

Description	Labor-Hours	Unit
Joint Reinforcing		
Wire Strips Regular Truss to 6" Wide	.267	C.L.F.
12" Wide	.400	C.L.F.
Cavity Wall with Drip Section to 6" Wide	.267	C.L.F.
12" Wide	.400	C.L.F.
Lintels Steel Angles Minimum	.008	lb.
Maximum	.016	lb.
Wall Ties	.762	C
Coping For 12" Wall Stock Units, Aluminum	.200	L.F.
Precast Concrete	.188	L.F.
Structural Reinforcing, Placed Horizontal,		
#3 and #4 Bars	.018	lb.
#5 and #6 Bars	.010	lb.
Placed Vertical, #3 and #4 Bars	.023	lb.
#5 and #6 Bars	.012	lb.
Acoustical Slotted Block		
4" Thick	.127	S.F.
6" Thick	.138	S.F.
8" Thick	.151	S.F.
12" Thick	.163	S.F.
Lightweight Block		
4" Thick	.090	S.F.
6" Thick	.095	S.F.
8" Thick	.100	S.F.
10" Thick	.103	S.F.
12" Thick	.130	S.F.
Regular Block		
Hollow		
4" Thick	.093	S.F.
6" Thick	.100	S.F.
8" Thick	.107	S.F.
10" Thick	.111	S.F.
12" Thick	.141	S.F.
Solid		
4" Thick	.095	S.F.
6" Thick	.105	S.F.
8" Thick	.113	S.F.
12" Thick	.150	S.F.
Glazed Concrete Block		
Single Face 8" x 16"		
2" Thick	.111	S.F.
4" Thick	.116	S.F.
6" Thick	.121	S.F.
8" Thick	.129	S.F.
12" Thick	.171	S.F.
Double Face		
4" Thick	.129	S.F.
6" Thick	.138	S.F.
8" Thick	.148	S.F.

Figure 9.11c

Installation Time in Labor-Hours for Block Walls, Partitions, and Accessories

Description	Labor-Hours	Unit
Joint Reinforcing Wire Strips		
4" and 6" Wall	.267	C.L.F.
8" Wall	.320	C.L.F.
10" and 12" Wall	.400	C.L.F.
Steel Bars Horizontal		
#3 and #4	.018	lb.
#5 and #6	.010	lb.
Vertical		
#3 and #4	.023	lb.
#5 and #6	.012	lb.
Grout Cores Solid		
By Hand 6" Thick	.035	S.F.
Pumped 8" Thick	.038	S.F.
10" Thick	.039	S.F.
12" Thick	.040	S.F.

Figure 9.11d

be significant. Allowances for waste are based on the individual type of stone. A general rule is that for stone, ashlar, or regular-shaped stone, the waste will vary between 4% and 10%. Irregular-shaped stones, such as rubble or fieldstone, often have higher wastes as a result of "unusable" stone in a delivered batch. Waste factors for lower-grade stone can approach 20%. Remember that some walls are dryset, or set with a minimum amount of mortar or none. Styles will vary with the type of stone and local practices. Stone is sometimes "dressed" at the site, which is the practice of shaping or cutting stone on site for both visual appearance and to fit the application. This can be extremely time consuming and difficult to estimate.

Masonry Reinforcement

The term *masonry reinforcement* refers to the use of steel reinforcing bars and wire mesh-type lateral reinforcing installed in the coursing of masonry units, and the vertical rebar grouted into the voids in concrete block. Reinforcing steel in masonry work adds tensile strength to the wall or partition in much the same way as in reinforced concrete. It also allows the reinforced masonry to move during a seismic event with minor damage in comparison to the unreinforced masonry, which collapses. Masonry reinforcing is classified in two groups: lateral (horizontal) and vertical.

Lateral Masonry Reinforcement

Lateral reinforcing can be further divided into two types: *wire mesh*, or *strip joint reinforcing*, and *horizontal steel rebar*. Rebar is frequently the same type and grade used in concrete applications. Both types provide reinforcement against lateral stresses, and horizontal movement. Wire mesh or strip joint reinforcing is accomplished by the use of wire mesh-type strips installed between the courses of masonry units. The most common types of wire strip joint reinforcement are the truss-type and the cavity-wall ladder type. Figure 9.12 illustrates the major types of joint reinforcement.

Typical Concrete Block Systems and Nomenclature

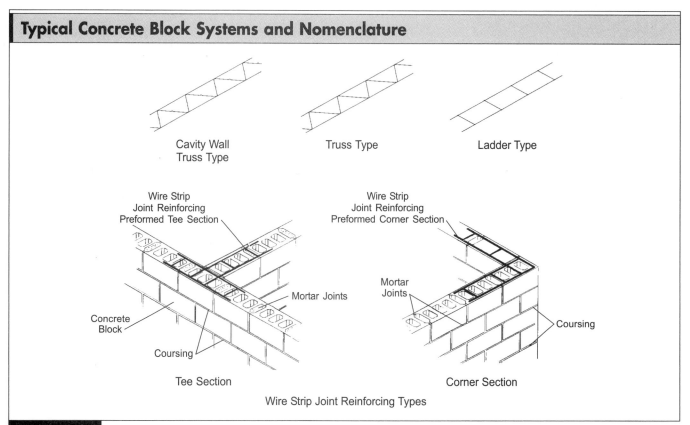

Cavity Wall Truss Type

Truss Type

Ladder Type

Wire Strip Joint Reinforcing Preformed Tee Section

Wire Strip Joint Reinforcing Preformed Corner Section

Mortar Joints

Mortar Joints

Concrete Block

Coursing

Coursing

Tee Section

Corner Section

Wire Strip Joint Reinforcing Types

Figure 9.12

Taking off Quantities

Horizontal joint reinforcement is taken off by the LF. Most plans and specifications are specific as to the location of horizontal joint reinforcement, which is typically specified by the course. To arrive at the total LF of joint reinforcement, count the number of courses that require joint reinforcement and multiply by the LF of reinforcement for each course. Materials and labor are priced per LF, which can be extended to 100 LF quantities by dividing the total linear footage by 100 and labeling the result with the unit CLF (100 LF).

Horizontal reinforcing in the form of rebar is typically used for bond beam applications. Steel reinforcing bars are laid within the trough of the bond beam and are grouted solid to form a continuous ring of lateral reinforcement at specific locations within the masonry wall or partition. Horizontal rebar in masonry is taken off by the LF. Plans and specifications designate the location of horizontal reinforcing, as well as the size of the bar, the number of bars to be used, and the lap of the bars.

Rebar quantities are determined by adding all linear footage at each location to arrive at a total LF. This total is then multiplied by the weight per foot of the specific bar designation. Figure 9.13 lists bar designations.

Calculate the weight of all bent bars for corners and intersections separately, and then add the weight to the total for that bar designation. Additional weight must be added for overlap of continuous bars. Include costs relative to storage and handling of the rebar, in addition to setting costs. Special grades of steel or coatings should also be noted for accurate pricing.

Reinforcing Steel Weights and Measures

| Bar Desig-nation No.** | Nominal Weight, Lb./Ft. | U.S. Customary Units | | | Nominal Weight kg/m | SI Units | | |
| | | Nominal Dimensions* | | | | Nominal Dimensions* | | |
		Diameter in.	Cross Sectional Area, in.²	Perimeter in.		Diameter, mm	Cross Sectional Area, cm²	Perimeter mm
3	0.376	0.375	0.11	1.178	0.560	9.52	0.71	29.9
4	0.668	0.500	0.20	1.571	0.994	12.70	1.29	39.9
5	1.043	0.625	0.31	1.963	1.552	15.88	2.00	49.9
6	1.502	0.750	0.44	2.356	2.235	19.05	2.84	59.8
7	2.044	0.875	0.60	2.749	3.042	22.22	3.87	69.8
8	2.670	1.000	0.79	3.142	3.973	25.40	5.10	79.8
9	3.400	1.128	1.00	3.544	5.059	28.65	6.45	90.0
10	4.303	1.270	1.27	3.990	6.403	32.26	8.19	101.4
11	5.313	1.410	1.56	4.430	7.906	35.81	10.06	112.5
14	7.65	1.693	2.25	5.32	11.384	43.00	14.52	135.1
18	13.60	2.257	4.00	7.09	20.238	57.33	25.81	180.1

*The nominal dimensions of a deformed bar are equivalent to those of a plain round bar having the same weight per foot as the deformed bar.
**Bar numbers are based on the number of eighths of an inch included in the nominal diameter of the bars.

Figure 9.13

Vertical Masonry Reinforcement

Vertical masonry reinforcement refers to steel rebar installed within the cells of hollow concrete block (CMU) walls, and grouted in place to form a single unit. When installed within an engineered design, the reinforced masonry walls resist stresses exerted by wind, earthquake, and other forces. In the typical application, the vertical bars are spaced at a predetermined "on center" spacing detailed on the drawings. Figure 9.14 illustrates a reinforced concrete block wall.

Taking off Quantities

Vertical rebar is the same type and grade of steel used in the horizontal masonry rebar applications. The takeoff is performed in a manner similar to vertical rebar in a cast-in-place concrete wall. The total length of the reinforced walls is divided by the on-center spacing to determine the number of bars. Once the quantity has been determined, it is multiplied by the length of the individual bars. Additional bars may need to be added per specification requirements at the corners or jambs of openings. These

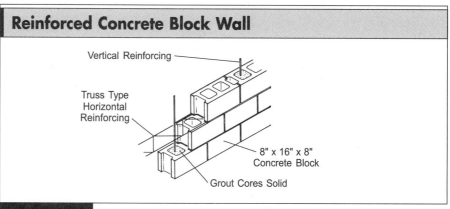

Reinforced Concrete Block Wall

Vertical Reinforcing

Truss Type
Horizontal
Reinforcing

8" x 16" x 8"
Concrete Block

Grout Cores Solid

Figure 9.14

should be added to the total. Calculate bar overlap based on the specific grouting conditions (covered later in this chapter). Convert it to weight, and add this to the total weight of rebar.

In order for the rebar to act as monolithic unit and provide the tensile strength to the compressive strength of the CMU, the two must be bonded together by grout, discussed in the next section.

Grout   Grout is a composition of Portland cement, sand, lime, and water mixed in similar proportions and strengths to mortar. Additional water is used to bring the consistency to a more fluid or plastic state. Grout is then pumped or poured into the cells of set concrete block that contain vertical or horizontal reinforcing bars. Vibrating or tamping may be required to ensure complete embedment of the rebar. Once the grout has cured, it forms a single solid unit of grout, block, and rebar.

Taking off Quantities

To determine the quantity of grout needed, calculate the volume of the cells to be filled. This is accomplished by determining the location and quantity of vertical columns (cells) to be filled, multiplied by the volume of each column of cells. This figure should be computed in CF, the typical unit of pricing. You may choose to convert the CF quantity to CY. (1 CY = 27 CF.) To simplify the calculation of grout quantities, use Figure 9.15. The quantity of grout specified in this table is listed according to specific spacing and various wall thicknesses, and is based on SF of wall area.

Low-Lift Grouting

Low-lift grouting calls for the placement of grout within the cells of an erected wall at a maximum of 4'. Grout is

> *There are two different methods of grout placement: high-lift and low-lift. Each have particular advantages and disadvantages. Most project specifications define which method is acceptable. In the absence of a specified method, consult the building code having jurisdiction. Some building codes do not allow the use of high-lift grouting.*

Volume of Grout Fill for Concrete Block Walls

Center to Center Spacing Grouted Cores	6" C.M.U. Per S.F. Volume in C.F.		8" C.M.U. Per S.F. Volume in C.F.		12" C.M.U. Per S.F. Volume in C.F.	
	40% Solid	75% Solid	40% Solid	75% Solid	40% Solid	75% Solid
All cores grouted solid	.27	.11	.36	.15	.55	.23
cores grouted 16" O.C.	.14	.06	.18	.08	.28	.12
cores grouted 24" O.C.	.09	.04	.12	.05	.18	.08
cores grouted 32" O.C.	.07	.03	.09	.04	.14	.06
cores grouted 40" O.C.	.05	.02	.07	.03	.11	.05
cores grouted 48" O.C.	.04	.02	.06	.03	.09	.04

Note: Costs are based on high-lift grouting method.

Low-lift grouting is used when the wall is built to a maximum height of 5'. The grout is pumped or poured into the cores of the concrete block. The operation is repeated after each five additional feet of wall height has been completed. High-lift grouting is used when the wall has been built to the full story height. Some of the advantages are: the vertical reinforcing steel can be placed after the wall is completed, and the grout can be supplied by a ready-mix concrete supplier so that it may be pumped in a continuous operation.

Figure 9.15

poured to within 1-1/2" of the top of the top block to allow for a keyway when additional lifts are poured. Low-lift grouting has the advantage of ensuring that cells are filled solid down to the previously poured lift. It also allows grout to be mixed in smaller quantities on site. The disadvantage is that setting production is limited to a maximum of six courses (48"). The setting is then stopped and the CMU is grouted. This is translated to an additional cost for delayed production in the erection of the wall.

High-Lift Grouting

High-lift grouting is the placement of grout in the cells after completion of the top course of the masonry work. This method requires that cleaning/ inspection holes be left out at the bottom of each cell. This allows access for cleaning mortar droppings out from within the cell to be grouted. This method requires that the grouting procedure be continuous to the top of each cell. It has the advantage of allowing the grouting operation to be performed in one application, in contrast to low-lift grouting, which is done in smaller portions and at various times. It also allows the vertical reinforcing to be placed after the wall has been completed. The major disadvantage is that it is difficult, if not impossible, to ensure that all rebar has been adequately surrounded by grout through the entire height of the cell. Some structural failures have been attributed to weak spots in the wall where voids have occurred and the rebar has deteriorated. Regardless of the specified method of grouting, the calculation for volume is the same.

Labor

The labor to perform grouting can be calculated per labor-hour per CY, or per labor-hour per SF of wall surface area. High-lift grouting most often requires the use of a grout pump. This is similar to the pump used in the placement of concrete as discussed in Chapter 8. Many larger masonry contractors own their own grout pumps. If the pump is to be rented, include this as part of the cost of grout placement. Rental can be calculated by the day or by the half day. Grouting can often require cleanup labor once completed.

Masonry Anchors & Ties

To anchor or tie multiple width masonry walls together, or a non-structural veneer brick wall to a structural backup wall, an anchor or tie must be used. Anchors or ties are manufactured of coated metals that will not deteriorate when in contact with the corrosive elements in mortar. They are available in a wide variety of shapes, sizes, and methods for fastening. Some of the more common types of anchors and ties are listed below.

- *Dovetail anchors*: Used to tie masonry veneers to cast-in-place concrete backup walls. The dovetail slot is poured within the forms and, when stripped, provides a vertical slot in which to attach the dovetail anchor.
- *Corrugated wall ties*: Hot-dip galvanized strips of corrugated metal for tying brick veneers to wood-framed or concrete block backup walls.
- *Box-type cavity wall anchors*: Loop-shaped metal wires of various gauges used to tie multiple-width masonry walls together.
- *Welded anchors*: Used to tie masonry veneers to structural steel columns and beams.

Anchors are embedded in the horizontal courses of masonry work and fastened to the backup wall by screws, welding, or embedment (in the case of dovetail slots). Ties for multiple width masonry walls are embedded in the respective courses of both walls. The spacing of anchors and ties is noted in the specifications. They are typically described in terms of both horizontal and vertical spacing. For example, *"ties and anchors will be spaced at 24" OC, both horizontally and vertically."* Review the masonry specification and the documents carefully to determine the specified tie and its method of installation/attachment. The cost of material will vary dramatically between different ties. The cost of the method of attachment will also vary with the actual application. For example, corrugated ties can be installed in the CMU backup wall as the block is laid up. However, the same tie attached to a metal stud and sheathed wall will have considerably more labor, as it is a completely separate application. Labor is typically calculated based on a specific quantity that is expected to be installed per hour of labor.

Taking off Quantities

Anchors and ties are taken off by the piece, and listed as each, EA. Frequently this quantity can be extended to sets of 100 (C) or per

1,000 (M). This requires that the area of wall to be anchored be calculated by the SF and then divided by the spacing specified. For example:

Calculate the ties required for 1,000 SF of masonry wall, with the ties spaced at 2' OC each way.

If the spacing is 2' each way, approximately one tie will be required for every 4 SF of wall.

1,000 SF/4 SF per tie = 250 ties

Allow approximately 5%–7% for waste resulting from handling. Also consider jurisdiction issues on union projects. Some collective bargaining agreements call for the installation of the ties by trades other than bricklayers, depending on the method of attachment.

Masonry Restoration

Masonry restoration refers to restorative work on masonry that is already in place. Most of this kind of work includes cutting out old mortar joints and *repointing* or refilling the existing joints with fresh mortar. This process is sometimes called *tuckpointing.* Masonry restoration may also include the removal and replacement of damaged or deteriorated individual masonry units, most often brick.

Cutting out old mortar joints is typically done by an electric saw or a grinder with a diamond or carborundum blade. The saw or grinder is set to a specific depth as required in the specifications, and is passed along the existing mortar joint until it is free of old mortar. Removing damaged or deteriorated brick is done in much the same manner.

Additional chipping by means of a hand mallet and chisel may be required to remove individual bricks. The newly cut and cleaned joint is then filled with mortar and tooled to achieve the desired joint. Replacement bricks are "buttered" with mortar and fitted into place. The replacement of individual bricks at areas subject to the most damage, such as outside corners, is most common. Removing old courses to create a bond for the new work is referred to as "toothing" or "toothing-in." Restoration work may also include sandblast cleaning of the surface area—the process of forcing fine sand or slag through a hose at high pressure. The abrasive force removes debris, graffiti, and the old surface. It should be noted that excessive sandblasting will damage the surface and remove the mortar from the joint. Some repointing of damaged joints may be necessary as a result.

Taking off Quantities

Sandblasting is taken off and priced by the square foot area to be cleaned. Openings for windows and doors are not deducted. The cost of sandblasting is affected by several factors. Costs can be reduced if the sand or slag can be salvaged. Often up to 60% of the material can be salvaged and reused. Brick with normal dirt and grime has higher production rates and success after the "first pass." Bricks with multiple coats of paint or waterproof coating may require multiple passes. Sandblasting, like most masonry restoration work, is a crew task where the production is based on a multi-person crew.

The standard takeoff unit for both cutting out the old joint and repointing is the SF. You may choose to separate the takeoff for each process for estimating purposes. Cutting out and repointing the old joint have different unit costs. The area is calculated by multiplying the length or width by the height of the surface to be tuckpointed. Labor to cut out old joints is based on production per hour and will vary with the age and condition of the brick and the mortar.

Labor

Labor costs to repoint old work have fewer variables. Consider the width of the mortar joint when calculating production and materials costs. Also include the cost of the carborundum wheels, and possibly even the costs of the grinders, as cutting out old mortar generates a lot of wear on tools and equipment. Removal and replacement of old brick can be taken off by the individual piece, EA, or by the SF. Individual brick to be replaced in random locations may be best taken off by the piece. Larger quantities grouped together with definable dimensions should be taken off and estimated by the SF. In either case, the quantities of each should be noted separately on the takeoff. Be sure to include an allowance for removing and replacing adjacent brick that may be damaged in the process. Matching existing brick and mortar colors often involves additional labor required for the multiple attempts to get it correct.

The cost of restoration work is affected by a variety of factors, including the type of staging to access the work. Movable staging, such as swing staging or motorized platforms, may best accommodate the frequent moves associated with tuckpointing. Typically, the cost for renting both types of staging exceeds the cost of conventional scaffolding. Evaluate and price the most efficient method. Another factor to consider is the need for temporary bracing when large quantities of damaged or deteriorated brick are removed. The possibility of collapse of old brickwork already weakened by the removal of old mortar is a realistic concern. Bracing should be evaluated by the individual work area. Ground labor to support the workers on the staging is usually required and must be accounted for in the estimate. Ground support provides mortar, materials, tools, and equipment for the crew above. Restoration work is labor-intensive and should not be underestimated.

Protection requirements for sandblasting procedures will vary with the size of the area being cleaned and the location of the work. Protection of surface features, such as windows, doors or ornaments, can slow productivity. Because the use of sandblasting equipment is environmentally regulated, check the requirements for individual areas. Work locations with dense populations generally require airborne particles to be contained. Enclosure of the work should be included in the estimated, and may consist of dismantling and re-erecting the containment enclosure several times as the work progresses. Cleanup of the spent sand or slag should also be included as part of the work. Maintenance and repair of the enclosures should also be considered for extended projects.

Masonry Cleaning

Some form of cleaning is required on all new masonry work to remove splattering of mortar and dust. Masonry cleaning is usually done after the work has set, but before the mortar has reached its full strength. Several methods can be used, including mild detergents and a coarse hand brush to scrub the surface. Stronger solutions containing chemicals, such as muriatic acid, may also be required. The basic process is the same, although protective gear may be required. An alternate method involves high-pressure washing. Water is forced through a nozzle at high pressure to remove the surface debris.

Taking off Quantities

Regardless of the method used, masonry cleaning is quantified by the SF of area to be cleaned. Different methods for the same project should be listed separately, as each will have a different cost. Solutions used in hand cleaning and power washing are usually diluted to a specified strength. Base the quantity of solution on the area to be covered. The quantity of solution often varies with the product used, and most often is a matter of judgment or may be stated in the specifications. Chemical cleaners, such as those used for paint removal, are often expensive and may require multiple coats applied by hand with rollers or brushes. Many of these chemicals are allowed to set before they are removed. This also requires protection laid over the ground so that the residual chemicals do not contaminate the surrounding soil.

Like most masonry restoration, cleaning often requires staging. On new work with standard pipe scaffolding, the work is usually cleaned before the staging is dismantled and moved. A ground crew may be needed for larger cleaning jobs to support the personnel doing the cleaning. Staging will be discussed in detail later in this chapter.

Toxic chemicals or solutions may also be governed by environmental regulations, and may require protection or special cleanup. Protective gear for workers can be costly and may reduce productivity. Disposal of the residual byproduct is costly, and should be investigated beforehand. Consult the specifications for the approved method of cleaning, and price the work accordingly. Substitutions of less expensive methods may not be acceptable. This can frequently be the work of a specialty contractor. It is recommended that you solicit subcontractor quotes for the work whenever the opportunity allows.

Masonry Insulation

Masonry insulation consists of installing rigid insulation boards between the veneer brick and the CMU backup wall. Another common method of insulating concrete block is to use masonry fill insulation, a granular material composed of water-repellent vermiculite or silicon-treated perlite. Both materials are poured from bags or blown in from trucks into the voids in cavity walls or the empty cells in concrete block. Review the specifications carefully for the methods required. It should also be noted that many states have adopted new energy codes, which focus on the exterior envelope in detail. Specifications referencing code requirements should be investigated carefully for materials and procedures.

Taking off Quantities

Masonry insulation is taken off based on the SF area to be insulated. The procedure for determining the quantity of masonry fill insulation is the same as that used for quantifying grout for reinforced cells. *(See "Grout" earlier in this chapter.)* The takeoff units are CF. Figure 9.15 can be used to calculate the volume of masonry fill insulation required, which can be extended into the typical sales quantities (bags) of the various products. Calculate the number of bags required, and allow a waste factor of 10%–12%. The labor to install masonry insulation, regardless of the material employed, can be significant. Masonry fill insulation costs are based on the quantity of CF that can be placed in a day. Rigid insulation is applied to the cavity wall by several methods, the most common of which is using the masonry tie to hold the insulation in place. Sometimes this requires the use of an adhesive to temporarily hold the sheet in place until the ties are installed. The labor costs include cutting the insulation as required to fit around openings in the exterior walls, which is included as part of the cost of the work. Exterior walls with many openings will reduce productivity, and unit costs should reflect this.

Flashings Flashings are impervious sheets of material commonly installed at the base of the exterior masonry walls to deflect water from going into the structure. Flashings are fabricated from a variety of different metals, including copper, lead-coated copper, asphalt-coated copper, steel, and some metals with proprietary coatings, such as Kynar®. The thickness of the metal sheet will affect the unit cost of the material as well as the cost of fabrication. Review the specification carefully for ownership of the flashings and its fabrication. Many specifications indicate that metal flashings should be fabricated by other trades, typically the roofing subcontractor, and provided to the masonry subcontractor. This is often because the flashings are intrinsic to weather-proofing the roof system. Other types of flashings can be specified under the masonry section of the specifications.

Taking off Quantities

Flashings are taken off and listed by the LF. Flashings of different compositions, thicknesses, and species should be listed separately, as this will affect the costs of the material. To determine the base costs of the materials, calculate the number of sheets of metal required. (Sheet metal flashings will be discussed later in the book under Division 7—Thermal

& Moisture Protection.) This is done by determining how many pieces can be produced from a single sheet of metal. An allowance for the overlap of the individual pieces must also be included. Labor costs for installation are reflective of the type of flashing. Some flashings are set in a bed of asphalt mastic and are mechanically fastened to the non-masonry backup wall. Others are "coursed" into the masonry CMU backup as the CMU is laid up. In either instance, the cost for installation is determined by the LF of flashings to be installed. Figure 9.16 shows a typical masonry cavity wall with insulation and flashings.

Cutting Masonry Units

It is not uncommon for brick or block to be cut on site. This can be time consuming if there is sufficient quantity, and can even require a dedicated individual to do the cutting. Be sure to include the cost of cutting masonry units, such as block and brick. Some block and brick materials are cut with a brick hammer and chisel, but when exposed surfaces requiring cuts, may need a gas or electric masonry saw with a diamond or carborundum blade.

Taking off Quantities

Cuts are taken off by the piece and can be listed as a total quantity for each type of masonry unit. The cost for minor cutting, especially with a hammer and chisel, may be negligible in the overall estimate. Projects that require extensive cutting must be evaluated accordingly. The cost of cutting masonry has two main components: the labor to cut and the carborundum saw blades. The cost of the labor is based on the number of pieces that can be cut per day or per hour. This depends on the density/hardness of the material being cut and the sophistication of the cut. Naturally, multiple passes through the saw with the same piece will entail more time. All masonry blades have a specific life, which will vary with the quality of the blade. That is to say that they will eventually become ineffective after so many cuts. Determine how many blade changes are required and include that as part of the cost. A masonry saw is basic equipment for the serious masonry subcontractor, and its cost is either calculated as part of indirect overhead or direct overhead of the company. Occasionally, the saw may be rented and then this cost must be included as part of the bid.

Formwork for Masonry

Some kinds of masonry work require the use of forms or braces to support installed work until it has cured and can support itself. Classic examples are the forms needed to hold brick or stone over half-round windows, or formwork to brace the bottom of a bond beam poured as a lintel for an opening.

Taking off Quantities

This work can be quantified by the opening or piece. Different types and applications should be listed separately in the estimate, as they are likely to have different costs. Material costs in most applications have multiple

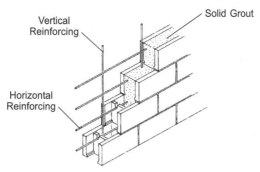

Vertical
Reinforcing

Solid Grout

Horizontal
Reinforcing

Interlocking Concrete Block

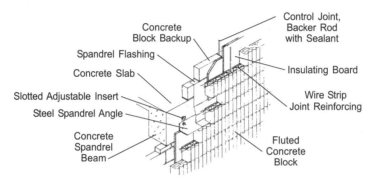

Concrete
Block Backup

Control Joint,
Backer Rod
with Sealant

Spandrel Flashing

Concrete Slab

Insulating Board

Slotted Adjustable Insert

Wire Strip
Joint Reinforcing

Steel Spandrel Angle

Concrete
Spandrel
Beam

Fluted
Concrete
Block

Block Face Cavity Wall System

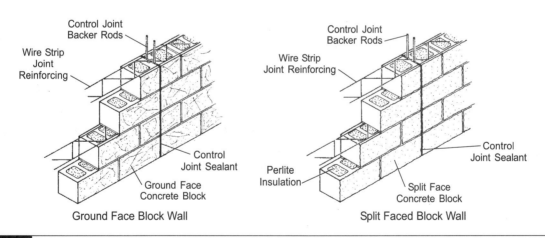

Control Joint
Backer Rods

Wire Strip
Joint
Reinforcing

Control
Joint Sealant

Ground Face
Concrete Block

Ground Face Block Wall

Control Joint
Backer Rods

Wire Strip
Joint Reinforcing

Control
Joint Sealant

Perlite
Insulation

Split Face
Concrete Block

Split Faced Block Wall

Figure 9.16

uses, and should be figured accordingly. Labor costs can be calculated several ways, most typically by the labor-hour per form. Remember that forms are temporary and also are required to be removed and dismantled as part of the cost. Review the specifications carefully to make sure that the formwork portion of the masonry is the work of the masonry subcontractor. It is not uncommon to include this work within another section, such as rough carpentry, in an effort to avoid jurisdictional issues with unions. It should also be noted that after most formwork is dismantled, there is a minor amount of remedial work to bring the masonry covered by the formwork up to the same standard as adjacent work.

Items Furnished by Other Trades

It is common for masonry contractors to install items furnished by other trades as part of the masonry scope of work. Typical examples are lintels (structural steel members that support the weight of masonry over openings in masonry walls), joist bearing plates (steel plates with anchors embedded in bond beam courses to tie bar joists to masonry walls), hollow metal door frames, sleeves for conduits and piping, and electrical boxes and conduits enclosed in masonry walls for receptacles and switches. These items must be installed as the various courses of masonry are laid. The specifications should clearly enumerate the items furnished by other trades and installed under the masonry scope of work. However, this is frequently done in a general statement that requires a careful review of all drawings for implied work.

While this work is often incidental, it still must be calculated, and included within the estimate. Larger lintels that must be installed at overhead doors have considerable weight and may require a piece of equipment to set in place. This is frequently done with a rubber tire fork-lift vehicle used for stocking brick, block, and mortar to staging. Since most materials are provided to the mason for installation, the cost of materials are negligible. There is, however, a labor and, potentially, an equipment component that must be acknowledged. Labor is based on the quantity of pieces installed per hour. Again, this will vary with the size and weight of the item to be installed, and should be considered on an individual basis.

Control Joints

Masonry walls of considerable straight length require the installation of a vertical control joint to allow for expansion and contraction of the wall. Control joints require the use of a compressible pre-molded joint filler (similar to the type used in concrete construction, discussed in Chapter 8) to break the bond between adjacent units in courses of brick or block masonry. The location of control joints should be clearly shown on both plan view and elevations of masonry walls on the drawings.

Taking off Quantities

Control joints are taken off by the vertical linear foot (VLF). Control joints of varying thickness (for different wall thicknesses) should be listed separately. While the costs of the actual joint filler is minimal, the labor costs are not. If control joints are placed in locations that do not fall on coursing, the block or brick must be cut at each course (both sides). This has a cost impact for both labor and equipment, as noted previously in this chapter. Figure 9.17 illustrates a control joint in a masonry wall.

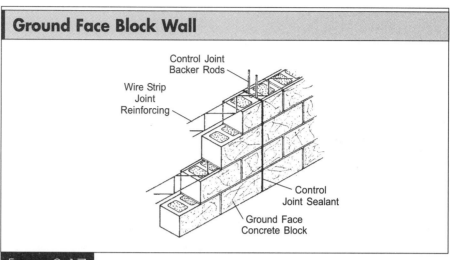

Ground Face Block Wall

Control Joint Backer Rods

Wire Strip Joint Reinforcing

Control Joint Sealant

Ground Face Concrete Block

Figure 9.17

Incidentals for Fireplace & Chimney Construction

Fireplace construction requires the masonry contractor to furnish and install some special masonry items, such as dampers, flues, clean-out doors, and fire brick. *Dampers* are cast-iron operable traps that regulate the draft of the fireplace. *Clean-out doors* are access doors and frames in varying sizes to allow the removal of ashes and debris. They are installed within the courses of masonry as the work proceeds, and are located at the lowest point in the fireplace. Masonry flues are noncombustible, heat-resistant, rectangular or round-shaped tubes made of fireclay to allow the passage of smoke from the fireplace, boiler, furnace, or solid fuel stove through the chimney. They vary in size as required by the design of the system.

Taking off Quantities

Clean-out doors are taken off by the piece (EA). Different sizes should be listed separately, as this will affect the cost. Flue lining is taken off and priced by the LF, measured from the top of the firebox to the very top of the chimney. Each size and shape should be listed separately for accurate pricing. Typically, there is only one damper per firebox, which should be listed by the piece (EA). Any special characteristics (such as manual or rotary operation) should be noted, as these can affect the cost.

Labor

Labor for the various components of a fireplace are often calculated on a labor-hour basis. It should be noted that many of the tasks in the construction of a fireplace and chimney require multiple personnel to complete efficiently. Staging or scaffolding for chimney construction is also a concern. Figure 9.18 illustrates a flue in perspective and plan view.

Freight of Masonry Units

Because most masonry units and stone materials are quite heavy, the cost for freight and delivery to the job site can be substantial. Be sure to secure a price from the supplier to include all shipping and handling costs.

Flue in Perspective and Plan View

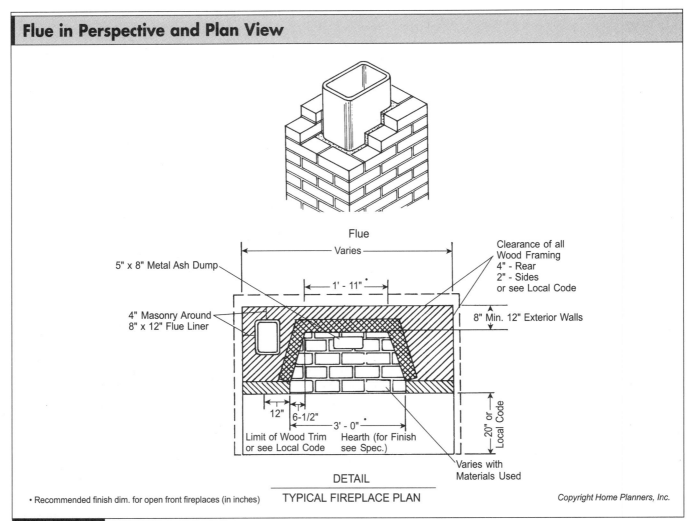

Flue

Varies

5" x 8" Metal Ash Dump

Clearance of all
Wood Framing
4" - Rear
2" - Sides
or see Local Code

1' - 11"

4" Masonry Around
8" x 12" Flue Liner

8" Min. 12" Exterior Walls

12" 6-1/2"

3' - 0"

20" or
Local Code

Limit of Wood Trim
or see Local Code

Hearth (for Finish
see Spec.)

Varies with
Materials Used

DETAIL

• Recommended finish dim. for open front fireplaces (in inches)

TYPICAL FIREPLACE PLAN

Copyright Home Planners, Inc.

Figure 9.18

Taking off Quantities

Freight costs can be taken off and priced either per ton or for the entire load as a lump sum (LS). Quantities listed by weight will require the approximate weight per 1,000 units (brick, block). Weight of stone may be by the pallet or shipping container. Both should be available from the supplier.

Staging & Scaffolding for Masonry Work

Staging and scaffolding, for the purpose of this discussion, will be considered interchangeable terms. Staging consists of a temporary elevated platform and a supporting structure erected against, within, or around the work to support workers, materials, and equipment. The most common type is conventional pipe scaffolding and planking, which is erected from the ground level and built or added to as required to maintain access to the work.

Taking off Quantities

The takeoff unit for staging is SF of surface area of the masonry. You may elect to convert the SF area to actual sections of scaffolding and planks needed. This conversion is based on the actual size of the available staging units. This type of takeoff will consist of frame sections, cross braces, outriggers (brackets attached to the side of vertical sections of staging to provide support for planking), and planks. As most masonry contractors own some quantity of staging and planking, the cost of materials may be negligible. If not enough staging is available, rental must be included. Because staging is an ongoing process as the work progresses and requires dismantling, moving, and re-erection, consider the number of moves based on productivity of the crew. This is a matter of judgment based on experience. Other types of staging may prove more efficient for some jobs. *(Refer to the "Masonry Restoration" section earlier in this chapter.)* Figure 9.19 is a table that provides various productivities for staging erection and dismantling.

Labor

The labor to erect, dismantle, and move staging is calculated on a labor-hour basis. Simple staging applications can often be done by a individual laborer, larger assemblies, or vertical building of staging require a multi-person crew.

Cleanup

Most masonry contracts provide for cleanup of debris generated by the work. Occasionally, the specifications will require that the masonry subcontractor is also responsible for removal and disposal of masonry debris. The amount of cleanup varies to some degree based on the contract or specifications, and the stage of the building progress when the work is done. Cleanup typically consists of picking up broken or discarded brick, block, or other such masonry units, as well as ties and forms, and scraping or sweeping mortar droppings. Masonry cleanup is most often accomplished by hand and quantified in labor-hours. The work is performed by laborers. Use judgment, based on experience, to determine the labor-hours necessary for the level of cleanup required. The cost for disposal in the form of dumpster rentals or landfill fees should be included.

Productivity in Scaffolding Assembly

This chart is a summary of the labor involved in assembling scaffolding and staging. It shows typical crews, expected daily outputs, and the expected labor-hours per unit for various areas of scaffolding erection.

Scaffolding	Crew Makeup	Daily Output	Labor-Hours	Unit
SCAFFOLD, Steel tubular, rented, no plank, 1 use per month				
Building exterior 2 stories	3 Carpenters	17.72	1.350	C.S.F.
4 stories	"	17.72	1.350	C.S.F.
6 stories	4 Carpenters	22.60	1.420	C.S.F.
8 stories		20.25	1.580	C.S.F.
10 stories		19.10	1.680	C.S.F.
12 stories		17.70	1.810	C.S.F.
One tier 3' high x 7' long x 5' wide 1 use per month	1 Carpenter	14.90	.537	C.S.F.
2 uses per month		14.90	.537	C.S.F.
4 uses per month		14.90	.537	C.S.F.
8 uses per month		14.90	.537	C.S.F.
5' high x 7' long x 5' wide 1 use per month		20.65	.387	C.S.F.
2 uses per month		20.65	.387	C.S.F.
4 uses per month		20.65	.387	C.S.F.
8 uses per month		20.65	.387	C.S.F.
6'-6" high x 7' long x 5' wide 1 use per month		26.85	.298	C.S.F.
2 uses per month		26.85	.298	C.S.F.
4 uses per month		26.85	.298	C.S.F.
8 uses per month		26.85	.298	C.S.F.
Scaffold steel tubular, suspended slab form supports to 8'-2" high				
1 use per month	4 Carpenters	31	1.030	C.S.F.
2 uses per month		43	.744	C.S.F.
3 uses per month		43	.744	C.S.F.
Steel tubular, suspended slab form supports to 14'-8" high				
1 use per month	4 Carpenters	16	2.000	C.S.F.
2 uses per month		22	1.450	C.S.F.
3 uses per month		22	1.450	C.S.F.
SCAFFOLDING SPECIALTIES				
Sidewalk bridge, heavy duty steel posts & beams, including parapet protection & waterproofing				
8' to 10' wide, 2 posts	3 Carpenters	15	1.600	L.F.
3 posts	"	10	2.400	L.F.
Sidewalk bridge using tubular steel scaffold frames, including planking	3 Carpenters	45	.533	L.F.
Stair unit, interior, for scaffolding, buy				Ea.
Rent per month				Ea.
SWING STAGING for masonry, 5' wide x 7', hand operated				
Cable type with 150' cables, rent & installation, per week	1 Struc. Steel Foreman 3 Struc. Steel Workers 1 Gas Welding Machine	18	1.780	L.F.
Catwalks, no handrails, 3 joists, 2" x 4"	2 Carpenters	55	.291	L.F.
3 joists, 3" x 6"	"	40	.400	L.F.
Move swing staging	1 Struc. Steel Foreman 3 Struc. Steel Workers 1 Gas Welding Machine	37	.865	L.F.

Figure 9.19

Conclusion   Masonry work is most often a crew task requiring incremental pieces be assembled to create the structural element or the veneer facing. In addition to the specific considerations discussed in this chapter, be sure to address the impact temperature extremes and the use of scaffolding or specialized equipment may have on your project.

Chapter Ten

Metals

C SI Division 5 includes one of the most versatile materials used in the construction industry—structural steel. Structural steel can best be defined as the steel members that make up the frame of a building, which will transmit the load to the foundation. Steel has the capacity to support large loads of a relatively compact size, in both compression and tension, making it an ideal material for flexural components. The variety of steel shapes and sizes available provides engineers with an economical solution to many structural design problems. Figure 10.1 lists the most common shapes and their respective designations. Structural steel is also available in different strengths or grades for particular loading or stress conditions. When estimating Division 5 work in general, the following categories must be considered:

- Structural steel
- Miscellaneous steel
- Open-web bar joists
- Metal decking
- Erection and cranes
- Field welding
- Items furnished for installation by other trades (such as steel lintels set by a mason)
- Shop and field priming/coatings
- Shop drawings

This chapter is limited to a discussion of the more common shapes of structural steel, open-web bar joists, and metal decking.

Structural Steel

Each steel shape, or *section,* is prefixed by a letter and numbers. These designations are more than simple identifications; they provide important information about the individual section. The letter stands for the classification of the piece by shape. The first number refers to the nominal depth in inches of the section. The second number refers to the weight in

Common Steel Sections

The upper section of this table shows the name, shape, common designation, and basic characteristics of commonly used steel sections. The lower portion explains how to read the designations used for the illustrated common sections above.

Shape & Designation	Name & Characteristics	Shape & Designation	Name & Characteristics
W	W Shape — Parallel flange surfaces	MC	Miscellaneous Channel — Infrequently rolled by some producers
S	American Standard Beam (I Beam) — Sloped inner flange	L	Angle — Equal or unequal legs, constant thickness
M	Miscellaneous Beams — Cannot be classified as W, HP or S; infrequently rolled by some producers	T	Structural Tee — Cut from W, M or S on center of web
C	American Standard Channel — Sloped inner flange	HP	Bearing Pile — Parallel flanges and equal flange and web thickness

Common drawing designations follow:

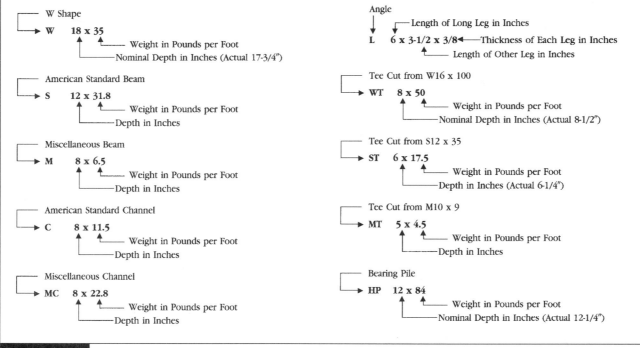

W Shape
W   18 x 35
 — Weight in Pounds per Foot
 — Nominal Depth in Inches (Actual 17-3/4")

American Standard Beam
S   12 x 31.8
 — Weight in Pounds per Foot
 — Depth in Inches

Miscellaneous Beam
M   8 x 6.5
 — Weight in Pounds per Foot
 — Depth in Inches

American Standard Channel
C   8 x 11.5
 — Weight in Pounds per Foot
 — Depth in Inches

Miscellaneous Channel
MC   8 x 22.8
 — Weight in Pounds per Foot
 — Depth in Inches

Angle
L   6 x 3-1/2 x 3/8 — Thickness of Each Leg in Inches
 — Length of Long Leg in Inches
 — Length of Other Leg in Inches

Tee Cut from W16 x 100
WT   8 x 50
 — Weight in Pounds per Foot
 — Nominal Depth in Inches (Actual 8-1/2")

Tee Cut from S12 x 35
ST   6 x 17.5
 — Weight in Pounds per Foot
 — Depth in Inches (Actual 6-1/4")

Tee Cut from M10 x 9
MT   5 x 4.5
 — Weight in Pounds per Foot
 — Depth in Inches

Bearing Pile
HP   12 x 84
 — Weight in Pounds per Foot
 — Nominal Depth in Inches (Actual 12-1/4")

Figure 10.1

pounds per linear foot of the section, which is critical in estimating the costs of the section—both in material and labor—since it is the key to its weight. For example:

> W12 x 22: *the W designates that the member is a wide flange section, the 12 indicates its approximate depth in inches, and the 22 refers to its weight per linear foot.*

Angle shapes are an exception to this rule. The first two numbers in an angle designation stand for the lengths of the "legs" of the particular angle, in inches. The third number is the thickness of each leg in inches. Some shapes, such as angles, do not include a weight designation. Determining the weight of angles, plate steel of various thicknesses, and tube steel requires the use of a table, such as those found in *Means Estimating Handbook, Second Edition.*

Structural steel is also available in different strengths, expressed as *yield stress.* Simply put, the yield stress, typically defined as *kips per square inch,* or KSI, is the maximum allowable stress that can be exerted on a material before it fails. (A *kip* is a unit of measure equal to 1,000 pounds.) The different grades of steel are named according to the number of the test conducted by the American Society of Testing and Materials (ASTM) to determine the characteristics of the species. Not all of the previously mentioned shapes are available in some of the more specialized grades of steel. Figure 10.2 lists common structural steel grades.

Drawings

Structural steel work is shown on structural drawings in plan view. Elevations, sections, and details are often added for clarity. Using schedules provided within the drawings to list columns, lintels, or repetitive steel features saves time during the takeoff. The details show the connections of individual pieces. Figure 10.3 is a simple structural steel drawing shown in plan view with the corresponding details to help illustrate some of the more common features.

Structural steel drawings include nomenclature unique to the work. One of these is the term "Do," which indicates duplication, similar to the expression "ditto." It is used to show repetitive use of the same designation beam, girder, joist, and so forth. The symbol < is used on drawings to identify angles. The number "2" before the symbol refers to a pair of angles.

Taking off Quantities

Structural steel is taken off by the length of the piece, converted to weight in pounds and extended to tons. Individual components should be listed according to shape and designation. Start with the largest member of the designation, and work down to the smallest. Pieces can be further classified by use (for example, beams, columns, and girders). Separating the pieces by application allows for pricing the erection and any special

Common Structural Steel Specifications

ASTM A36 is the all-purpose carbon grade steel widely used in building and bridge construction. The other high-strength steels listed in this table may each have certain advantages over ASTM A36, depending on the application. They have proven to be economical choices where, due to lighter members, the reduction of dead load and the associated savings in shipping cost can be significant.

Steel Type	ASTM Designation	Minimum Yield Stress in KSI	Shapes Available
Carbon	A36	36	All structural shape groups, and plates & bars up thru 8″ thick
	A529	42	Structural shape group 1, and plates & bars up thru 1/2″ thick
High-Strength Low-Alloy Manganese-Vanadium	A441	40	Plates & bars over 4″ up thru 8″ thick
		42	Structural shape groups 4 & 5, and plates & bars over 1-1/2″ up thru 4″ thick
		46	Structural shape group 3, and plates & bars over 3/4″ up thru 1-1/2″ thick
		50	Structural shape groups 1 & 2, and plates & bars up thru 3/4″ thick
High-Strength Low-Alloy Columbium-Vanadium	A572	42	All structural shape groups, and plates & bars up thru 6″ thick
		50	All structural shape groups, and plates & bars up thru 4″ thick
		60	Structural shape groups 1 & 2, and plates & bars up thru 1-1/4″ thick
		65	Structural shape group 1, and plates & bars up thru 1-1/4″ thick
High-Strength Low-Alloy Columbium-Vanadium	A992	50	All structural shape groups
Corrosion-Resistant High-Strength Low-Alloy	A242	42	Structural shape groups 4 & 5, and plates & bars over 1-1/2″ up thru 4″ thick
		46	Structural shape group 3, and plates & bars over 3/4″ up thru 1-1/2″ thick
		50	Structural shape groups 1 & 2, and plates & bars up thru 3/4″ thick
Weathering High-Strength Low-Alloy	A588	42	Plates & bars over 5″ up thru 8″ thick
		46	Plates & bars over 4″ up thru 5″ thick
		50	All structural shape groups, and plates & bars up thru 4″ thick
Quenched and Tempered Low-Alloy	A852	70	Plates & bars up thru 4″ thick
Quenched and Tempered Alloy	A514	90	Plates & bars over 2-1/2″ up thru 6″ thick
		100	Plates & bars up thru 2-1/2″ thick

Figure 10.2

coatings that apply, rather than the materials. Referring to Figure 10.3, the weight of the steel can be calculated for each individual member. For example:

Calculate the weight of the W12 x 22 beams between column lines 1 and 2 shown in Figure 10.3. From the designation number, it can be determined that the W12 x 22 beam weighs 22 lbs. per LF, and the plan shows 7 beams 20'-0" long. Therefore, the following calculation can be made:

7 beams x 20' each x 22 lbs./LF = 3,080 lbs. = 1.54 tns

Many structural steel drawings provide column lengths. The highest elevation on a column or beam is called the *top of steel* and is shown on the drawings as TOS. The proposed elevation for the top of the leveling plate is also given. The difference between the two is the length of the column. All structural steel is priced by weight in tons. This includes costs for milled materials, fabrication labor, erection, and all other miscellaneous tasks, such as priming, coatings, and trucking to the site.

Structural Steel Plan

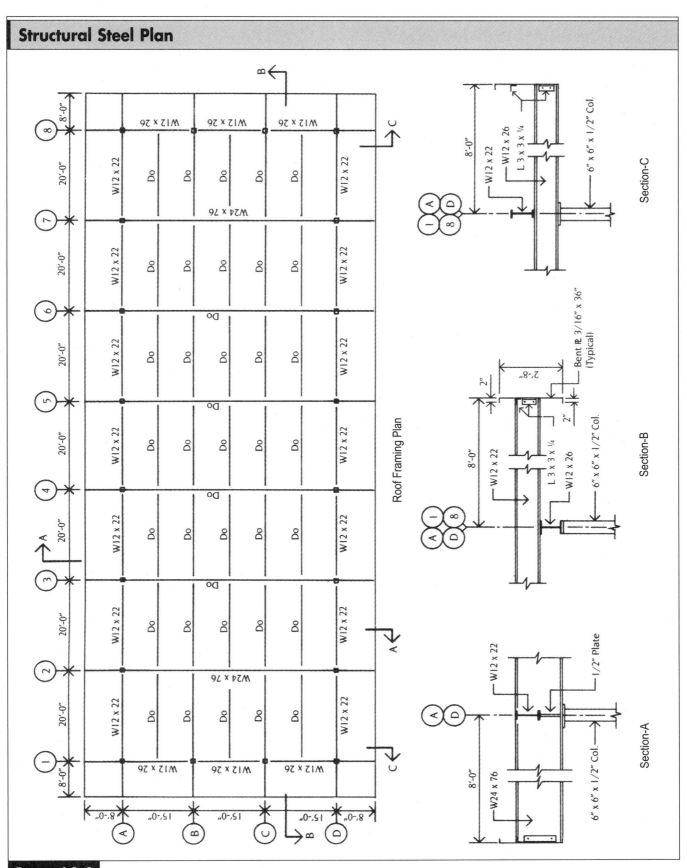

Figure 10.3

165

Carefully take off the lengths of the various members, from centerline of columns to centerline of columns. No deduction is required for connections.

Open-Web Steel Joists

Steel joists are manufactured by welding hot-rolled or cold-formed sections to angle web or round bars to form a truss. Standard open-web and long-span steel joists were developed as a cost effective alternative to wood frame construction. Steel joists' capacity to carry loads spanning greater distances has made them popular for all types of light-occupancy construction. They also can be used in fire-rated construction, and their open webbing allows the passage of mechanical piping and electrical conduits without drilling or coring holes.

Classification

Steel joists can be classified according to one of the following three categories or series:

- **K-Series:** Open-web, parallel-chord steel joists manufactured in standard depths of 8", 10", 12", 14", 16", 18", 20", 22", 24", 26", 28", and 30" with lengths up to 60'.
- **LH-Series:** Long-span, open-web steel joists manufactured in depths of 18", 20", 24", 28", 32", 36", 40", 44", and 48" with lengths up to 96'.
- **DLH-Series:** Deep, long-span, open-web steel joists manufactured in depths of 52", 56", 60", 64", 68", and 72" with lengths up to 144'.

Figure 10.4 shows the typical details for all three series' open-web joists and the different types of designs available.

LH- and DLH-Series are also available with top chords that are pitched or parallel to the bottom chords. The ends of the joists can be square ends or underslung. Joist designations are defined as follows:

24K10

The first number, 24, is the depth in inches of the joist.

The letter, K, indicates that it is a K-Series joist.

The last number, 10, indicates the load capacity/size of the chords.

Taking off Quantities

In Figure 10.5, open-web steel joists are shown as they would appear in plan view of a typical structural drawing. They are quantified by the pound and then extended to tons. They are typically taken off by the LF and quantity of each series and designation, then converted to weight. This requires referring to a table that lists the weights per foot of the different species of bar joist. Consulting the plan view of a typical open-web, K-Series steel joist (Figure 10.5 and Figure 10.6), it is possible to calculate the total weight of the K-Series steel joists for pricing. For example:

Calculate the weight of the K-Series steel joists in Figure 10.5.

Joists shown are 16K4. A takeoff shows a quantity of 10 with a span of

Standard Joist Details

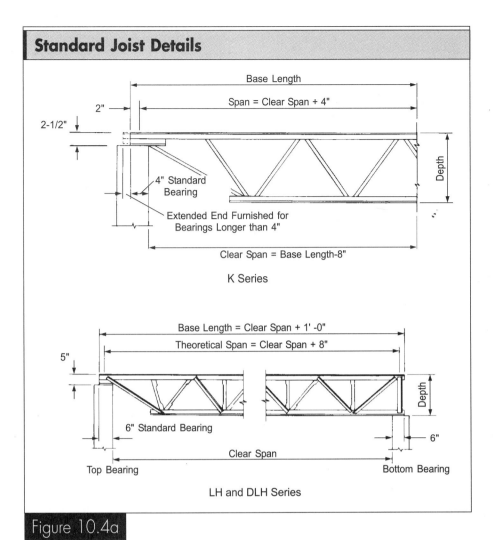

Figure 10.4a

30'-0". Locating a 16K4 joist in the table in Figure 10.5, we can see that it has a weight of 7.0 lbs. per LF.

10 EA x 30' LF = 300 LF x 7.0 lbs./LF = 2,100 lbs. = 1.05 tns.

Once the total weight of the bar joists has been calculated, multiply the weight by the cost of erection to determine the in-place cost.

Separate bar joists by designation number and series for accurate pricing. Steel joists that are welded in place should be listed separately from those that are connected by nuts and bolts. Check the documents carefully and coordinate mechanical drawings for doubling joists at rooftop equipment. Once the bar joists have been set and fastened, a brace is added to protect against lateral movement called *bridging*. It provides stability to prevent wracking of the joists. Bridging is most often accomplished with small, lightweight steel angles bolted or welded perpendicular to the span of the joist. The locations of the courses of bridging are shown on the structural plans and are determined in accordance with the joist manufacturer's recommendation.

Standard Joist Details

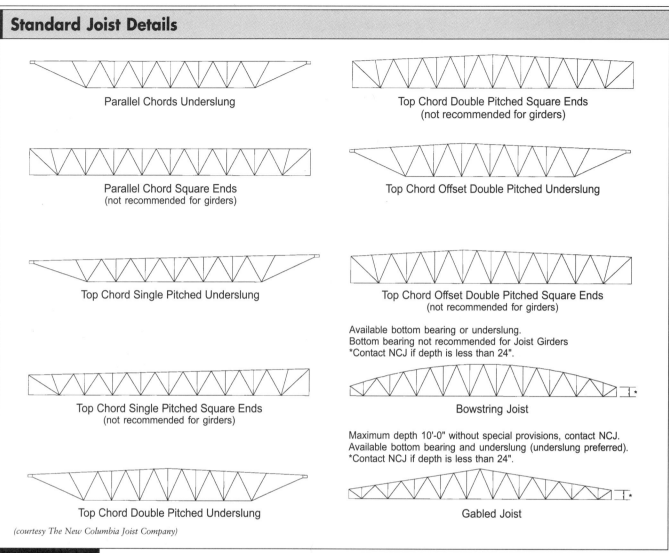

Parallel Chords Underslung

Parallel Chord Square Ends
(not recommended for girders)

Top Chord Single Pitched Underslung

Top Chord Single Pitched Square Ends
(not recommended for girders)

Top Chord Double Pitched Underslung

Top Chord Double Pitched Square Ends
(not recommended for girders)

Top Chord Offset Double Pitched Underslung

Top Chord Offset Double Pitched Square Ends
(not recommended for girders)

Available bottom bearing or underslung.
Bottom bearing not recommended for Joist Girders
*Contact NCJ if depth is less than 24".

Bowstring Joist

Maximum depth 10'-0" without special provisions, contact NCJ.
Available bottom bearing and underslung (underslung preferred).
*Contact NCJ if depth is less than 24".

Gabled Joist

(courtesy The New Columbia Joist Company)

Figure 10.4b

There are two main types of bridging:

- *Horizontal*: Two continuous steel members, one fastened to the top chord, and one fastened to the bottom chord.
- *Diagonal*: Members running diagonally from the top of one chord to the bottom chord of the adjacent joist.

It is important that the terminations of bridging are securely fastened to the wall or beam, regardless of the bridging installation method. This helps tie the bar joists to the structure itself. Both horizontal and diagonal bracing are taken off and priced by the linear foot (LF). Bridging mechanically fastened with nuts and bolts should be listed separately from welded bridging, as they have different installation costs.

Metal Decking

Metal decking consists of specially formed sheets of steel applied perpendicular to the span of the joists. These sheets serve as a substrate for the installation of roofing materials, such as rigid insulation and

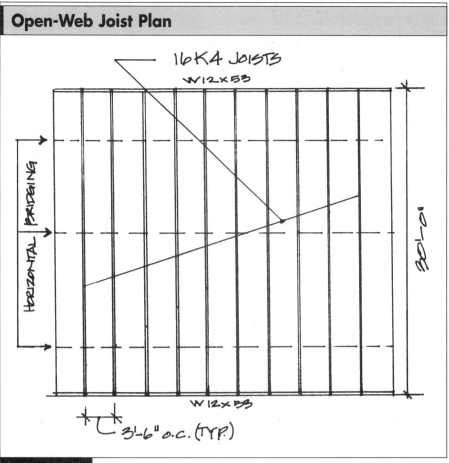

Open-Web Joist Plan

16 K4 JOISTS
W12×53
HORIZONTAL BRIDGING
30'-0"
W12×53
3'-6" o.c. (TYP.)

Figure 10.5

membrane, or as permanent forms for concrete floor slabs. Metal decking is fabricated from steel sheets in 18-, 20-, or 22-gauge thicknesses. The typical width is 30" with standard lengths ranging from 14' to 30', depending on specific project needs. The depth of the decking section can vary with type and application, but is usually 1-1/2" to 2-1/2". Special coatings and colors are available, but the most common finish is galvanized. Individual sections are fabricated with interlocking end and side laps for added rigidity.

Classification

Metal decking can be classified in two main categories for estimating purposes:

- Corrugated, undulated, or "corruform" concrete-fill permanent forms, also used for roofing and siding of industrial-type buildings.
- Cellular-type with well-defined, bent contours in trapezoidal or rectangular pitches or depths, used as permanent concrete forms for larger-span spacings or heavier live load applications.

The approximate weights per linear foot as shown in the following table do not include any accessories or connection plates.

Joist Designation	8K1	10K1	12K1	12K3	12K5	14K1	14K3	14K4	14K6	16K2	16K3
Depth (in.)	8	10	12	12	12	14	14	14	14	16	16
Approx. Wt. (Lbs./Ft.)	5.1	5.0	5.0	5.7	7.1	5.2	6.0	6.7	7.7	5.5	6.3
Joist Designation	16K4	16K5	16K6	16K7	16K9	18K3	18K4	18K5	18K6	18K7	18K9
Depth (in.)	16	16	16	16	16	18	18	18	18	18	18
Approx. Wt. (Lbs./Ft.)	7.0	7.5	8.1	8.6	10.0	6.6	7.2	7.7	8.5	9.0	10.2
Joist Designation	18K10	20K3	20K4	20K5	20K6	20K7	20K9	20K10	22K4	22K5	22K6
Depth (in.)	18	20	20	20	20	20	20	20	22	22	22
Approx. Wt. (Lbs./Ft.)	11.7	6.7	7.6	8.2	8.9	9.3	10.8	12.2	8.0	8.8	9.2
Joist Designation	22K7	22K9	22K10	22K11	24K4	24K5	24K6	24K7	24K8	24K9	24K10
Depth (in.)	22	22	22	22	24	24	24	24	24	24	24
Approx. Wt. (Lbs./Ft.)	9.7	11.3	12.6	13.8	8.4	9.3	9.7	10.1	11.5	12.0	13.1
Joist Designation	24K12	26K5	26K6	26K7	26K8	26K9	26K10	26K12	28K6	28K7	28K8
Depth (in.)	24	26	26	26	26	26	26	26	28	28	28
Approx. Wt. (Lbs./Ft.)	16.0	9.8	10.6	10.9	12.1	12.2	13.8	16.6	11.4	11.8	12.7
Joist Designation	28K9	28K10	28K12	30K7	30K8	30K9	30K10	30K11	30K12		
Depth (in.)	28	28	28	30	30	30	30	30	30		
Approx. Wt. (Lbs./Ft.)	13.0	14.3	17.1	12.3	13.2	13.4	15.0	16.4	17.6		

Figure 10.6

Other, more unique types of decking include long-span decking that ranges in depth from 4-1/2" to 7-1/2" fabricated from 14-, 16-, 18-, or 20-gauge sheet steel. Acoustical decking provides sound deadening capabilities, while still maintaining a structural load capability.

Taking off Quantities

Metal decking is taken off by the SF of area to be covered and extended to the square (SQ), where one SQ is equal to 100 SF. Allowances should be made for overlap at the sides and ends of the individual sheets, in accordance with the specification section of the design requirements noted on the drawings. Metal decking of different gauges, shapes, or finishes should be listed separately in the takeoff, as this will affect the cost.

Metal decking that serves as a permanent concrete form will require the use of sheet metal angles fastened to the perimeter of the decking and openings to act as an edge form for the placement of the concrete. These angles are taken off by the LF and should be listed by size and method of installation for proper pricing. They are priced by the LF for both material and installation costs. *(See "Edge Forms," Chapter 8.)* Another special task to check for is the installation of shear studs. *Shear studs* connect the composite floor systems to the structural steel through the decking. This is a separate task often performed last, just prior to the placement of the concrete. Shear studs are taken off and priced by the piece, based on their spacing and locations.

Labor

Review the specifications carefully for installation requirements. For example, thinner-gauge decking that is welded may require the use of thickening washers placed at the point of fusion, to avoid burning through the decking. This practice is common for metal of 20-gauge or higher (thinner metal). Decking that is fastened to the structure via welding is often required to be "stitched" with self-tapping screws at the side and end laps at specific spacing. Also analyze the specifications for field touch-up requirements for the galvanized finish at the welds. This can be a time-consuming process and should be listed separately in the takeoff. It can be quantified by square foot area or labor-hours to perform the work. Installation is priced by the square.

Since decking is typically loaded to the roof or floor with a crane, there is an equipment component in the price. The installation and welding tasks require a crew. The decking must be spread, with the required overlap and side lap, while welders follow behind and tack it to the deck. Review the specifications carefully for cutting the deck for openings, for items such as ducts, curbs, hatches, and miscellaneous penetrations. This can often be time consuming and require the opening to be reinforced from underneath with angles. Also consider labor to perform punchlist tasks, which are almost inevitable with this type of work. Figure 10.7 illustrates the various types of steel decking.

Light-Gauge Metal Framing (LGMF)

LGMF refers to the method of construction that uses a high-tensile-strength, cold-rolled steel formed in the shape of joists, studs, track, and channel. All components are fabricated of structural grade steel in 12-, 14-, 16-, and 18-gauge thicknesses. The various sections are designed to provide the load-bearing characteristics of steel or wood framing at a reduced weight and cost. Light-gauge framing is also non-combustible and does not warp, shrink, or swell in contrast to wood. Sections are available with a galvanized coating or red zinc chromate paint that resists rusting. Slots or channels are factory-punched within the web of the section to allow the passage of wiring, piping, and horizontal bracing. LGMF can be shop-fabricated and delivered ready for assembly, thereby reducing on-site costs and increasing quality control.

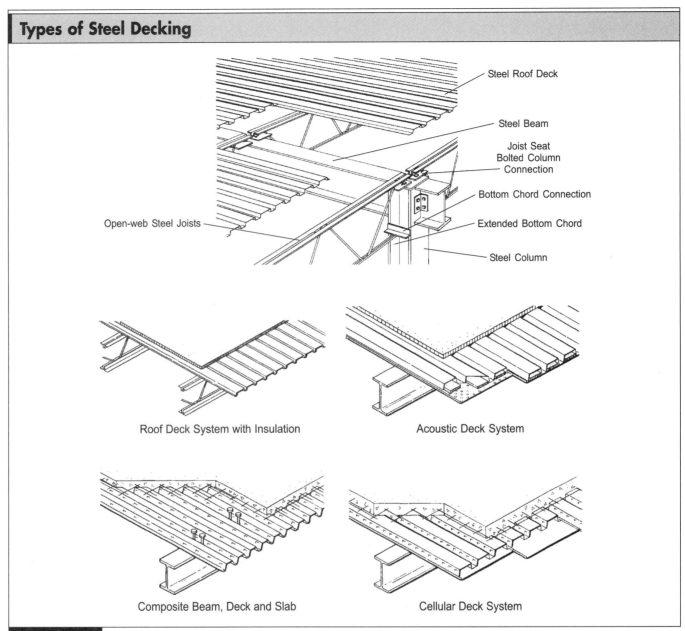

Steel Roof Deck

Steel Beam

Joist Seat
Bolted Column
Connection

Bottom Chord Connection

Extended Bottom Chord

Steel Column

Open-web Steel Joists

Roof Deck System with Insulation

Acoustic Deck System

Composite Beam, Deck and Slab

Cellular Deck System

Figure 10.7

On-site cutting of the sections is done with a "chop" saw outfitted with a high-speed metal-cutting blade. Layout and erection are similar to the procedures used for wood framing components. Fastening the various components can be done by bolting, screwing with self-tapping screws, or welding. Again, be sure to review the documents for touching-up welds with a zinc-based coating, a frequent requirement to maintain the integrity of the galvanizing. This can be a time-consuming process if done in the field.

Joists

Joist sections are available in 6", 8", 10", and 12" depths, and flanges in 1-5/8" or 2-1/2" widths. The most common lengths are from 8' to 30' in 2' increments. Joists are used in floor and roof construction with the typical 12", 16", and 24" on-center spacings familiar in wood frame construction. Joist and wall bridging can be done with special C-shaped channels that are inserted into the punched slots provided by the manufacturer. The spacing and location of the bridging components are found in the specifications or on the structural drawings.

Taking off Quantities

LGMF components are taken off by the LF. Special channels for use as box joists (sill or head plates in wood construction) are also taken off by the LF, as well as the C-shaped stiffener used within the walls or joist framing system. Sections of different shapes, sizes, gauges, and coatings (as well as the method of fastening) should be listed separately for accurate installation pricing. For projects that require fabricating panels off-site, the costs for materials and fabrication can be converted to the SF area of the panelized system. Labor for fabrication off-site must be added to the cost of erection on site. The two costs should be figured separately, as the labor rates and productivities can be different.

Studs & Track

Studs are the vertical components of a wall system, and are C-shaped with folded flanges. The specifications determine the on-center spacing requirements. Steel track refers to the horizontal component to which the steel stud is fastened. It is typically located at the top and bottom perimeters of the wall. Figure 10.8 illustrates a load-bearing wall. Steel studs and track are available in 1-5/8", 2-1/2", 3-5/8", 4", and 6" depths. Standard gauges are 14, 16, and 18. They are also available in 20- and 25-gauge thicknesses, but these are not considered to be of load-bearing capacity, and will be discussed in Chapter 14, Finishes (Division 9).

Taking off Quantities

There are four basic methods for estimating metal studs and track:

1. Take off the stud and track separately by the LF. Price studs and track totals separately for materials and labor costs.
2. Take off the wall by the LF, where one LF of wall is equal to one LF of length by the height. For example, 76 LF of wall that is 8' high is quantified and listed as 76 LF. Convert material and labor costs to linear foot of wall based on a specific height.
3. Calculate the SF area of the wall (length times height). For example, the wall cited in Method #2, 76 LF × 8' high, would be listed in the takeoff as 608 SF. Convert material and labor costs to SF.
4. Calculate the SF area as in Method #3. Estimate the cost of panel fabrication and the cost of erection separately. Include equipment costs required for erection.

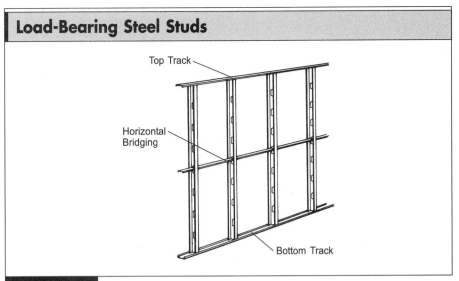

Load-Bearing Steel Studs

Top Track

Horizontal Bridging

Bottom Track

Figure 10.8

Regardless of the method selected, be sure to separate walls of different stud widths, gauges, heights, methods of fastening, on-center spacings, and applications. Added materials for openings in the wall must also be calculated. Similar to wood construction, openings in light-gauge, load-bearing metal stud walls must be framed to support the load transmitted from above. This involves the use of headers, cripple studs, sills, and doubled jamb studs. Openings and their components may be taken off and priced by the opening (EA) based on size, or by the individual component (e.g., doubled studs per LF, headers per LF, or sills per LF). The choice of estimating method should be based on the type of openings. For example, openings for numerous doors and windows of the same size may best be quantified per opening (EA).

Specialized equipment, such as staging for installation, may also be needed. Equipment should be listed separately, based on length of time required. Charges for erection, dismantling, or moving should also be included.

Miscellaneous & Ornamental Metals

Miscellaneous and ornamental metals are frequently specified under CSI Section 05500—Metal Fabrications, and can be shown on both the architectural and structural drawings. Exterior railings are also shown on site improvement drawings. Miscellaneous and ornamental metals are typically separated into two categories for takeoff purposes. *Miscellaneous* refers to the various items that do not fit into one specific classification. *Ornamental* refers to railings and special metal fabrications for stairs.

It is not uncommon for projects with limited structural steel to still have a considerable number of miscellaneous and ornamental metal items. This category encompasses a diverse range of items that are furnished and delivered, and sometimes installed. The following sections describe the more common items and their respective takeoff and estimating procedures.

Lintels

These are structural members, typically installed in masonry walls over windows or doors, to support the load of the masonry above the opening. The most common type of lintel is the steel angle. These can be cut from stock lengths of various-sized steel angle stock. They are longer than the width of the opening in order to span the opening and provide bearing on either side. The amount of bearing is dictated by the specifications and/or applicable building code, contingent on the size of the opening and the load above it. Angles can be supplied as either individual units, or composite units of multiple angles, welded together for walls of multiple masonry widths.

Taking off Quantities

Like most steel items, lintels are taken off by the individual piece and converted to weight for pricing. This is done by adding the bearing requirement for each side to the width of the opening in LF, multiplying the LF by the number of pieces, and then multiplying by the weight per LF to obtain a weight in pounds.

For buildings with a substantial masonry scope of work, the structural documents may list the lintels in a lintel schedule, which refers to the lintel by name, such as L1, L2, L3, and the species of angle. It also specifies the size in length, and whether the unit is an individual or a composite of angles welded together. Lintels should be listed separately from structural steel items on a takeoff, because the unit price per pound for smaller sections is considerably more than for structural sections. They also are frequently required to be galvanized as a finish coating to protect against the weather. This process has an added cost impact. Lintels are a furnished-and-delivered item only. Installation is typically included as part of the masonry scope of work, because the lintels must be installed as the masonry courses progress.

Pipe Railings

Pipe railings are commonly found at interior and exterior stairs or ramps for pedestrian traffic. They are constructed of welded-steel pipe in configurations to match the profile of the stair or ramp. Diameters of the pipe can range from 1-1/4" to 1-1/2". The welds are ground flush, and the railing is often primed, galvanized, or finish-painted ready for installation. They are installed by the use of sleeves, which are slightly bigger than the diameter of the pipe, embedded in the wet concrete. They can also be installed by coring a hole in the concrete and grouting the rail in place with the use of hydraulic cement. For applications in materials other than concrete, the railings may incorporate the use of a flange welded to the point of attachment that has holes punched for bolted fastening.

Taking off Quantities

The most common unit of takeoff and pricing for railings is by the LF of completed rail. Railings of various diameters and different methods of installation and finishes should be listed separately. Review the documents carefully for all types and locations of railings. The method of attachment and finishes are among the primary determinants in the cost.

Ladders

Permanently-installed ladders for access to high roofs from low roofs, from elevator pits, and from the interior to the roof are typically constructed of flat steel bar stock, with rungs of round steel bars. They are fabricated by welding the rungs perpendicular to the flat stock at the specified spacing. Angles or brackets are welded to the flat stock for fastening to the masonry or concrete wall. Standard finishes include primer, finished paint, and galvanizing ready for on-site finish paint. As with railings, the cost of ladders is impacted by the specific method of attachment and finish. Ladders are typically taken off by the vertical linear foot (VLF) or by the individual piece (EA). They are priced by the same units.

Grates

Grates are fabricated items used to allow the flow of air or water while supporting vehicular or pedestrian traffic. They are composed of parallel flat bar stock with intermediate round bars welded between. Grates typically include angles for support that are bolted to the adjacent masonry or concrete surfaces. Grating is also used for the intermediate landings and treads in industrial application stairs, and for exterior fire escapes. In these applications, other parts need to be included in the estimate, such as toe plates and metal stringers to support the treads.

Taking off Quantities

The standard unit of takeoff and pricing for grating is SF. The LF measurement of support angles should be included as part of the takeoff and price. Figure 10.9 illustrates the use of grating as landings and treads on a stair. Review the specifications for coatings, such as galvanizing or Color-Galv.

Metal Pan Stairs

Steel stairs may be of the metal pan type, which requires placing concrete into the treads and landings as the wearing surface. They can also be constructed of diamond plate steel or metal grating (see previous section on grating). Metal pan stairs are typically fabricated off site in multiple pieces, which usually include stringers with treads and risers attached to landing components.

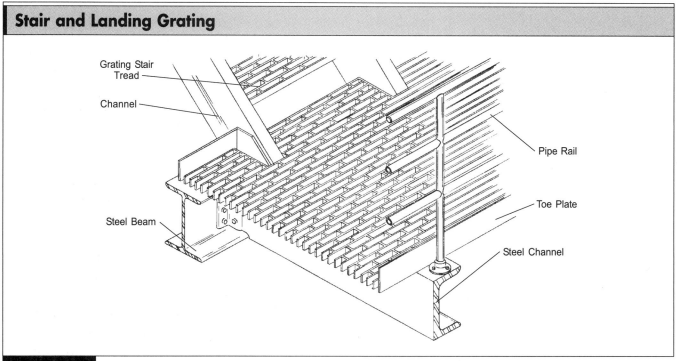

Grating Stair Tread

Channel

Steel Beam

Pipe Rail

Toe Plate

Steel Channel

Figure 10.9

Taking off Quantities

The cost of fabrication should be kept separate from the cost of installing the stairs. Steel stair takeoff and its supporting structural members should be kept separate from the other miscellaneous metals categories. Stairs are frequently priced per riser, which would include the treads and supporting stringers. The quantity and size of the tread and riser combination will affect the price. Sizes of landings should be taken off and priced separately by the square foot of area. Other parts, such as railings, toe rails, or miscellaneous filler pieces, are taken off and priced separately. Also remember to include the cost of the concrete to fill the pan and the landing deck. These costs can be included as part of the stair estimate or can be included in Division 3—Concrete.

Bear in mind that the placement of concrete in the stairs can be labor-intensive. It may also require the use of a concrete pump, if there is sufficient quantity. Since the process is fairly messy, be sure to include labor to clean the concrete from adjacent work. Figure 10.10 illustrates the basic components of a metal pan stair and the typical associated labor-hours.

Joist-Bearing Plates/Embedded Items

Joist-bearing plates are small pieces of steel of varying thicknesses, the most common being 1/2" or 3/4", with approximate dimensions of 4" × 6". Welded to the bottom of the flat plate are hooked anchor bolts. The anchor bolts of the joist-bearing plate are embedded in the bond beam course of a masonry wall. Once the grout has cured, the joist-bearing plate

Installation Time in Labor-Hours for Stair Systems

Description	Labor-Hours	Unit
Concrete		
Stairs C.I.P.	.600	L.F. tread
Landings C.I.P.	.253	S.F.
Steel Custom Stair 3'-6" Wide	.914	riser
Steel Pan		
Stair Shop Fabricated 3'-6" Wide	.914	riser
Landing Shop Fabricated	.200	S.F.
Concrete Fill Pans	.070	S.F.
Spiral Stair		
Aluminum 5'-0" Diameter	.711	riser
Cast Iron 4'-0" Diameter	.711	riser
Steel Industrial 6'-0" Diameter	.800	riser
Included Ladder (Ships' Stair) 3'-0" Wide	1.067	V.L.F.
Wood Box Stair Prefabricated 3'-6" Wide		
4' High	4.000	flight
8' High	5.333	flight
Open Stair Prefabricated 8" High	5.333	flight
Curved Stair 3'-3" Wide		
Open 1 Side 10' High	22.857	flight
Open 2 Sides 10' High	32.000	flight
Railings 1-1/2" Pipe, 2 Rail		
Aluminum	.200	L.F.
Steel	.200	L.F.
Wall-Mounted	.150	L.F.
Rails Ornamental		
Bronze or Stainless	.611	L.F.
Aluminum	.767	L.F.
Wrought Iron	.834	L.F.
Composite Metal, Wood or Glass	1.467	L.F.

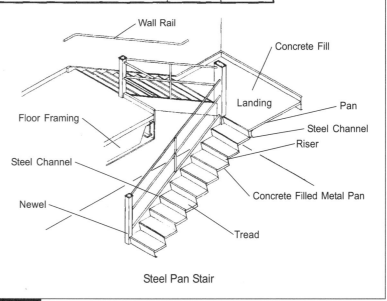

Steel Pan Stair

Figure 10.10

is held secure for the attachment of bar joists. Bar joists are welded to the exposed portion of the joist-bearing plate. Similar versions of longer lengths, called *end wall-bearing plates*, which run parallel to bar joists, are fabricated and installed to support the deck at the masonry end walls of the structure.

Taking off Quantities

Joist-bearing plates are taken off and priced by the piece (EA). This is accomplished by counting the number of joist ends that bear on masonry walls. The end wall-bearing plates are taken off and priced by the linear foot. The major portion of the cost is the fabrication. Consult the documents for installation requirements. Most joist-bearing plates are furnished-and-delivered items only. Their installation is typically part of the masonry scope of work and proceeds as the top course is filled with grout.

Lally Columns

Lally columns for residential construction are used to transmit live and dead loads from the structural members above to the isolated footings. They are typically 3-1/2" diameter concrete-filled steel pipe columns, with separate cap and base plates. Lally columns are available in a variety of stock lengths from 7' to 12' in one foot increments. Columns can be cut on site using a heavy-duty pipe cutter.

Taking off Quantities

Lally columns are taken off and priced by the individual piece based on the even foot length. To obtain the length of the column, calculate the distance from the bottom of the load-bearing beam to the top of the column, and round up to the nearest foot. The cost of cutting, usually minor, should be included as part of the installation.

Steel Window Guards

Steel window guards or grates are fabricated from a variety of direct sized bar or round stock, most commonly 1/2" x 1/2" bar or 1/2" diameter rod welded to flat stock at the perimeter. Other types of security grating include heavy gauge, diamond-shaped wire mesh welded to a frame constructed of 1-1/2" x 1-1/2" angles welded as a picture frame. They are typically fabricated off site, then delivered and installed by bolting.

Taking off Quantities

Window guards are taken off and priced by the square foot. Multiple guards of the same size can be priced by the piece, especially for installation purposes. The cost of bolts, anchors, shields, and fasteners in general should be included as part of the installation cost. Review the specifications for guard finishes, as they will impact cost.

Miscellaneous Costs

Estimating structural steel and miscellaneous metals often requires items that are not easily categorized. Among them are shop drawings, shop painting, and field erection.

Shop Drawings

Prior to the actual fabrication of any structural steel components, the steel fabricator is required to produce a set of working drawings, or shop drawings, that show the actual connection details, heights, and lengths of the various structural members, such as beams, columns, and joists. This is part of a checks and balances system between engineers and contractors to avoid costly errors. In addition, shop drawings provide lintel schedules and show base and cap plate details. Shop drawings are reviewed by the architect or structural engineer for conformance and are approved for fabrication. The fabricator then uses them as a guideline for fabrication and, ultimately, erection.

Taking off Quantities

Pricing the production of shop drawings is a difficult task with many variables, and is a direct function of the complexity of the steel design. The more complicated the steel fabrication, the more details, in the form of shop drawings, are required. Shop drawings can be priced by the individual sheet required; 24" x 36" sheets are considered standard. The alternate method involves pricing the shop drawings per ton of steel.

Shop Priming of Structural Steel

After the various steel components have been fabricated, they are generally primed prior to leaving the shop, unless the steel will be spray-fireproofed or encased in concrete. The type of primer paint is typically identified in the specifications. Consider any touch-up that may be required in the field if primer has been damaged by welding or handling. The cost of shop priming is based on the amount of steel to be primed in tons. As a guide, ordinary structural steel members contain approximately 175 to 250 SF of surface area per ton. Based on the cost of the specified paint and its recommended coverage per gallon, you can calculate the cost of materials per ton.

Labor costs will depend on the application method used, most commonly spraying. Review the specifications for the number of coats required and any specified coating film thicknesses. Field touch-up is priced as a separate item, and is quantified by labor-hours.

Field Erection of Structural Steel

All of the components of a structural steel frame are erected by a crew rather than a single individual. The size of the crew is determined by the complexity and scope of the project. The erection of structural steel must include the handling and distribution on site, crane setup and moving, crane rental, and the materials and labor for on-site welding. Most erection crews provide a foreman or other form of supervision during the initial phase of the process. (Typically, steel erection crews come en masse to erect the frame. The "buttoning up" work takes several weeks after with a lot smaller crew.) There are a variety of items that will affect the productivity of an erection crew. The most common ones are weather and temperature, on-site accessibility, experience of the crane operator, and number of connections. Always review historical data as a basis for pricing erection. Steel erection is a special task, and should be left to those familiar with the work who have the appropriate tools and safety equipment.

Taking off Quantities

Structural steel erection is taken off and priced by the ton. The quantity of steel in tons can be obtained from the material takeoff previously done. Structural steel members should be separated from joist and decking for accurate pricing. The major portion of the steel will first be erected and bolted or welded. The joist will then be set and the deck landed on the various floors or roof as quickly as possible so that crane time can be minimized. As the frame is squared and plumbed, it is braced for safety purposes. The crew will install fall protection at the outside perimeter and interior openings in accordance with OSHA guidelines. The remaining tasks of installing and tightening bolts to the required torque, welding bar joists, and fastening decking take somewhat longer, and are usually done by a detail crew after the main erection crew is finished.

Conclusion

As a common component in the commercial construction marketplace—and to a somewhat limited degree residential—steel often accounts for a large portion of the cost of a project. For that reason, a detailed and comprehensive takeoff and estimate may require additional time to check calculations and verify quantities.

Chapter Eleven

Wood & Plastics

Wood and plastics are covered in CSI Division 6. Although there are numerous sections within this division, for estimating purposes, all tasks can be classified into one of four major categories:

- Rough carpentry, framing, and blocking
- Finish carpentry
- Architectural millwork
- Casework and cabinetry

Within these four major groups are most of the tasks you would encounter in a residential or light commercial construction project. While not essential, it is beneficial to have a working knowledge of carpentry, especially framing.

For the purpose of this chapter, we will use the terms *rough carpentry* and *framing* interchangeably to refer to building structures with wood structural components, including framing-grade lumber and sheathings. Wood trusses may also be used. Pre-engineered and pre-fabricated structural components, such as composite joists, are often used in place of conventional framing lumber. In recent years, these products have gained in popularity and are the rule rather than the exception. Their greatest popularity is for framing floor and roof systems.

Finish carpentry refers to materials and techniques for finish-grade wood trims for windows, doors, baseboards, and moldings on the building's interior. It also includes installing details, both interior and exterior, from standard lumberyard stock, as well as paint and stain-grade wood species. *Architectural millwork* is classified as custom-fabricated moldings and trims, most often used in the structure's interior. This work is typically defined as first-class. *Casework and cabinetry* refers to the installation of pre-fabricated (mass-produced) or custom-fabricated casework, such as bookshelves, countertops, and cabinets.

Rough Carpentry & Framing

In light commercial construction, most rough carpentry and framing details are shown on a portion of the structural drawing set called *framing plans*. As the name would imply, the majority of information is provided in plan view, supported by details and sections. The framing plan, a modified version of structural drawings showing the "skeleton" of the structure, illustrates the structural wood members used to construct the frame of the building. The building cross-section and wall section provide essential information for taking off and accurately pricing the wall framing and sheathing, roof framing and sheathing, and the roof/ceiling assembly. Note that in residential construction, specifically renovation work, there may be no framing plan. In this circumstance, the builder must rely on the building code as a guideline to frame within the parameters of the architectural drawings.

Taking off Quantities

Prior to the start of the lumber takeoff, begin with a thorough review of the plans. This includes both the architectural and structural (framing) plans. The purpose is to become familiar with the structure and coordinate the work between both design disciplines. Next, read the specifications for the grade and species of lumber to be used. *Grade* can be defined as quality, both visual and, more importantly, structural. Different species have different structural integrity (strength), and, as a result, different prices. This is also true of sheathings. The species of wood that makes up the sheathing will be a major determinant in the price. Define all materials in the lumber list by species, grade, and any other special requirements, such as pressure-treated or fire-retardant woods, as this will affect the price.

The most accurate procedure for estimating lumber quantities is to perform a detailed and comprehensive takeoff of each piece of lumber and sheathing included in the work. Shortcuts to this procedure can often result in errors or omissions that can be costly. The completed *lumber list*, as it is called, is then sent to various lumber suppliers for price quotes. When this is done correctly, it provides current pricing of wood materials. Performing the takeoff allows you to gain a full understanding of the project and is essential when estimating the cost of associated labor.

Platform Framing

All of the estimating techniques described in this chapter are based on *platform* or *western framing*. In platform framing, the load-bearing walls start at the top of the subfloor sheathing and continue to the underside of the platform or floor above. An alternate method, called *balloon framing*, starts the exterior and load-bearing walls at the top of the pressure-treated sills, and continues to the underside of the ceiling joists. Platform framing is the more common method employed for residential/light commercial projects.

Dressed Lumber

Lumber prepared for frame construction is called *dressed* lumber. The term "dressed" refers to the surfacing of the rough lumber, accomplished by a thickness planer. This process provides a uniform size and shape with a smooth surface. Lumber that has been surfaced on all four sides is called *S4S*. Once the lumber has been surfaced, it is smaller than its original dimensions. For example, a 2" x 4" piece of rough lumber measures 1-1/2" x 3-1/2" after being dressed. The 2" x 4" dimension is called the *nominal* dimension, and 1-1/2" x 3-1/2" the *actual size*. Most rough carpentry work can be classified as frame construction, which includes the use of sheathings and structural grade lumber, such as 2" x 4", 1" x 6", and 2" x 8". Framing lumber has nominal dimensions from 2" to 6" in thickness and 4" to 14" in width. The length of the lumber differs by the species and availability, but most commonly ranges from 8' to 20' in 2' increments. Larger-dimensioned lumber, such as 2" x 10", 2" x 12", 4" x 6", and 6" x 8", is available in lengths up to 24'.

Framing Assemblies

The framing of a structure can be broken down into three main systems, or assemblies. An *assembly* is a series of components that together form a larger system or portion of work. The four main assemblies are:

- Floor framing
- Wall/partition framing
- Roof/ceiling framing
- Exterior trims and miscellaneous items

As with most estimating procedures, it is best to start at the beginning of a task and proceed as the project would be built. It is also important to include all incidental materials that are part of the assembly, so that nothing is omitted. For the sake of clarity, the following discussion will cover the procedure for the material takeoff portion of the work only. Estimating labor will follow after the takeoff of all four assemblies has been discussed.

Floor Framing Assembly

The floor framing assembly consists of all framing materials from the top of the subfloor down. This includes the subfloor sheathing, joists, box or band joists, cross bridging, girders, sills, and sill sealers. In addition, ancillary items, such as fasteners, adhesives, and joist hangers, should also be included in the assembly in which they occur. Figure 11.1 illustrates the floor framing assembly with the floor framing plan and a cross-section through the floor frame.

Girders and Sills: When the width of the structure is greater than the floor joist can span, a built-up or single-piece member called a *girder* is used. The girder is located at a specific point, frequently the midpoint in the width, to reduce the overall span of the joists. The girder is supported at specified intervals by lally columns that transmit the load to the

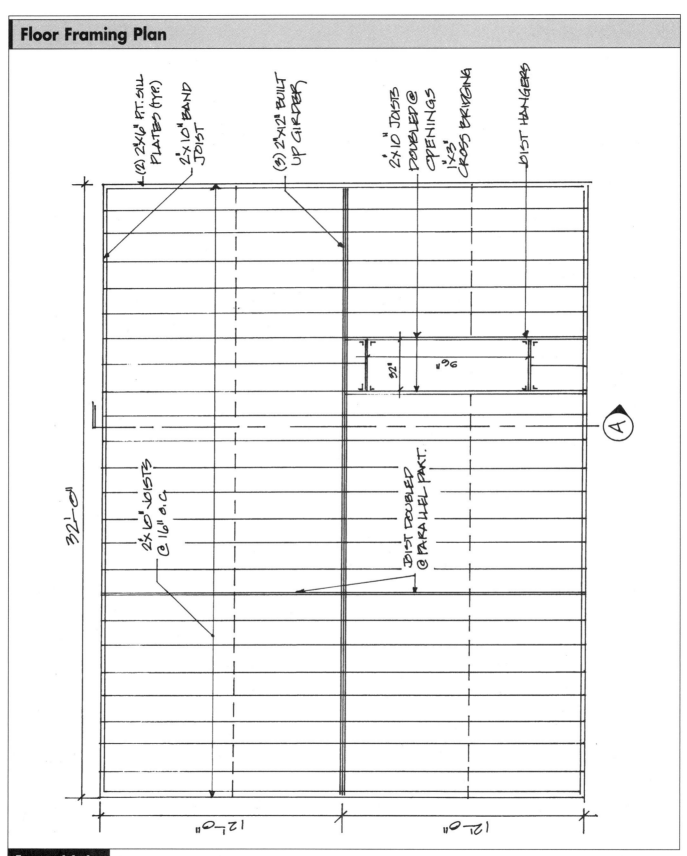

Figure 11.1a

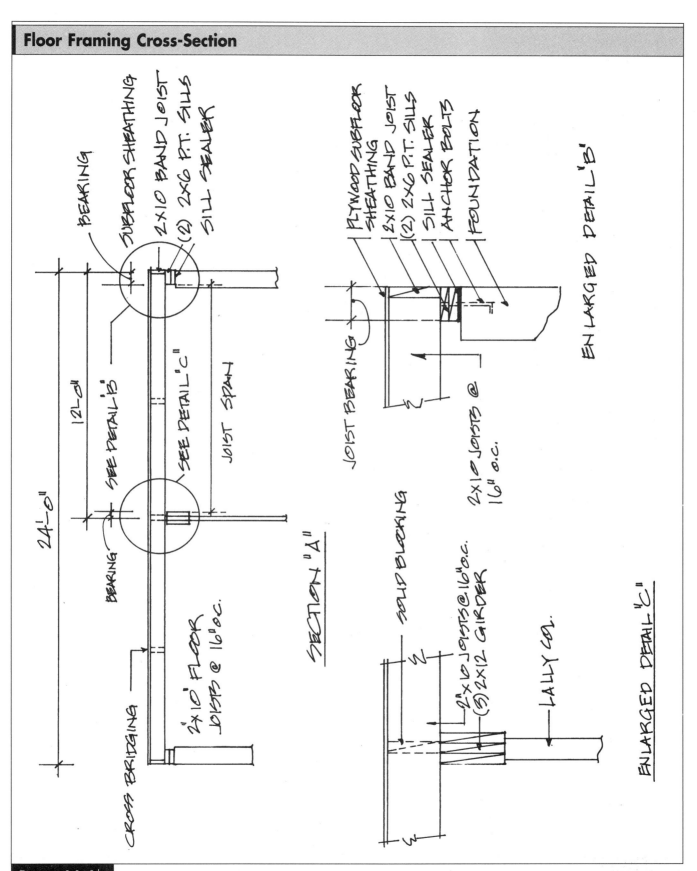

CROSS BRIDGING

2"x 10" FLOOR JOISTS @ 16" O.C.

BEARING

SEE DETAIL "B"

SEE DETAIL "C"

JOIST SPAN

BEARING

12'-0"

24'-0"

BEARING

SUBFLOOR SHEATHING

2x10 BAND JOIST

(2) 2x6 P.T. SILLS

SILL SEALER

SECTION "A"

PLYWOOD SUBFLOOR SHEATHING

2x10 BAND JOIST

(2) 2x6 P.T. SILLS

SILL SEALER

ANCHOR BOLTS

FOUNDATION

JOIST BEARING

2x10 JOISTS @ 16" O.C.

ENLARGED DETAIL "B"

SOLID BLOCKING

2"x 10" JOISTS @ 16" O.C.

(5) 2x12 GIRDER

LALLY CO.

ENLARGED DETAIL "C"

Figure 11.1b

187

footings. (Both lally columns and footings are defined in prior chapters of this text.) Sills are anchored to the top of the foundation wall by anchor bolts to provide a nailable bearing surface for the joist and box joist. Sills, or sill plates, are typically 2" x 6" or 2" x 8" and are doubled up on some plans. Because they are bolted to the concrete or masonry foundation, sills are *pressure-treated*, which refers to the process of treating wood with chemical preservatives under high pressure to protect against decay. The thin, compressible material installed between the sill and the top of the foundation wall is called the *sill sealer*, which acts as a barrier against insects and air infiltration and is made of synthetic materials resistant to decay.

Joists: The structural members that provide support for the floor are called *joists*. Joists are spaced at regular intervals, most commonly 12", 16", or 24" on center, and span the space between the girder and the sill on the foundation wall. A *box* or *band joist* (also known as a *rim joist*) runs perpendicular to the joists at their ends. It completes the platform or box that the floor framing resembles. To maintain the spacing at the midpoints and to prevent the joists from rolling or buckling, cross bridging is installed, located at approximately 8' on center for joists that span more than 16'. Cross bridging pieces are typically 1" x 3" or 1" x 4" cut to fit diagonally between the top of one joist and the bottom of the next. In addition to cross bridging, solid blocking can be installed at right angles to the joists between them. Solid blocking is used as a fire stop between joists at the center of a bearing partition or girder. The flooring laid perpendicular to the joists is called the *subfloor*, and is typically plywood or similar structurally-rated sheathing. The specifications frequently require that the sheathing be glued and nailed to the joists.

Taking off Quantities: Girders are taken off by the LF. Built-up girders with multiple members of the same size should be counted, then multiplied by the length to arrive at the LF. The length should include the clear span plus the required bearing at each end of the girder. The girder's lumber should be converted to stock sales lengths, which will be discussed in more detail in the following sections.

Sill sealer is taken off by the LF of the foundation wall requiring sills. The total quantity should be rounded to the nearest sales unit. For example, if the nearest sales unit is one roll (120 LF per roll) and the total linear footage required is 110 LF, then the lumber list should reflect one roll. Sill pieces are taken off by the LF and multiplied by two for sills that are doubled. Then converted them to stock sales length. If 240 LF were required, this could be listed in the takeoff several ways, such as: 20 pieces – 12' or 15 pieces – 16'. A combination of different lengths could also be used.

To determine the quantity of floor joists, divide the length of the floor frame (in feet) by the spacing (in feet), plus one joist for the end. The takeoff should list the quantity of each length of joist separately, and be reported in the lumber list as the total quantity of pieces of a specific length. The length refers to the span of the joist plus the required bearing at each end. For example, referring to Figure 11.1:

The length of the floor frame is 32' divided by 16" OC (1.33') = 24 joists + 1 joist at the end = 25 joists.

The overall length of the span from the outside foundation wall to the center of the girder is 12'. The result is 25 pieces of 12' joists on each side of the girder, or a total of 50 pieces of 12' joists.

To complete the frame, the band joist must be calculated. Band joists run perpendicular to the joists and can be taken off and extended to the total quantity of pieces of a specific length. Referring to Figure 11.1, the joists are perpendicular to the 32' length of the frame.

Therefore, 32' x 2 sides = 64 LF band joist. This can be extended to 8 pieces – 8' long or 4 pieces – 16' long.

The quantity of floor joists and band joists to be reported in the lumber list would be:

50 pieces – 12'

4 pieces – 16'

It should be noted that in order for the floor framing lumber to be complete, be sure to include the joists that are doubled at the stair openings and under the partitions, as shown in Figure 11.1. The actual size of the joists required should be extended to the stock sales length. For example, if the actual length of the joists needed were 11'-6", report it in the lumber list as a 12' length.

Cross bridging is shown at midspan between the foundation walls and the girder. It is taken off by the LF and again extended to typical practical stock lengths. To determine the actual LF needed, the length of a typical piece is calculated by using the Pythagorean Theorem. Referring to Figure 11.2, the following calculation can be made:

The length of a piece of cross bridging "C" is C = 17.2" or 17-1/4", since there are 2 pieces per bay: 2 x 17-1/4" = 34-1/2". The 34-1/2" could be rounded to 36" or 3'.

There are 32' of joists on each side of the girder, totaling 64 LF. To determine the number of bays, divide 64 LF by the 1.33' spacing, which equals 48 bays.

48 bays x 3' per bay equals 144 LF of bridging material. The 144 LF could then be converted to 12 pieces – 12'.

The subfloor sheathing is taken off by the SF. Since subflooring in today's market is a form of sheathing, you can determine the quantity of sheets required by dividing the SF area by the area of an individual sheet. Sheathing is typically manufactured in 4' x 8' sheets, with an area of 32 SF. The subfloor sheathing is laid with the 8' length of the sheet perpendicular

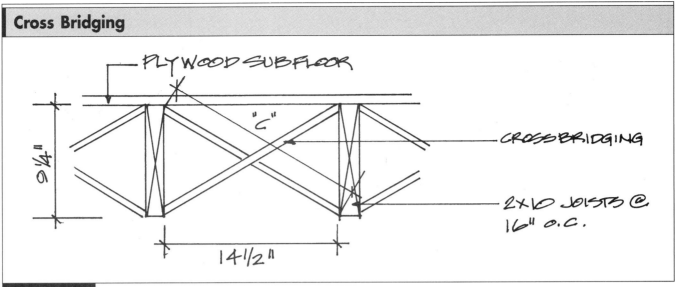

Figure 11.2

to the joists. For the example shown in Figure 11.1, the subfloor requirements would be determined by a simple calculation of the total area divided by 32 SF per sheet.

The floor area = 32' x 24' = 768 SF, divided by 32 SF per sheet = 24 sheets.

Since the plywood for all floor frames does not work out to the exact sheet (as in our example), you may need to make adjustments for odd-dimensioned frames. This may require counting actual sheets placed over the frame.

To reduce squeaking caused by movement in the subfloor, the sheathing is typically glued to the deck with subfloor adhesive. Calculating the amount of adhesive needed often depends on experience. A general rule of thumb is that a one-quart tube of adhesive should cover approximately five sheets of sheathing. This rule is subject to change with the weather, handling, and care taken in the application. Colder weather or poor handling will reduce the number of sheets covered by as much as one-third.

Study the drawings for the ends of joists that "hang" or do not rest on anything. Most building codes require joist hangers to support these members. Fasteners, including nails and screws, are most often sold by the pound. Check the specifications and/or manufacturer's recommendations for nailing and fastening schedules that indicate the spacing on-center for fasteners. Most estimators quantify nails as a lump sum (LS) item. As a reminder, *always* use the dimensions shown on the drawings for calculating quantities. Scaling should be a last resort when no other options are available.

Wall/Partition Framing Assembly

The wall and partition framing consists of the exterior walls and sheathing, the interior load-bearing partitions, and the interior non-load-bearing partitions. Load-bearing walls carry live and dead loads from a part of the structure above, such as a floor, roof, or ceiling. A major component of the load-bearing wall is the *header*, which spans the openings in load-bearing walls above windows and doors. Headers are structural members that transmit the load from above the opening to the framing on either side. Typical header construction consists of 2" x 6", 8", 10", or 12" (nominal) framing lumber nailed together with 1/2" plywood spacers to equal the thickness of the wall. Figure 11.3 illustrates a typical wood header.

The vertical members that support the header are called *trimmers* or *jack studs*. Jack studs are nailed to full studs at each side of the header, sometimes referred to as *king studs*.

All partitions and walls have horizontal members that hold the studs, or vertical members, at the desired spacing, called *plates*. The plate at the top of the wall is referred to as the top plate, and the one at the bottom is called the *sill plate* or *sole plate*. Most load-bearing wall construction requires that the top plate be doubled. The horizontal member that runs parallel to the header at the window sill height is called the sill. The short studs that fill in under the windowsill or above the header are called *cripples*. Figure 11.4 illustrates typical load-bearing wall framing.

Wood Header

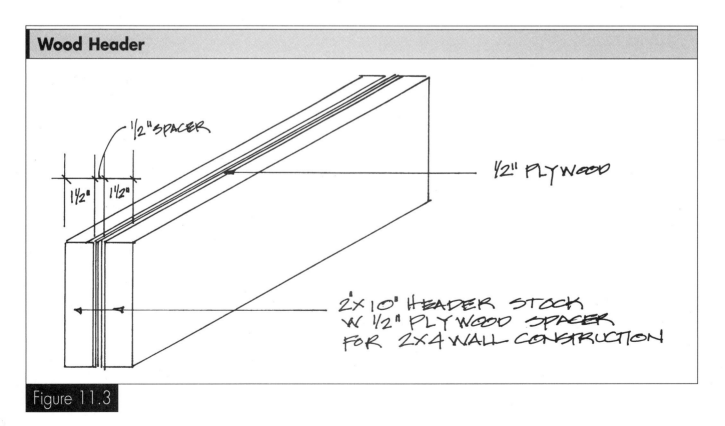

Figure 11.3

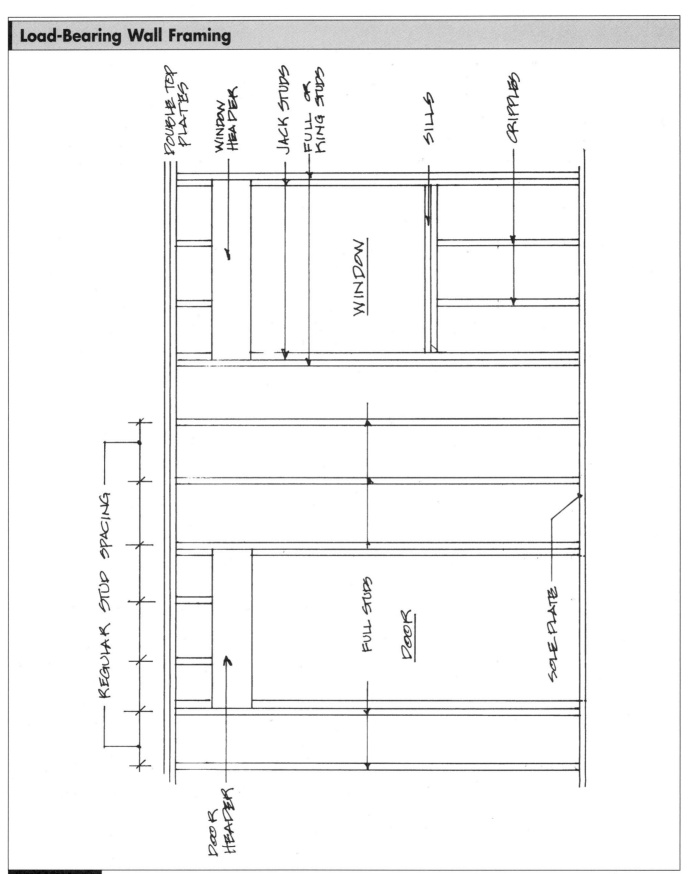

Figure 11.4

192

To complete the exterior wall system, plywood or similarly rated sheathing is installed over the framed wall. This helps give the wall rigidity and braces it against the wind. Just as in floor framing, wall sheathing is nailed with the 8' length perpendicular to the studs.

Taking off Quantities: Wall/partition takeoff starts with the exterior walls. The sole plate and double top plate are taken off by the LF by first determining the length of the wall and multiplying it by three (if there is a double top plate). Determining the quantity of studs required is more a matter of experience than a mathematical formula. When determining the number of studs required, provide for additional studs for outside corners, backer studs that provide nailing for intersecting partitions, and jack studs for openings. Since counting individual studs can be time consuming, it is common practice to use a multiplying factor to account for these additional studs, based on the number of intersecting partitions, openings, and corners. Factors can range from 1.10 to 1.35 studs per LF of wall length. A reasonable average would be 1.25 studs per LF of wall. For example, if the perimeter of the exterior wall were 100 LF, then the number of studs required would be:

100 LF x 1.25 studs per LF = 125 studs

The height (length) of the stud is calculated by referring to the wall section on the architectural drawings for the sole plate to top plate dimension, and subtracting the width of the three plates. Figure 11.5 shows a partial wall section for determining the stud height.

The example in Figure 11.5 shows that the height of the stud is the plate-to-plate dimension of 8', less the thickness of three 2" x 4" studs: 3 times 1-1/2" or 4-1/2". The stud height is 96" (8') minus 4-1/2" or 91-1/2" (7'-7-1/2"). The actual stud length would have to be extended from 7'-7-1/2" to 8' stock lengths, unless *precuts* were available. Precuts are studs that have been precut at the lumberyard to standard lengths for common wall types.

Window and door header lengths are determined by adding the rough opening width to the required bearing on each side. This is typically the thickness of a 2" x 4" or 2" x 6" stud, or 1-1/2". The *rough opening* is the clear width and height between the framing into which the window or door will fit. It is expressed as *width by height*, and can be found on the window or door schedules. The size of the stock (2" x 6", 2" x 8", 2" x 10", etc.) for the header should be shown on the architectural wall section, the structural framing plan, or as a note on the structural detail drawings. In the absence of a specified stock size, consult the engineer or, as a minimum, refer to the applicable building code. To convert the length of the header to the correct stock length, verify the quantity of pieces needed based on the wall thickness. Figure 11.6 illustrates the rough opening and header size.

Partial Wall Section

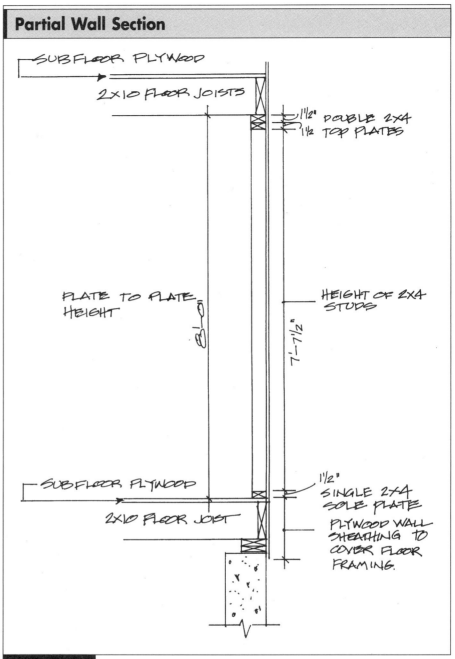

SUBFLOOR PLYWOOD

2X10 FLOOR JOISTS

1 1/2" DOUBLE 2X4
1 1/2" TOP PLATES

PLATE TO PLATE HEIGHT

8'-0"

HEIGHT OF 2X4 STUDS

7'-7 1/2"

SUBFLOOR PLYWOOD

2X10 FLOOR JOIST

1 1/2" SINGLE 2X4 SOLE PLATE

PLYWOOD WALL SHEATHING TO COVER FLOOR FRAMING.

Figure 11.5

In Figure 11.6, the length of the header is the width of the rough opening, 36" plus the bearing dimension of the jack studs on either side of the opening, or 2 times 1-1/2" = 3" for a total of 39". However, since the header is composed of two pieces that are each 39" long, the length could be extended to 78" or 6'-6". The stock length for a single header, in this example, would be one 8' piece.

Exterior wall sheathing is taken off by the SF and can be extended to the number of sheets required, in the same manner as subfloor sheathing. Note that the vertical height of exterior wall sheathing does not start at

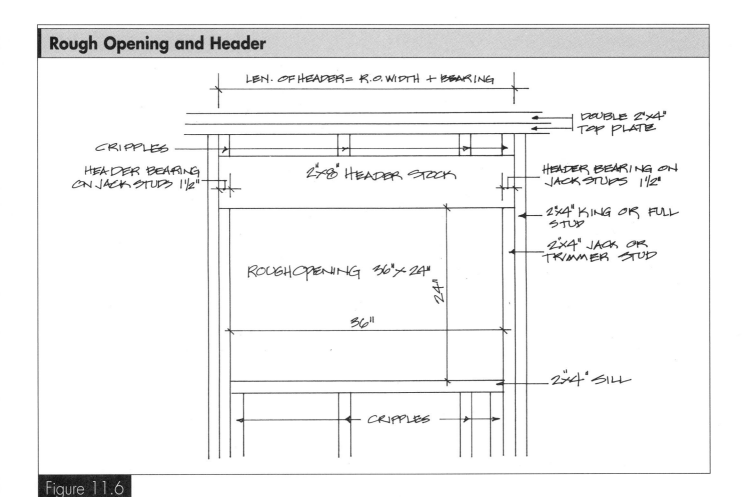

LEN. OF HEADER = R.O. WIDTH + BEARING

DOUBLE 2"X4" TOP PLATE

CRIPPLES

HEADER BEARING ON JACK STUDS 1½"

2"X8" HEADER STOCK

HEADER BEARING ON JACK STUDS 1½"

2"X4" KING OR FULL STUD

2"X4" JACK OR TRIMMER STUD

ROUGH OPENING 36"X 24"

24"

36"

2"X4" SILL

CRIPPLES

Figure 11.6

the sole plate, but at the bottom of the pressure-treated sills. To determine the vertical height of the wall sheathing, again refer to the wall section on the architectural drawings and calculate the vertical dimension from the pressure-treated sills to the top plate of the uppermost story. This dimension is, in turn, multiplied by the perimeter of the exterior wall. This dimension may not be consistent for the entire perimeter because of changes in story heights and roof lines. Deductions for windows, doors, and other exterior openings should be based on the size of the opening and the method of framing. Common field practice calls for sheathing over openings and cutting them afterward. In this case, deductions do not apply, and the cut-out pieces are considered waste. To check the quantity of sheathing, refer to the exterior wall elevations on the architectural drawings. Additional sheathing for gable-ends that extend beyond the top plate must be taken off with consideration for waste resulting from cutting at angles to match the roof pitch. There is no standard waste factor that can be applied; it must be determined on an individual basis. Ranges for waste can vary from 3% to 10%, based on the complexity of the frame.

The procedure for taking off interior load-bearing partitions is the same for exterior walls, except that there is no wall sheathing. Non-load-bearing partitions are similar, but do not require double top plates or structural headers. Increase the length of the stud by 1-1/2" for interior partitions with the same plate-to-plate height. It should also be noted that the multiplier for interior partitions is usually higher than the recommended 1.25 studs per LF used on exterior walls. Due to the increased amount of intersecting partitions at the interior of the space, more corner and backer studs are typically used.

Become familiar with the common framing practices in your region so that additional stock for items such as braces or spring boards for "plumbing up" exterior walls can be taken into account. This additional stock should be taken off and included as part of the lumber list.

Roof/Ceiling Framing Assembly

Conventional, or *"stick,"* framing, uses individual members, rather than trusses, to construct the roof. Before starting the takeoff, become familiar with the roof and ceiling framing system by studying the architectural and structural drawings, specifically the building cross-sections, wall sections, elevations, roof framing plans, and corresponding details.

Roof Pitch: *Rafters* are structural members that follow the slope, or pitch, of a conventionally framed roof. *Pitch* is the angle or inclination of the roof, expressed as a ratio between the horizontal *run* of the roof and its vertical *rise*. It is typically noted on the architectural drawings as an incremental ratio per 12" of run.

Figure 11.7 illustrates a typical symbol used to designate pitch, where the pitch of the roof is 8" of rise for every 12" of run. The rafters are supported at the base by the top plate at the top of the exterior wall. In the same way that floor joists are spaced along the pressure-treated sills, rafters are spaced along the top plate. Common spacing is 12", 16", or 24" on center. The part of the rafter that extends beyond the face of the exterior wall is called the *rafter tail* or *tail*. It provides the nailing for the fascia and soffit (discussed later in this chapter) and constitutes the roof's overhang. The highest point of the rafter terminates at a perpendicular member in the horizontal plane called the *ridge* or *ridge board*.

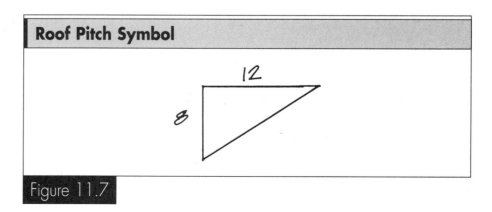

Roof Pitch Symbol

Figure 11.7

Ceiling Joists: To complete the triangular shape of the roof frame, horizontal members called ceiling joists provide the floor of the attic space or ceiling of the floor below. Ceiling joists extend from the top plates of bearing walls and span the space, much like floor joists that span from sill to girder or sill. Ceiling joists for gable-end roofs run parallel to rafters. Strapping (called *furring* when applied to walls) typically comprises 1" x 3" (nominal) boards nailed to the interior side of the ceiling joists. It is used to maintain the spacing of ceiling joists between bearing points and to provide furring for the ceiling finish. Strapping runs at right angles to the ceiling joists in the same horizontal plane. Strapping is commonly spaced at 12" or 16" on center.

Collar Ties: To increase the rigidity of the roof frame, horizontal members called *collar ties* are installed from rafter to rafter on opposite sides of the ridge. Collar ties are typically located in the top third of the imaginary triangle created by the roof frame. The *roof sheathing* extends from the rafter tail to the ridge board along the top surface of the rafter and provides a substrate for the application of the roofing. Figure 11.8 shows a typical roof frame as viewed in a building cross-section.

Hip Roofs: Another type of roof with intersecting roof planes is a *hip roof*. The member that forms the outside intersection of the hip roof is a *hip rafter*. The member at the inside intersection is referred to as the *valley*

Section at Roof Frame

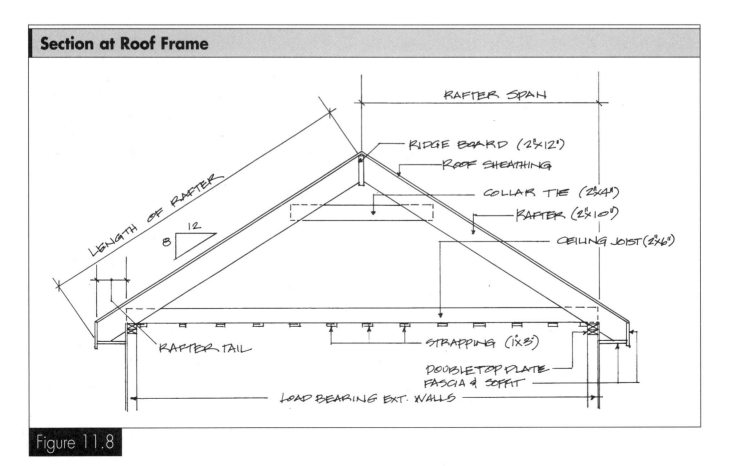

Figure 11.8

rafter. In addition to the common rafters, smaller rafters called *jack rafters* rise from the top plate and terminate at the hip or valley rafters. Figure 11.9 illustrates a hip roof frame.

Hip Roof Frame

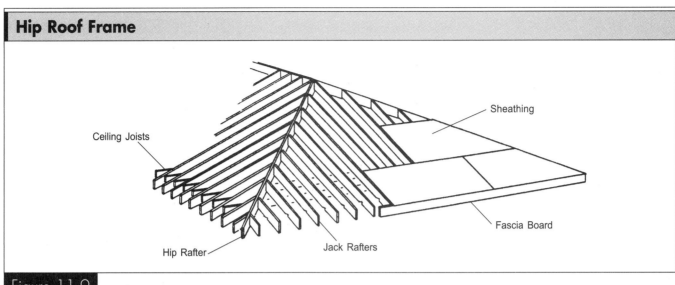

Figure 11.9

Taking off Quantities: The quantity of common rafters required is determined by the same method used to calculate the number of floor joists. *(Refer to the floor frame assembly discussed previously in this chapter.)* Divide the overall length of the structure by the spacing (both in feet) and include one additional common rafter for the end. Also be sure to include double rafters at openings in the roof for dormers, skylights, or other requirements noted on the drawings. It is important to include the rafters from both sides of the ridge. Once the quantity has been determined, calculate the length of the rafters and stock to be included in the lumber list.

Determining Common Rafter Lengths: If a vertical line passing through the center of the ridge were intersected by a horizontal line from the rafter tail to the center of the ridge, the intersection would form a right angle. By adding the rafter to these two imaginary lines, the shape would be a right triangle, subject to the rules of the Pythagorean Theorem. *(See Chapter 3.)* Figure 11.10 illustrates the imaginary triangle from the roof frame in Figure 11.8.

To determine the length of the rafter, first calculate the total run, "B," by adding the rafter span to the overhang. The *rafter span* is the horizontal distance from the face of the ridge to the outside face of the exterior wall sheathing. Determine the distance from the outside of the wall sheathing to the center of the ridge using the dimensions on the architectural

Calculating Rafter Length

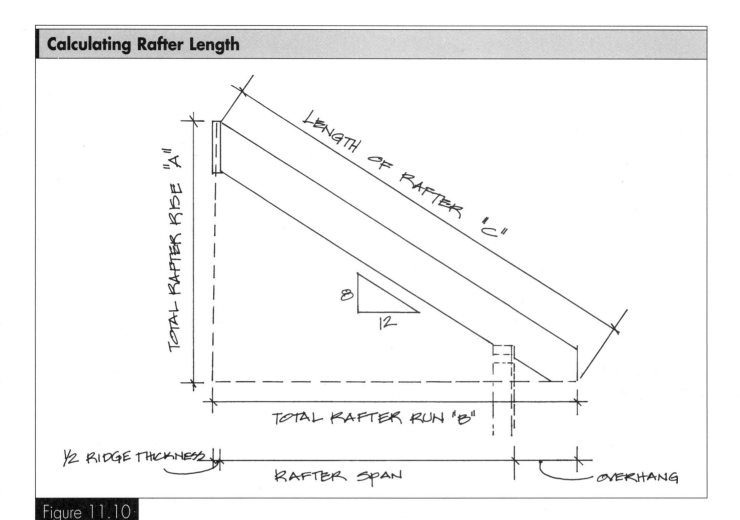

LENGTH OF RAFTER "C"

TOTAL RAFTER RISE "A"

8
12

TOTAL RAFTER RUN "B"

½ RIDGE THICKNESS

RAFTER SPAN

OVERHANG

Figure 11.10

drawings. For example, in Figure 11.10, if the dimension from the center of the ridge to the outside of the sheathing is 14', you could determine the total run of the rafter by the following calculations:

$$B = + \ 14' \quad \textit{(center of the ridge to outside of the sheathing)}$$
$$+ \ 1' \quad \textit{(overhang)}$$
$$- \ 3/4" \quad \textit{(half the thickness of the ridge)}$$
$$B = \quad 14'\text{-}11\text{-}1/4" = 14.94' = \textit{total run of the rafter}$$

Once the total run of the rafter, "B," is determined, then calculate the total rise of the rafter, "A." Since the pitch, or rise-to-run ratio, remains constant over the length of the rafter, the pitch can be used to determine "A."

The 8:12 pitch used in the example can be expressed as a decimal (8 divided by 12 = .67). This decimal equivalent of the pitch is a *unitless* value, with no units, such as feet or inches. It is a constant used as a multiplier. The calculation for determining "A" is as follows:

$$A = .67 \ x \ B = .67 \ x \ 14.94 = 10'$$

199

With values for "A" and "B," use the Pythagorean Theorem: $A^2 + B^2 = C^2$.

$$Where \; C = \sqrt{A^2 + B^2} = \sqrt{(10)^2 + (14.94)^2} = 17.97 \; or \; 17\text{'-}11\text{-}11/16\text{"}$$

After determining the length of the rafter in the previous example, we can now conclude that a stock length of 18' is required. It should be noted that not all roofs have equal pitches for both sides of the ridge. Roofs with varying pitches require separate calculations for each set of rafters. For most gable-end roofs, the measurement used to determine the quantity of rafters and sheathing is the length of the building. Some designs have end rafters that project beyond the plane of the gable-end with an overhang. This is called a *lookout frame*. Refer to the elevations, sections, and details to determine whether additional rafters, sheathing, or other lumber are needed.

The quantity of ceiling joists is determined by the same method used to determine floor joists. Divide the length of the building (in feet) by the spacing of the ceiling joist (in feet). Add one joist for the end. The actual length of the joist is determined by the dimensions provided on the plans. Since ceiling joists typically bear on exterior walls and interior partitions, the length is the dimensions between various walls of rooms, plus sufficient bearing. Again, the actual length is extended to the stock length for inclusion in the lumber list.

Collar ties are taken off using the same method as ceiling joists. The length is determined by their placement on the drawings. The Pythagorean Theorem can be used if necessary for determining the exact length. It can then be extended to the stock length of the material required.

Strapping is taken off and listed by the LF. First, calculate the length and width of the ceiling joists to be strapped. Since strapping is nailed perpendicular to the long length of the ceiling joists, determine the quantity of pieces needed by dividing the length (in feet) by the spacing (in feet). Multiply the quantity by the width of the building (length of the strapping). The total linear footage can then be added to the lumber list. Strapping is typically priced by the LF, so it is not necessary to extend it to stock lengths. Since strapping is installed end to end, the materials can be sold as random length. *Random length* refers to various pieces of different stock length adding up to the total required footage.

To take off roof sheathing, multiply the length of the building by the length of the rafter. (Both must be in the same units.) For practical purposes, the length of the rafter can be rounded up to the nearest foot. In the previous example, the 17'-11-11/16" would naturally be rounded to 18' stock. Just like subfloor and sidewall sheathing materials, extend the SF area to sheets by dividing the total area by 32 (SF per sheet). Round up to the nearest full sheet.

Determining Hip/Valley Rafter Length: Determining the length of the hip and valley is similar to the procedure for common rafters, but with one additional calculation. Since hip and valley rafters are most often at

45° to the common rafter, the dimension of "B" must be adjusted to reflect the additional length, using the Pythagorean Theorem. If the "B" dimension of 14.94' for the common rafter in the previous example is used, determine the total run, or "B" dimension, for the hip rafter in question:

Since the run of the hip rafter is 45° to the run of the common rafter (in the horizontal plane as measured at the top of the wall), the length of each leg of the triangle would be the same. Using the Pythagorean Theorem, the hypotenuse is the total run, or B_h dimension, for the hip rafter. For example:

$$B_h = \sqrt{(14.94)^2 + (14.94)^2} = 21.12$$

This represents the total run of the hip rafter. The total rise of the hip rafter, A_h, must equal the total rise of the common rafter, since they both meet at the ridge. This means that total rise "A" of the common rafter and total rise "A_h" of the hip rafter are the same.

If the previous "A" value of 10' is used with the "B_h" value for the hip, 21.12', then:

Length of the hip rafter $C_h = \sqrt{(10)^2 + (21.12)^2} = 23.37 = 23'\text{-}4\text{-}5/16"$

You would need 24' stock for the hip rafter. This same calculation applies in determining the length of the valley rafter.

Many building codes require rafter clips to anchor the rafter to the top plate, including common, hip, valley, and jack rafters. The quantity can be determined by counting the number of rafters and multiplying by two for both sides of each rafter. This requirement would be included in the specifications governing the work of the framing.

Occasionally, hip rafters intersect with common rafters at angles other than 45°; these are irregular and are sometimes called *bastard hip rafters.* The length of bastard rafters can be calculated in the same way as conventional hip rafters, except that the length of the triangle leg perpendicular to the rafter (in the horizontal plane) is not the same as the run of the common rafter and must be determined separately. This is a mathematical calculation based on the angle of the irregular hip rafter.

The length of jack rafters is calculated by the same method as common rafters, but can be time consuming. Consult framing texts with tables for jack rafter lengths based on the pitch and run of the common rafter. Hand-held calculators designed for contractors are also helpful in calculating the length of common, hip, valley, and jack rafters at the push of a button.

The ridge board is taken off by the LF. The length of the ridge in a gable-end framed structure is determined by the overall length of the building, plus the length of the lookout frame, if any. The *lookout frame* is the overhang at the gable-ends of the building. For a hip roof, the ridge is the length between the intersections of the hip or valley rafters at either end of the roof. Ridge boards, like other framing members, should be extended to the stock lengths and quantity required and included in the lumber list for pricing.

Blocking: Blocking consists of small pieces of wood installed between studs or other structural members for reinforcing or installation of other work, such as cabinetry, trim, windows, doors, or mechanical equipment. Blocking is not always shown on drawings, but the experienced estimator knows that certain items require it. Review the architectural drawings for such items as cabinetry, finish trim, millwork, toilet accessories, toilet partitions, handrails at stairs and corridors, windows or doors installed in masonry or metal stud-framed openings, or similar installations that would require special wood blocking for anchoring the work. Review the electrical and mechanical drawings for blocking that may be required for the installation of this work. Blocking is also required to attach water piping as it exits the wall for plumbing fixtures, such as sinks, toilets, or tubs. It is also needed to support piping within walls or joists. Electrical devices in walls or floors between existing framing may also require blocking, along with backer boards for electrical panels. Study the specifications for specific items that may require blocking. Frequently, blocking is required for the installation of work excluded from the contractor's agreement, such as equipment installed by the owner or under separate agreement.

Dimensional lumber, such as 2" x 8" and 2" x 10", used for blocking is typically taken off by the LF, and can be converted to random length materials or specific lengths if required. Sheathing used for blocking, backer boards, or as spacers within headers is taken off by the SF area and, again, converted to sheets.

Certain classifications of construction, such as fire-resistant work, may require fire-treated wood. Quantities of fire-treated wood should be listed separately, as the cost for such materials is considerably more. In addition to regular blocking, *fire blocking* is required by building codes to slow the transmission of fire through a wall or stair construction and interior cavity. Again, fire blocking is not always shown on the drawings. In structures with balloon framing, it is required at the floor level of all walls passing through the floor. Determining the need for blocking is often a matter of experience or good practice. You should be familiar with the local codes having jurisdiction over the project.

Stair Framing: Stairs are a combination of incremental vertical members, called *risers*, and incremental horizontal runs, called *treads*. The structural members that support the individual treads and risers are called *stringers*. At the framing stage of the work, stringers are installed with a temporary tread as a means of access for the workers. Finish treads and risers will be discussed later in this chapter. Stairs are shown on the architectural drawings. Refer to the various floor plans to determine the location, size of the stair, number of treads and risers, and the incremental rise and run of the stair. Riser and tread sizes are designated on the plan of the stair itself. Figure 11.11 shows a stair in plan view with the designated

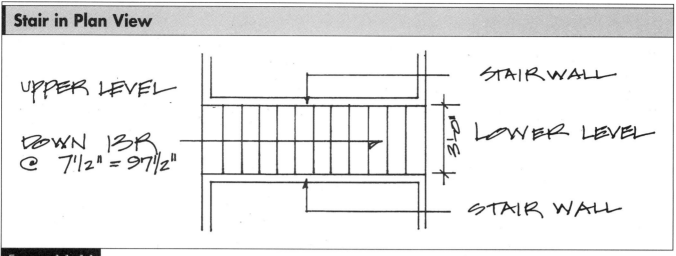

UPPER LEVEL

DOWN 13R
@ 7'|2" = 97'|2"

STAIR WALL

LOWER LEVEL

STAIR WALL

3'-0"

Figure 11.11

riser height. If the same stair is sectioned, it will be evident that the sum of the risers equals the floor-to-floor dimension of the stairs. *(See Figure 11.12.)*

To calculate the length of the stair stringers, determine the diagonal measurement between the total rise and total run of the stairs. This is the hypotenuse of the right triangle created by the rise and run of the stair. For stairs that have been designed to a specific riser and tread size, multiply the number of risers by the incremental riser height. The same calculation can be used for the treads. For example, in Figure 11.11, the following calculations would result:

> *13 risers at 7-1/2" = 97-1/2" or 8'-1-1/2" total rise*
> *12 treads at 10-1/4" = 123" or 10'-3" total run*

Once the total rise and run of the stairs have been determined, calculate the length of the stair stringers using the Pythagorean Theorem. The vertical leg, "A," of the triangle is the total rise of the stair, and the horizontal leg, "B," of the triangle is the total run of the stair. Substituting the numbers from the previous example, the following calculations result:

> *Length of stringer*
> *"C" = $\sqrt{(8.125)^2 + (10.25)^2}$ = 13.07 or approx. 13'-1"*
> *Therefore, the length of stock needed is 14'.*

The number of stringers required for a stair is based on the width of the stair. In the absence of a specific number of stringers on the drawings, refer to local building codes.

Stair stringer stock is taken off and listed by the LF, converted to a multiple of certain length members, such as 3 – 14'. Takeoff units for temporary stair treads are by the piece or by the LF. For example, from Figure 11.12:

> *The stair width is 3'. Therefore, 12 treads are required at 36" or 3' EA, or a total of 36 LF.*

Section View of Stairs

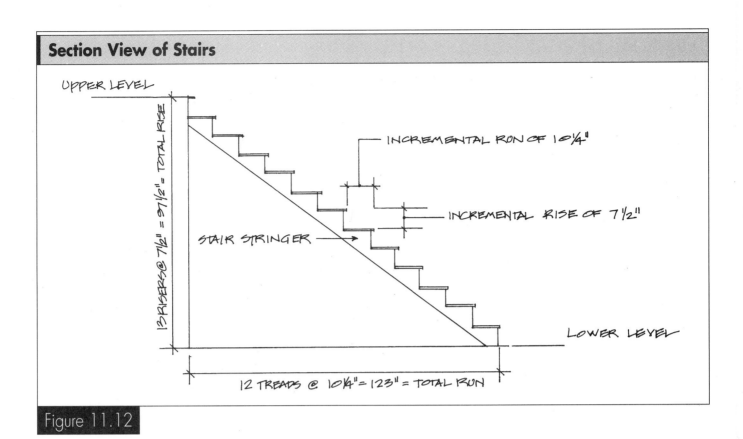

UPPER LEVEL

13 RISERS @ 7½" = 97½" = TOTAL RISE

INCREMENTAL RUN OF 10¼"

INCREMENTAL RISE OF 7½"

STAIR STRINGER

LOWER LEVEL

12 TREADS @ 10¼" = 123" = TOTAL RUN

Figure 11.12

Composite Members: As an alternative to conventional structural grade lumber for framing floor and roof systems, special members have been fabricated from structural woods and plywood, under strict engineering guidelines. These are generally referred to as *composite members* and are used in place of floor and ceiling joists, roof rafters, headers, and other load-bearing members. Composite members used in floor, ceiling, and roof framing look similar to structural steel "I" beams, with flanges constructed of structural grade lumber and webs of plywood or *oriented strand board* (OSB). Headers and similar load-bearing members that act as beams are generically referred to as *laminated veneer lumber*, or LVL, composed of veneers of structural plywood laminated together under pressure to form a structural member.

Composite members offer several advantages over conventional framing lumber. Because of their engineered design, strict manufacturing standards, and quality control, they can span greater unsupported lengths with more spacing in between. They are not subject to the shrinking and movement normally associated with conventional lumber, thereby reducing "squeaking" and deflection. Composite members are available in a variety of cross-sectional sizes and lengths up to 60'. They are handled, cut, and installed using methods similar to conventional framing. *(See the "Floor and Roof Framing Systems" section earlier in this chapter)*. Review the structural drawings, paying special attention to floor and roof framing plans, sections, and details showing load-bearing members and exterior wall openings. Specifications should be reviewed for the required product or manufacturer.

Since composite members are a manufactured product, special accessories or components are required. Familiarize yourself with the particular product specified, so that no components are left out. As a result of the increased spans allowed by composite members, some form of equipment may be required to handle or set in place individual joists or rafters. Carefully review the lengths of larger composite members, such as girders, hip and valley rafters, and ridge beams. These costs must be included in the estimate.

Composite members are taken off by the LF and listed for pricing according to depth, width, and length of the member. List the various members according to the manufacturer's model or designation number, if available, for accurate pricing. Many manufacturers have model numbers that indicate load carrying capabilities. Composite members have increased dramatically in popularity and availability in the last decade and are now regularly stocked by most lumber companies. Since composite members are used in place of conventional framing members, the methods and procedures for determining the lengths of common rafters, hip rafters, floor joists, headers, cross bridging, and beams will apply.

Trusses: Trusses are prefabricated structural components composed of a combination of wood members, usually in a triangular arrangement, to form a rigid framework. They are used as an alternative to the roof and ceiling framing in conventional "stick" framing. The architectural roof framing plans or the structural framing plans show the roof truss system. The plan view should show the span, on-center spacing, and the number of trusses required to complete the system. Details are often included to show the shape of the truss in elevation view. This view should provide the configuration of the truss members, the span and overall length of the trusses, the pitch of the top chord of the trusses, and the bracing requirements.

Installed trusses require lateral bracing, or bracing parallel to the length of the building, applied to the underside of the top chords of the trusses. Additional bracing applied to the vertical members closest to the center is called *cross bracing*, which prevents lateral movement in the same way that cross bridging does for floor frame systems. *Diagonal bracing*, or bracing of the bottom and top chords against buckling, may also be required. A combination of all three types of bracing may be needed, depending on the design. The bracing requirements and associated materials are not always shown on the contract documents, and are sometimes referred to only as "in accordance with manufacturer's specifications."

Taking off Quantities: Trusses are taken off by the individual piece and must be detailed in the lumber list separately according to length, span, pitch, and type. To determine the number of trusses, divide the length of the trussed area by the spacing. Special trusses for end conditions, such as gable-end trusses, should be identified separately. Trusses that are specifically designed for a particular project often necessitate pricing by the manufacturer. This can take time, since engineering design is required first. Be sure to submit trusses for pricing well in advance of the bid dates.

Bracing for trusses is taken off and listed by the LF. Typical sizes are 1" x 4" or 2" x 4", but review the design carefully for location, size, and type. Quantities can be reported as random length or converted to stock lengths.

Trusses are large and awkward to handle, and all but the smallest require some type of hoisting equipment to set correctly and safely. The type of equipment is based on the size of the trusses, access to the structure, and number of stories in the building, as well as project coordination. Other auxiliary types of equipment, such as spreader bars, may be required.

Exterior Trims

To enclose the framing system and make the work more visually appealing, exterior wood trim is used. Exterior wood trims are typically 1" x 3", 1" x 4", and so on, up to 1" x 12" in size. The species of wood depends on the specification or may be noted on the drawings. Refer to architectural drawings, specifically the elevations, wall, and roof sections, which should show the configuration and sizes of the exterior trims. Vertical trim pieces at the corners of the structure are called *corner boards*. Horizontal trim at the foundation line is called the *water table*, and trim at the top of the exterior wall running around the perimeter of the building is called the *frieze board*. Horizontal trim attached to the vertical portion of the rafter tail is called the *fascia board*, and the trim at the underside of the rafter tail is called the *soffit*. Exterior trim that follows the rafter line on gable-end roofs is called the *rake board*, while smaller trim applied on top of the rake board is called a *rake molding*.

Taking off Quantities: Exterior trim and moldings are taken off by the LF. Exterior trims should be listed according to size in width and thickness, species of wood, and type or function of the trim piece. Most trims are listed in the lumber list as the stock lengths. To minimize visible joints, the longest practical lengths are typically used. Review the details of the trim for any special blocking required for the installation of the trim boards. Frequently, special moldings are applied to exterior trims to enhance the design. These are taken off and separated on the lumber list by manufacturer, wood species, and model number. Pre-manufactured moldings are priced by the LF and, are again, ordered in the longest manageable lengths. Special pieces fabricated from synthetics are also extremely popular in response to their longevity, maintenance-free characteristics, and availability. Due to the wide range of items, it is essential to identify products by manufacturer, model, dimensions, and quantity so that they may be accurately priced.

Estimating Framing Labor

In general, framing and rough carpentry is a crew task. Most framing crews consist of multiple personnel who perform a specific task within the crew, such as supervision, layout, cutting, and prefabricating items like headers, gable-end trusses, stair stringers, and so forth. The most efficient framing crews are those who have worked together and are familiar with one another's work habits.

At the risk of using an overworked cliché, an experienced framing crew should work "like a finely-tuned Swiss watch." In order to be efficient, each member of the crew must meet the expected production set by the schedule. An average seven-member framing crew would likely have one working supervisor/foreman who, in addition to coordinating the crew and doing layout, also produces work. Three experienced carpenters typically lead the work, supported by two less experienced carpenters or apprentices. The apprentices will assemble and stand walls, carry stock, and provide much of the labor to perform the more mundane or repetitive tasks, such as nailing plywood to framing. Last but not least, one mill carpenter would cut stock to specific lengths for headers, joists, rafters, and various other stock. This is typically a seasoned individual capable of multi-tasking and "feeding" pieces to other members of the crew, so as not to delay the work.

With a crew of this makeup, it is clear that not all crew members are on the same pay scale. Foremen or supervisors typically earn 8%–10% more than lead or production carpenters. Organizations with collective bargaining agreements also acknowledge supervisory skills with additional compensation. Lead or experienced carpenters in the same crew receive roughly the same compensation. Apprentices' pay scales run the gamut from 50%–80% of the lead carpenter's pay, depending on experience and reliability. Apprentice programs for union employees are rigidly structured. A mill carpenter's pay may vary based on performance and reliability, with earnings at least matching the lead carpenter's rate, and frequently somewhere between that of a lead carpenter and a foreman. While this all may seem rather vague, it is meant to serve as a guideline to estimate framing labor. Larger projects with repetitive work may require larger crews with still only one supervisor. Historical data is always the best guideline for determining both correct crew size and productivity.

The labor costs for framing a structure are typically broken down into crew-days based on each level of assembly, just as with the takeoff portion of the work. Price the labor portion of the four major assemblies *after* the lumber list has been done. Once the lumber list has been completed, you should be thoroughly familiar with the intricacies of the structure, and ready to start the labor portion of the estimate. Recognizing that crew size is dependent on the individual project, you are free to make adjustments as needed. Too large a crew becomes counterproductive, with not all hands producing. Too small a crew causes the project to drag on with measurably slow progress. Study the details of the project, and "fit" crew members into various positions as if the project were actually being built, rather than estimated. For larger framing companies with more than one crew working at a time, it is not uncommon for the crew size to be reduced once the first three assemblies have been completed. A reduced crew size allows focus on miscellaneous or "pick-up" items, such as strapping, stair stringers, fire blocking, blocking details at eaves, and other odds and ends.

It is important to construct the ideal crew for each assembly. For example, the cost for an optimal crew of seven could be assembled as follows (assuming all labor burdens have been including in the sample wages):

1 Supervisor/carpenter at $27.50 per hour	=	*$27.50*
3 Lead carpenters at $25.00 per hour	=	*$75.00*
2 Apprentice carpenters at $15.00 per hour	=	*$30.00*
1 Mill carpenter at $26.00 per hour	=	*$26.00*
Total crew cost per hour		*$158.50*

Total crew cost per day = $158.50/hr x 8 hr. = $1,268 per day.

Now analyze the time in crew days that it would take to frame each of the four assemblies. Again, if we create a hypothetical example:

Floor Frame Assembly (1st floor):	*2 crew days*
Wall and Partition Assembly (1st floor):	*2 crew days*
Floor Frame Assembly (2nd floor):	*1 crew day*
Wall and Partition Assembly (2nd floor):	*2 crew days*
Roof and Ceiling Assembly:	*4 crew days*
Stair Frame and Misc. Blocking:	*1 crew day*
Total crew days to frame:	*12 crew days*
Total crew cost to frame:	*12 crew days x $1,268 = $15,216*

If the crew was reduced to two lead carpenters and one apprentice to install exterior trim, recalculate the crew cost to $65 per hour, or $520 per day. If it was determined that it would take 4 crew days to trim the exterior, the process could be repeated:

4 crew days x $520 = $2,080

Finish Carpentry

Finish carpentry can be defined as the use of finish woods (in contrast to dimensional framing lumber) in a variety of shapes, sizes, profiles, and species, applied to provide a finished appearance to windows, doors, stairs, and other features on the interior and exterior of the building. In contrast to architectural millwork (to be discussed later in this chapter), finish carpentry is the application of stock trim pieces versus custom-fabricated woodwork. For the purposes of this text, it is classified as the materials than can be purchased off-the-shelf at the local lumberyard or home improvement store. Finish carpentry also includes the use of square edge stock commonly referred to as *dressed wood*.

Study the architectural drawings for the location, size, and configuration of the interior finish carpentry. Pay special attention to the interior elevations and the wall sections that may illustrate finish carpentry work. Finish carpentry details are often used to clarify or enlarge a particular section or elevation. Interior trim materials, such as casings, baseboard, cornice, chair rails, railings, and skirt and cheek boards, are taken off and priced by the LF. Quantities can be determined by measuring the perimeter of the room, door, window, or wall. Other interior finish woodwork, such as wainscoting, is taken off and priced by the SF. Stair parts, such as newel posts, balusters, treads, and risers, are taken off by the individual piece (EA), according to size and spacing.

As in all types of carpentry work, the takeoff for finish carpentry items should be separated according to the size, species, grade, and intended application of the wood. Waste factors for materials should account for both the quality of the product and difficulty of the application. Waste factors for finish carpentry materials range from a conservative 4% to a liberal 15%.

Estimating labor costs for installing trim work is calculated by the LF, based on two factors:

- Production of each individual carpenter
- Difficulty of the application

In contrast to framing, finish carpentry tasks are measured by the production of the individual carpenter versus the production of the entire crew. Even if multiple carpenters are performing the same task, production is measured as an average of the total output. This allows you to price the labor based on reasonable expectations supported by past performance.

Assessing the level of skill required by the craftsman to perform the task, however, can be difficult. For example, casing a window without a sill or apron is easier than installing cornice moldings at the ceiling line. The pay

Terminology for Finish Carpentry

The trim around window perimeters and the sides and head of doors is called casing. *The wood trim at the base of the wall that runs along the perimeter of the room is called the* baseboard. *Horizontal trim that runs parallel to the baseboard approximately 3' above it is called the* chair rail. *A wood surface may be applied between the chair rail and baseboard, in the form of paneling, raised panels, or vertical or horizontal strips, referred to as* wainscoting. *Horizontal trim at the intersection of the walls and ceilings is called the* cornice.

To complete stairs, finish treads and risers are necessary. Additional stair parts, such as newel posts to support the railings, are also considered finish carpentry, as are the railings that run between the newel posts and provide enclosure to the stair. Balusters, or individual vertical members, are attached to the railing. Skirt boards are trim pieces at the exterior of an open stair running parallel to the stringer. A similar trim at the interior of a stair is called a cheek board.

scale would reflect the skill level of the carpenter, and a daily rate would have to be calculated. If the cost for the finish carpenter is $27 per hour, the daily cost would be $216. If the same carpenter installed an average of 200 LF of wood base in an eight-hour day, the labor cost per LF would be:

$216 per day/200 LF per day = $1.08 per LF

Architectural Millwork

Custom-fabricated trims, molding, casings, cornices, and any other woodwork component from rough stock is referred to as architectural millwork. Work is typically done in a millwork shop according to quality control guidelines using machinery and equipment that is not considered portable. Unique or one-of-a-kind designs can be prepared specifically for the project. The woodwork is fabricated from a higher grade or species of hardwood, in comparison to the softer woods that comprise the major portion of finish carpentry products. The mill shop selects the rough stock and planes, joints, shapes, sands, and even finishes the trims in the shop to fulfill the design. Quality control measures, such as maintaining temperature and humidity requirements to stabilize the work, matching grain to provide continuity, and pre-treating wood for the uniformity of color when finished, are all considered within the realm of architectural millwork.

Taking off Quantities

Takeoff procedures parallel those of finish carpentry work. However, translating the LF requirements of the finish materials into the quantity of rough stock needed is somewhat more difficult. The difficulty lies in that you must determine how much rough material should be purchased in order to mill the required quantity of dressed wood, while accounting for natural imperfections, waste, and losses due to fabrication. Hardwood, or finish woods "in the rough," in general have their own system of measurement called *board foot measure* (BFM), that is the basis for pricing. One board foot is equal to the volume of a piece of wood 1" thick by 1' square. When calculating in BFM, nominal dimensions are used.

To calculate the board footage of any piece of wood, the following formula is applied:

$$BFM = \frac{t \times w \times l \times n}{12} \text{ where:}$$

BFM = board foot measure in feet

t = nominal thickness in inches

w = nominal width in inches

l = length in feet of the individual piece

n = number of pieces

> *For example: How many board feet are in a 2" x 6" board that is 16' long?*

$$BFM = \frac{2" \times 6" \times 16' \times 1 \text{ piece}}{12} = 16 \text{ board feet (BFM)}$$

Estimating architectural millwork can be broken down into three main phases of the process. They are as follows:

- Milling (material and shop labor)
- Shaping and finishing (material and shop labor)
- Installation (minor material and field labor)

Milling is the process of converting wood from a rough state to a dressed product. It includes planing, or dressing, the horizontal or widest portion of the stock. Additionally, the stock is passed through the joiner, which squares the edges with reference to the widest portion of the material. The material can be cut to a specific size and length of square-edged stock, then run through various sanding machines to prepare it for finishing, or can proceed to additional milling steps. These additional steps may include cutting a profile on the face of the wood, as in the case of a cornice or sculptured molding. This process is called *shaping*, and, depending on the elaborateness of the profile, can require multiple passes through the shaper to achieve the finished product. Once the profile has been completed, it is then sanded and prepared for finishing.

Finishing is the process by which the square-edged stock or profiled trims are stained and/or sealed. Frequently, the work is conditioned to accept the stain more uniformly. The stain is applied and allowed to dry, then finished with a variety of sealers, such as urethanes or lacquers. Once the material has been finished, it can then be shipped to the project for installation.

Labor

All of the shop processes—milling, shaping, and finishing—are labor intensive, as a result of the care and attention required to produce the finished product. Be sure to analyze each step in the process to assign labor-hours and, ultimately, costs for the work. Installation labor costs follow the same guidelines as those for finish carpentry. They are based solely on the production of the individual carpenter. Note that installation production rates on finished architectural millwork can be significantly less than for its finish carpentry counterpart. This is often due to the level of workmanship that is expected of a custom millwork project and the added care in the joinery. Also consider on-site staging or platforms for installing the work, as well as touch-up of the finish.

Casework & Cabinetry

Casework and cabinetry, for the sake of this text, can be defined as the purchase and installation of production line wood or laminate cabinets, bookcases, vanities, countertops, and the like. These products are mass-produced and sold as individual units in an enormous variety of shapes, sizes, compositions, and price ranges. Estimating fabrication and finish costs for custom cabinetry requires special estimating experience and follows a similar procedure outlined in the architectural millwork section discussed previously.

Most cabinetry, including kitchen and bathroom, can be classified as one of three main types for estimating purposes:

- *Base units*: Installed on the floor and terminate at the underside of the countertop.
- *Wall units*: Fastened on the wall above the countertop, terminating below the ceiling line.
- *Full height units*: Continuous cabinets that start at the floor and terminate at the top of the wall cabinets.

Casework consists of modular or prefabricated units, such as bookcases, retail display cases, storage cabinetry, and shelving. All production line cabinetry and casework is prefinished at the factory. Cabinetry consists of the box or shell of the cabinet, called the *carcass*, and the door or drawers that are applied to the carcass, depending on its function. Wood cabinetry and casework is prefinished in much the same manner as architectural woodwork. It is stained and then sealed with a clear urethane or lacquer coating. An alternative method of construction and prefinishing of casework and cabinetry is to cover the exposed surfaces with a thin sheet of resin-impregnated paper, called *plastic laminate*. Plastic laminate, available in a variety of colors and textures, is also used to cover the surfaces of kitchen countertops and bathroom vanity tops.

Taking off Quantities

To begin the takeoff process, review the architectural drawings with specific attention to interior elevations, floor plans, sections, and details of the cabinetry. Many architectural drawing sets include separate plans or elevations for cabinetry and casework. These plans provide detailed dimensions that allow you to determine stock sizes offered by manufacturers.

Review the specifications for the manufacturer, model, and series of the cabinetry, casework, or plastic laminate shown, as this is a major determinant in the materials' cost. Cabinetry and casework are taken off by the individual piece (EA) and listed by the quantity of each piece. Individual pieces should be separated according to size, function, and type. A sample cabinet takeoff might look as follows:

ABC Manufacturing Co.; Premium line, "Colonial Series" in Medium Oak finish

36", 2-door sink base unit – 1 EA

42", corner base unit with Lazy Susan – 1 EA

24", 2-door base unit with 1 drawer – 3 EA

30" wide x 36" high wall cabinet with 2 doors – 3 EA

36" wide x 84" high full height pantry with 2 doors – 1 EA

3" x 36" filler pieces – 3 EA

Special accessories, such as sliding trays, baskets, sliding cutting boards, or adjustable shelving within the unit, should also be noted. This list is then submitted to the sales representative or retailer for pricing. Review the quote carefully for completeness, accuracy, and inclusions, such as freight or handling costs.

Cabinet hardware, such as knobs or pulls, should be counted and listed separately, as these are not always provided with the cabinetry and may constitute an additional cost for both materials and installation.

Plastic laminate countertops with a standard 25" depth are taken off and priced by the LF for material cost. This is typically done by measuring the countertop from the abutting wall. Alternate units of the takeoff and pricing include the SF of countertop surface. Plastic laminate sheets for field installation as backsplashes are taken off and priced by the SF. Plastic laminate for field applications should be converted to the manufacturer's available sheet size. Not all textures and colors are available in every size. Waste must also be considered, and will vary in accordance with the availability of product, size of the sheet, and application.

Also include material costs for contact cement and any special tools or equipment required for installation. Countertops can be manufactured with a backsplash, an integral vertical return that abuts the wall. Separate unattached backsplashes may also be used and may require a separate listing in the takeoff. They are taken off and priced by the LF based on the height of the backsplash. The standard height is 4", although custom heights can vary. Other types of backsplashes can include sheet plastic laminate adhered to the wall surface. The material costs are priced by the SF. Convert the required SF to the available sheet size. Sheets can vary in size from 30" x 72" to 60" x 144". Not all colors and patterns are available in every size. Check manufacturers' stock when pricing the needed materials. This same process is applicable to custom-fabricated tops that exceed standard widths and shapes.

Labor

Labor costs are calculated by the labor-hours expended to install the casework and countertops. Due to the limited amount of space in most applications, the installation crew typically consists of two individuals. Include unloading, assembling (if required), and installing the cabinets, casework, and countertops, as well as the installation of the hardware, such as pulls and knobs. While most casework comes completely assembled, this is not always the case. It is advisable to ask about the level of field assembly required. Installing casework requires first-class workmanship, yet a skilled crew can be productive. Installation in existing spaces can be more time consuming due to the shimming of cabinets and scribing of fillers needed to meet existing walls and floors that are out of level and plumb. Also note the substrate to which the cabinetry will be attached. Masonry substrates require more time than wood or drywall substrates. Detail work, such as scribing fillers that are adjacent to walls and ceilings, can also be time consuming and should be reviewed carefully.

Labor to install trims, such as valances, skirt boards, kicks, and cornices, should be estimated separately as an addition to the cost of installing the carcasses. Also include labor for adjusting draws, doors, latches, and the like. Labor for countertop installation can be expressed by the LF of countertop for standard 25"-deep tops or by the SF for irregular sized surfaces.

Conclusion

In order to accurately estimate carpentry tasks, a thorough review of the documents is required. In addition, a clear understanding of the different types of tasks and the level of workmanship required is helpful in correctly determining labor costs.

Chapter Twelve

Thermal &
Moisture Protection

CSI Division 7—Thermal & Moisture Protection covers work that protects the structure from the elements. *Waterproofing* and *dampproofing* include coatings below and above grade to prevent moisture migration. *Insulation* materials reduce the transmission of heating or cooling through the exterior envelope. *Roofing* provides a watertight surface for the uppermost surface of the structure. *Siding* provides protection from the elements on the vertical surfaces of the structure. To provide a water- and moisture-tight envelope, *caulking* and *sealants* are also used to fill in spaces and seal surface areas. Miscellaneous items such as skylights, roof accessories, gutters, and downspouts are also part of Division 7.

Most of the work in this division is detailed on the architectural drawings. Be sure to check the roof plan for the location and extent of roofing work. Also consult:

- *Details and sections of the roof system* for flashing and sheet metal details, insulation at the roof envelope, and roof accessories.
- *Wall sections and details* for information about thermal insulation, air barriers, and vapor barriers at the exterior walls.
- *Building sections* for insulation materials at the floor level.
- *Wall and foundation sections and details* for surfaces to be waterproofed, dampproofed, or insulated below grade.
- *The specifications* to help determine appropriate products and installation methods. Items such as caulking and sealants are not always detailed at every required location on the drawings. Consult the specifications to verify the location and extent of caulking.

Waterproofing

The purpose of waterproofing is to prevent water from penetrating through structures. Waterproofing is not to be confused with dampproofing, which is most often below grade at the foundation level. Check the specifications for particular waterproofing products and application methods.

Methods of Waterproofing

The *integral method* involves special additives mixed with concrete for use in poured foundations. *Membrane waterproofing* is applied to the surface of the protected area. *Metallic*, or *trowel-coat, waterproofing* involves a fine iron powder mixed with oxidizing agents applied to the surface area. The compound is typically applied with trowels or brushes, and fills the pores of the concrete or masonry. As the iron particles rust, they expand to form a barrier impervious to water. *Liquid membrane waterproofing* is an elastomeric synthetic rubber material brushed or sprayed on cold to form a seamless, flexible, waterproof film that bonds to most masonry or concrete substrates.

Integral Method

The quantity of admixture to be added to the concrete mix is based on the manufacturer's recommendations. Liquid and powder admixtures are batched at a ready-mix plant to maintain quality control. For estimating purposes, this is often reflected as an additional cost for the concrete per cubic yard. There is no additional cost for placement labor or waste factors.

Membrane Waterproofing

Membrane waterproofing consists of one or more layers of asphalt-saturated fabric or rubber membranes applied with an adhesive after the surface has been cleaned and primed, and all holes have been filled. The adhesive can be synthetic- or asphalt-based, compatible with the primer and fabric. Lapping at sides and ends is as dictated by the specifications or the manufacturer. Additional materials (required for lap) will vary from 6%-10% of the area to be waterproofed. Materials and labor are priced by the SF area or square to be waterproofed. Become familiar with the particular product and its application so that you can accurately price labor and materials. While all waterproofing products perform the same basic function, labor and material cost varies. Some products are applied cold, and others at specific temperatures.

Metallic Waterproofing

Metallic, or trowel-coat, waterproofing requires specific preparation of the concrete or masonry surface prior to application. The surface should be "roughed up" by mechanical means, then thoroughly washed to remove residual material. Holes, cracks, and penetrations should be filled and patched. This can be labor-intensive and costly. Visit the site, if possible, to verify conditions prior to estimating. Many trowel-coat or brushed products require multiple coats. The minimum recommendation is two coats, although some products require as many as five or six coats. Metallic waterproofing is priced by the SF of surface area to be covered.

Liquid Membrane Waterproofing

Liquid membrane waterproofing requires cleaning the substrate and filling cracks and holes prior to application. Since liquid membrane waterproofing is priced by the SF and varies by product, find out as much as you can about coverage of the specified product. Verify the number of coats specified, and convert this information to gallons of material. Labor is priced by the SF based on productivity per day.

Taking off Quantities

Quantities for each method should be taken off, listed, and priced separately. Use conservative production rates for preparation of older buildings. Waterproofing is a crew task frequently requiring a minimum of two workers.

The standard units for takeoff for both the membrane and metallic methods are SF, which can be converted to squares (each 100 SF). The SF area to be protected is determined by the amount of surface area below grade. Consult the grading and drainage drawing (part of the Site Plan) to determine accurate locations and heights of foundation walls. For foundation applications, multiply the foundation perimeter by the distance from the finish grade at the exterior to the bottom of the footing.

Dampproofing

Dampproofing, typically applied to the foundation area below grade to prevent moisture penetration, is not intended to resist water pressure and should not be confused with waterproofing. The most common methods are spraying, painting, or troweling a bituminous-based, tar-like coating on the protected areas, uniformly covering the areas below grade. Another method, called *parging*, involves plastering a cement-based mixture over the area to be protected. Liquid-applied dampproofing is also common and follows the same procedure for estimating liquid-applied waterproofing.

Taking off Quantities

Dampproofing is done by a crew of two workers. Daily production is their combined effort. Standard units for takeoff for all types of dampproofing are SF or squares. The procedure for determining areas is the same for waterproofing. Quantities for bituminous applications should be separated according to method of application, as labor costs will differ. Parging should be listed by the thickness and number of coats. The standard thickness is 1/2", applied in two coats. Like waterproofing, dampproofing requires surface preparation, also taken off and priced by the SF of surface area.

Special preparation tasks, such as cleaning or roughing the surface area, as noted in the specifications or required by the manufacturer, should be included separately. This work should be taken off and estimated separately. Some dampproofing products may require a primer coat prior to dampproofing, also estimated in square feet of surface area.

Insulation

In residential and light commercial construction, insulation is used to reduce heating or cooling loss through the exterior of the structure or to unheated or uncooled areas within the structure. Insulation materials are rated for *thermal resistance*, expressed as the material's *R-value*. The higher the R-value, the more effective the insulation. Higher R-values usually translate to higher costs for materials. Consult the architectural plan views, elevations, sections, and details that provide the location of the materials. In addition to the building envelope, insulation information can be found on building sections, wall sections, and details, particularly on the sections through the exterior envelope of the structure. The specification should also be reviewed for product information that may provide pricing criteria. Figure 12.1 shows a section and details illustrating the location of insulation.

Insulation is available in various forms, sizes, thicknesses, and R-values. In wood and light-gauge metal frame construction, blankets or rolls of insulation, called *batts*, are installed between the studs or joists at the exterior walls, roof, or floor of the structure. Insulation is available with an attached paper or foil facing that acts as a vapor barrier. (Vapor barriers will be discussed in detail later in this chapter.) Rigid insulation is used where a particular shape must be maintained, such as under concrete slabs, at the exterior of foundation walls, for roof decks, and over exterior sheathings under siding materials. Some common types include expanded polystyrene, often called "beadboard," and extruded polystyrenes, such as Styrofoam. More complex rigid insulations used as part of roofing systems are called *polyisocyanurates*. These are faced with asphalt-impregnated felts, generally have a high R-value per inch of thickness, and are a common component in flat roof systems.

Taking off Quantities

Batt Insulation

Batt or roll insulation is taken off and estimated by the SF, and should be listed separately according to width, R-value, and its location within the building (e.g., roof, walls, floors, etc.). For wood or metal framing, the width refers to the space between each stud or joist. For example, wood studs spaced at 16" on center require 15"-wide material. Materials should also be listed separately by vapor barrier facings, such as kraft paper and foil facing. Consult the specifications for the required R-values and specific product information.

Labor costs reflect the amount of material that can be installed per day. Labor to install insulation is based on individual (versus crew) productivity. Consider costs for staging to access high ceilings or roof caps. Large open areas should be separated from smaller "cut-up" areas in the takeoff, as this will affect productivity.

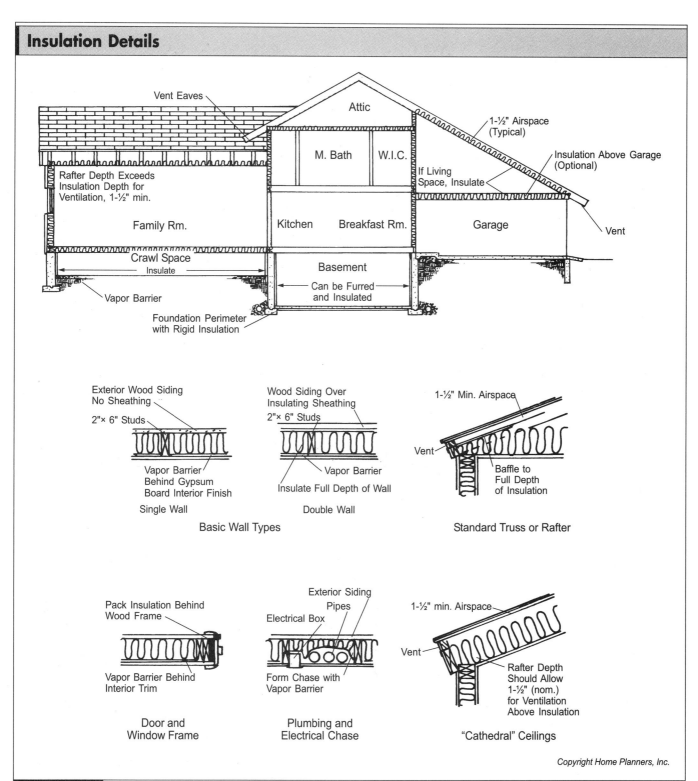

Vent Eaves

Attic

1-½" Airspace (Typical)

M. Bath

W.I.C.

Insulation Above Garage (Optional)

Rafter Depth Exceeds Insulation Depth for Ventilation, 1-½" min.

If Living Space, Insulate

Family Rm.

Kitchen

Breakfast Rm.

Garage

Vent

Crawl Space

Insulate

Basement

Can be Furred and Insulated

Vapor Barrier

Foundation Perimeter with Rigid Insulation

Exterior Wood Siding No Sheathing

2"× 6" Studs

Vapor Barrier Behind Gypsum Board Interior Finish

Single Wall

Wood Siding Over Insulating Sheathing

2"× 6" Studs

Vapor Barrier

Insulate Full Depth of Wall

Double Wall

Basic Wall Types

1-½" Min. Airspace

Vent

Baffle to Full Depth of Insulation

Standard Truss or Rafter

Pack Insulation Behind Wood Frame

Vapor Barrier Behind Interior Trim

Door and Window Frame

Exterior Siding

Pipes

Electrical Box

Form Chase with Vapor Barrier

Plumbing and Electrical Chase

1-½" min. Airspace

Vent

Rafter Depth Should Allow 1-½" (nom.) for Ventilation Above Insulation

"Cathedral" Ceilings

Figure 12.1

Rigid Insulation

Rigid insulation is taken off and priced by the SF, according to the type of material used, application, method of installation, R-value, and size. You may convert the square feet to sheets of the individual product based on the size needed. The most common size sheets are 24" x 96" and 48" x 96".

Labor for installing rigid insulation is based on individual productivity. The most common installation methods are mechanical fastening with screws and washers, using adhesives, and laying the material in place for underslab applications. Check the specifications for the method of attachment, and make sure all fasteners and adhesives have been included. Installation costs will vary significantly with the method of installation. Consider costs associated with staging or hoisting of materials. These costs should be listed separately in the estimate. Many roofing systems include insulation as part of the roofing system specifications. The cost of this insulation is part of the roof estimate, and care should be taken not to duplicate quantities in the takeoff.

Loose-Fill Insulation

Loose-fill insulation in the form of mineral wool (a form of molten rock) and expanded volcanic rock materials, such as perlite and vermiculite insulation, is often used to insulate cavity spaces, cells of concrete blocks, and attic spaces. It can be installed by spraying, pouring by hand, or machine-blowing. Calculate the volume based on R-value per inch of in-place thickness. Loose-fill insulation is sold in bags of varying volume, which can be converted to the number of bags required for accurate material pricing.

Labor costs are based on the amount placed per day. Hand-placement is considerably slower than machine-blowing, which is more productive using a two-person crew than by an individual. Be sure to include the cost of equipment for machine-blowing. Regardless of the placement method, loose-fill insulation can be a messy operation. Waste factors can vary from 10%-20% depending on the method of installation. Include time for cleanup after the work has been completed.

Vapor Barriers

Vapor barriers prevent the transmission of moisture (caused by temperature and humidity changes) between the building interior and exterior. They are typically applied at the warm side of walls, floors, roofs, and ceiling construction. The most common vapor barrier is *polyethylene sheeting*, a plastic film available in thicknesses designated by *mils* (1/1000th of an inch), the most common of which are 4- and 6-mils.

Taking off Quantities

Vapor barriers are taken off by the SF and separated by thickness. The SF area can be extended to number of rolls and the required roll size. Be sure to consider side and end laps, which will vary from 5%-10% of the overall area.

Other material costs will include attachment, such as staples and tape to seal the seams at the lap. The specifications should stipulate lap dimensions, method of attachment, and requirements for sealing the seams. Do not deduct for openings, which are usually cut out afterwards, with the residual pieces treated as waste. Review the specifications carefully for other types of vapor barriers in addition to polyethylene. Occasionally, the underslab vapor barrier material and installation may be specified in Division 3—Concrete. These products and installation tend to be of a more sophisticated nature.

Labor

Labor to install vapor barriers is priced by the SF of area to be covered using the gross area versus the net area. Underslab labor costs are typically less than wall or ceiling applications. Installation of polyethylene sheeting is most efficient as a two-person task. Staging or lifts for access to high areas should be figured separately. Labor costs should reflect reduced productivity when staging is used.

Air Infiltration Barriers

Air infiltration barriers protect against drafts caused by wind and water penetration. They are installed at the exterior of the sidewall sheathing under the siding with a barrier (such as Tyvek® Homewrap®). Since the efficiency of the building insulation is influenced by humidity and the exterior temperature, the best scenario is a drywall cavity free of moisture, which allows air to migrate through the wall. Less sophisticated products, such as asphalt felt paper, can also be used.

With recent changes to energy codes in many states, air infiltration barriers have become a focal point of design in light commercial projects. Designs often include expensive membrane products that require specific application temperatures, priming of the substrate, and integral terminations at exterior wall openings. These new products and their related details are expensive and labor-intensive to install. Review the specified product carefully and search for any installation details to help determine pricing. Additional sources of product information can be obtained from manufacturers' literature or Web sites.

Refer to the architectural wall sections for the location and the exterior elevations for the limits of air infiltration barriers. Check the specifications for the particular product and installation criteria. Deductions for window or door openings are not usually taken into account.

Taking off Quantities

Air infiltration barriers are taken off and priced by the SF, measuring the area of the exterior wall sheathing to be covered. Convert the area to roll size, according to the manufacturer or specifications. Include additional materials for side and end laps. Installation is most productive with two people. For framed-in-place walls, consider supplemental staging to access the building exterior. For wood-framed walls that are tilted up after fabrication, labor costs will be reduced. Installation labor will vary dramatically with different products. Obtain manufacturers' recommendations for installation times or productivity rates, when available.

Exterior Siding

Exterior siding is available in a variety of materials, the most common being wood, metal, and vinyl. Wood siding is manufactured in bevel, shiplap, and tongue-and-groove patterns to be installed horizontally as exterior cladding. Bevel siding, commonly referred to as *clapboard*, is installed with exposures ranging from 3" to 6". (*Exposure* refers to the portion of the clapboard that is exposed to the weather.) Clapboard is available in lengths from 3' to 20' in 1'-0" increments. Cedar is the most common wood for clapboard siding, but redwood, pine, fir, and spruce are also available. *(See Figure 12.2.)*

Clapboard Siding

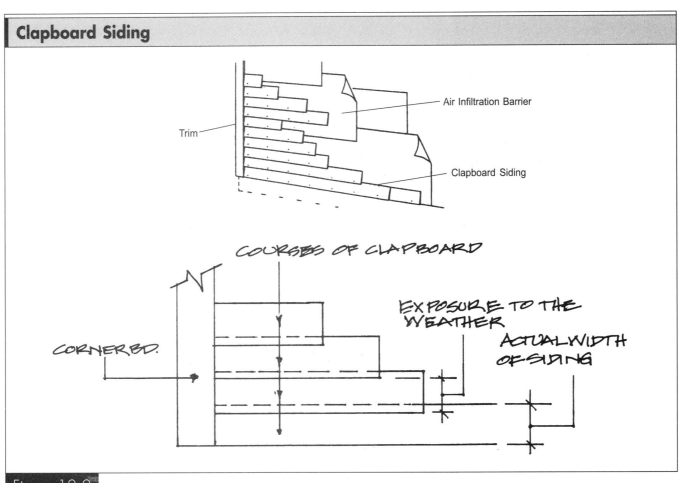

Air Infiltration Barrier

Trim

Clapboard Siding

COURSES OF CLAPBOARD

EXPOSURE TO THE WEATHER

ACTUAL WIDTH OF SIDING

CORNER BD.

Figure 12.2

Shakes and shingles are other types of wood siding that can be installed at the exterior sidewall with typical exposures from 4" to 9". Shakes and shingles range in length from 12" to 24", and can be from 2-1/2" to 14" in random widths or sawn to widths of 4", 5", or 6". Shakes and shingles are most often red or white cedar, and vary in grade and price. *(See Figure 12.3.)*

Simulated wood clapboard is also available, manufactured from metals such as thin-gauge steel and aluminum, and vinyl siding [extruded polyvinyl chloride (PVC)]. This type of siding is installed horizontally with preset exposures from 4" to 8". Most panels are approximately 8" to 9" in height and 12' to 12'-6" in length. Finishes range from smooth to wood-grain textures in a variety of colors. Pre-formed siding requires accessories for proper installation that must be included as part of the takeoff. These include inside and outside corners, "J" channels for

Wood Siding

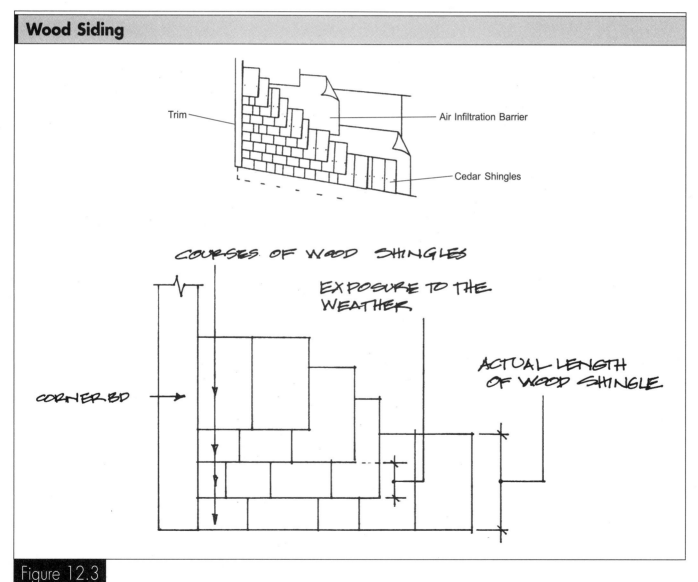

Figure 12.3

223

terminations of siding, horizontal starter strips, and finish trims, as well as soffit and fascia pieces and trims.

Other more commercial siding materials include:

- *Corrugated metal panels*: Fastened to a girt system with a screw and washer assembly.
- *Insulated metal panels*: Smooth in appearance, with a concealed fastening system.

Custom shapes and architectural details, such as interior and exterior corners, window and door head and jamb trim, and special termination trim pieces, are also available.

Taking off Quantities

Consult the architectural drawings for wall sections showing details of the siding. They will provide dimensions for calculating heights. Exterior elevations should confirm the dimensions for the takeoff. Floor plans can be used to check locations and running dimensions obtained from the elevations. Familiarity with the specified products helps to accurately price material and labor costs.

Individual siding components are taken off separately, using the following guidelines:

- *Wood siding*: by the SF or square (each 100 SF) for pricing. Note the grade and species of the siding and the exposure. Changing the exposure from 5" to 4" for white cedar shingles, for example, requires a 20% increase in material.
- *Pre-formed metal and vinyl siding*: by the SF, converted to the square for pricing.
- *Trim pieces*: by the LF. Trims for vinyl siding, such as starter strips, inside and outside corners, and "J" channels, are also taken off and priced by the LF, but may be converted to the manufacturer's individual sales length.
- *Accessories*: by the SF for soffit and fascia materials. Other accessories and trim pieces, such as "F" channels, are taken off and priced by the LF.
- *Decorative vinyl shutters*: by the individual piece or pair (PR) according to size, style, and color.

Special Considerations

Siding is installed over the exterior sheathing and air infiltration barrier. Shingles without cornerboards require mitering. Take off the vertical length of exterior corners to be mitered separately, and list them by the LF. Price this work by the LF. This type of application is considerably more labor-intensive, which must be considered for accurate pricing. When an exterior wall intersects a roof, there is generally flashing, and custom cutting of siding materials is required. This fitting, or *scribing*, should also be calculated in LF of the abutting surfaces.

Waste must be included for all types of siding and associated trims. Waste will vary with the quality of the product. Natural products, such as clapboards and wood shingles, have higher waste factors because of natural imperfections. Lower grades of natural wood and manufactured products will also have higher waste factors. Generally speaking, as the quality of the product decreases, the amount of waste increases. The final or net quantity of siding materials should include deductions for openings, such as doors or windows. Openings smaller than 4 SF are usually not deducted.

Labor

Labor priced by the square (SQ). Production rates will vary dramatically depending on the product. Wood siding is typically installed by one person. Productivity is measured on the individual output. Vinyl siding can be a crew task, depending on the size of the façade. Vertical metal siding is installed by a multiple-person crew. Production in squares per day is based on the combined effort of the crew.

Most siding applications require staging or a lift to access areas above ground. This must be included in the cost. Note that façades with many interruptions, referred to as "cut-up," dramatically reduce productivity. Include trims at windows, doors, and exterior openings. Cut-up areas with reduced production rates should be separated from wide-open areas in the takeoff as each will have different productivity rates.

Roofing

A roofing system consists of many different parts that work together to form a watertight envelope at the top of the building. The major components are:

- Insulation (applied to the roof deck)
- Waterproofing membrane or layer
- Protective surfacing
- Flashings and counterflashings
- Metal perimeter termination devices

See Figure 12.4 for the standard terminology associated with flat roofing systems.

Check the architectural drawings, specifically building sections, roof plans, and larger scale plans showing the details at the roof line. Specifications also identify the type of roofing system and information on individual components, such as the membrane, insulation, flashings, and so forth.

Figure 12.5 shows a typical roofing plan and details for a shingle roof. The importance of understanding the manufacturer's particular requirements cannot be stressed enough. Many specifications require a manufacturers' representative to be on site during installation in order to warranty the installation. This cost, in most cases, is borne by the contractor.

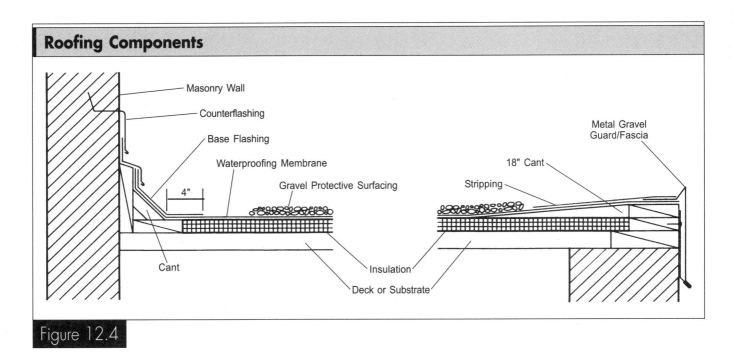

Figure 12.4

For estimating purposes, roof systems can be categorized into four basic types:

- Built-up
- Single-ply
- Metal
- Shingles/tiles

Each will be discussed in detail in the following sections. A combination of one or more roof systems in one project is not uncommon.

Built-Up Roof Systems

A built-up roof consists of felt, bitumen, and surfacing. *(See Figure 12.6.)* The felts, which are made of glass, organic, or polyester fibers, serve much the same purpose as reinforcing steel in concrete. They provide tensile reinforcement to resist pulling forces in the roofing material. Felts installed in layers allow more bitumen to be applied to the whole system. Bitumen (coal-tar pitch or asphalt) is the "glue" that holds the felts together and serves as waterproofing.

Surfacing materials are smooth gravel or slag, mineral granules, or a mineral-coated cap sheet that protect the membrane from mechanical damage. Gravel, slag, and mineral granules may be embedded into the still-fluid flood coat. Built-up roof systems can contain two to four plies, or layers of felt with asphalt bitumen or coal-tar pitch. All systems may be applied to rigid deck insulation or directly to the structural roof deck. Flashings, counterflashings, metal gravel stops, and treated wood cants are also needed to complete the system.

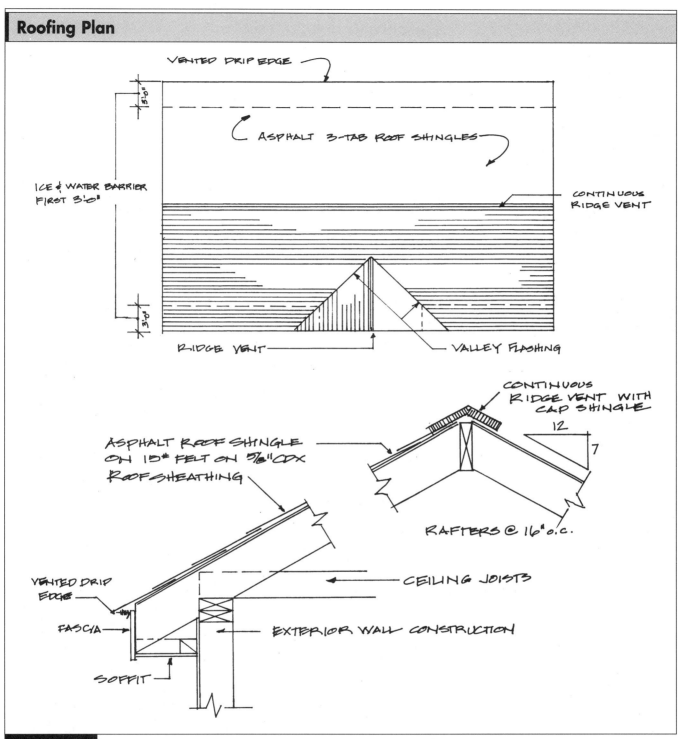

VENTED DRIP EDGE

ASPHALT 3-TAB ROOF SHINGLES

ICE & WATER BARRIER FIRST 3'-0"

CONTINUOUS RIDGE VENT

RIDGE VENT

VALLEY FLASHING

CONTINUOUS RIDGE VENT WITH CAP SHINGLE

12
7

ASPHALT ROOF SHINGLE ON 15# FELT ON 5/8" CDX ROOF SHEATHING

RAFTERS @ 16" O.C.

CEILING JOISTS

VENTED DRIP EDGE

FASCIA

EXTERIOR WALL CONSTRUCTION

SOFFIT

Figure 12.5

227

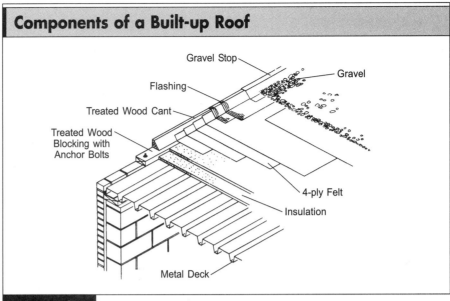

Components of a Built-up Roof

Gravel Stop

Gravel

Flashing

Treated Wood Cant

Treated Wood Blocking with Anchor Bolts

4-ply Felt

Insulation

Metal Deck

Figure 12.6

Taking off Quantities

Take off individual components in the built-up roof system separately, using the following guidelines:

- *Roof insulation and felts*: by the SF and extended to the SQ (100 SF).
- *Bitumen*: based on the coverage required in the specifications. (Can be listed by weight based on the weight per SF specified by the manufacturer.)
- *Mineral surfacing*: by the weight specified per SF and converted to total weight in pounds or tons.
- *Flashings, counterflashings, gravel stops, and treated wood or fiber cants*: taken off and listed by the LF.

Separate all items according to type of metal, gauge of metal, and overall size of the flashings. Price materials separately from labor. Individually priced materials can be combined to develop a price for materials per square (SQ).

Include additional items, such as collars, sleeves, or penetrations through the roof, in the takeoff. Count and list them individually as "EA," according to the size of each item and its use. Items supplied and installed by other trades, such as rooftop curbs for HVAC units or smoke and access hatches flashed into the roof system, may also need to be included. Roof accessories have added material and labor costs to install.

Labor

With the exception of minor repairs, built-up roofing is always a crew task. Productivity is based on the work of all members of the crew, typically calculated as squares per day. Roof demolition should be taken off and priced separately, as it is labor-intensive. Costs for disposing of old roofing or debris from new work should be calculated separately.

Built-up roof work is most often performed by large crews. Detail work, such as flashing in vents through the roof and curbs, is frequently only "temped-in" until a pick-up crew can complete some of the more time-consuming details. Roof metal installation rates are based on linear foot of production per day. (This will be discussed in greater detail later in this chapter.)

Weather conditions are important as extremes can reduce productivity and quality. Anticipated production rates should be scaled back during seasons when these conditions are likely. See Figure 12.7 for labor productivity guidelines.

Single-Ply Roofing Systems

Single-ply, or elastomeric, roofing can be broken down into three categories:

- Thermosetting
- Thermoplastic
- Composites

All three use a PVC or rubber sheet material, or *membrane*, applied over the top of the insulation or approved substrate to serve as a waterproofing surface.

Single-ply roofing can be applied loose-laid and ballasted, partially adhered, and fully adhered. Loose-laid systems involve fusing, welding, or gluing the side and end laps of the membrane to form a continuous non-adhered sheet, held in place by a layer of gravel. Partially-adhered single-ply membrane is attached (with strips or plate fasteners) to the roof substrate. Because the system allows movement, ballast is not required. Fully-adhered systems are uniform and continuously adhered to the manufacturer-approved base. Figure 12.8 shows a single-ply roofing system and estimating guidelines for labor.

Taking off Quantities

The takeoff procedure and units are the same for single-ply roofing as for built-up systems. Square feet can be extended to the square (100 SF). The components to be priced are:

- Insulation
- Membrane
- Hardboard base (if applicable)
- Metal fascia, or *gravel stop*

Take off and price metal fascias, flashings, counterflashings, and termination strips by the LF. Include treated wood nailers (for both built-up and single-ply systems) for support at the edge of the rigid insulation and for nailing the fascia or gravel stop.

The roofer may furnish and install wood blocking at the roof perimeter or under curbs, or it can be included under MasterFormat Section 06100—Rough Carpentry. Review the specifications to determine what section the wood blocking work is included in.

Installation Time in Labor-Hours for Built-Up Roofing

Description	Labor-Hours	Unit
Built-up Roofing		
Asphalt Flood Coat with Gravel or Slag		
Fiberglass Base Sheet		
3 Plies Felt Mopped	2.545	Sq.
On Nailable Decks	2.667	Sq.
4 Plies Felt Mopped	2.800	Sq.
On Nailable Decks	2.947	Sq.
Coated Glass Fiber Base Sheet		
3 Plies Felt Mopped	2.800	Sq.
On Nailable Decks	2.947	Sq.
Organic Base Sheet and 3 Plies Felt	2.545	Sq.
On Nailable Decks	2.667	Sq.
Coal Tar Pitch with Gravel or Slag		
Coated Glass Fiber Base Sheet and		
2 Plies Glass Fiber Felt	2.947	Sq.
On Nailable Decks	3.111	Sq.
Asphalt Mineral Surface Roll Roofing	2.074	Sq.
Walkway		
Asphalt Impregnated	.020	S.F.
Patio Blocks 2" Thick	.070	S.F.
Expansion Joints Covers	.048	L.F.

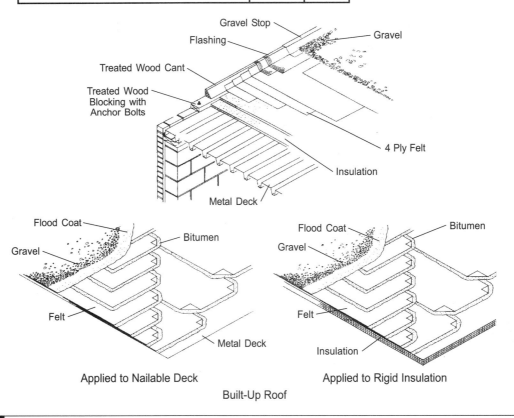

Built-Up Roof

Applied to Nailable Deck   Applied to Rigid Insulation

Figure 12.7

Installation Time in Labor-Hours for Single-Ply Roofing

Description	Labor-Hours	Unit
Single Ply Membrane, General		
Loose-Laid and Ballasted	.784	Sq.
Mechanically Fastened	1.143	Sq.
Fully Adhered, All Types	1.538	Sq.
Modified Bitumen, Cap Sheet		
Fully Adhered Torch Welding	.019	S.F.
Asphalt Mopped	.028	S.F.
Cured Neoprene for Flashing	.028	S.F.

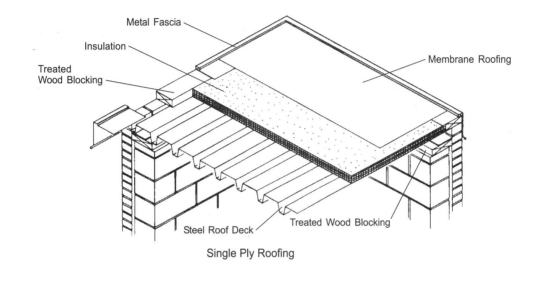

Single Ply Roofing

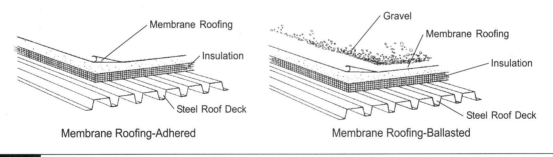

Membrane Roofing-Adhered

Membrane Roofing-Ballasted

Figure 12.8

As with all roofing work, it is important to consider how the materials will be hoisted to the roof. This can be done by a roof crane, a hired crane, or a variety of other methods. Hoisting is not always identified in the specifications as a direct responsibility of the roofer. Often, the responsibility for hoisting on a commercial project is included in Division 1—General Requirements, under Section 01500—Temporary Facilities. Address the issue with the architect or engineer if the documents do not specify hoisting.

Metal Roof Systems

For estimating purposes, metal roofing systems can be divided into two groups: pre-formed and formed metal. *Pre-formed metal roofs*, available in long lengths of varying widths and shapes, are constructed from aluminum, steel, or composite materials, such as fiberglass. Aluminum roofs can be left natural or pre-painted. Steel roofs are usually galvanized or painted. Most manufacturers require the product to be factory-painted in order to warranty its finish. Pre-formed metal roofing is installed on sloped roofs according to the manufacturer's recommendation for minimum pitch. Lapped ends may be sealed with a pre-formed sealant to match the deck configuration. Pre-formed roofing is a cost-effective, durable alternative to other types of roofing for large buildings with shallow pitch or flat roof surfaces.

Formed metal roofing, typically selected for aesthetic reasons, is installed on sloped roofs that have been covered with a base material, such as plywood or concrete. Typical base materials include copper, lead, and zinc alloy. Flat sheets are joined by tool-formed batten-seam, flat-seam, and standing-seam joints. Formed metal roofing is typically more expensive—both material and installation—than pre-formed roofing.

Taking off Quantities

Takeoff is done by the SF, and can be listed by the individual piece. Specific components are as follows:

- *Pre-formed sealant material*: by the LF. Determine quantities by calculating the SF of roof surface to be covered with the manufacturer's recommended allowances for side and end laps.
- *Formed metal roofing*: by SF and converted to the SQ (each 100 SF).
- *Trim pieces* (battens for the seams and finish end pieces): by the LF or individual piece.

Formed metal roofing is most often used in custom applications and one-of-a-kind designs. It requires field measurement and shop drawings for fabrication. Be sure to include these costs in the estimate.

Takeoff for both types of metal roofing should be separated according to type of metal, manufacturer, finish, and particular application. Check the specifications for sheet material species, weight, and other characteristics, including color or special coatings on the exposed face of the metal, to help ensure accurate pricing. Include any hoisting and staging requirements.

Unlike most roofing work, formed metal roofing has both fabrication labor and field labor. Be sure to include shop time to cut, bend, and fabricate the pieces—work typically performed by sheet metal workers. Separate field installation and shop fabrication costs for accurate pricing.

Roof Shingles and Tiles

Shingles and tiles are popular for sloped roofs with a pitch of 3" or more per foot. Both are *watershed* materials, designed to direct water away from the building by means of the slope, or *pitch*, of the roof. Shingles are installed in layers with staggered joints over roofing felt underlayment. Nails or fasteners are concealed by the course above. Shingle materials include wood, asphalt, fiberglass, metal, and masonry tiles. Asphalt and fiberglass shingles are available in a variety of weights and styles; three-tab is the most common. The components and quantities of the roof system can be derived from the architectural roof plans, building sections, and roof details. *(See Figure 12.9.)*

Wood shingles may be either shingle or shake grade, and are most commonly cedar. Metal shingles are either aluminum or steel and are generally pre-finished. Slate and clay tiles are available in a variety of shapes, sizes, colors, weights, and textures. Since these are heavier materials, they require specialized installation techniques and a stronger structural roof system. Product costs vary widely by grade of material and manufacturer.

Shingled Roof

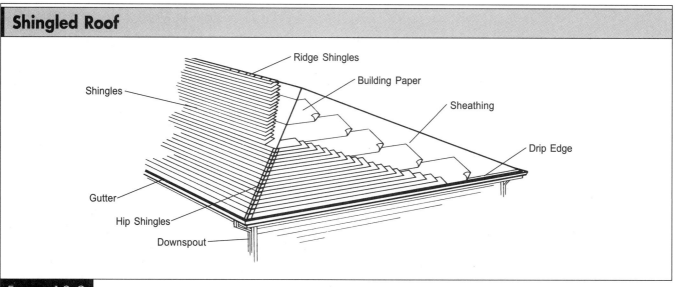

Figure 12.9

Shingle and tile roof systems require additional components to complete the assembly. Special metal trim pieces called *drip edge* protect the edge of the roof deck and allow water to drip off the roof edge. These are made of a corrosion-resistant metal, typically aluminum. (Drip edge may be omitted with wood shingles or slates when the edge of the shingle or slate projects beyond the roof edge.) Metal flashings may be specified for the valleys of shingled and tiled roofs. Valley flashing can be lead-coated copper, copper, or zinc alloy. Ridge vents ventilate the attic space, allowing air to transfer from the attic or rafter space to the outside, and thereby prevent moisture build-up along the underside of the roof sheathing. Ridge-venting materials are available in a variety of styles and compositions.

Shingle and tile roof systems require special shingles, called *cap shingles*, at the ridge or hip of the roof. A cap shingle may be a regular three-tab shingle modified for use as a cap, as in the case of asphalt or fiberglass shingles, or a special pre-fabricated cap, as with some clay or metal tile designs.

Special membrane material installed under shingles at the eaves, rakes, and hips and valleys of the shingle or tile roof is called an *ice/water barrier*. Most products are a bitumen-based, self-adhering membrane for use in cold climates where ice and water may dam along the eaves and valleys and cause water to back up under the roof shingles.

Taking off Quantities

Shingle and tile roofing are taken off by the SF and extended to the square (100 SF). In the case of asphalt or fiberglass shingles, squares can be converted to individual bundles for pricing. Additional takeoff guidelines are as follows:

- *Underlayment felts*: by the SF, converted to rolls.
- *Wood shingles and slate tiles*: by the SF, converted to cartons or bundles.
- *Special hip and ridge tiles or cap shingles*: by the LF. Can be converted to the individual piece (as in the case of metal or clay tiles).
- *Drip edge (vented or non-vented)*: by the LF. Can be converted to the individual piece (most commonly 10'-0" long) and listed as EA.
- *Ridge vent*: by the LF. Can be converted to the individual piece (EA) or roll.
- *Ice/water barriers*: by the SF. Can be extended to the manufacturer's size roll.

Be sure to include hand and pneumatic nails in the estimate. Hand nails are priced by the pound (lb.), and pneumatic nails by the box. Review the materials specified for manufacturer, weights per square, model numbers, and any other information that will help to accurately price them.

Labor

Unit prices for labor to install shingle and tile roofs are based on crew productivity. Crews on shingle roofing projects tend to be smaller than on built-up and single-ply roofs, as the shingle installation is repetitive, and most roofers on the crew perform the same tasks. Also, shingle roofs tend to be smaller in size than flat roofs. Figure 12.10 shows labor-hour guidelines for shingle or tile roofs.

Adjust for steep-pitched roofs, weather extremes, or "cut-up" roofs (roofs with many penetrations, such as dormers, skylights, or pipes).

Flashing and Sheet Metal Work

Flashing refers to pieces of sheet metal or impervious flexible membrane material used to seal and protect joints in a building and prevent leaks. It can be custom-fabricated, as in the case of rigid through-wall flashings, or purchased off-the-shelf, as with roll aluminum and step flashing materials. Sheet metal work involves pre- or custom-formed metal fabrications, such as parapet caps, gravel stops, and cleat strips, which make the roofing system weathertight. Concealed flashing is made of sheet metal or membrane material. Sheet metal fabrications and exposed flashings can be fabricated from a variety of materials, such as copper, lead-coated copper, aluminum, galvanized steel, lead, or zinc alloy. Flashing can be formed on site, or pre-formed in the shop prior to installation.

Flashing is also used for window/door heads and masonry applications. Flashing details are often shown in the plan, sections, and roof details. Plan view and elevation drawings show their locations. Consult the specifications for material characteristics such as metal gauge, color, or special coatings that may affect the price.

Taking off Quantities

Stock (off-the-shelf) flashing is taken off by the LF for rigid or roll form materials. Convert the LF into pieces or rolls for pricing. Pre-manufactured flashing for pipe and conduit penetrations is taken off and priced by the piece. For accurate quantities, cross-reference the mechanical and electrical drawings for penetrations for piping and conduits. Custom-fabricated sheet metal work often requires shop drawings based on dimensions verified in the field. To determine the quantity of sheet metal required to fabricate the various pieces, calculate the number of sheets. Be sure to include waste. Sheet metal is available in a variety of different sized sheets, depending on the manufacturer and product.

Labor

Labor for flashing and sheet metal work must be evaluated separately. Off-the-shelf materials have an installation labor component only. The materials are purchased and installed as part of the normal roofing process, with only minor adjustments to their stock shapes. Most of this work is priced by the LF. Custom-fabricated sheet metal work, such as parapet caps, gravel stops, and edge cleats, require both shop fabrication

Installation Time in Labor-Hours for Shingle and Tile Roofing

Description	Labor-Hours	Unit
Shingles, Manual Nailed		
Aluminum	1.600	Sq.
Ridge Cap or Valley, Manual Nailed	.047	L.F.
Fiber Cement		
500 lb. per Sq.	3.636	Sq.
Starters	2.667	C.L.F.
Hip and Ridge	8.000	C.L.F.
Asphalt Standard Strip		
Class A 210 to 235 lb. per Sq.	1.455	Sq.
Class C 235 to 240 lb. per Sq.	1.600	Sq.
Standard Laminated		
Class A 240 to 260 lb. per Sq.	1.778	Sq.
Class C 260 to 300 lb. per Sq.	2.000	Sq.
Premium Laminated		
Class A 260 to 300 lb. per Sq.	2.286	Sq.
Class C 300 to 385 lb. per Sq.	2.667	Sq.
Hip and Ridge Shingles	.024	L.F.
Slate Including Felt Underlay	4.571	Sq.
Steel	3.636	Sq.
Wood		
5" Exposure, 16" long	3.200	Sq.
5-1/2" Exposure, 18" long	2.909	Sq.
Panelized 8' Strips 7" Exposure	2.667	Sq.
Ridge	.023	L.F.
Shingles, Pneumatic Nailed		
Asphalt Standard Strip		
Class A 210 to 235 lb. per Sq.	1.143	Sq.
Class C 235 to 240 lb. per Sq.	1.280	Sq.
Standard Laminated		
Class A 240 to 260 lb. per Sq.	1.422	Sq.
Class C 260 to 300 lb. per Sq.	1.600	Sq.
Premium Laminated		
Class A 260 to 300 lb. per Sq.	1.831	Sq.
Class C 300 to 385 lb. per Sq.	2.133	Sq.
Hip and Ridge Shingles	.019	L.F.
Wood		
5" Exposure	2.462	Sq.
5-1/2" Exposure	2.241	Sq.
Panelized 8' Strips 7" Exposure	2.000	Sq.
Tiles		
Aluminum		
Mission	3.200	Sq.
Spanish	2.667	Sq.
Clay,		
Americana, 158 Pc/Sq.	4.848	Sq.
Spanish, 171 Pc/Sq.	4.444	Sq.
Mission, 192 Pc/Sq.	6.957	Sq.
French, 133 Pc/Sq.	5.926	Sq.
Norman, 317 Pc/Sq.	8.000	Sq.
Williamsburg, 158 Pc/Sq.	5.926	Sq.
Concrete	5.926	Sq.

Figure 12.10

and field installation time. As discussed previously with formed metal roofing, separate these different labor costs for accurate pricing. Figure 12.11 provides guidelines for installation labor.

Gutters and Downspouts

Gutters and downspouts are metal or wood fabrications used to channel precipitation from the roof surface to the ground. Most metal gutters and downspouts are pre-fabricated and available in a variety of colors and sizes. Custom-fabricated metal gutters and downspouts follow the installation procedure identified above in sheet metal work. Wood gutters are shaped from a variety of wood species that are decay-resistant.

Taking off Quantities

Gutters and downspout materials are taken off and priced by the LF, separated according to composition, size, gauge of metal, and application, as well as special colors or finishes. The method of gutter installation should be noted on the takeoff for accurate pricing. Simple installations may include fastening directly to the fascia with nails or screws, as in the case of wood gutters. Other installations require more complicated hanging/fastening systems. Check the specifications for materials, accessories, and method of installation required. Exterior elevation drawings and sections at the eave of the roof provide essential information for accurate takeoff and pricing. Figure 12.12 illustrates gutters and downspouts with normal labor-hours.

Roof Accessories

Roof accessories include skylights, roof hatches, HVAC curbs, and smoke vents. Most are taken off and priced by the individual piece (EA) according to size, function, and any special characteristics. Manufacturer, make, model, type of glazing (for skylights), and size are critical characteristics for accurate pricing.

Labor to install roof accessories is priced by the individual piece or per SF of surface area the feature occupies, as in the case of large skylights. Other cost considerations include assembly labor, if required. Many skyroofs (large, linear or vaulted series of connected skylights) require some assembly prior to installation. Consideration should also be given to hoisting the materials to the roof. Most roof accessories are bulky and heavy, precluding hand-loading. Be sure to examine the specification for hoisting responsibility. Figure 12.13 shows roof accessories and labor-hour guidelines.

Caulking and Sealants

Caulking and sealants provide a water, vapor, and air barrier between joints or gaps of adjacent, but dissimilar, materials. A classic example is the joint between a steel door frame and a masonry wall opening. Caulking and sealants are manufactured for a full range of applications, such as interior or exterior use, expansion and contraction, service

Installation Time in Labor-Hours for Flashing, Expansion Joints, and Gravel Stops

Description	Labor-Hours	Unit
Flashing Aluminum Mill Finish	.055	S.F.
Fabric-Backed or Mastic-Coated, 2 Sides	.024	S.F.
Copper Sheets		
16 oz.	.070	S.F.
20 oz.	.073	S.F.
24 oz.	.076	S.F.
32 oz.	.080	S.F.
Paperbacked, Fabric-Backed, or		
Mastic-Backed, 2 Sides	.024	S.F.
Lead-Coated Copper, Paperbacked,		
Fabric-Backed, or Mastic-Backed	.024	S.F.
Lead 2.5 lbs. per S.F.	.059	S.F.
Polyvinyl Chloride or Butyl Rubber	.028	S.F.
Copper-Clad Stainless Steel Sheets Under 500 lbs.		
.015" Thick	.070	S.F.
.018" Thick	.080	S.F.
Stainless Steel Sheets or		
Terne Coated Stainless Steel	.052	S.F.
Paberbacked 2 Sides	.024	S.F.
Zinc and Copper Alloy, .020" Thick	.052	S.F.
Expansion Joint, Butyl or Neoprene Center with		
Metal Flanges	.048	L.F.
Neoprene, Double-Seal Type with		
Thick Center, 4-1/2" Wide	.064	L.F.
Polyethylene Bellows with		
Galvanized Flanges	.080	L.F.
Roof Expansion Joint with		
Extruded Aluminum Cover, 2"	.070	L.F.
Roof Expansion Joint, Plastic Curbs,		
Foam Center	.080	L.F.
Transitions, Regular, Minimum	.800	Ea.
Maximum	2.000	Ea.
Large, Minimum	.889	Ea.
Maximum	2.667	Ea.
Roof to Wall Expansion Joint with Extruded		
Aluminum Cover	.070	L.F.
Wall Expansion Joint, Closed Cell Foam on		
PVC Cover, 9" Wide	.064	L.F.
12" Wide	.070	L.F.
Gravel Stops		
4" Face Height	.055	L.F.
6" Face Height	.059	L.F.
8" Face Height	.064	L.F.
12" Face Height	.080	L.F.

Figure 12.11

Installation Time in Labor-Hours for Gutters and Downspouts

Description	Labor-Hours	Unit
Gutters		
Aluminum	.067	L.F.
Copper Stock Units		
4" Wide	.067	L.F.
6" Wide	.070	L.F.
Steel Galvanized or Stainless	.067	L.F.
Vinyl	.073	L.F.
Wood	.080	L.F.
Downspouts		
Aluminum		
2" x 3"	.042	L.F.
3" Diameter	.042	L.F.
4" Diameter	.057	L.F.
Copper		
2" or 3" Diameter	.042	L.F.
4" Diameter	.055	L.F.
5" Diameter	.062	L.F.
2" x 3"	.042	L.F.
3" x 4"	.055	L.F.
Steel Galvanized		
2" or 3" Diameter	.042	L.F.
4" Diameter	.055	L.F.
5" Diameter	.062	L.F.
6" Diameter	.076	L.F.
2" x 3"	.042	L.F.
3" x 4"	.055	L.F.
Epoxy Painted		
2" x 3"	.042	L.F.
3" x 4"	.055	L.F.
Steel Pipe, Black, Extra Heavy		
4" Diameter	.400	L.F.
6" Diameter	.444	L.F.
Stainless Steel		
2" x 3" or 3" Diameter	.042	L.F.
3" x 4" or 4" Diameter	.055	L.F.
4" x 5" or 5" Diameter	.059	L.F.
Vinyl		
2" x 3"	.038	L.F.
2-1/2" Diameter	.036	L.F.

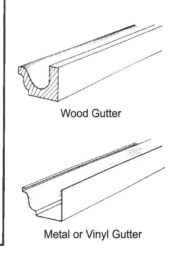

Wood Gutter

Metal or Vinyl Gutter

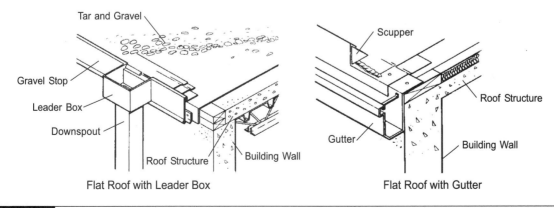

Flat Roof with Leader Box

Flat Roof with Gutter

Figure 12.12

Description	Labor-Hours	Unit
Roof Hatches with Curb		
2'-6" x 3'-0"	3.200	Ea.
2'-6" x 4'-6"	3.556	Ea.
2'-6" x 8'-0"	4.848	Ea.
Smoke Vents		
4'-0" x 4'-0"	2.462	Ea.
4'-0" x 8'-0"	4.000	Ea.
Plastic Roof Domes Flush or Curb Mounted		
Under 10 S.F.		
Single	.200	S.F.
Double	.246	S.F.
10 S.F. to 20 S.F.		
Single	.081	S.F.
Double	.102	S.F.
20 S.F. to 30 S.F.		
Single	.069	S.F.
Double	.081	S.F.
30 S.F. to 65 S.F.		
Single	.052	S.F.
Double	.069	S.F.
Ventiliation, Insulated Plexiglass Dome		
Curb Mounted		
30" x 32"	2.667	Ea.
36" x 52"	3.200	Ea.
Skyroofs		
Translucent Panels 2-3/4" Thick	.081	S.F. Horiz.
Continuous Vaulted to 8' Wide		
Single Glazed	.200	S.F. Horiz.
Double Glazed	.221	S.F. Horiz.
To 20' Wide Single Glazed	.183	S.F. Horiz.
Over 20' Wide Single Glazed	.160	S.F. Horiz.
Pyramid Type to 30' Clear Opening	.194	S.F. Horiz.
Grid Type 4' x 10' Modules	.200	S.F. Horiz.
Ridge Units Continuous to 8' Wide		
Double	.246	S.F. Horiz.
Single	.160	S.F. Horiz.

Roof Hatch

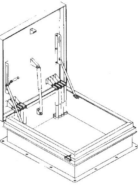

Smoke Vent

Circular Dome Skylight

Domed Skylight

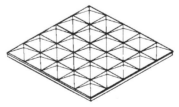

Pyramid Skylights in Grid Form

Skyroofs

Figure 12.13

temperature range, and compatibility with the material to be sealed. Sealants can be used straight from the tube, or may be multi-components that require mixing before application.

Joint sealants at exterior applications are normally applied over a backup material that controls the depth of the joint. They serve as bond breaks to allow free movement of the joint and prevent water penetration. The backup material, called *backer rod*, is available in a variety of compositions, such as butyl, neoprene, polyethylene, or rubber.

Check the architectural drawings (elevations, wall sections, and details) that show window and exterior door installations. Consult details illustrating the connection of dissimilar materials for caulking and sealant work.

Taking off Quantities

Take off interior caulking separately from exterior joint sealants. Check the specifications for the location and type of caulking and sealants needed, and note their respective application within the takeoff. Caulking and joint sealants are taken off and priced by the LF. Separate them according to the size of the bead, interior or exterior application, and type of material. Backup materials are taken off and listed by the LF according to size, composition, and application.

Many types of caulking and sealants are available, ranging from inexpensive latex caulking used by painters, to expensive two-part elastomeric compounds used where flexibility and longevity are critical. Determining the quantity in gallons, quarts, or tubes often involves the manufacturer's specifications for LF per gallon. Figure 12.14 shows LF quantities per gallon of material based on different joint sizes.

Consider whether staging or power lifts are required to access windows or other features above ground level. Mobile lifts or boom lifts are most often employed for this work, as they have the required reach and mobility for accessing the work.

Estimating Guide for Caulking

Lineal Feet per Full Gallon (231 cu. in.)		Width of Joint						
		1/4"	3/8"	1/2"	5/8"	3/4"	7/8"	1"
Depth of Joint	1/4"	308	205	154	123	102	88	—
	3/8"	205	136	102	82	68	58	—
	1/2"	154	102	77	61	51	44	38
	3/4"	102	68	51	43	34	30	26

Example: One full gallon is sufficient material to fill a joint 1/2" wide and 3/8" deep and 102' long.

Cartridges: When figuring feet per cartridge for a particular joint size divide lineal feet shown above by 12.

Figure 12.14

Stucco

Stucco, a cement plaster used to cover exterior wall and ceiling surfaces, is usually applied to a wood, metal lath, concrete, or masonry base. It is composed of Portland cement, lime, and sand, with water as the mixing agent, and is typically applied in a three-coat system. The *scratch coat* is the first, applied directly to the substrate. The *brown coat* is next, applied over the scratch coat that builds up the surface. The final coat is the *finish coat*. Stucco can be applied directly to the substrate, as in the case of masonry or concrete walls, or over a metal lath installed on a wood surface. Stucco provides a durable, weather-resistant surface that is virtually maintenance-free and impervious to moisture. The finish coat can be troweled in a variety of textures and then painted.

The completed stucco system requires special trim pieces to achieve square and plumb corners at the intersection of wall and ceiling surfaces. Other trims are also needed at the intersection of stucco with other materials, similar to J-bead. Expansion and control joints, used to control cracking, are also required.

Architectural drawings should be reviewed for the location of stucco surfaces, with special attention to exterior elevations, exterior reflected ceiling plans, and exterior sections and details. Consult the specifications for the particular mixing proportions of water, Portland cement, sand, and lime to achieve the required strength, as well as the texture and thickness of the finish coat. Specifications also note the type and location of the various trim pieces, such as outside corners, expansion joints, and metal lath (if applicable).

Taking off Quantities

Stucco is taken off by the SF by measuring the length and width of the surfaces to be covered. The SF can then be converted to square yards (SY) for pricing. Quantities of metal lath can be determined from the SF area and converted to standard-sized sheets of the particular product. Allowances for overlap at the sides and ends of the individual sheets should also be included in the takeoff, based on the manufacturer's recommendations or the specifications. Trims, such as inside and outside corner beads, control joints, and J-beads, are taken off and priced by the LF and can be converted to the manufacturer's standard unit length (typically 8' or 10'). Convert SY of stucco to the individual components of Portland cement, sand, and lime by weight, and metal lath based on the proportions in the specifications for more accurate material pricing.

Labor for Stucco Applications

The stucco process is a crew task and should be priced based on the productivity of the entire crew. The principal trade is plastering. However, the crew may also include plasterer tenders to mix the stucco; stock materials; erect, dismantle, and relocating staging; and cleanup. Assemble and price the proper crew based on the individual project. Productivity will be reduced if an elevation has a lot of openings or is generally "cut-up," in comparison to wide open areas that several plasterers can work on simultaneously. Small walls between windows and entry soffits are often substantially more costly per SY than open areas, due to the amount of prep and cleanup required.

Because stucco uses water as a mixing agent, it is subject to freezing and may require temporary enclosures and heating during its curing period. *(See "Temporary Facilities & Controls" in Chapter 6—Division 1.)* Temporary staging or scaffolding may also be necessary to access the work.

Exterior Insulation and Finish System

An *exterior insulation and finish system* (EIFS), sometimes referred to as synthetic stucco, is an exterior siding material with the durability of stucco, plus thermal insulation value. It is composed of expanded polystyrene insulation board and a cementitious base coat applied in varying thicknesses, with a synthetic woven mesh that acts as reinforcement. The top or finish coat is an acrylic stucco, available in a variety of textures and colors. The insulation is adhered or mechanically fastened to the sidewall substrate of plywood, masonry, or gypsum sheathing. The base coat is troweled onto the insulation, similar to a conventional stucco system, and the mesh reinforcing is embedded in the base coat. The finish coat is applied after the base coat has had sufficient time to dry.

Refer to the architectural drawings for plan view and elevations to find the dimensions required for determining quantities. Corresponding sections and details of the system will provide additional information for an accurate estimate. Special conditions, such as returns at windows and doors or the termination at dissimilar materials, also affect material and labor pricing. Check the reflected ceiling plan, which should show exterior soffits over entries or windows, as the product is often used as an exterior ceiling finish. Control and expansion joints are required per the manufacturer's recommendations to control expansion and contraction.

Expansion and control joints are typically shown on the exterior elevations. In the absence of expansion or control details on the drawings, consult the specifications for the recommended spacing. The specs should indicate the individual product as well as the manufacturer's standard application and installation procedures. EIFS includes a wide variety of products that are similar in composition, design, and performance. It is recommended that you become familiar with the specified product and its system prior to starting the takeoff or estimating the EIFS work.

Taking off Quantities

EIFS is taken off by the SF of surface area to be covered. Separating out the individual components, such as polystyrene insulation, base coat, reinforcing mesh, and finish coat, may be required for more accurate pricing, depending on the individual product, but as a rule, this is not required. All components are taken off by the SF, and their individual material costs are added together to arrive at a total cost per SF. Base and finish coats may require conversion of SF quantities to gallons of material needed for the particular thickness specified. Control and expansion joints are taken off and priced by the LF and should be noted separately in the takeoff. This helps determine normal production rates before work is slowed by an expansion joint. List expanded polystyrene insulation according to its thickness (in inches) and application, such as soffits, fascias, walls, and ceilings. Also list finish coats with different textures, colors, or thicknesses separately. Deduct openings greater than 2 SF. Consider temporary heat and protection, and any staging required to access the work.

Labor costs for installing EIFS follow the same procedure as for stucco. In fact, the crews consist of the same trades and, in some cases, the same size crew. Productivity in SF per day is not comparable to stucco, as the process is different. Again, your own historical data is the best basis for comparison.

Firestop Systems & Sprayed Fireproofing

Firestop systems consist of an assembly of fire-resistive materials used to fill the space around penetrations through walls and floors. These penetrations are for piping, conduits, ductwork, and similar services to pass from room to room or floor to floor, in most cases through fire-rated wall or floor assemblies. Typically, sleeves are installed as the wall or floor assembly is being constructed or installed remedially in existing work. The sleeve is 1"–2" larger in diameter than the pipe or conduit that will pass through it. Rectangular openings for ductwork are similarly oversized.

Once the pipe or duct has been installed, the oversized space at the perimeter of the sleeve must be filled with a fire-resistive material. The most common method is to fill most of the space with a rock wool or slag fiber insulating material, hand-packing it into the sleeve. It is held back from the edge of the sleeve approximately 1-1/2" at either end to allow space for the intumescent filler. An *intumescent filler* is a non-combustible material, similar in consistency to mortar or caulking, that resists the transfer of fire or toxic gases through the penetration. It solidifies once it dries and maintains its shape without shrinking or cracking. The product can be troweled, pumped, or poured into place. Other types of intumenscent fillers are similar in appearance to caulking in a tube, and are placed in much the same manner as regular caulking. Other applications include packing the firestop at the top of the partition or between the metal stud or masonry partition.

Determining the quantities of firestop materials required depends on the individual product used. Most manufacturers provide printed data or on-line services for converting opening sizes into materials required. Consult the specifications for the required system and its application. Also consult the mechanical and electrical specifications to avoid duplication of firestop costs; it is frequently the responsibility of the individual trade to firestop their own penetrations.

Labor Costs

Labor costs are calculated based on the quantity of material that can be installed by a single individual per day. (Many manufacturers provide guidelines.) Consider critical factors that affect productivity, such as accessibility or room to perform the work, staging requirements, or any formwork required to hold the material in place.

Sprayed Fireproofing

This insulating material is sprayed directly on a building's structural components to achieve a fire endurance rating. Its main function is to insulate and resist the transfer of heat from fire to the structural members, thereby delaying their becoming deformed and failing. The most common type of sprayed fireproofing is *cementitious*, a composition of Portland cement or gypsum binders with inorganic fibers, fillers, aggregates, and additives. When mixed with water and spray-applied, it has a high bond strength to steel beams and decks, as well as bar joist. Consult the specifications for the materials to be used and the required thicknesses. Most specifications refer to a UL (Underwriters Laboratory) design or ASTM testing number as a standard.

Taking off Quantities

Quantities are calculated as a volume in cubic feet (CF), based on thickness (inches converted to feet) multiplied by SF of surface area to be covered. The manufacturer's guideline is the best source for determining quantity. Labor costs are based on the production of the crew and the equipment. Productivity varies by application. Other cost considerations include accessibility, surrounding conditions, and staging requirements. Sprayed fireproofing can be extremely messy and warrants a liberal waste allowance. Costs for protection of adjacent work of other trades must also be included, along with detailed cleanup. Consider the impact of sprayed fireproofing work in multiple phases, if necessary, and touch-up of sprayed surfaces that may be damaged by other trades. Figure 12.15 shows average labor-hours.

Conclusion   The work of Division 7—Thermal and Moisture Protection includes a variety of different and unique tasks that prevent the structure from being rendered useless by the elements of nature. A thorough understanding of the individual product and how it is installed is helpful in producing an accurate estimate for this division.

Installation Time in Labor-Hours for Fireproofing Structural Steel

Description	Labor-Hours	Unit
Fireproofing - 10" Column Encasements		
Perlite Plaster	.273	V.L.F.
1" Perlite on 3/8" Gypsum Lath	.345	V.L.F.
Sprayed Fiber	.131	V.L.F.
Concrete 1-1/2" Thick	.716	V.L.F.
Gypsum Board 1/2" Fire Resistant,		
1 Layer	.364	V.L.F.
2 Layer	.428	V.L.F.
3 Layer	.530	V.L.F.
Fireproofing – 16" x 7" Beam Encasements		
Perlite Plaster on Metal Lath	.453	L.F.
Gypsum Plaster on Metal Lath	.408	L.F.
Sprayed Fiber	.079	L.F.
Concrete 1-1/2" Thick	.554	L.F.
Gypsum Board 5/8" Fire Resistant	.488	L.F.

Figure 12.15

Chapter Thirteen

Doors & Windows

CSI Division 8 includes windows, doors and frames, finish hardware, and glass and glazing. Hardware for this division includes items such as hinges, locksets, passage sets, thresholds, weather stripping, door closers, and panic devices. Doors and windows are available in a multitude of sizes with various functions, insulating values, finishes, and glass types.

The size, location, quantity, and specific information for each door or window are included on the architectural drawings. Plan and elevation view drawings show their locations, operations, and quantities.

The specifications define door quality either by gauge of steel facing or species of wood veneer. Figure 13.1 illustrates some of the more common operations of doors as seen in plan view and their associated details. Figure 13.2 illustrates common window types. Consult the details to clarify the type and specific operations of windows.

Architectural Drawings

The architectural drawings include both a door schedule and a window schedule. *(Refer to the "Schedules" section of Chapter 1.)* Schedules are laid out in block column form and list all the information concerning each item. Many projects have detailed drawings of the head, sill, and jambs of the doors, frames, or windows for the purpose of clarification and to provide adequate detail to estimate the work.

Window Schedules

Windows are laid out according to:
- Designation (usually by letter)
- Size in width by height
- Material composition of the sash and frame
- Manufacturer and model number
- Type or function (e.g., fixed, double-hung, casement, or awning)
- Glazing requirements

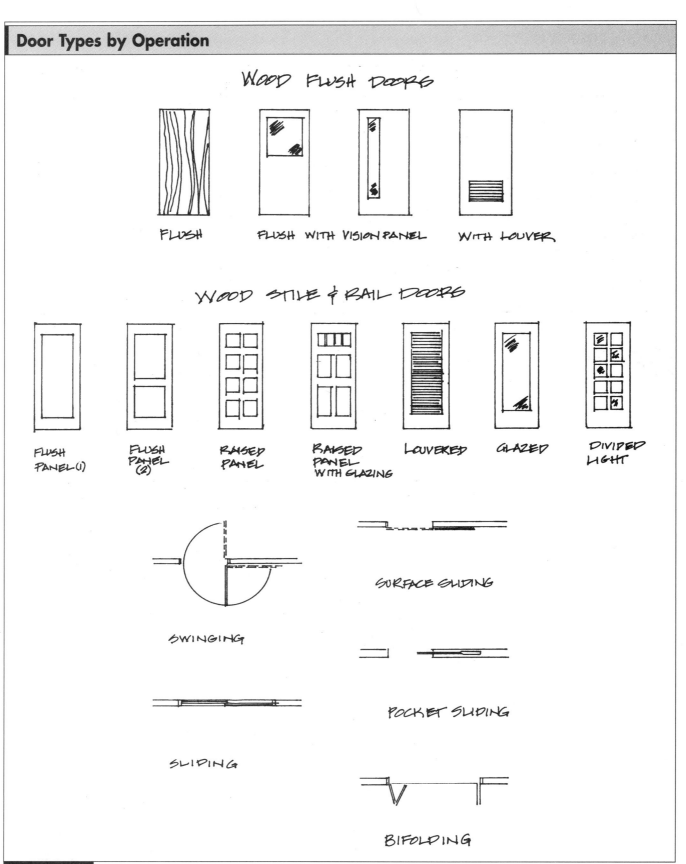

WOOD FLUSH DOORS

FLUSH FLUSH WITH VISION PANEL WITH LOUVER

WOOD STILE & RAIL DOORS

FLUSH PANEL (1) FLUSH PANEL (2) RAISED PANEL RAISED PANEL WITH GLAZING LOUVERED GLAZED DIVIDED LIGHT

SWINGING

SURFACE SLIDING

SLIDING

POCKET SLIDING

BIFOLDING

Figure 13.1

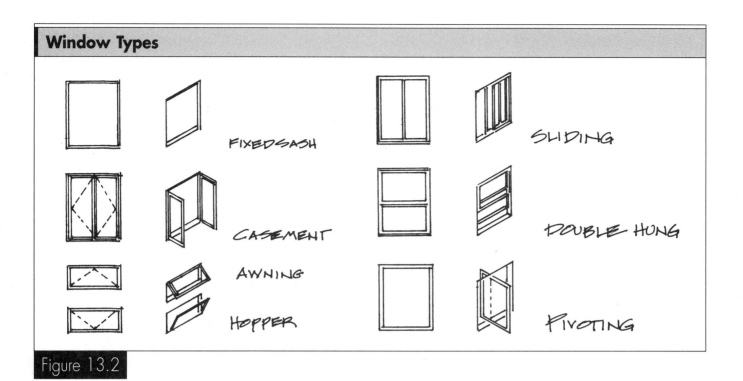

Window Types

Figure 13.2

The schedule sometimes lists the size of the rough opening for the installation of the window, rather than the size of the window itself. Figure 13.3 is a typical window schedule with related details.

Door Schedules

Door schedules typically list each door opening by a specific number, or designation, called the *door mark*. This mark can also be used to identify the location of the door within the structure. Prefixes to the door mark indicate the floor on which the door is located. For example, B05 specifies door #5 in the basement level. Listed beside the mark in the schedule are the following details:

- The door size (width by height)
- Material composition (steel, wood, or glass, etc.)
- Frame type and material composition
- Frame size
- Fire rating requirements (if any)
- Louver or vision panels (if required)
- The hardware set
- A "remarks" column for specific instructions

Figure 13.4 is a typical door schedule showing some of the corresponding details of the head, jamb, and sill.

Hardware Schedules

Doors require special hardware, called *finish hardware*. The finish hardware schedule is different from window and door schedules in that it does not always appear in column form on the architectural drawings.

Window Details

MARK	MANUF/MODEL	TYPE	ROUGH OPEN.	GLASS	JAMB	REMARKS
A	ANDER/C24	CASEMENT	4'-0½" × 4'-0½"	HIGH PERFORM.	4 9/16"	GRILLES, SCREENS
B	ANDER/C34	CASEMENT	6'-0½" × 4'-0½"	"	"	" "
C	ANDER/CW14	CASEMENT	2'-4⅞" × 4'-0½"	"	"	" "
D	ANDER/CW25	CASEMENT	4'-9" × 5'-0⅜"	"	"	" "
E	ANDER/24210	DOUBLE HUNG	2'-6⅛" × 3'-1¼"	"	"	" "
F	ANDER/2842	DOUBLE HUNG	2'-10⅛" × 4'-5¼"	"	"	" "
G	ANDER/30-364618	30° BAY	7'-0" × 4'-10¾"	"	"	" "
H	ANDER/A330	AWNING	3'-0½" × 3'-0½"	"	"	" "
I	ANDER/AW31	AWNING	3'-0½" × 2'-4⅞"	"	"	" "
J	ANDER/CW13	CASEMENT	2'-4⅞" × 3'-0½"	"	"	" "
K	ANDER/C12	CASEMENT	2'-0⅝" × 2'-0⅝"	"	"	" "

WINDOW SCHEDULE

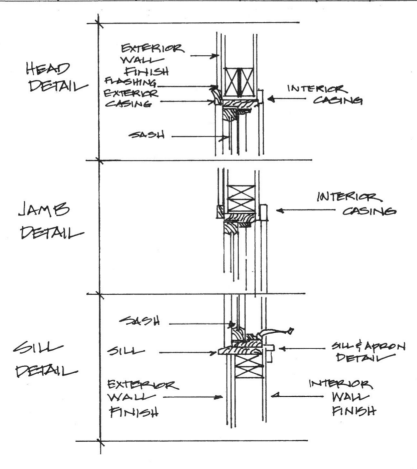

HEAD DETAIL — EXTERIOR WALL FINISH, FLASHING, EXTERIOR CASING, SASH, INTERIOR CASING

JAMB DETAIL — INTERIOR CASING

SILL DETAIL — SASH, SILL, EXTERIOR WALL FINISH, SILL & APRON DETAIL, INTERIOR WALL FINISH

Figure 13.3

Wood Door Frame Detail

DOOR SCHEDULE								
NO.	SIZE	TYPE	MATL	FRAME	TRSH.	CLOSER	HARDWARE	REMARKS
101	3° x 7° x 1¾"	A	WD/GL	WD.	ALUM.	✓	BRASS PUSH BAR/PULL LOCKSET	MORGAN M-5911
102	3° x 7° x 1¾"	A	"	WD	"	✓	"	"
103	2⁶ x 7° x 1¾"	A	"	WD.		✓	"	"
104	3° x 6⁸ x 1⅜"	B	WD	WD	MARBLE		PRIVACY SET	MORGAN 5 CROSS PANEL
105	3° x 6⁸ x 1⅜"	B	WD.	WD	"		"	"
106	BY WALK - IN MANUFACTURER							2-6" WIDE MAX.
107	3° x 6⁸ x 1⅜"	D	WD	WD			SPRING HINGE	BY OWNER
108	3° x 7° x 1¾"	C	H.M.	P.M.		✓	EXISTING	EXIST H.M. DOOR
109	3° x 7° x 1¾"	C	H.M.	P.M.		✓	"	"

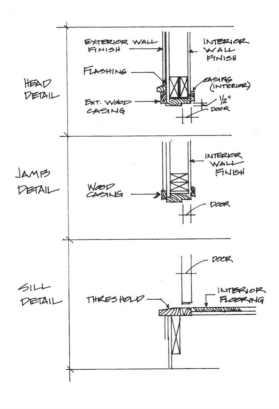

Figure 13.4

251

It lists the items needed to outfit a particular door, called the *hardware set*, typically noted by a number. Each piece of hardware is listed by manufacturer, model number, size, and color or appearance, called the *finish*. The finish should be noted as part of the hardware takeoff, as it has a major impact on material pricing. The following is a sample description of a hardware set that might be encountered in a set of specifications.

Hardware Set #4
- 1-1/2 pair 4-1/2" Stanley CB Series Hinges
- Corbin 977L-9500 Series Mortise Lockset
- LCN 4010 CUSH Series Closer
- Ives 436 B Floor Stop
- Ives #20 Silencers

"Hardware Set #4" in the above example may apply to several different doors on one job. The door schedule may include a column that lists hardware sets that are applicable to particular doors. In the absence of such a column, the finish hardware section of the specifications will list the applicable doors under the individual hardware sets. Both practices are common, and should be reviewed carefully for an accurate quantity of each hardware set.

Hollow Metal Frames & Doors

Hollow metal frames and doors are typically used for commercial projects that require durable, heavy-duty door and frame systems, and where aesthetics are not a primary concern. Hollow metal components are sometimes referred to as steel doors and frames. They are available in a wide variety of sizes, ratings, functions, and price ranges. Installation labor is predominantly, but not exclusively, a carpentry task. The work can be an individual task or may require two tradespeople.

Hollow Metal Frames

Hollow metal frames are formed of 18-, 16-, or 14-gauge steel and are made to accommodate 1-3/8" and 1-3/4" wood or metal doors. They come in a variety of standard wall thicknesses, sometimes called *throat*, typically 4-3/4", 5-3/4", 6-3/4", and 8-3/4". They are available pre-finished, galvanized, primed, or unfinished. Hollow metal frames can be installed in wood frame walls, masonry walls, metal stud and drywall walls, or a combination of all three materials. They are available in two standard levels of fabrication: *knockdown* (KD), where the frame is disassembled into the two jambs and the head piece and re-assembled on site; and *welded assembly*, where the frame is welded at the factory at the corners to produce a true frame for site installation. Figure 13.5 illustrates some typical hollow metal door frame applications.

Taking off Quantities

Hollow metal door frames are taken off and priced by the individual frame or piece (EA). Takeoff quantities should be separated according to

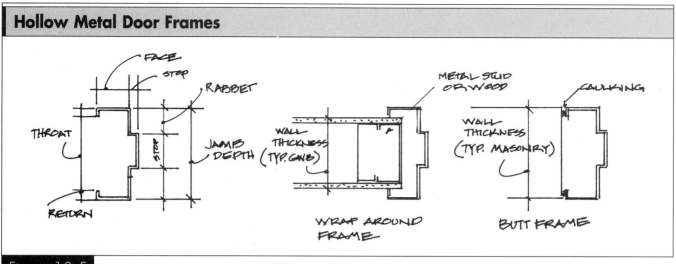

Figure 13.5

type (knockdown or welded), size in width by height, finish, gauge of the frame, and throat size. Any special fabrications required for installation, such a dimpled jambs for anchors or tee-anchors for masonry applications, should be noted. The height of the head (standard 2" or can be 4" to match certain masonry coursing) should also be noted for pricing. Be sure to note any special preparation of or machining to the frame. Modifying frames in the field can be labor-intensive and difficult at best. All machine prepping of the door frame should be done during fabrication to minimize on-site costs.

Labor

Labor to install hollow metal door frames is priced by the individual piece, per frame. The type of door frame (welded or knockdown), the size, installation type (drywall, wood, or masonry), and whether the frame is installed in the course of new work or as a retro-fit application are all critical details for accurate labor pricing. Welded frames are installed as the wall or partition is being built, whereas KD frames are installed after the wall or partition has been completed. Welded frames often require two tradespeople to erect and set, although a KD frame is an individual task. The labor to install hollow metal frames is often included as part of the work of the trade that is responsible for building the wall or partition. This is especially true of welded frames, since they are integral to the wall construction.

The specification section for masonry might state that the installation of hollow metal frames in all masonry walls and partitions must be done by a mason as the walls or partitions are being constructed. Note that many specifications require that door frames with fire ratings be filled solid with non-combustible material. Welded frames installed in masonry walls are filled with mortar as the wall or partition is constructed. Welded frames installed in drywall walls and partitions are frequently filled with plaster. Due to the installation process of the frame in the drywall opening, this is a labor-intensive and often difficult task.

Hollow Metal Doors

Hollow metal doors are constructed of 16-, 18-, or 20-gauge face sheets, with interior metal framing for a 1-3/8" or 1-3/4" finished thickness. They are available in a variety of styles, including flush, small vision panels, full or half glass, and louvered. Building codes require doors and frames in certain locations to be fire-rated. Typical fire-rating capacity labels are:

- C label for a 3/4-hour rating
- B label for a 1-1/2- to 2-hour rating
- A label for a 3-hour rating

A door's rating is based on its physical composition and capacity to slow the transmission of fire. Doors are subjected to testing by independent organizations, such as Underwriters Laboratories (UL). Other restrictions and qualifications also govern labeled doors and frames, such as glass size for vision panels and fire-rated louvers. Labeled doors and frames are considerably more expensive than other doors.

Review the architectural drawings, particularly the floor plans and elevations, for door locations and quantities. The door schedule should identify any special fire-rating (label), undercutting, louvers, and hardware sets. Consult the drawings for rated wall types. Doors within the rated wall should match with a comparable rating.

Taking off Quantities

Metal doors are taken off and priced by the individual piece (EA), according to size, thickness, type, gauge of metal, and finish/style. Any special preparations for a deadbolt, openings for louvers or vision panels, or undercutting must be noted. Double door sets are noted as a pair (PR) in the takeoff, with the same qualifications. An individual door within a pair is referred to as a *leaf*. Figure 13.6 illustrates some of the more common designations for steel doors.

Labor

Hollow metal doors are typically installed by carpenters. The actual installation on the frame, referred to as *hanging the door*, requires installing the hinges first. This is typically a two-person task due to the awkwardness and weight of most steel doors. Installation is most often included as part of the hardware package installation labor in an effort to save an estimating step. *(See the "Finish Hardware" section of this chapter.)* Also consult the general notes at the end of the "Doors & Frames" section.

Wood Doors & Frames

Wood doors come in many types, materials, sizes, and thicknesses. They can be supplied separately for hollow metal frames, or can be specified pre-hung. *Pre-hung* refers to a packaged unit, consisting of a finished door

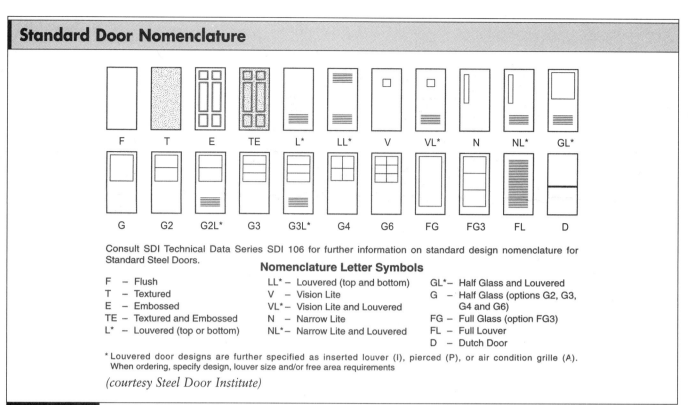

Consult SDI Technical Data Series SDI 106 for further information on standard design nomenclature for Standard Steel Doors.

Nomenclature Letter Symbols

F — Flush
T — Textured
E — Embossed
TE — Textured and Embossed
L* — Louvered (top or bottom)

LL* — Louvered (top and bottom)
V — Vision Lite
VL* — Vision Lite and Louvered
N — Narrow Lite
NL* — Narrow Lite and Louvered

GL* — Half Glass and Louvered
G — Half Glass (options G2, G3, G4 and G6)
FG — Full Glass (option FG3)
FL — Full Louver
D — Dutch Door

* Louvered door designs are further specified as inserted louver (I), pierced (P), or air condition grille (A). When ordering, specify design, louver size and/or free area requirements

(courtesy Steel Door Institute)

Figure 13.6

on a frame, trim, and hinges. Wood doors can be classified in one of two categories. The first, *flush doors*, are flat slab doors that are either solid-core or hollow-core. Solid-core wood doors are made of particle board or mineral core composition with a wood veneer facing. They are used where increased fire resistance, sound insulation, and dimensional stability are specified. *Hollow-core* doors are used for interior applications and have a honey-combed cardboard/wood core with a wood veneer facing. They are less stable than solid-core doors and have no real thermal or sound-insulating value. They are mainly used in the residential market.

The second major classification is stile and rail doors. *Stile* and *rail* doors have vertical (stile) and horizontal (rail) members that provide the framework for wood, glass, or louver center panels. Wood doors are manufactured in widths ranging from 2' to 4', with smaller widths available in some styles. Heights range from 6'-6" to 9'-0", and thicknesses are 1-3/4", 1-3/8", and 1-1/8" for some residential-grade bi-fold and sliding closet doors.

Wood doors for high-end residential and commercial applications are available in a variety of wood veneers, ranging from oak and birch to exotic hardwoods. Consult the architectural drawings and door schedules (as noted above for metal doors) for sizes, quantities, and styles. Review the specifications for quality terms such as *book-matched* and *balanced*, which indicate matching grains within the door veneers.

Taking off Quantities

Wood doors are taken off and priced by the piece (EA). They are listed in the takeoff according to size (width by height, thickness); composition (solid- or hollow-core); species of wood; type of door (flush or stile and rail); and any special features, such as fire-rating label, vision panels, and preparation for special hardware. Wood frames are taken off and priced by the piece and specified according to size of the door they fit, wall thickness, species and quality of wood (paint- or stain-grade), and any preparation to the frame, such as for hinges, locksets, or deadbolts. Pre-hung units are taken off and priced by the piece, which in this case, is the complete assembly. They are listed according to the size and type of the door itself, wall thickness, species and quality of door and frame wood, labels, vision panels, and any additional characteristics that would aid in accurate pricing. Double doors are taken off and priced by the pair (PR), with the above-mentioned qualifications.

Many high-end residential and commercial wood doors are available pre-finished from manufacturers. Often, wood door specifications require that doors are prefinished at the manufacturer's to maintain the warranty. Be sure to note this in the takeoff so that there is no duplication of finishing costs. In addition, wood doors should always be machined and prepped for hardware off-site when this option is available. While it will clearly add to the cost of the door, it reduces on-site costs for labor, provides quality control not available in the field, and saves time.

Labor

Wood door frames are installed by carpenters. Lightweight residential interior pre-hung units are frequently installed by an individual carpenter, while exterior pre-hung entry units often require two carpenters. Labor costs are based on carpenter labor-hours per door frame. Pre-hung units with the door and frame attached are also estimated by the carpenter labor-hours to install. Pre-machined, pre-finished doors are hung as part of the installation of the finish hardware. (See the hollow metal section earlier in this chapter.)

Sliding Glass Doors

Sliding glass doors, commonly referred to as *sliders*, consist of a stile and rail door with a full glass panel, sold as a single unit. Slider units range from 5' to 12' in width and from 6'-8" to 8'-0" in height. The stiles and rails can be wood or aluminum, or can be covered with a metal or vinyl coating, referred to as *cladding*, at the exterior. The panels are insulated, tempered safety glass. Slider units are noted on the plan view and exterior elevation drawings. Refer to the specifications and door schedule for the information necessary for pricing. Similar units that swing, as opposed to slide, are also available.

Taking off Quantities

Sliding glass door units are taken off and priced by the piece (EA) or unit. "Piece" refers to the entire unit or assembly of doors, hardware, and track. The slider should be specified in the takeoff by the manufacturer and model number, when sufficient for accurate pricing. If the manufacturer and model number are not specified, the unit should be listed by the size (width by height), composition, wall thickness the unit will occupy, type of glazing, screens or grilles, hardware, and the color of the finish (if applicable). Swinging glass door units are qualified the same way, with a special notation about the number and location of operable panels.

Labor

There is a wide selection of sliding and swinging doors on the market, with dramatically different prices and quality. Some are shipped assembled and ready for installation, while others require some assembly prior to installation. Assembly requirements should be noted in the takeoff and included as part of the installation costs. Installation typically requires two carpenters, although assembly can often be done by a single carpenter.

Special Doors

Special doors include folding doors, pocket doors, and surface sliding doors.

Folding Doors

These are accordion or bi-fold doors that fold or stack against a wall or jamb. Folding doors over 150 square feet in area are referred to as *folding partitions*. Both folding doors and partitions are typically provided with tracks and all related hardware for installation. Available finishes include wood, fabric, and vinyl. Folding doors and partitions are often used to separate space within a room, and therefore may require resistance to sound transmission, expressed as the door's sound transmission class (STC). (This is analogous to the R-value of insulation.) In general, the higher the sound-insulating value, the more expensive the door.

Pocket Doors

These are installed within the framework of a wall so that when opened, the door can be stored within the wall cavity. They are used in residential applications where special constraints preclude the use of swing or bi-fold doors. Pocket doors are available as a package unit with all necessary hardware and the track, in a variety of compositions, finishes, styles, and sizes.

Insulating Door Units

Steel insulating door units for residential entrances are composed of thin steel sheets over a wood-and-foam insulating core. They are typically provided pre-hung in a wood frame with an integral aluminum threshold, bored for locksets and/or deadbolts. Sizes range from 2'-8" to 3'-0" in width and 6'-6" or 6'-8" in height. Steel doors are provided primed for field-applied paint, and fiberglass units are unfinished, ready for field-applied stains or paints.

Storm Doors

These provide protection of the entrance from weather and allow air passage through the screen in warm weather. Aluminum storm doors are lightweight, and pre-finished with interchangeable glass sashes and screens, set within a matching aluminum frame. The storm unit is surface-applied by screwing through flanges, attached to the frame jambs and head, to the surface of the exterior door trim. Handles, latches or locksets, and hydraulic closers are included as part of the unit. Storm door units are available in sizes to fit most exterior entry units, in a variety of colors and designs.

Taking off Quantities

Folding doors and partitions are taken off and priced by the square foot of the occupied opening. The takeoff description should note size (width by height), composition of the door and finishes, method of door operation (manual or electrical), STC classifications, fire rating (if applicable), and any special locking hardware.

Pocket doors are taken off and listed by the piece (EA), according to size (width by height), composition (wood or plastic), and thickness of the wall. The takeoff designation should include all components necessary in the unit so that they can be priced as a single unit.

Steel and fiberglass insulating entry units are taken off and priced by the piece and listed according to size, wall thickness, function (in-swing or out-swing), design or model, exterior casing type, and the preparation for the door (boring for lockset or deadbolt). The piece designation includes the complete unit.

Storm door units are taken off and listed by the piece according to size, design, special options (e.g., insulated glazing, or locksets), and color of finish. Size is often designated according to the size of the entry unit. They are priced by the individual piece or unit, with the designation "each" (EA).

Labor

Special doors are installed by carpenters. Costs are based on carpenter labor-hours and will vary dramatically with the type of door and application. For most special doors, installation requires two carpenters. Folding partitions often require two or more carpenters. Consult applicable manufacturers' literature on individual units for guidelines in assembly and installation. Pocket doors require some level of assembly prior to installation, and the amount of work depends on the manufacturer and quality of the unit.

General Notes on Doors

Doors and frames are typically delivered to the job FOB (freight on board) and require handling from the truck to storage or immediate distribution. Handling and distribution can be costly for projects with a large quantity of doors and frames. Review the specifications for any special handling or storage requirements. Costs for labor to distribute doors, frames and hardware from the storage area to the actual opening must be included in the labor portion of the estimate. Many carpenter unions require that finished products, including doors and frames, be distributed by carpenters instead of laborers. Distribution should be included as a separate item in the labor portion of the estimate.

Occasionally, the handling or direction of a door's swing may affect the price (especially for exterior residential door units that swing out instead of the normal in-swing). Similar requirements for metal doors should be noted. It is not uncommon for doors to need some minor adjustments. Allow labor time for adjusting the swing of the door after it has been hung. Because pre-hung units come with the casing attached or included, it is necessary to specify the type of casing for accurate pricing of the unit. Finishing of wood and metal doors will be discussed later in Chapter 14, "Division 9—Finishes." Accurate pricing of doors and frames often requires contemporaneous pricing by a material supplier. Door and frame takeoffs should be provided to material suppliers for up-to-date prices.

Folding partitions for commercial applications may need to be fire-rated to meet building codes. Review the specifications carefully for this requirement. Larger folding partitions may require special structural details to accommodate the weight of the partition itself. This is not usually part of the scope of the partition manufacturer or installer; clarification of the limits of the work is essential for accurate pricing.

Overhead & Coiling Doors

Overhead doors, such as garage doors, are constructed of wood stiles and rails with hardboard flush inserts, or thin steel face sheets over a steel frame and foam insulating core. Face sheets can be flush or may have an embossed design. Special designs are also manufactured to include glass lights within individual panels. Wood door finishes are either unfinished or primed for field painting. Metal doors are usually provided pre-finished in the manufacturer's standard colors.

Standard door openings range from 8' to 18' in width and 7' to 12' in height. Custom sizes are also available, but may constitute an additional cost. Overhead doors are typically provided with the necessary hardware for installation, as well as locking mechanisms for security. Other types of overhead doors, called *coiling doors* or *rolling shutters*, are taken off and priced per opening based on the square foot area of the coiling door. Material composition (steel, stainless steel, or aluminum) of the door and its operation will affect the price. Added costs for steel jambs and heads for mounting, hoods, or guides must be included. Review door schedules, architectural plans, and elevations for information on overhead doors, and consult the specifications for special requirements or manufacturers.

Taking off Quantities

Overhead doors are taken off and listed by the piece according to size (width by height), thickness of the door panels, composition and finish of the panels, door style or design, manufacturer's model number (if applicable), and special options such as glass lights, electrical operators, safety devices, and security mechanisms. Additional information, such as R-value or the amount of overhead clearance distance (from the head of the door to the ceiling above), may also be required for accurate pricing. Custom-sized overhead doors are taken off and qualified by the same units. Overhead doors are typically priced by the square foot area of each door. Special functions, such as door operation or high R-values, will affect the square foot cost.

Labor

Overhead doors are installed by specialty subcontractors. Always solicit a price for a furnished and installed overhead door to ensure accurate pricing. Installation costs for overhead doors are calculated per labor-hour per door. Labor costs are based on the productivity of the crew or individual, depending on the size of the door and its application. Labor costs for the electrical wiring portion of a motorized overhead door should be calculated in Division 16—Electrical.

Entrances & Storefronts

These consist of metal framework surrounding fixed or operable windows and entrance doors. The framework is manufactured from aluminum alloy and can be extruded into a variety of shapes and sizes. Finishes are anodized in a number of colors (or clear) to prevent oxidation from exposure. Durable coatings are available in a range of colors.

Insulated or plain glazing panels manufactured off-site are installed within channels of the extruded framework to provide a weather-tight window or wall system. Specialty glazing can be used to obscure structural elements, or insulating non-glazed panels may be incorporated into the design. Entrance doors of the same construction with hinges or pivots can be manually operated or motorized, and may be purchased with panic and finish hardware. Figure 13.7 illustrates a typical storefront and details.

The precise location and width of the entrance and storefront system is noted on the architectural floor plans. Additional drawings showing sections through the head, jamb, and sills of the various windows are usually provided on a separate sheet, called *window details*. Elevation views are found on the exterior elevations. Review the specifications for the type of glass (laminated safety or tempered), frame system, manufacturer, door and window systems and hardware, samples, and shop drawings.

Taking off Quantities

Each individual component of the glass and glazing system is taken off and priced separately for better accuracy. The aluminum framework is

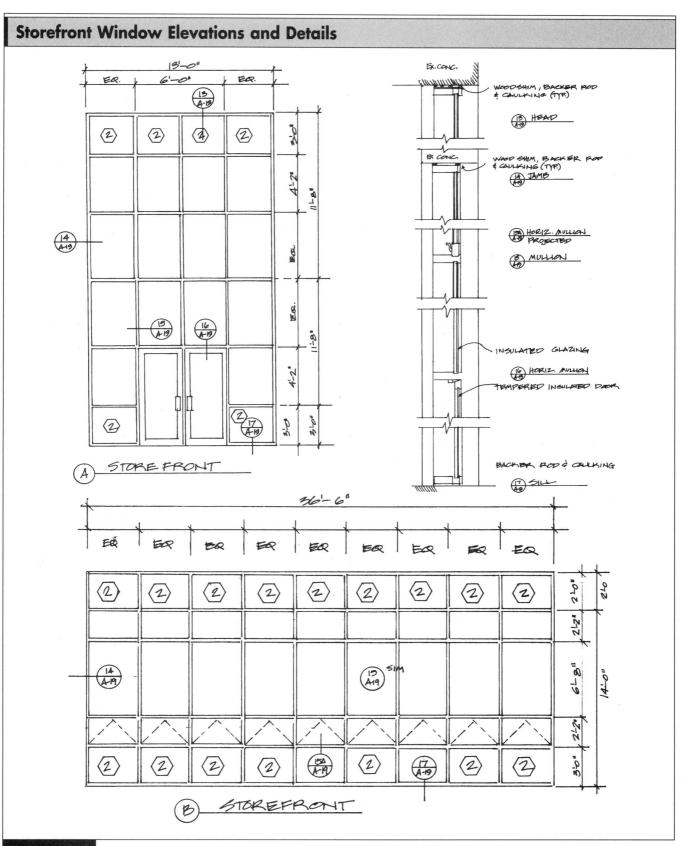

A STOREFRONT

B STOREFRONT

Figure 13.7

taken off and priced by the LF, including all vertical and horizontal mullions, jambs, heads, and sills. Extruded sections should be separated according to size, thickness of the material (gauge), finish, and shape. Aluminum flashings at the sills, or head of the system, should be taken off by the LF. Flashings over 12" in width may be converted to SF.

Caulking and sealants at the perimeter of the unit and between metal components are taken off and priced by the LF. Be careful not to duplicate work that is specified under Section 07900—Caulking and Sealants. Frequently, specifications require that the storefront section in Division 8 cover caulking and sealing of storefront work, in an effort to maintain one source of responsibility for weather-tightness of the system.

Glass and insulated glass panels are taken off and priced by the square foot of the area of the individual insulated glass panels that fit within an extruded frame system. These should be listed in the takeoff separately according to size (width by height), thickness of the insulating panel or pane of glass, type of glass (e.g., clear, tinted, or spandrel), and special treatment of glass (e.g., tempered or laminated safety glass). Insulated non-glazed panels are taken off and priced by the SF according to the size, thickness, facing or finish of the panel, and insulating material within the panel. Convert SF area into sheets depending on the various manufacturers' sized sheets.

Windows are taken off and priced by the piece (EA) according to size (width by height), function (e.g., casement, awning, hopper, or sliding), hardware requirements, material and finish of the sash, and glass type.

Doors are taken off and priced by the piece (EA) according to size (width by height), thickness, stile and rail materials, hardware (such as hinges or pivots), panic devices, locking mechanisms, and type of glass. Finish door hardware for aluminum entrances may be specified under this section or can be included as part of Section 08700—Finish Hardware.

Custom fabrication of glass panels and their framework require shop drawings showing the exact sizes of each fabrication. Field measurement and verification of the rough opening sizes are needed. The cost of shop drawings is considered as part of the cost of the work, and should be accounted for in the takeoff. Shop drawings are listed as a lump sum (LS).

Labor

There are two classifications of labor: shop fabrication and field installation labor. Both must be included in the estimate to be complete. Aluminum extrusions that make up the storefront system come from the manufacturer in stock lengths and are then cut to specific sizes and assembled in accordance with the shop drawings. Assembled window sashes and doors fit into the frame. Frames are delivered to the site unglazed and installed within the pre-measured rough openings. Once secured in place, the frames are glazed; stops and gasketing are set; and doors, finish hardware, and window sashes are installed.

Be sure to calculate labor for both the fabrication and installation process, which are crew tasks. The individuals that perform the work are referred to as *glaziers*. Crews consist of two or more glaziers, depending on the size of the storefront. Fabrication labor should be kept separate from installation labor. Fabrication of glass panels within the frame is typically priced by the square foot area of the panel. Installation costs are based on labor-hours per square foot area of the frame, including doors and windows. Additional labor costs for installation of doors, finish hardware, and glazed and non-glazed panels must be included. Again, include labor costs for adjustments to door and window hardware once installed.

Wood & Plastic Windows

Windows are furnished as complete, factory-assembled units, including frame, sash, operating hardware, weather stripping, and glazing. Wood windows are constructed of kiln-dried, clear, straight-grain woods, usually western pine. Frames are treated with a water-repellent preservative, and are available primed and ready for field-applied paint, factory-painted, aluminum-clad, or vinyl-clad. Plastic windows, featuring jambs, heads, sills, and sashes, are made of various grades of PVC. Insulated glass panels are set within plastic stiles and rails. Wood and plastic windows come in literally hundreds of sizes within the various types of operation. Combinations of various styles and sizes are often joined together in the factory or field to produce a desired appearance.

Review architectural floor plans and elevations for the locations of various window types. Window schedules (see Figure 13.3) should be studied for the specific manufacturer, model, and size of the individual or combined unit. Occasionally, special details or sections through the unit may be used for clarification. The specifications should be studied for detailed information on the type of glazing, finish of the window, cladding color (if applicable), and accessories, such as screens or grilles. Acceptable manufacturers and required warranties are also listed in the specifications.

Taking off Quantities

Wood and plastic windows are taken off and priced by the individual unit or piece (EA). Quantities should be noted according to manufacturer, model or size, function (e.g., double-hung, casement, awning, or fixed sash), wall thickness, type of exterior finish, color of the finish, type of insulating glass, and exterior casing (for non-clad wood windows). Special options, such as grilles, screens, or blinds, can be taken off and priced separately or included as part of the actual window cost. For larger window units, such as bays or bows, many manufacturers offer the option of making normally fixed sashes operable, such as the center sashes in a four- or five-lite bow window. This often constitutes an additional cost, and should be noted in the takeoff for accurate pricing.

Many manufacturers fabricate windows to custom specifications, which can be expensive and require considerable lead times. To accurately price custom window fabrication, contact the manufacturer and obtain a direct quote, including any shipping costs. While most wood windows are manufactured for a normal wall thickness (2" x 4" construction), those constructed of thicker framing members (such as 2" x 6") require finish wood pieces to bring the jambs, head, and sill out flush to the interior finish surface. These are called *extension jambs* and are additional to the cost of the window.

Labor

Most wood and plastic window applications require two carpenters. For replacement windows set within an existing frame, the task can often be accomplished by an individual carpenter from the interior of the building. Labor costs are based on labor-hours per window or, alternately, the quantity of windows that can be installed by a crew in a eight-hour day. Consider staging or lifts for windows above the first floor.

Metal Windows

These are more frequently used for commercial applications. They can be "stock units" (standard models that the manufacturer keeps in stock for fast delivery), or custom-fabricated to meet the specific needs of an individual project. Metal windows are comparable in operation, glazing, and most options to wood and plastic windows. Aluminum windows are pre-manufactured and available in a wide variety of operations, sizes, colors, and glazing.

Taking off Quantities

For stock units, metal windows are taken off and priced by the individual piece (EA). Trims and receiver channels at the perimeter of the window are taken off and priced by the linear foot of the perimeter. Custom-fabricated windows are taken off and priced by the square foot of the window itself. All considerations noted under the wood and plastic window section above (with the exception of the extension jambs) must be acknowledged for accurate pricing. For custom fabrications, shop drawings are often required. Pricing should be quoted by the manufacturer to ensure accuracy.

Labor

Installation is typically performed by a multi-person crew. Productivity is measured by unit-per-day installed by a specific crew. Labor costs per window unit can be assigned as labor-hours per unit. It should be noted that, as in the case of entrance and storefront systems, metal window specifications may require caulking and sealing. Review the specifications so that there are no duplications. Additional labor should be added for installing screens and hardware that do not come assembled from the factory.

General Notes on Windows

Specifications for commercial projects may require the window and storefront system installer to clean all glass (inside and out) prior to acceptance by the owner. Warranties on the glazing portion of windows and storefront systems, typically issued by the manufacturer, may require a site test or inspection by the manufacturer's technical representative. Depending on the manufacturer, this may have an associated cost. Check the specifications carefully for any "attic stock" or replacement glazing panels that must be provided as part of the base contract.

Finish Hardware

The most common examples of finish hardware are hinges, locksets, latch sets, closers, stops, deadbolts, thresholds, weatherstripping, and panic devices. Most hardware is available in a variety of finishes, designated by the U.S. Code Symbol Designation.

Consult the architectural drawings and door schedule, which typically follows two basic formats for noting finish hardware. The first and most common method is to designate the particular hardware set for each door by a number, as illustrated in the example at the beginning of this chapter. The second method uses a series of columns included in the door schedule, each of which is headed by a particular item of finish hardware. The row lists the door mark and corresponding hardware items with a number that defines the specific item in the specifications.

Taking off Quantities

Hardware items are taken off by counting the individual units and are listed as EA. The individual pieces can be grouped into hardware sets for pricing. Items should be separated according to the manufacturer, series model, type, finish, and any other means of identification specified, such as Federal Specification Series

The following is a list of the most common U.S. Code Symbol numbers and their respective finishes:

- *US P - Primed paint coat*
- *US 3 - Polished brass*
- *US 4 - Satin brass*
- *US 9 - Polished bronze*
- *US 10 - Satin bronze*
- *US 10B - Satin bronze, oil-rubbed*
- *US 14 - Polished nickel*
- *US 15 - Satin nickel*
- *US 20 - Statuary (light) bright bronze*
- *US 26 - Polished chrome*
- *US 26D - Satin chrome*
- *US 28 - Satin aluminum, anodized*
- *US 32 - Polished stainless steel*
- *US 32D - Satin stainless steel*

Designation or American National Standards Institute (ANSI) series number. Note that the finish on hardware can have a direct impact on its cost and may require lead time. Some of the less expensive finishes, such as US 28, are readily available. Others, such as US 32, are special order and may require long lead times for delivery. Consult the supplier for delivery schedules so that temporary hardware items are included in the estimate, if necessary.

Many construction projects require temporary cores for locksets during construction, with permanent ones installed at turnover. This is typically noted in the specifications and may be an additional cost. Most doors supplied to project sites have been prepped for the hardware off site.

Occasionally, doors are mortised and bored for hardware on site. Be sure to verify how the doors will be supplied prior to pricing the hardware installation.

Pricing hardware material is a specialized discipline requiring advanced knowledge and experience beyond that of the average estimator. A simple addition of a number or letter to a model can have a dramatic impact on an item's function and price. For projects with detailed finish hardware requirements, solicit pricing and lead times from suppliers in advance of the bid date.

Labor

Finish hardware is typically installed by finish carpenters. Occasionally, the installation portion of the finish hardware is specified under Section 06200—Finish Carpentry. Finish hardware installation requires first-class workmanship, and is measured by the productivity of the individual carpenter.

Review the documents to determine whether the doors will be provided pre-machined, which will impact the costs of the finish hardware installation. Other concerns include receiving, cataloging, and distributing the hardware to the individual locations. On larger commercial projects with many doors, such as hotels, schools, and apartment buildings, these costs can be labor-intensive and must be included in the estimate. Labor costs are calculated as labor-hours per hardware set. The cost in labor-hours must be determined for each set, then multiplied by the quantity of each. For example, referring to Hardware Set #4 (with minor modifications) introduced previously in the chapter:

Labor-hours to install Hardware Set #4	
1-1/2 pair 4-1/2" Stanley CB Series Hinges (1-1/2 pr.)	.50 hours
Hang and swing door	.30 hours
Corbin 977L-9500 Series Mortise Lockset (1 ea.)	1.00 hours
LCN 4010 CUSH Series Closer (1 ea.)	1.40 hours
Ives 436 B Floor Stop (1 ea.)	.30 hours
Ives #20 Silencers (3 ea.)	.20 hours
Adjust hardware and door	.50 hours
Subtotal for labor-hours for HS #4	4.20 hours

If the 4.20 labor-hours for each Hardware Set #4 is multiplied by the takeoff quantity of 12 for Hardware Set #4, then:

HS #4 = 12 sets x 4.20 labor-hours per set = 50.40 labor-hours.

The 50.40 labor-hours could then be multiplied by the billing rate of $48.50 per labor-hour to arrive at the costs for installing all Hardware Sets #4:

50.40 labor-hours x $48.50 per labor-hour = $2,444.40.

The labor-hours could alternately be calculated for *all* hardware sets on the project before pricing is done. This method can save some estimating time and reduce the level of detail. Remember to calculate individual labor-hours to the nearest 5-minute increment (.083 labor-hours) whenever possible. Rounding should be at the final summary of all labor-hours for the entire hardware package. Figure 13.8 provides some guidance for calculating installation labor-hours on specific types of hardware. This figure should be consulted as a guide only, and your own historical data should always be used first.

Be sure to note the labor-hours for retrofit situations on remodeling jobs, where existing hardware is removed and replaced, on a door by door basis. Aligning and adjusting hardware on this type of application can be painstakingly slow. Verify that doors with closers are adjusted to meet the requirements of the Americans with Disabilities Act (ADA).

Glass & Glazing

All glass and mirrors that are not specifically part of a storefront, entry unit, or pre-manufactured windows make up the category of glass and glazing. Most glass used in construction today is called *float* glass, which refers to its manufacturing process. Float glass undergoes *annealing*, which is a heating treatment that increases the toughness of the finished product. Specific examples of glass and glazing include: glass for vision panels within doors, fire-rated glass for rated doors, glass for sidelights and transoms, glass for interior borrowed lights, and non-framed mirrors. Glass materials under this section can be classified into one of the following types for estimating purposes.

- **Insulated glass:** A composite of multiple pieces (panes) of glass with a sealed or gas-filled space between them, which helps reduce the loss of heat or cooling through the unit. Units are custom-made to specific sizes and thicknesses for individual applications. A variety of different types of glass can be used for the individual panes, which can affect the price.
- **Tempered glass:** Heat-treated annealed glass that has a high strength. When tempered glass breaks, it ruptures into cube-shaped fragments. This fragmenting helps reduce serious injury that would normally occur with pointed fragments.
- **Laminated glass:** A "sandwich" unit of multiple panes of glass with a high-strength, transparent plastic film between each layer. It is available in various thicknesses, and is frequently referred to as *safety glass*. Safety glass will crack under sufficient impact, but will remain intact.
- **Wired glass:** Contains wire within the thickness of the glass sheet and is used for protective applications, such as fire door vision panels. Its purpose is to maintain the shape and integrity of the glass in the event of a fire. The glass will crack from the heat, but maintain its shape due to the wire.
- **Coated glass:** Float glass that has a thin reflective metallic coating. Some coatings reduce glare, some reduce heat loss, and others are heat-absorbing. The majority of coated glass is used for energy conservation applications.

Installation Time in Labor-Hours for Finish Hardware

Description	Labor-Hours	Unit
Astragals, 1/8" x 3"	.089	L.F.
Spring Hinged Security Seal with Cam	.107	L.F.
Two Piece Overlapping	.133	L.F.
Automatic Openers, Swing Doors, Single	20.000	Ea.
Single Operating, Pair	32.000	Pair
Sliding Doors, 3' Wide Including Track and		
Hanger, Single	26.667	Opng.
Bi-parting	40.000	Opng.
Handicap Opener Button, Operating	5.333	Pair
Bolts, Flush, Standard, Concealed	1.143	Ea.
Bumper Plates, 1-1/2" x 3/4" U Channel	.200	L.F.
Door Closer, Adjustable Backcheck, 3 Way Mount	1.333	Ea.
Doorstops	.250	Ea.
Kickplate	533	Ea.
Lockset, Non-Keyed	.667	Ea.
Keyed	.800	Ea.
Dead Locks, Heavy Duty	.889	Ea.
Entrance Locks, Deadbolt	1.000	Ea.
Mortise Lockset, Non Keyed	.889	Ea.
Keyed	1.000	Ea.
Panic Device for Rim Locks		
Single Door, Exit Only	1.333	Ea.
Outside Key and Pull	1.600	Ea.
Bar and Vertical Rod, Exit Only	1.600	Ea.
Outside Key and Pull	2.000	Ea.
Push Pull Plate	.667	Ea.
Weatherstripping, Window, Double Hung	1.111	Opng.
Doors, Wood Frame, 3' x 7'	1.053	Opng.
6' x 7'	1.143	Opng.
Metal Frame, 3' x 7'	2.667	Opng.
6' x 7'	3.200	Opng.

Figure 13.8

- **Mirrors:** Sheets of float glass, usually 1/8" or 1/4" in thickness, to which a reflective coating has been applied. The coating is then sealed to protect against moisture and handling damage. Mirrors that have been cut from larger pieces require dressing of the edges. The most common form of edgework is a plain polished edge, although beveled edges are sometimes specified for a particular application. Mirrors can be installed using adhesives applied to the back, or can be supported by special tracks and hardware. Trim pieces may also be required to cover vertical and horizontal seams or inside and outside corners.

All types of glass and mirrors are shown on the exterior and interior elevations of architectural drawings for wall applications, and on reflected ceiling plans for ceiling applications. Plan view architectural drawings should be cross-referenced to verify quantities, sizes, and location. The specifications should be reviewed for the type, thickness, and method of application, as well as for the associated trim pieces or setting materials needed. Consult the door schedules for glass in vision panels and borrowed lights.

Taking off Quantities

All glass and mirror materials are taken off and priced by the SF and should be separated in the takeoff according to size, type, color, thickness, edge treatment, and method of installation for accurate pricing. You may elect to take off the quantity of edge treatment for mirrors separately, by measuring the perimeter of the individual pieces and listing them by the LF. Adhesives for mirrors are taken off by the SF and extended to the gallon or manufacturer's typical sales unit for pricing. SF quantities are determined by the individual product's coverage. Setting blocks are calculated by the perimeter of the individual glass size.

Cutting special shapes or boring holes in glass or mirrors for custom applications can be expensive and should be noted in the takeoff for accurate pricing. Some types of glass can only be drilled or cut in the factory.

Conclusion

Much of the work of CSI Division 8—Doors & Windows involves specialty suppliers or subcontractors. Whenever possible, secure pricing from potential suppliers or subcontractors to ensure accurate and timely pricing.

Chapter Fourteen

Finishes

CSI MasterFormat Division 9 includes a variety of interior finish work, such as drywall and metal stud partitions, plaster, tile, acoustical ceilings, wood and resilient flooring, carpeting, and painting. Although this work does not typically represent a major segment of the total project cost, it does account for a large amount of time in the schedule. Finishes have the largest impact on the aesthetic value of the building, and time is often required to produce the necessary quality, which is always expected to be first-class.

Finish work is detailed on the architectural drawings. Quantities are derived from floor plans, reflected ceiling plans, interior elevations, and the related details that support the design. The details and sections often provide the additional information for accurately defining the work, as well as critical dimensions for changes in finishes.

Room finish schedules, also found in the architectural set of drawings, provide more information about the finishes of floors, walls, and ceilings. They display information in a table format for easy reference. Each room is assigned a number, and the specific finishes for each surface are listed. Some finish schedules list each wall separately, referring to it by its compass location (north, south, east, or west). This allows the architect to call out different finishes on each wall if desired. Finish schedules are most often found on commercial projects with a large number of rooms.

While the drawings are essential for determining finish quantities, the specifications are necessary for determining the quality and individual characteristics of each specified product. Specifications also define the quality of workmanship and acceptable standards of installation. Special installation methods or techniques are also outlined.

Due to the large variety of finish products available, it is critical that you become familiar with each new product specified. Simple changes in a model number or color of a finish material can have a significant cost impact on both material and labor. The Internet is often a valuable source of information where you can learn about new products and installation techniques.

For estimating purposes, Division 9 work can be classified into one of the following general categories:

- Plaster systems
- Gypsum wallboard systems
- Metal stud framing and furring
- Tile
- Acoustical ceiling systems
- Flooring
- Painting and wallcoverings

Plaster Systems

Once the major choice for wall and ceiling surfaces, plaster has seen a steady decline in popularity since the introduction of its competitor, gypsum drywall. Plaster still has an appeal with residential contractors, however, due to its more durable finish. The plaster system, commonly called *lath and plaster,* consists of a rigid substrate, *lath,* and a coating of plaster. Lath has evolved from wood strips, to perforated metal sheets, to sheetrock, and finally to its current form, a gypsum base, called *blueboard.* Blueboard is fastened to the wood or metal framing as a base for the application of plaster. Most plaster in residential/light commercial construction is applied using a thin (1/8") coat, called *skim coat plaster.*

The gypsum base is a gypsum-core board faced with a multi-layer, specially-treated paper that allows the skim coat or *veneer* plaster to bond to the base. Veneer plasters are designed to be applied in one- or two-coat systems for a strong, abrasion-resistant surface. Common blueboard sheets are 4' in width by 8', 10', or 12' in length. Other sizes are also available on special order. Standard thicknesses are 3/8", 1/2", and 5/8". Gypsum base is applied by screwing or nailing it to the framing. Plaster base is also manufactured for fire-rated applications and with a vapor-backing to retard the transmission of moisture. Veneer plaster is sold dry in 50- or 80-pound bags. When mixed with water to a paste-like consistency, it can be troweled onto the surface of the base. Coverage is based on the individual product, the specified thickness, and the type of finish.

An alternate type of plaster system, called a *conventional three-coat* system, requires the first two coats to be mixed with sand, perlite, or vermiculite aggregates in varying proportions. Three separate coats are applied, called *scratch, brown,* and *finish coats.* Each coat is allowed to dry prior to the application of the next. Conventional plaster systems are extremely labor-intensive and therefore costly, and, as a result, have suffered a reduction in popularity.

Taking off Quantities

Materials for both types of lath and plaster work are taken off by the square foot (SF) of surface area and converted to sales units for pricing. For accurate material pricing, the individual components, such as base, plaster, trims, and joint reinforcing tape, can be priced separately, then combined to arrive at the price of the system.

Skim coat plaster systems are priced by the square foot. Conventional plaster systems are priced by the square yard (SY). The takeoff should separate wall and ceiling applications due to labor pricing considerations. Openings less than 4 SF in area are not deducted, while openings without plaster *reveals*, or returns, are deducted in full. Reveals at openings should be calculated at 1.5 times their actual size. Special configurations, such as arches, pilasters, columns, decorative features, and special patterns, should be separated in the takeoff and priced on an individual basis. Allow one fastener for each square foot of plaster base. Multiple layers will follow the same procedure. The size and type of each fastener is determined by the thickness of the lath and the corresponding requirement in the specifications.

Labor

Regardless of the system, plastering is a crew task. Multiple trades comprise the crew. Carpenters hang the gypsum base, sheetrock, or metal lath. The tenders mix the plaster, erect and dismantle staging, distribute materials, stock the plasterers, and clean up. Plasterers cover the base with each coat to the desired finished texture. Plastering, similar to masonry and finish carpentry, is considered a *craft*, and only high-quality workmanship is acceptable.

Gypsum Wallboard Systems

Gypsum wallboard, more commonly known as *drywall*, is a manufactured product of powdered gypsum mixed with water and sandwiched between two layers of treated paper. It has become the system of choice in recent years. Because of its gypsum and mineral core, drywall, like plaster base, does not support combustion. It is manufactured in the same thicknesses and sheet sizes as plaster base. It can be used for a number of applications, including for fire-ratings, moisture resistance, and foil-backed for retarding vapor transmission. Other special products, such as 1"-thick shaft-wall liners for use in cavity-wall applications and gypsum sheathing for exterior curtain walls, also fall within the gypsum drywall category.

Drywall is installed with screws on metal or wood framing in the same manner as plaster base. Taping and finishing conceals the joints, and results in a smooth surface ready for paint or other finishes. Drywall ceiling installations can be covered with a textured finish to achieve an acoustical finish.

Taking off Quantities

Drywall is taken off and priced by the square foot (SF). Individual components can be converted to typical sales units, such as sheets, then priced separately in order to arrive at a square foot price. The procedure for taking off and pricing drywall is the same as for plaster base. Multiple layers of drywall for special fire-rated assemblies should be separated in the takeoff, since the level of finish differs at each layer. Taping and finishing is also listed in the takeoff by the square foot of area to be finished. The level of finish required should also be noted (for example: fire-coat only, or full tape and finish). Textured finishes for ceilings are listed in the takeoff separately by the square foot. Different application methods, such as spray or handwork, should also be separated.

Consult the architectural drawings, plans, elevations sections, and details. In addition, small cross-sectional views of the different walls and partitions used in the project, called *wall types*, are helpful. They illustrate the different components of the particular assembly. Like lath and plaster work, drywall should be priced separately based on the location and application. Costs for items such as staging to access the work or special equipment for spraying must also be included in the estimate. Deductions in openings follow the same rules as with lath and plaster.

Labor

Hanging drywall is a crew task, and most often done by carpenters. Production is based on the crew's combined output. Taping and finishing is done by *tapers*. Taping, however, is an individual task measured by the production of an individual. Consider additional costs for staging to finish drywall located above reach from the floor. It is common practice to carry an allowance for drywall touch-up after the surfaces have been primed. Figure 14.1 illustrates labor-hours for installation of various wallboard systems on wood partitions.

Metal Stud Framing & Furring

A popular choice for partitions and ceilings on commercial projects is metal stud framing and furring because it does not support combustion. The materials covered in this chapter are limited to non-load-bearing applications. For load-bearing applications, consult Division 5 in Chapter 10 of this book.

Non-load-bearing metal framing and furring is manufactured from cold-rolled galvanized metal, and is available in a variety of sizes, thicknesses (gauge), and shapes. The most common sizes of metal stud and track are 1-5/8", 2-1/2", 3-5/8", 4", and 6" with thicknesses of 20 and 25 gauge. Standard lengths range from 8' to 16' in 2' increments. Longer lengths of the larger sizes can be special ordered. Metal stud framing is fastened with framing screws, while furring can be attached with screws or power-actuated fasteners.

Metal stud partitions are framed in much the same way as wood partitions. Channel-shaped runners, called *tracks*, are positioned at the top and bottom of the partition and are similar to wood plates in wood framing. The tracks are anchored to the floor and overhead structure with screws, or in the case of concrete or steel, a power-actuated fastener. Metal studs are installed perpendicular to the track by fastening the flanges of the stud and track together with self-tapping screws. The studs are located within the track at the on-center spacing. Figure 14.2 illustrates a typical non-load-bearing metal stud partition assembly.

Installation Time in Labor-Hours for Wallboard Systems

Description	Labor-Hours	Unit
Metal Lath Diamond Expanded		
2.5 lb. per S.Y.	.094	S.Y.
3.4 lb. per S.Y.	.100	S.Y.
Gypsum Lath		
3/8" Thick	.094	S.Y.
1/2" Thick	.100	S.Y.
Gypsum Plaster		
2 Coats	.381	S.Y.
3 Coats	.460	S.Y.
Perlite or Vermiculite Plaster		
2 Coats	.435	S.Y.
3 Coats	.541	S.Y.
Wood Fiber Plaster		
2 Coats	.556	S.Y.
3 Coats	.702	S.Y.
Drywall Gypsum Plasterboard Including Taping		
3/8" Thick	.015	S.F.
1/2" or 5/8" Thick	.017	S.F.
For Thin Coat Plaster Instead of Taping Add	.013	S.F.
Prefinished Vinyl Faced Drywall	.015	S.F.
Sound-deadening Board	.009	S.F.
Walls in Place		
2" x 4" Studs with 5/8"		
Gypsum Drywall Both Sides Taped	.053	S.F.
2" x 4" Studs with 2 Layers Gypsum Drywall		
Both Sides Taped	.078	S.F.

Figure 14.1

Non-Load-Bearing Metal Stud Partition

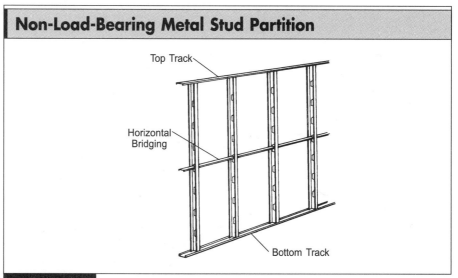

Top Track

Horizontal Bridging

Bottom Track

Figure 14.2

Special steel framing components for use in cavity shaft and fire-rated construction are manufactured in 20-, 22-, 24-, and 25-gauge thicknesses and are galvanized to resist corrosion. Their components are similar to regular metal stud framing, but include support for 1" thick shaft wall liner panels. Components are available in 2-1/2", 4", and 6" widths and lengths from 8' to 28', depending on the shape and width specified. Some of the more common shapes encountered in shaft wall construction are C-H studs installed between abutting liner panels, E studs used to cap panels at vertical intersections of walls, and J and C runners used as tracks at the top and bottom of cavity wall construction. Cavity wall framing materials are all non-load-bearing. Figure 14.3 shows the different types of studs and track used in cavity wall construction.

Other specialty members, such as cold-rolled channels (CRC) for use as main runners in ceiling suspension systems, are manufactured in 3/4", 1-1/2", and 2" sizes. The material is 16-gauge cold-rolled galvanized steel and is available in 16' and 20' lengths. It is typically suspended by a wire tied to the structure above. CRC channels are spaced at a maximum of 4'-0" on-center longitudinally, with a hat channel fastened transversely to the CRC at 12", 16", or 24" on-center by wire or special clips. Figure 14.4 shows different types of metal-framed ceiling systems.

Taking off Quantities

Metal studs and track are taken off by the LF. Track and studs are separated by gauge, type, size, and length of studs. Quantities are determined by dividing the length of the partition (in feet) by the stud spacing (also in feet) and adding additional studs for the end and for intersecting partitions. Doubled-up metal studs at the door and window jambs, heads, and sills are also needed. Although there are no structural headers required at non-load-bearing partitions, a piece of track is required to terminate the drywall at the head of the door and window and at the window sill.

Furring channels are taken off by the linear foot and separated according to type, size, gauge, and application (attached to wood, masonry, concrete, etc.).

CRC channels are taken off by the linear foot according to size and location. To determine the linear foot quantity, divide the length of the ceiling (in feet) by the on-center spacing (in feet). Multiply the result by the length of the individual pieces.

Cavity wall framing members are taken off by the linear foot and separated according to size, type, and length of the individual piece. The quantity of J and C runners is determined by measuring the length of the partition at the top and bottom. The number of C-H studs can be found by dividing the length of the partition (in feet) by the spacing (in feet) and adding additional studs for the ends or for corners. Additional quantities of track should also be considered for openings in cavity walls for doors,

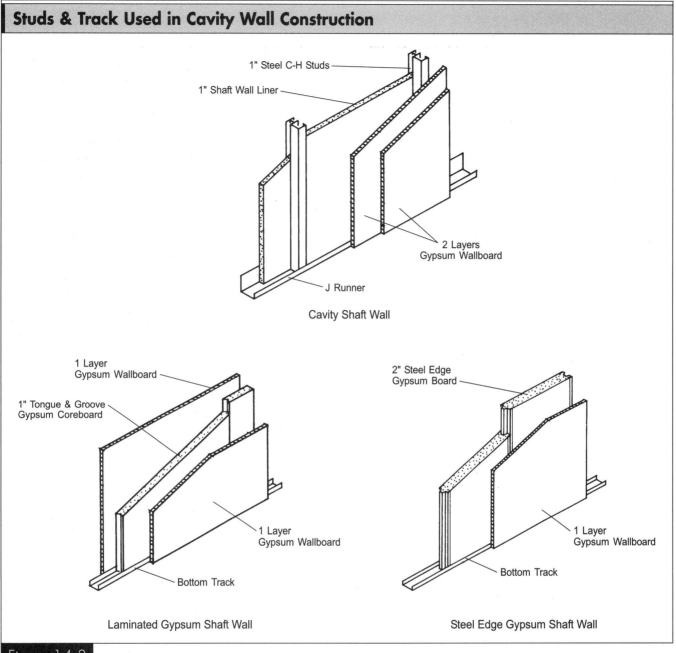

1" Steel C-H Studs

1" Shaft Wall Liner

2 Layers Gypsum Wallboard

J Runner

Cavity Shaft Wall

1 Layer Gypsum Wallboard

1" Tongue & Groove Gypsum Coreboard

1 Layer Gypsum Wallboard

Bottom Track

Laminated Gypsum Shaft Wall

2" Steel Edge Gypsum Board

1 Layer Gypsum Wallboard

Bottom Track

Steel Edge Gypsum Shaft Wall

Figure 14.3

as with standard metal partitions previously noted. The quantity of screws or power-actuated fasteners for framing is typically calculated at one fastener per linear foot of stud in the absence of a detailed specification for fastening. Power-actuated fasteners are typically expensive and are calculated by the linear foot of track, top and bottom of the partition, and the total length of furring channels by the on-center spacing as dictated by the specifications.

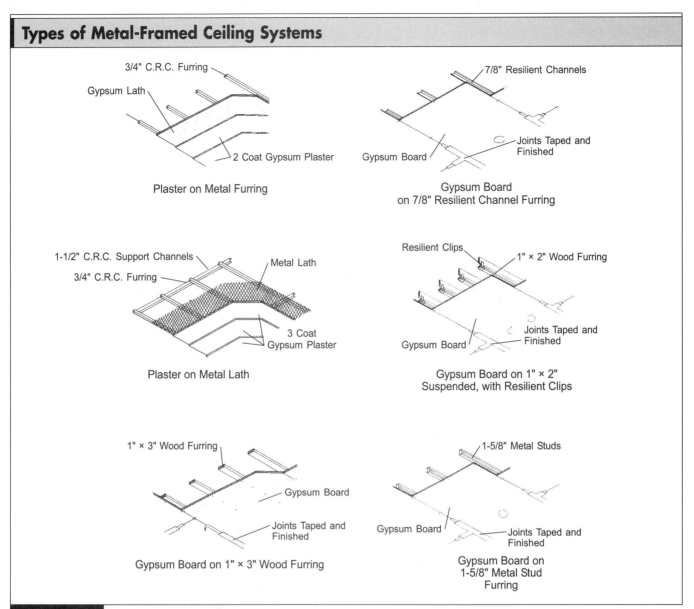

3/4" C.R.C. Furring

Gypsum Lath

2 Coat Gypsum Plaster

Plaster on Metal Furring

7/8" Resilient Channels

Joints Taped and Finished

Gypsum Board

Gypsum Board
on 7/8" Resilient Channel Furring

1-1/2" C.R.C. Support Channels

Metal Lath

3/4" C.R.C. Furring

3 Coat
Gypsum Plaster

Plaster on Metal Lath

Resilient Clips

1" × 2" Wood Furring

Joints Taped and Finished

Gypsum Board

Gypsum Board on 1" × 2"
Suspended, with Resilient Clips

1" × 3" Wood Furring

Gypsum Board

Joints Taped and Finished

Gypsum Board on 1" × 3" Wood Furring

1-5/8" Metal Studs

Gypsum Board

Joints Taped and Finished

Gypsum Board on
1-5/8" Metal Stud
Furring

Figure 14.4

Labor

Metal framing and furring is installed by multiple carpenters. Typical crews consist of pairs of carpenters working together. Production is measured by the crew's daily output. A laborer to handle and distribute materials may also be part of the crew when the work requires it. Production is measured by the linear foot of completed partition. This includes installing the track (top and bottom), studs, and special framing members at door or window openings. Productivity can also be based by the square foot of framed partition.

Additional costs for equipment, such as staging or lifts, including erection, dismantling, or delivery charges, must be included for accurate pricing. Framing partitions around ductwork, piping, conduits, and the like will substantially reduce productivity, as will numerous window or door openings. Take this into account when calculating labor-hours. Figure 14.5 provides a guideline for determining labor-hours for framing and furring.

Tile Tile, manufactured from clay, porcelain, or stone, is available in an ever-changing variety of sizes, shapes, colors, textures, patterns, finishes, and thicknesses. Tile provides a hard, durable, and virtually maintenance-free surface for both interior and exterior use. It is considered an excellent choice where wear and tear and longevity are concerned. In addition to standard tile pieces, often referred to as *field tile*, special

Installation Time in Labor-Hours for Steel Stud Partition Systems

Description	Labor-Hours	Unit
Non-Loadbearing Stud, Galv., 25 Gauge, 1-5/8" Wide,		
16" On Center	.019	S.F.
24" On Center	.016	S.F.
2-1/2" Wide,		
16" On Center	.020	S.F.
24" On Center	.016	S.F.
20 Gauge, 1-5/8" Wide,		
16" On Center	.018	S.F.
24" On Center	.016	S.F.
2-1/2" Wide,		
16" On Center	.019	S.F.
24" On Center	.016	S.F.
25 Gauge or 20 Gauge, 3-5/8" or 4" Wide		
16" On Center	.020	S.F.
24" On Center	.017	S.F.
6" Wide,		
16" On Center	.022	S.F.
24" On Center	.018	S.F.
Loadbearing Stud, Galv. or Painted, 18 Gauge, 2-1/2" Wide,		
16" On Center	.019	S.F.
24" On Center	.016	S.F.
3-5/8" or 4" Wide,		
16" On Center	.020	S.F.
24" On Center	.017	S.F.
6" Wide,		
16" On Center	.022	S.F.
24" On Center	.018	S.F.
Loadbearing Stud, Galv. or Painted, 16 Gauge, 2-1/2" Wide,		
16" On Center	.020	S.F.
24" On Center	.017	S.F.
3-5/8" or 4" Wide,		
16" On Center	.021	S.F.
24" On Center	.018	S.F.
6" Wide,		
16" On Center	.024	S.F.
24" On Center	.019	S.F.

Figure 14.5

shapes or trim pieces are also available. Some of the more common wall trims are bullnose, cove base, inside and outside corner pieces, custom transition shapes, and accessories such as toilet paper holders, towel bars, and soap dishes.

The characteristics of the tile material itself, installation method, and setting materials influence the overall cost of the work. Tile can be set with water-resistant pre-mixed adhesives—the most common method of tile installation in residential applications. Another common method is using dry-set Portland cement mortar, commonly referred to as *thin-set mortar*. Thin-set mortar is available in bags of varying sizes, and is mixed with water to obtain a toothpaste-like consistency. Specialty types of thin-set mortars for flexibility, exterior applications, and epoxy-based thin-sets are also available and in wide use.

Tile comes in individual pieces or back-mounted sheets for faster installation. It can be set with small spaces between the pieces for a grid-like appearance. The size of the spacing, called the *grout joint*, depends on the size, type, location, and specified design of the tile. Some ceramic tile is manufactured with pre-set spacing, as with back-mounted sheets; others are spaced by the tile setter. Once the tile has set, the joints between the tile are grouted to provide a continuous surface. The excess is cleaned off with a sponge or by other means to leave the surface clean.

Review the architectural drawings, plans, elevations, and reflected ceiling drawings for the location of tile work. Sections and details may add the necessary perspective to accurately price the work. Sections can be used to confirm wall tile heights shown on elevations, and details can provide information on the substrate or trim pieces required to complete the installation. Room Finish Schedules should also be consulted as a check and balance against other architectural drawings for locations of tile work. A comprehensive review of the technical specifications is also essential for the specific proprietary information on the products, setting method, and grout. Without this information, accurate pricing of the tile work will be compromised.

As the varieties of tile are numerous, for the purpose of this text and estimating tile work in general, discussion will be limited to two classifications: manufactured tile (ceramic and quarry tile) and natural tile (marble and granite tile).

Manufactured Tile

Ceramic and quarry tile are manufactured from clay, porcelain, or similar materials and baked in a kiln to a permanent hardness. Ceramic tile can be glazed or unglazed. Glazed tile can have an impervious glassy facial finish available in a multitude of colors, shapes, and sizes. Special trim pieces, such as bullnose tile, are used as transition pieces to terminate the tile work at adjacent surfaces. Other special trims include pieces that are used at the intersection of wall and floor tile, called *coves* or *cove base*, are available with inside and outside corners. Ceramic accessories, such as soap dishes, toilet paper holders, and towel bars, are also manufactured to match the field tile.

Ceramic mosaic tiles are small, with a face area of less than six square inches. They are mounted on pre-spaced backing sheets for ease of installation and are manufactured glazed or unglazed in various colors, patterns, or designs. Ceramic mosaic tile is used primarily for floor or decorative wall applications. Figure 14.6 shows the typical use and location of field and trim ceramic tile pieces.

Another extremely hard, durable form of tile, called *quarry tile*, is manufactured for use primarily as a floor tile. It is long-wearing and resembles brick pavers. It is available with abrasive chips embedded in the wearing surface for non-skid applications. Trim pieces similar to ceramic wall tile trims are also available to match.

Taking off Quantities

Tile and accessories are taken off separately, using the following guidelines:

- *Field tile for both ceramic and quarry tile*: taken off and priced by the SF area. Quantities should be separated according to finish (glazed or unglazed), and location (floor or wall).
- *Accent tile*: listed separately by the SF.
- *Trim pieces*: by the LF, converted to the number of pieces required.
- *Inside and outside corners*: by the individual piece (EA).

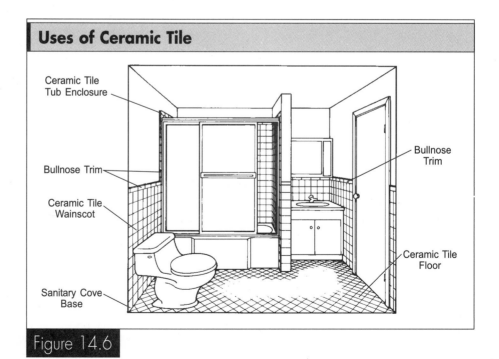

Uses of Ceramic Tile

Ceramic Tile Tub Enclosure

Bullnose Trim

Ceramic Tile Wainscot

Sanitary Cove Base

Bullnose Trim

Ceramic Tile Floor

Figure 14.6

Deductions for door and window openings should be made in full. Returns, or reveals, at doors and window openings should be included. The quantity of tile in square foot area can be converted to boxes of tile based on the individual sales unit. Tile setting materials, such as thin-set or adhesive, are calculated by the square foot of tile to be set. These quantities are then converted to typical sales units based on the manufacturer's coverage. Required bonding additives are determined by the manufacturer's formula of dry materials to liquid. This is then converted to the appropriate sales unit, most often gallons. Calculating grout follows the same procedure for setting materials. The square foot area and size of the grout joint (width and depth) are required. Identify the grouting and cleaning phase separately from the actual tile setting process.

Labor

Ceramic and quarry tile setting is done by tile layers or setters, with assistance from laborers, sometimes referred to as *tile setters' helpers*. Productivity is measured by the crew's daily output. Crews can range from a single tile setter in small applications, such as a residential bathroom, to several tile setters and helpers for commercial projects. The quality of workmanship is always estimated as first-class due to the highly aesthetic nature of tile. Special designs may reduce productivity. Additional layout time should also be allowed for in the estimate. Applying adhesive to the substrate and setting the tile on the wall or floor is considered a single process. The labor required to grout and clean the tile is also estimated as a separate task.

The cost of cutting tile with a hand cutter must be included as part of the setting costs. Harder or more dense types of tile, such quarry tiles and those that require unusual cuts, may need an electric or gas water-cooled saw with a diamond blade. Projects with a large number of cuts may even require an individual setter or helper dedicated to making cuts. This cost, along with the cost of the saw and blade replacement due to wear and tear, must be included in the estimate.

Delays, or time lapses, between setting and grouting tile, allow for the materials to cure and harden. Be sure to account for the costs in down-time for tile setters. The cost of cleaning agents should also be included.

Because of the weight and bulk of tile, shipping and handling costs can be significant. Secure the delivery price whenever possible.

Natural Tile

This type of tile has been cut and polished from natural stone and rock, such as marble and granite. The popularity of natural tile has risen exponentially as a result of the increased varieties and availability. Marble and granite tile, cut from larger blocks into uniform sizes, commonly come 12" x 12" in 1/2" thicknesses. The face or exposed surface is factory-polished to a high gloss. Other types of natural tile, such as slate for floor and wall applications, is less uniform in size and thickness and suggests a more rustic appearance. Slate tile is packaged by square footage. The setting materials used for ceramic and quarry tiles can also be used for stone tiles, although specialty products for certain types of marble tiles may be required. Trim pieces are not typically manufactured for stone tiles. Consequently, the external corners may require field mitering. Grouting joints between natural tiles is accomplished in the same manner as in ceramic and quarry tile. Grouted surfaces can be cleaned with water and light detergents, in contrast with acid for ceramic and quarry tile work.

Taking off Quantities

Natural tiles are taken off by the SF, extended to the quantity of individual pieces required for material pricing. They should be separated according to application or location (wall or floor), size, types of stone, and setting method. Cutting or mitering can be labor-intensive in large quantities and must be done with a wet saw. (Refer to the previous section on cutting tile.)

Labor

As with manufactured tiles, natural tiles are installed by tile setters and helpers. Crews rarely consist of less than two people due to the nature of the work. Review the considerations in the ceramic tile labor section earlier in this chapter, since most are applicable to natural tile. Other considerations include costs for sealing the surface and special epoxy setting materials for installing certain colored marble tiles. Sealing of natural surfaces can be expensive in both material and labor costs. Refer to the specifications and additional literature on the specific product. Installation productivity can be significantly reduced with certain types of epoxy setting adhesives, due to the small coverage per unit.

For all tile work, factor in waste due to tile damage, breakage, or mishandling. Specifications may require you to provide additional materials to be turned over to the owner upon completion. This is commonly called *attic stock*, and allows the owner to make repairs and replacement of tile outside of the warranty. Attic stock is often specified as a percentage of each style, color, or type on site. Common percentages range from 2% to 10%, depending on the size of the project.

Figure 14.7 provides a guideline to determine labor-hours for setting various types of tiles.

Acoustical Ceiling Systems

Designed to absorb and reduce sound transmission while still providing access above the ceiling, acoustical ceiling tiles are available in a variety of sizes, colors, patterns, and textures. For estimating purposes, most acoustical ceiling systems can be classified in one of three groups:

- Acoustical ceiling systems attached directly to ceiling substrates.
- Suspended acoustical ceiling tiles with a concealed spline.
- Acoustical ceiling tiles installed in an exposed suspension system.

Installation Time in Labor-Hours for Floor and Wall Tile Systems

Description	Labor-Hours	Unit
Flooring Cast Ceramic 4" x 8" x 3/4" Pressed	.160	S.F.
Hand Molded	.168	S.F.
8" x 3/4" Hexagonal	.188	S.F.
Heavy Duty Industrial Cement Mortar Bed	.200	S.F.
Ceramic Pavers 8" x 4"	.168	S.F.
Ceramic Tile Base, Using 1" x 1" Tiles, 4" High,		
Mud Set	.195	L.F.
Thin Set	.125	L.F.
Cove Base, 4-1/4" x 4-1/4" High, Mud Set	.176	L.F.
Thin Set	.125	L.F.
6" x 4-1/4" High, Mud Set	.160	L.F.
Thin Set	.117	L.F.
Sanitary Cove Base, 6" x 4-1/4" High, Mud Set	.172	L.F.
Thin Set	.129	L.F.
6" x 6" High, Mud Set	.190	L.F.
Thin Set	.137	L.F.
Bullnose Trim, 4-1/4" x 4-1/4", Mud Set	.195	L.F.
Thin Set	.125	L.F.
6" x 4-1/4" Bullnose Trim, Mud Set	.190	L.F.
Thin Set	.129	L.F.
Floors, Natural Clay, Random or Uniform,		
Thin Set, Color Group 1	.087	S.F.
Color Group 2	.087	S.F.
Porcelain Type, 1 Color, Color Group 2,		
1" x 1"	.087	S.F.
2" x 2" or 2" x 1", Thin Set	.084	S.F.
Conductive Tile, 1" Squares, Black	.147	S.F.
4" x 8" or 4" x 4", 3/8" Thick	.133	S.F.
Trim, Bullnose, Etc.	.080	L.F.
Specialty Tile, 3" x 6" x 1/2", Decorator Finish	.087	S.F.
Add For Epoxy Grout, 1/16" Joint,		
1" x 1" Tile	.020	S.F.
2" x 2" Tile	.020	S.F.
Pregrouted Sheets, Walls, 4-1/4", 6" x 4-1/4",		
and 8-1/2" x 4-1/4", S.F. Sheets,		
Silicone Grout	.067	S.F.
Floors, Unglazed, 2 S.F. Sheets		
Urethane Adhesive	.089	S.F.
Walls, Interior, Thin Set, 4-1/4" x 4-1/4" Tile	.084	S.F.
6" x 4-1/4" Tile	.084	S.F.
8-1/2" x 4-1/4" Tile	.084	S.F.
6" x 6" Tile	.080	S.F.

Figure 14.7a

Installation Time in Labor-Hours for Floor and Wall Tile Systems

Description	Labor-Hours	Unit
Decorated Wall Tile, 4-1/4"x 4-1/4"		
Minimum	.018	Ea.
Maximum	.028	Ea.
Exterior Walls, Frostproof, Mud Set,		
4-1/4" x 4-1/4"	.157	S.F.
1-3/8" x 1-3/8"	.172	S.F.
Crystalline Glazed, 4-1/4" x 4-1/4", Mud		
Set, Plain	.160	S.F.
4-1/4" x 4-1/4", Scored Tile	.160	S.F.
1-3/8" Squares	.172	S.F.
For Epoxy Grout, 1/16" Joints, 4-1/4" Tile,		
Add	.020	S.F.
For Tile Set in Dry Mortar, Add	.009	S.F.
For Tile Set in Portland Cement Mortar, Add	.055	S.F.
Regrout Tile 4-1/2" x 4-1/2", or Larger, Wall	.080	S.F.
Floor	.073	S.F.
Ceramic Tile Panels Insulated, Over 1000		
Square Feet,		
1-1/2" Thick	.073	S.F.
2-1/2" Thick	.073	S.F.
Glass Mosaics 3/4" Tile on 12" Sheets,		
Color Group 1 and 2 Minimum	.195	S.F.
Maximum (Latex Set)	.219	S.F.
Color Group 3	.219	S.F.
Color Group 4	.219	S.F.
Color Group 5	.219	S.F.
Color Group 6	.219	S.F.
Color Group 7	.219	S.F.
Color Group 8, Gold, Silvers and Specialties	.250	S.F.
Marble Thin Gauge Tile, 12" x 6", 9/32", White		
Carara	.250	S.F.
Filled Travertine	.250	S.F.
Synthetic Tiles, 12" x 12" x 5/8",		
Thin Set, Floors	.250	S.F.
On Walls	.291	S.F.
Metal Tile Cove Base, Standard Colors,		
4-1/4" Square	.053	L.F.
4-1/8" x 8-1/2"	.040	L.F.
Walls, Aluminum, 4-1/4" Square, Thin		
Set, Plain	.100	S.F.
Epoxy Enameled	.107	S.F.
Leather on Aluminum, Colors	.123	S.F.
Stainless Steel	.107	S.F.
Suede on Aluminum	.123	S.F.
Plastic Tile Walls, 4-1/4" x 4-1/4",		
.050" Thick	.064	S.F.
.110" Thick	.067	S.F.

Figure 14.7b

Installation Time in Labor-Hours for Floor and Wall Tile Systems

Description	Labor-Hours	Unit
Quarry Tile Base, Cove or Sanitary, 2" or 5" High, Mud Set		
1/2" Thick	.145	L.F.
Bullnose Trim, Red, Mud Set, 6" x 6" x 1/2" Thick	.133	L.F.
4" x 4" x 1/2" Thick	.145	L.F.
4" x 8" x 1/2" Thick, Using 8" as Edge	.123	L.F.
Floors, Mud Set, 1000 S.F. Lots, Red,		
4" x 4" x 1/2" Thick	.133	S.F.
6" x 6" x 1/2" Thick	.114	S.F.
4" x 8" x 1/2" Thick	.123	S.F.
Brown Tile, Imported, 6" x 6" x 7/8"	.133	S.F.
9" x 9" x 1-1/4"	.145	S.F.
For Thin Set Mortar Application, Deduct	.023	S.F.
Stair Tread and Riser, 6" x 6" x 3/4", Plain	.320	S.F.
Abrasive	.340	S.F.
Wainscot, 6" x 6" x 1/2", Thin Set, Red	.152	S.F.
Colors Other Than Green	.152	S.F.
Window Sill, 6" Wide, 3/4" Thick	.178	L.F.
Corners	.200	Ea.
Terra Cotta Tile on Walls, Dry Set, 1/2" Thick		
Square, Hexagonal or Lattice Shapes, Unglazed	.059	S.F.
Glazed, Plain Colors	.062	S.F.
Intense Colors	.064	S.F.

Figure 14.7c

Acoustical ceiling tiles are manufactured in increments of 12" in each direction, with 12" x 12", 24" x 24", and 24" x 48" the most common. Other non-acoustic ceiling tiles can be installed within a suspension system, or *grid*. Decorative, thin metal panels, either embossed or plain, in chrome or brass finishes are available. Vinyl-coated gypsum panels are manufactured for ceilings that require washable surfaces, such as kitchens and food processing areas.

Suspension systems consist of aluminum or steel main runners of light, intermediate, or heavy-duty construction with snap-in cross tees in one- to five-foot lengths. Main runners are hung from the supporting structure with tie wire. Small metal angles, called *wall angles*, are attached to the perimeter wall or vertical surface at the ceiling height to complete the grid. Components of the suspension system are available in colored or metallic plating.

Review the architectural floor and reflected ceiling plans to determine the location and quantities of components. Cross-referencing the roof finish schedule can help confirm locations and provide additional information, such as the type of ceiling, height of ceiling above the finished floor, and any special fire-rated assemblies. Quantities are determined by measuring the length and width of the room. Additional information, including the "length of the hang" of suspension systems, can be obtained from building cross-sections.

Consult the specifications for the actual products and their various characteristics for accurate material pricing. Critical characteristics, such as color, STC (sound transmission classification) rating, surface finish, fire-rating, and seismic requirements are major price determinants. Also review the specifications for attic stock requirements.

Taking off Quantities

Acoustical ceiling systems can be taken off two ways: by the square foot area of the room, or by the individual components of the system. The latter is recommended for more accurate pricing, as it accounts for the square foot area of the actual acoustical ceiling tile or panel. Dimensions of the room should be rounded to the nearest 1'-0" for 12" tile and nearest 2'-0" for 2' x 2' or 2' x 4' tiles. This can then be converted to the number of pieces or units required. Suspension components, such as the main runners, cross-tees, wall angles, and hanging wire, should be taken off by the linear foot and converted to the individual piece. Hold-down clips, if required, are calculated by the individual piece. All quantities should be separated according to size, color, type, manufacturer, model, texture, and finish. Some acoustical tiles are *directional*, where the pattern on the exposed face has a direction, and cut pieces from one side may not be used on the opposite side. This can significantly contribute to waste. The description in the takeoff should provide as much information as possible for pricing.

Labor

Acoustical ceiling systems are installed by carpenters. Productivity can be measured by the output of an individual carpenter or the combined efforts of a crew by completed square foot area per day. Large open areas should be distinguished in the takeoff from small confined areas, as different productivities will result. Another factor that will affect productivity is the support structure from which the ceiling will hang. Tying hanging wire to open web bar joists is less labor-intensive than anchors drilled or "shot" into the concrete deck above. The length of the ceiling hang is also a determining factor. The longer the hang, the slower the process. Other considerations include staging or lifts required to access the work. Be sure to include erecting, dismantling, delivery, and rental costs if required.

Fire-rated systems or those with hold-down clips can significantly reduce productivity, as do sloped or splayed ceilings and soffits. These features all require additional time to install. Special tiles that recess the tile in the grid, called *reveal edge* tiles, are sometimes cut to fit a grid opening. The cut edge must be grooved to replicate the reveal edge. This process, called *kerfing* the tile, is done with a knife by hand on-site, and may, with sufficient quantity, require a separate individual to maintain the progress of the project. Figure 14.8 provides guidelines for installation labor-hours of different types of acoustical ceiling systems.

Distribution and handling of acoustical ceiling materials can be significant. Labor should be included for stocking materials if the quantity is sufficient. Consider added labor for cleanup and disposal of debris, if required in the contract.

Installation Time in Labor-Hours for Ceiling Systems

Description	Labor-Hours	Unit
Ceiling Tile Stapled, Cemented or Installed on Suspension System, 12" x 12" or 12" x 24", Not Including Furring		
Mineral Fiber, Plastic Coated	.020	S.F.
Fire Rated, 3/4" Thick, Plain Faced	.020	S.F.
Plastic Coated Face	.021	S.F.
Aluminum Faced, 5/8" Thick, Plain	.021	S.F.
Metal Pan Units, 24 ga. Steel, Not Incl. Pads, Painted, 12" x 12"	.023	S.F.
12" x 36" or 12" x 24", 7% Open Area	.024	S.F.
Aluminum, 12" x 12"	.023	S.F.
12" x 24"	.022	S.F.
Stainless Steel, 12" x 24", 26 ga., Solid	.023	S.F.
5.2% Open Area	.024	S.F.
Suspended Acoustic Ceiling Boards Not Including Suspension System		
Fiberglass Boards, Film Faced, 2' x 2' or 2' x 4', 5/8" Thick	.012	S.F.
3/4" Thick	.016	S.F.
3" Thick, Thermal, R11	.018	S.F.
Glass Cloth Faced Fiberglass, 3/4" Thick	.016	S.F.
1" Thick	.016	S.F.
1-1/2" Thick, Nubby Face	.017	S.F.
Mineral Fiber Boards, 5/8" Thick, Aluminum Faced, 24" x 24"	.013	S.F.
24" x 48"	.012	S.F.
Plastic Coated Face	.020	S.F.
Mineral Fiber, 2 Hour Rating, 5/8" Thick	.012	S.F.
Mirror Faced Panels, 15/16" Thick	.016	S.F.
Air Distributing Ceilings, 5/8" Thick, F.R.D. Water Felted Board	.020	S.F.
Eggcrate, Acrylic, 1/2" x 1/2" x 1/2" Cubes	.016	S.F.
Polystyrene Eggcrate	.016	S.F.
Luminous Panels, Prismatic	.020	S.F.
Perforated Aluminum Sheets, .024" Thick, Corrugated, Painted	.016	S.F.
Mineral Fiber, 24" x 24" or 48", reveal edge, Painted, 5/8" Thick	.013	S.F.
3/4" Thick	.014	S.F.
Wood Fiber in Cementitious Binder, 2' x 2' or 4', Painted, 1" Thick	.013	S.F.
2" Thick	.015	S.F.
2-1/2" Thick	.016	S.F.
3" Thick	.018	S.F.
Access Panels, Metal, 12" x 12"	.400	Ea.
24" x 24"	.800	Ea.

Figure 14.8

Flooring

Flooring includes an almost infinite number of different and perpetually changing products. For estimating purposes, flooring can be classified in three general categories:

- Wood
- Resilient
- Carpet

Material costs for flooring products range from economy to luxury grade. It is critical that you become familiar with the characteristics of the specified products to accurately price both materials and installation. Special concerns that have a cost impact include preparing the substrate, maintaining temperature and humidity conditions, washing/waxing or vacuuming of the finish product, and protecting the installed work. Be sure to study the architectural drawings and specifications in detail to determine the full scope of flooring work. In the absence of detailed specifications, the estimator must consider costs that relate to complying with "industry standards" or manufacturers' requirements.

Wood Flooring

This type of flooring comes in a wide variety of styles, grades, species, and patterns for interior use. It is manufactured in solid and laminated planks or parquet. *Laminated flooring*, high-grade wood veneers laminated over a lesser grade base material, is sold pre-finished. Solid wood flooring can be pre-finished or unfinished, and is classified by grade and quality. Common hardwood flooring materials are milled from oak, ash, maple, beech, walnut, cherry, and mahogany. Other exotic hardwoods include teak, ebony, zebrawood, and rosewood. Popular softwood flooring materials include fir, pine, cedar, and spruce.

Unfinished wood flooring requires repeated machine sanding with increasingly finer-grit sand paper, followed by the application of a finish coating. Finish coatings can vary from polyurethanes to tung oil and may require more than one application. Review the architectural drawing set carefully with special attention to floor plans and corresponding flooring details that illustrate the transition between different types of flooring. Room finish schedules will confirm locations and types of flooring materials. Specifications will provide the wood type, species, size, and pattern. The grade and quality of the material should also be identified in the wood floor specifications section. For unfinished materials, the specifications should also define the steps in the sanding process, the finishing product, and the number of coats. This is extremely important to accurately price the materials and labor for the particular system. In the absence of a formal specification, as is often the case in the residential sector, consult the manufacturer's literature for recommendations in order to maintain the warranty.

Taking off Quantities

Wood flooring is taken off by the SF of floor area. It should be identified according to type (plank, strip, or parquet), finish (pre-finished or unfinished), species (oak, maple, ash, etc.), size (width and thickness), and method of application (adhesive, face, or blind nailed). Any patterns should also be noted. Grade and quality of unfinished wood flooring materials are critical in determining accurate quantities and pricing.

Waste is directly related to grade and quality of the wood. The lesser the grade, the more waste to be included in the takeoff as a result of natural imperfections. Pre-finished materials are more closely regulated during the quality control process, and, as a result, generally have little waste. Patterns and designs influence quantities and waste, as well.

The square foot quantity of unfinished flooring materials is often converted to *board foot measure* (BFM) for pricing. *(See Chapter 11— Wood & Plastics.)* Board foot quantities depend on the profile and thickness of the individual species and type of flooring. Be sure to differentiate between large, open areas, and small rooms or closets that might affect productivity. Fasteners, adhesives, vapor barriers, and building paper are taken off by the square foot and converted to the sales unit of the individual product.

Takeoff for Refinishing: The quantity of flooring to be refinished is calculated by the square foot of surface area to be refinished. The species of wood and the various stages of sanding should also be noted. Finishing can be separated in the takeoff from sanding for more accurate pricing, but this is not mandatory. Finishing should be defined by the product and the number of coats required. The square foot area multiplied by the number of individual coats can help determine the gallons of product needed, based on the manufacturer's recommended coverage.

Labor

Wood flooring can be installed by carpenters or floor installers. While the installation of pre-finished wood flooring has become extremely homeowner-friendly, use of unfinished wood flooring still remains more complicated and the domain of the professional flooring contractor. Depending on the size of the project, crews can consist of a single individual or several flooring installers and laborers to distribute the flooring material. Productivity is based on the individual flooring installer. Patterns and designs generally reduce productivity, as do small, confined work areas. Blending new flooring into existing flooring is also particularly time-consuming. It often requires the removal of existing flooring and the labor-intensive process of weaving new into old. Include any additional costs for handling and distributing the flooring, as well as equipment costs. Pneumatic nail guns have become increasingly popular for flooring installation and, as a result, have increased productivity in general. Figure 14.9 provides guidelines for estimating installation labor-hours for wood flooring.

Installation Time in Labor-Hours for Wood Flooring

Description	Labor-Hours	Unit
Wood Floors Fir, Vertical Grain, 1" x 4", Not Including Finish	.031	S.F.
Gym Floor, in Mastic, Over 2 Ply Felt, #2 and Better 25/32" Thick Maple, Including Finish	.080	S.F.
33/32" Thick Maple, Including Finish	.082	S.F.
For 1/2" Corkboard Underlayment, Add	.011	S.F.
Maple Flooring, Over Sleepers, #2 and Better Including Finish, 25/32" Thick	.094	S.F.
33/32" Thick	.096	S.F.
For 3/4" Subfloor, Add	.023	S.F.
With Two 1/2" Subfloors, 25/32" Thick	.116	S.F.
Maple, Including Finish, #2 and better, 25/32" Thick, on Rubber Sleepers, with Two 1/2" Subfloors	.105	S.F.
With Steel Spline, Double Connection to Channels	.110	S.F.
Portable Hardwood, Prefinished Panels	.096	S.F.
Insulated with Polystyrene, Add	.048	S.F.
Running Tracks, Sitka Spruce Surface	.129	S.F.
3/4" Plywood Surface	.080	S.F.
Maple, Strip, Not Including Finish	.047	S.F.
Oak Strip, White or Red, Not Including Finish	.047	S.F.
Parquetry, Standard, 5/16" Thick, Not Including Finish, Minimum	.050	S.F.
13/16" Thick, Select Grade, Minimum	.050	S.F.
Maximum	.080	S.F.
Custom Parquetry, Including Finish, Minimum	.080	S.F.
Maximum	.160	S.F.
Prefinished White Oak, Prime Grade, 2-1/4" Wide	.047	S.F.
3-1/4" Wide	.043	S.F.
Ranch Plank	.055	S.F.
Hardwood Blocks, 9" x 9", 25/32" Thick	.050	S.F.

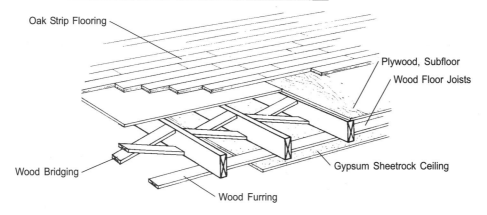

Oak Strip Flooring

Plywood, Subfloor

Wood Floor Joists

Wood Bridging

Gypsum Sheetrock Ceiling

Wood Furring

Figure 14.9a

Installation Time in Labor-Hours for Wood Flooring

Description	Labor-Hours	Unit
Acrylic Wood Parquet Blocks,		
12" x 12" x 5/16", Irradiated, Set in Epoxy	.050	S.F.
Yellow Pine, 3/4" x 3-1/8", T & G, C and		
Better, Not Including Finish	.040	S.F.
Refinish Old Floors, Minimum	.020	S.F.
Maximum	.062	S.F.
Sanding and Finishing, Fill, Shellac, Wax	.027	S.F.
Wood Block Flooring End Grain Flooring,		
Creosoted, 2" Thick	.027	S.F.
Natural Finish, 1" Thick	.029	S.F.
1-1/2" Thick	.031	S.F.
2" Thick	.033	S.F.
Wood Composition Gym Floors		
2-1/4" x 6-7/8" x 3/8", on 2" Grout Setting		
Bed	.107	S.F.
Thin Set, on Concrete	.064	S.F.
Sanding and Finishing, Add	.040	S.F.

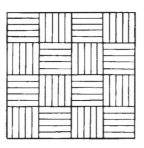

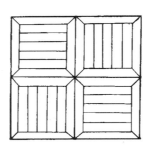

Random Patterns of Parquet Flooring

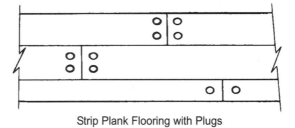

Strip Plank Flooring with Plugs

Figure 14.9b

Labor for Refinishing Flooring: Labor to refinish floors, including sanding and coating, is calculated and priced by the square foot. Incidental costs of sandpaper, rollers, and brushes for applying the finish, and equipment must be included. Refinishing floors (versus new finishing) may require protection of adjacent work and the associated costs. Cleanup, vacuuming, hand sanding, and touch-up also must be addressed in the labor portion of the estimate.

Resilient Flooring

Resilient flooring is designed for areas where flooring durability, low-maintenance, and longevity are of primary concern. Materials include asphalt tiles, vinyl composition tiles (VCT), cork tiles, and rubber tiles. Sheet materials include rubber, vinyl, and polyvinyl chloride. Rubber and vinyl accessories for resilient flooring include bases, thresholds, transition strips, stair treads and risers, and nosings. Resilient flooring materials are installed with adhesives, though some are manufactured with a self-adhering backing.

Consult the floor plans for information on the quantities and accessories, and the room finish schedules for locations and limits of flooring within individual rooms. Review the technical specifications section for critical information necessary to accurately price materials and installation. Product data will also help you price the correct product. Other unique considerations that have a cost impact, such as protection of completed flooring, washing and waxing, and substrate preparation, are identified within the specifications.

Taking off Quantities

Resilient flooring is taken off by the square foot by calculating the area of the floor. Resilient tiles are priced by the SF, and can be converted to sales units of the individual product. Sheet goods quantities are extended from the SF to the SY for pricing. All takeoff quantities should be separated according to size, type, thickness, method of installation, location, or any other identifying characteristics. Accessories, such as base, transitions strips and thresholds, are taken off by the LF, while stair treads, risers, and nosings of a repetitive size are taken off by the piece (EA). Adhesives are calculated by converting the square footage of flooring to units (most often gallons) of the individual product. Coverage will vary with the subfloor condition and the manufacturer's recommendations.

Other considerations include allowances for waste, which will vary with layout and patterns. Flooring tiles laid in a diagonal pattern, for example, will require additional quantities. Most specifications call for layout to start at the center of the room so that the cuts on opposite walls are equal. You may choose to increase the measurements of the room to the nearest full tile on either side. Because of the thinness and flexibility of resilient products, defects in the subfloor easily "telegraph" through the flooring. Consequently, the subfloor materials and the quality of its surface preparation are very important. Subfloor preparation, even for new construction, is required and should be included in the estimate. The quantity is expressed by the SF of subfloor.

Labor

Resilient floor tile and sheet goods are installed by floor tile layers and priced by the SF and SY, respectively. Productivity of a crew composed of multiple individuals is measured by the total output in square feet per day. Installation of base, treads, risers, and nosing is priced by the individual piece. Costs for prep work should be separate in the takeoff from actual tile or base installation, and are calculated by the square foot of subfloor that can be prepped in a day. Floor prep costs are extremely subjective and will vary dramatically depending on the conditions of the substrate. Floor prep costs are most accurate when the subfloor can be viewed prior to pricing. Other labor costs, such as washing and waxing or protection of newly installed floors, are calculated based on the square foot area. Since most resilient flooring products are heavy and bulky, include costs for delivery, stocking, and distribution throughout the building. Figure 14.10 provides a guideline for calculating labor.

Carpeting

A popular flooring material for both residential and commercial construction, carpet provides a comfortable, sound absorbing, and attractive finish surface. It is manufactured from a variety of different materials, including nylon, wool, acrylic, polyester, and rayon, and is specified by weight, pile thickness, and density. Special carpets for commercial applications, such as fire-rated materials and anti-static carpet for use in computer rooms, are also available. Commercial grade carpeting is manufactured in rolls and tiles, but residential is available mainly in rolls. The size of the roll will vary with type, manufacturer, quality, and model. Rolls are generally available in 12- and 15-foot widths. Occasionally, 9- and 18-foot-wide rolls are available in limited patterns. Carpet tiles are available in 18" x 18", 24" x 24", and 36" x 36" sizes. Carpeting can be installed on cushion material called *padding*.

Accessories for carpeting include metal or rubber edging and specialty carpeting for stair runners. Most carpeting is installed using one of two methods: directly gluing the carpet to the floor substrate, or using pad underlayments and fastening the carpet in one section at the perimeter of the room.

The architectural drawings, floor plans, and room finish schedules will provide the location and limits of specific types of carpeting. Review the specs for manufacturer, model, size (roll width), color, weight, and method of installation for correct pricing. Other special requirements, such as seaming, patterns, vacuuming, and protection, are also detailed in the specifications.

Installation Time in Labor-Hours for Resilient Flooring

Description	Labor-Hours	Unit
Resilient Asphalt Tile, on Concrete, 1/8" Thick		
Color Group B	.015	S.F.
Color Group C and D	.015	S.F.
For Less Than 500 S.F., Add	.002	S.F.
For Over 5000 S.F., Deduct	.007	S.F.
Base, Cove, Rubber or Vinyl, .080" Thick		
Standard Colors, 2-1/2" High	.026	L.F.
4" High	.027	L.F.
6" High	.027	L.F.
1/8" Thick, Standard Colors,		
2-1/2" High	.026	L.F.
4" High	.027	L.F.
6" High	.027	L.F.
Corners, 2-1/2" High	.026	Ea.
4" High	.027	Ea.
6" High	.027	Ea.
Conductive Flooring, Rubber Tile,		
1/8" Thick	.025	S.F.
Homogeneous Vinyl Tile, 1/8" Thick	.025	S.F.
Cork Tile, Standard Finish, 1/8" Thick	.025	S.F.
3/16" Thick	.025	S.F.
5/16" Thick	.025	S.F.
1/2" Thick	.025	S.F.
Urethane Finish, 1/8" Thick	.025	S.F.
3/16" Thick	.025	S.F.
5/16" Thick	.025	S.F.
1/2" Thick	.025	S.F.
Polyethylene, in Rolls, No Base Incl.,		
Landscape Surfaces	.029	S.F.
Nylon Action Surface, 1/8" Thick	.029	S.F.
1/4" Thick	.029	S.F.
3/8" Thick	.029	S.F.
Golf Tee Surface with Foam Back	.033	S.F.
Practice Putting, Knitted Nylon Surface	.033	S.F.
Polyurethane, Thermoset, Prefabricated in Place, Indoor		
3/8" Thick for Basketball, Gyms, etc.	.080	S.F.

Figure 14.10a

Taking off Quantities

Carpeting and padding is taken off by calculating the area of the room in SF, extended to the pricing unit of SY, where 1 SY equals 9 SF. Carpet tile quantities are calculated the same way, but instead of extending the quantities to SY, they are converted to the required number of pieces. Separate different types of carpet according to manufacturer, model, type, style, and method of installation for accurate pricing. Patterns or combinations of different carpeting should also be noted, as they are sometimes labor-intensive. Protection or cleaning requirements of completed work should be taken off separately.

Installation Time in Labor-Hours for Resilient Flooring

Description	Labor-Hours	Unit
Stair Treads and Risers		
Rubber, Molded Tread, 12" Wide, 5/16"		
Thick, Black	.070	L.F.
Colors	.070	L.F.
1/4" Thick, Black	.070	L.F.
Colors	.070	L.F.
Grit Strip Safety Tread, Colors 5/16" Thick	.070	L.F.
3/16" Thick	.067	L.F.
Landings, Smooth Sheet Rubber,		
1/8" Thick	.029	S.F.
3/16" Thick	.030	S.F.
Nosings, 1-1/2" Deep, 3" Wide, Residential	.057	L.F.
Commercial	.057	L.F.
Risers, 7" High, 1/8" Thick, Flat	.046	L.F.
Coved	.046	L.F.
Vinyl, Molded Tread, 12" Wide, Colors,		
1/8" Thick	.070	L.F.
1/4" Thick	.070	L.F.
Landing Material, 1/8" Thick	.040	S.F.
Riser, 7" High, 1/8" Thick, Coved	.046	L.F.
Threshold, 5-1/2" Wide	.080	L.F.
Tread and Riser Combined, 1/8" Thick	.100	L.F.

Figure 14.10b

Many specifications have strict seaming requirements and may call for the layout of "drops" of carpeting or seaming drawings for approval. Seams should be minimized during installation, as they will increase the waste of the carpet if remnants cannot be used elsewhere. For example, if a room measuring 10'-3" x 20'-3" has an area of 23 SY, but a 12-foot wide carpet is used, one piece 12' x 21' or 28 SY must be purchased. The difference represents a 22% waste. Carpeting with special designs or repeating patterns requires careful calculation to allow for matching the pattern at seams. A classic example is carpet that simulates an Oriental or Persian rug.

Labor

Regardless of the method of installation, carpet is typically installed by floor tile layers. The crew most often consists of two individuals to handle the awkward and bulky carpet rolls. Productivity is measured in SY installed per crew per day. Large open areas and small confined spaces should be priced separately, as should patterned carpeting. Figure 14.11 provides labor-hour guidelines for the installation of various types of carpeting and applications.

Painting

Finishing and painting are often required to protect surfaces from wear and deterioration, and to provide a decorative appearance. The work typically includes preparation of the surface to receive the paint or finish, and may involve sanding, filling in holes, and removing dust or oils. More extensive preparation can involve stripping old finishes, applying wood conditioner, or applying primers to neutralize the substrate, as in the case of galvanized finishes. Painting and finishing products run the full spectrum from latex and alkyd or oil-based paints and stains, to epoxy coatings and urethanes. Application methods include spraying, rolling, and brushing. All three may be used on the same project or even in the same process.

Installation Time in Labor-Hours for Carpeting

Description	Labor-Hours	Unit
Carpet Commercial Grades, Cemented		
Acrylic, 26 oz., Light to Medium Traffic	.216	S.F.
28 oz., Medium Traffic	.229	S.F.
35 oz., Medium to Heavy Traffic	.242	S.F.
Nylon, Non Anti-Static, 15 oz., Light Traffic	.229	S.F.
Nylon, With Anti-Static, 17 oz., Light to Medium Traffic	.211	S.F.
20 oz., Medium Traffic	.216	S.F.
22 oz., Medium Traffic	.216	S.F.
24 oz., Medium to Heavy Traffic	.229	S.F.
26 oz., Medium to Heavy Traffic	.229	S.F.
28 oz., Heavy Traffic	.229	S.F.
32 oz., Heavy Traffic	.242	S.F.
42 oz., Heavy Traffic	.258	S.F.
Needle Bonded, 20 oz., No Padding	.143	S.F.
Polypropylene, 15 oz., Light Traffic	.143	S.F.
22 oz., Medium Traffic	.182	S.F.
24 oz., Medium to Heavy Traffic	.182	S.F.
26 oz., Medium to Heavy Traffic	.182	S.F.
28 oz., Heavy Traffic	.205	S.F.
32 oz., Heavy Traffic	.205	S.F.
42 oz., Heavy Traffic	.216	S.F.
Scrim Installed, Nylon Sponge Back Carpet		
20 oz.	.242	S.Y.
60 oz.	.267	S.Y.
Tile, Foam-Backed, Needle Punch	.014	S.F.
Tufted Loop or Shag	.014	S.Y.
Wool, 30 oz., Medium Traffic	.229	S.Y.
Wool, 36 oz., Medium to Heavy Traffic	.242	S.Y.
Sponge Back, Wool, 36 oz., Medium to Heavy Traffic	.143	S.Y.
42 oz., Heavy Traffic	.229	S.Y.
Padding, Sponge Rubber Cushion, Minimum	.108	S.Y.
Maximum	.123	S.Y.
Felt, 32 oz. to 56 oz., Minimum	.108	S.Y.
Maximum	.123	S.Y.
Bonded Urethane, 3/8" Thick, Minimum	.094	S.Y.
Maximum	.107	S.Y.
Prime Urethane, 1/4" Thick, Minimum	.094	S.Y.
Maximum	.107	S.Y.

Figure 14.11

Floor plans, interior elevations, and reflected ceiling plans can help define the painting work. Interior elevations frequently illustrate wood trims that require finishes, and exterior elevations will provide dimensions for exterior siding and trims. Room finish schedules should also be reviewed for individual locations and any limitations of painting/finishing work. Consult the mechanical and electrical drawings for the painting of pipes, conduits, and unfinished equipment as a means of identification. Roof drawings can be helpful in determining the quantities of rooftop equipment or gas piping to be painted.

Study the technical specifications carefully for the location and summary of finishing work, type of products to be used, application methods, number of coats, and level of preparation required. Colors, finishes, and any patterns or borders should also be noted, as any type of detail work will reduce productivity.

Taking off Quantities

For estimating purposes, separate all of the work into two main classifications, exterior and interior, in the takeoff. While both share similar methods, techniques, and materials, there are some characteristics unique to each venue. The principal difference is that exterior work is affected by weather and temperature, while interior is not.

Exterior

Exterior work includes painting or staining exterior trims, siding, soffits, shutters, columns, doors and frames, windows, decks, porches, and rooftop equipment. Other less common items to be painted include metal railings, flagpoles, bollards, gates, and grating.

Take off exterior components separately, using the following guidelines:
- *Trims and soffits less than 12" in width:* by the LF.
- *Trims and soffits larger than 12" in width:* extended to SF for pricing.
- *Siding:* by the SF of surface area to be painted. Openings for windows and doors less than 10 SF are not deducted.
- *Shutters, columns, doors, frames, and windows:* by the piece (EA). Descriptions in the takeoff should include the size of each item, number or sides (doors and shutters), number of coats, and any special preparatory work.
- *Deck and porch surfaces:* by the SF.
- *Railings and balusters:* by the LF. Balusters can also be taken off by the individual piece.
- *Exterior stairs:* by the individual components. Treads and risers by the piece (EA), and stringers, skirts, or cheek boards by the LF.
- *Small rooftop equipment:* by the individual piece. Larger units can be taken off by the SF of surface area on the unit.

Note the method of application (brush, spray, or roller) for each takeoff item, as well as the number of coats and whether the work is stain, paint, or epoxy. Surface preparation should always be listed separately. Special techniques, such as *back priming*—the process of priming all surfaces of trims before installation even if not exposed, should be taken off and priced separately.

Interior

Interior work includes painting or staining walls, ceilings, doors and frames, windows, standing and running trims, wood shelving, casework, wainscoting, stair parts, and concrete floors. All work should be listed separately in the takeoff and described according to type, item to be painted, coating (paint or stain), number of coats, color, product, and method of application.

Generally, coverage of paints and finishes will vary with the surface being finished (its porosity), the number of coats (the first coat will cover less due to absorption into the surface), and the product itself. Consider the manufacturer's recommended coverage for the individual product and make adjustments, if necessary, for the porosity of the surface being painted. Also review the specifications for the requirement of "attic stock" paint. It is not uncommon, especially with commercial projects, for the painter to be required to provide one gallon of unopened paint of each color to be turned over to the owner at the end of the project.

Wall and ceiling painting is taken off and priced by the SF of surface area to be painted. Wall area is calculated by multiplying the perimeter of the room by its height. Openings larger than 4 SF are deducted in full; openings smaller than 4 SF are negligible. Ceiling area is calculated by multiplying the length by the width of the surface. Walls and ceilings are listed separately in the takeoff for pricing purposes. Interior wood trims, such as baseboards, cornices, chair rails, door and window casings, railings, and stair cheek or skirt boards, are taken off and priced by the LF. Stair components, such as balusters, treads, risers, and newel posts, are taken off and priced by the individual piece, and again are listed separately in the takeoff according to type. Painting of windows and accessories, such as grilles, is taken off and priced by the piece (EA). Interior doors and frames are taken off and priced by the individual unit (EA). Remember to differentiate between single and double door units in the takeoff.

Casework, cabinetry, and shelving are typically finished off site during the manufacturing process. However, when these items are field-finished, they are taken off and priced by the SF of surface area to be finished, or by the individual piece for repetitive items of the same size. Take off wainscoting and wood ceilings by the SF of surface area, and be sure to note the type of work, such as raised panel wainscoting or tongue-and-groove ceilings.

Concrete floors are taken off and priced by the square foot of floor area to be painted. The area is computed by multiplying the length by the width of the space. Verify whether preparation of the floor is necessary, such as sandblasting, acid-etching, or washing.

Painting of pipes and conduits is taken off and priced by the LF. Quantities should be separated according to pipe diameter. Most piping requires cleaning and priming. The solvents required to remove the oils and coatings from the pipes should be included as part of the preparatory work.

Labor

Productivity of painting can be measured by the individual painter or by a crew, depending on the task. Since painting and finishing work has a high aesthetic value, it often proceeds at a slow pace and requires greater care. This is especially true of interior painting or finishing in high-end residential work.

Ordinary workmanship, such as used in painting industrial or warehouse buildings, would most likely not be suitable for residential or commercial applications, such as a home, restaurant, or library that require first-class workmanship. When estimating painting work, consider the class or workmanship required by the specifications or by the nature of the project.

Productivity and cost will vary dramatically with the method of application of the product. It is important to select the proper method for the particular task. Large open areas with little interference from other work are ideal for paint spraying. Paint rolling is necessary when the area is small or obstacles would interfere with the path of spray. Detailed work on trims and cutting-in around other features, such as casework or cabinetry, is done by brush. The method of application is critical to pricing the labor portion of the work and should be noted in the takeoff.

The quality and longevity of a paint job frequently depends on the level of preparation. Preparation time and costs will vary from surface to surface. Repainting work that has a sound surface in good condition often requires only minimal time to correctly prep. Conversely, steel that has rusted or wood with flaking, scaling, or peeling paint may require considerable time to prepare the surface. If the opportunity arises, examine the existing substrate before preparing the estimate. Figure 14.12 provides labor-hour guidelines for the application of various coatings.

Be sure to account for staging, ladders, platforms, and any other equipment necessary to access the work. Productivity will always decrease as a result of frequent moves of a ladder or setting up staging.

Most specifications require that the painter do minor touch-up work after the installation of work of other trades. Since this can be labor-intensive and costly, consult your own historical data on similar projects to allow adequate labor-hours. Most materials used in touch-up work are left over from the main work.

Wallcoverings

There is a wide selection of materials that can be applied as decorative treatment to interior walls in residential and commercial projects. Wallcoverings are manufactured, printed or woven, in fabric, paper, vinyl, leather, suede, cork, wood veneers, and foils. They are available in a variety of weights, backings, and quality.

Application Time in Labor-Hours for Painting

Description	Labor-Hours	Unit
Cabinets and Casework		
Labor Cost Includes Protection of Adjacent		
Items Not Painted		
Primer Coat, Oil Base, Brushwork	.020	S.F.
Paint, Oil Base, Brushwork		
1 Coat	.021	S.F.
2 Coats	.040	S.F.
Stain, Brushwork, Wipe Off	.022	S.F.
Shellac, 1 Coat, Brushwork	.021	S.F.
Varnish, 3 Coats, Brushwork	.034	S.F.
Doors and Windows		
Labor Cost Includes Protection of Adjacent		
Items Not Painted		
Flush Door and Frame, per Side, Oil Base,		
Primer Coat, Brushwork	.571	Ea.
Paint		
1 Coat	.320	Ea.
2 Coats	.640	Ea.
3 Coats	.889	Ea.
Stain, Brushwork, Wipe Off	.800	Ea.
Shellac, 1 Coat, Brushwork	.667	Ea.
Varnish, 3 Coats, Brushwork	1.600	Ea.
Panel Door and Frame, per Side, Oil Base,		
Primer Coat, Brushwork	.615	Ea.
Paint		
1 Coat	.667	Ea.
2 Coats	1.330	Ea.
3 Coats	2.000	Ea.
Stain, Brushwork, Wipeoff	1.330	Ea.
Shellac, 1 Coat, Brushwork	1.000	Ea.
Varnish, 3 Coats, Brushwork	2.670	Ea.
Windows, Including Frame and Trim, per Side		
Colonial Type, 2' x 3', Oil Base, Primer Coat		
Brushwork	.333	Ea.
Paint		
1 Coat	.364	Ea.
2 Coats	.615	Ea.
3 Coats	.800	Ea.
3' x 5' Opening, Primer Coat, Brushwork	.533	Ea.
Paint		
1 Coat	.615	Ea.
2 Coats	1.000	Ea.
3 Coats	1.380	
4' x 8' Opening, Primer Coat, Brushwork	.667	Ea.
Paint		
1 Coat	.800	Ea.
2 Coats	1.330	Ea.
3 Coats	1.860	Ea.

Figure 14.12a

Application Time in Labor-Hours for Painting

Description	Labor-Hours	Unit
Standard, 6 to 8 Lites, 2' x 3', Primer	.308	Ea.
Paint		
1 Coat	.333	Ea.
2 Coats	.615	Ea.
3 Coats	.800	Ea.
3' x 5', Primer	.471	Ea.
Paint		
1 Coat	.533	Ea.
2 Coats	.800	Ea.
3 Coats	1.000	Ea.
4' x 8', Primer	.571	Ea.
Paint		
1 Coat	.667	Ea.
2 Coats	1.000	Ea.
3 Coats	1.330	Ea.
Single Lite Type, 2' x 3', Oil Base, Primer Coat, Brushwork	.200	Ea.
Paint		
1 Coat	.216	Ea.
2 Coats	.400	Ea.
3 Coats	.571	Ea.
3' x 5' Opening, Primer Coat, Brushwork	.296	Ea.
Paint		
1 Coat	.320	Ea.
2 Coats	.571	Ea.
3 Coats	.800	Ea.
4' x 8' Opening, Primer Coat, Brushwork	.571	Ea.
Paint		
1 Coat	.615	Ea.
2 Coats	1.000	Ea.
3 Coats	1.230	Ea.
Miscellaneous		
Fence, Chain Link, Per Side, Oil Base, Primer Coat, Brushwork	.013	S.F.
Spray	.010	S.F.
Paint 1 Coat, Brushwork	.014	S.F.
Spray	.010	S.F.
Picket, Wood, Primer Coat, Brushwork	.039	S.F.
Spray	.031	S.F.
Paint 1 Coat, Brushwork	.040	S.F.
Spray	.031	S.F.
Floors, Concrete or Wood, Oil Base, Primer or Sealer Coat, Brushwork	.007	S.F.
Roller	.006	S.F.
Spray	.006	S.F.
Paint 1 Coat, Brushwork	.008	S.F.
Roller	.007	S.F.
Spray	.006	S.F.

Figure 14.12b

Application Time in Labor-Hours for Painting

Description	Labor-Hours	Unit
Stain, Wood Floor, Brushwork	.007	S.F.
Roller	.006	S.F.
Spray	.006	S.F.
Varnish, Wood Floor, Brushwork	.008	S.F.
Roller	.007	S.F.
Spray	.006	S.F.
Grilles, per Side, Oil Base, Primer Coat, Brushwork	.020	Ea.
Spray	.016	Ea.
Paint 1 Coat, Brushwork	.021	Ea.
Spray	.016	Ea.
Paint 2 Coats, Brushwork	.040	Ea.
Spray	.032	Ea.
Gutters and Downspouts, Oil Base, Primer Coat, Brushwork	.025	L.F.
Paint 1 Coat, Brushwork	.027	L.F.
Paint 2 Coats, Brushwork	.049	L.F.
Pipe, to 4" Diameter, Primer or Sealer Coat, Oil Base, Brushwork	.020	L.F.
Spray	.015	L.F.
Paint 1 Coat, Brushwork	.021	L.F.
Spray	.015	L.F.
Paint 2 Coats, Brushwork	.040	L.F.
Spray	.029	L.F.
To 8" Diameter, Primer or Sealer Coat, Brushwork	.040	L.F.
Spray	.025	L.F.
Paint 1 Coat, Brushwork	.046	L.F.
Spray	.025	L.F.
Paint 2 Coats, Brushwork	.080	L.F.
Spray	.043	L.F.
To 12" Diameter, Primer or Sealer Coat, Brushwork	.067	L.F.
Spray	.050	L.F.
Paint 1 Coat, Brushwork	.073	L.F.
Spray	.050	L.F.
Paint 2 Coats, Brushwork	.133	L.F.
Spray	.100	L.F.
To 16" Diameter, Primer or Sealer Coat, Brushwork	.083	L.F.
Spray	.067	L.F.
Paint 1 Coat, Brushwork	.089	L.F.
Spray	.067	L.F.
Paint 2 Coats, Brushwork	.160	L.F.
Spray	.123	L.F.
Trim, Wood, Including Puttying Under 6" Wide Primer Coat, Oil Base, Brushwork	.009	L.F.
Paint, Brushwork		
1 Coat	.009	L.F.
2 Coats	.016	L.F.
3 Coats	.027	L.F.

Figure 14.12c

Application Time in Labor-Hours for Painting

Description	Labor-Hours	Unit
Over 6" Wide, Primer Coat, Brushwork	.013	L.F.
Paint, Brushwork		
1 Coat	.018	L.F.
2 Coats	.027	L.F.
3 Coats	.042	L.F.
Cornice, Simple Design, Primer Coat, Oil Base, Brushwork	.029	S.F.
Paint, Brushwork		
1 Coat	.032	S.F.
2 Coats	.050	S.F.
Ornate Design, Primer Coat	.053	S.F.
Paint		
1 Coat	.057	S.F.
2 Coats	.089	S.F.
Balustrades, per Side, Primer Coat, Oil Base, Brushwork	.027	S.F.
Paint		
1 Coat	.028	S.F.
2 Coats	.047	S.F.
Trusses and Exposed Wood Frames		
Primer Coat Oil Base, Brushwork	.010	S.F.
Spray	.007	S.F.
Paint 1 Coat, Brushwork	.011	S.F.
Spray	.007	S.F.
Paint 2 Coats, Brushwork	.016	S.F.
Spray	.013	S.F.
Stain, Brushwork, Wipe Off	.013	S.F.
Varnish, 3 Coats, Brushwork	.029	S.F.
Siding Exterior		
Steel Siding, Oil Base, Primer or Sealer Coat, Brushwork	.009	S.F.
Spray	.005	S.F.
Paint 2 Coats, Brushwork	.012	S.F.
Spray	.006	S.F.
Stucco, Rough, Oil Base, Paint 2 Coats, Brushwork	.012	S.F.
Roller	.008	S.F.
Spray	.006	S.F.
Texture 1-11 or Clapboard, Oil Base Primer Coat, Brushwork	.006	S.F.
Spray	.004	S.F.
Paint 1 Coat, Brushwork	.006	S.F.
Spray	.004	S.F.
Paint 2 Coats, Brushwork	.013	S.F.
Spray	.008	S.F.
Stain 1 Coat, Brushwork	.006	S.F.
Spray	.004	S.F.
Stain 2 Coats, Brushwork	.013	S.F.
Spray	.008	S.F.

Figure 14.12d

Application Time in Labor-Hours for Painting		
Description	**Labor-Hours**	**Unit**
High Build Epoxy, 50 Mil		
Minimum	.021	S.F.
Maximum	.084	S.F.
Laminated Epoxy with Fiberglass		
Minimum	.027	S.F.
Maximum	.055	S.F.
Sprayed Perlite or Vermiculite 1/16" Thick		
Minimum	.003	S.F.
Maximum	.013	S.F.
Vinyl Plastic Wall Coating		
Minimum	.011	S.F.
Maximum	.033	S.F.
Urethane on Smooth Surface 2 Coats		
Minimum	.007	S.F.
Maximum	.012	S.F.
3 Coats		
Minimum	.010	S.F.
Maximum	.017	S.F.
Ceramic-like Glazed Coating, Cementitious		
Minimum	.018	S.F.
Maximum	.023	S.F.
Resin Base		
Minimum	.013	S.F.
Maximum	.024	S.F.

Figure 14.12e

Wallcoverings are installed with adhesives, and some require special pastes. Preparation of the wall surface is necessary to ensure proper bonding of the wallcovering and includes minor sanding and repairing of defects in the wall, and applying *sizing,* or primer for proper adhesion.

Review the architectural drawings, with particular attention to floor plans and elevations. Room finish schedules will provide the location of wallcoverings within specific rooms. Reflected ceiling drawings or room finish schedules should be reviewed for the vertical heights of the walls. The technical specifications should be consulted for information on individual products, including model and manufacturer, surface preparation, and adhesives. Special requirements in commercial applications, such as fire-treated wallcoverings that do not support combustion, should also be noted in the specs. Waste on wallcoverings can range from a low of 10% for a product with a basic pattern, to as much as 60% for wallcoverings with intricate patterns.

Taking off Quantities

Wallcoverings are taken off by the SF of surface area, calculated by multiplying the LF of the wall by its height. Deductions are taken for windows, doors, and openings in excess of 4 SF. The SF area is then converted to wallcovering rolls, which typically contain 36 SF. The total number of rolls can be determined and then priced. Wallcoverings are generally produced in double and triple roll units called *bolts*. Commercial wallcoverings are manufactured in widths ranging from 21" to 54" and in lengths up to 100-yard bolts. For an accurate quantity, the linear footage of the walls to be covered (in feet) can be divided by the width of the wallcovering (in feet), which results in the number of "strips." Calculate the number of strips per bolt by dividing the length of the bolt by the height of the hang. Adjustments in the number of strips per bolt will be required based on the repetition of the pattern, if applicable. The number of strips required (rounded up to the nearest whole number) is divided by the number of strips per bolt (rounded down to the nearest whole number) to determine the number of bolts required.

Quantities of adhesives or paste are calculated by dividing the total square foot area to be covered by the manufacturer's recommended coverage per sales unit (typically the gallon). Coverage may be expressed in rolls.

Labor

Wallcoverings are typically installed by paperhangers and painters, and productivity is measured by the daily output of each worker. For larger projects, it is not uncommon for a paperhanger to have a helper for trimming and pasting. Due to the high aesthetic value of wallcoverings, the quality of workmanship must always be estimated as first-class. Calculate the cost of wall preparation, including sizing, separate from the actual cost of hanging the wallcovering. Layout and cleanup should also be included as part of the cost of the work. While the surface area of the wall is increased to include waste and repeating patterns, remember to calculate labor based on the actual area of the walls to be covered. Figure 14.13 provides guidelines for wallcovering installation labor-hours.

Conclusion

Always pay careful attention to the plans and specifications when estimating finishes in general. Their aesthetic value cannot be overstated—often one of the most important and noticed features to the owner. Accurate estimating of both materials and labor costs is a by-product of understanding the requirements set forth in the documents.

Installation Time in Labor-Hours for Wallcoverings

Description	Labor-Hours	Unit
Wallcovering		
Aluminum Foil	.029	S.F.
Copper Sheets, .025" Thick		
Vinyl Backing	.033	S.F.
Phenolic Backing	.033	S.F.
Cork Tiles, Light or Dark, 12" x 12"		
3/16" Thick	.033	S.F.
5/16" Thick	.034	S.F.
1/4" Basketweave	.033	S.F.
1/2" Natural, Non-directional Pattern	.033	S.F.
Granular Surface, 12" x 36"		
1/2" Thick	.021	S.F.
1" Thick	.022	S.F.
Polyurethane Coated, 12" x 12"		
3/16" Thick	.033	S.F.
5/16" Thick	.034	S.F.
Cork Wallpaper, Paperbacked		
Natural	.017	S.F.
Colors	.017	S.F.
Flexible Wood Veneer, 1/32" Thick		
Plain Woods	.080	S.F.
Exotic Woods	.084	S.F.
Gypsum-based, Fabric-backed, Fire Resistant for Masonry Walls		
Minimum	.020	S.F.
Average	.023	S.F.
Maximum	.027	S.F.
Acrylic, Modified, Semi-rigid PVC		
.028" Thick	.048	S.F.
.040" Thick	.050	S.F.
Vinyl Wallcovering, Fabric-backed		
Lightweight	.013	S.F.
Medium Weight	.017	S.F.
Heavy Weight	.018	S.F.
Grass Cloths with Lining Paper		
Minimum	.020	S.F.
Maximum	.023	S.F.

Figure 14.13

Chapter Fifteen

Specialties

Specialties include items that are manufactured off site and shipped pre-finished, and often pre-assembled, for easy on-site installation. Specialty items are generally more common in commercial than residential projects. This division includes a wide variety of familiar, but hard to categorize, items such as:

- Chalkboards, tack boards, and bulletin boards
- Directories and signage
- Metal lockers
- Fire extinguishers and cabinets
- Flagpoles
- Toilet partitions and accessories
- Postal specialties
- Pre-fabricated fireplaces
- Wood-burning stoves
- Metal wall louvers
- Display cases
- Turnstiles
- Canopies
- Partitions
- Storage and shelving
- Coat racks and wardrobes

Specialties has often been referred to as the "catch-all" division. The items included in this section are often added after the finishes on the project are complete, and therefore occur in the latter part of the schedule. Specialty items can be installed by your own forces or subcontracted to a specialty subcontractor.

Most of the work will be depicted on the architectural drawings. All plan views, elevations, and schedules should be reviewed carefully for reference notes and illustrations. Occasionally, typical details will be presented in latter sheets of the architectural drawings to set a standard for the project. Classic examples include fire extinguishers and cabinets, toilet partitions and accessories, signage, and metal lockers. The work of Division 10 is not relegated exclusively to the interior of the building, and as a result, be sure to consult the site drawings for items such as site signage and flagpoles. The architect does not always provide the graphic detail for Division 10 work that is frequently found with other items, but more commonly relies on the language of the specifications to define the scope of work. Review the specifications for items not shown on the drawings. Often designers will provide the name of a distributor and contact information for a particular product. This is a fairly good indicator that substitutions will most likely not be accepted. Coordination with other discipline drawings, such as mechanical drawings for wall louvers, is also recommended to verify quantities and sizes.

Many of the items of this section come furnished and delivered only. Therefore, it is essential to obtain current pricing for each product. This is often as simple as searching the specified manufacturer's Web site or soliciting a price. Web sites often provide illustrations or information that allow you to determine if assembly is required or if there are other unique features of the product that affect pricing.

Taking off Quantities

The most common takeoff method is by the individual piece, each (EA). Some specialty items such as fire extinguishers, toilet accessories, signage (both interior and exterior), prefabricated fireplaces, lockers, and flagpoles can be repetitive and are best estimated by counting and assigning a lump sum price. Other items, such as chalkboards and tack boards, toilet partitions, and metal wall louvers, are priced by the SF area of the individual piece. Be sure to consider equipment costs for setting items. For example, most flagpoles require some type of crane to install. This cost must be included in the estimate.

Labor

Labor for this division is also estimated by the piece (EA). For example, the labor cost for installing interior signage can be calculated by the quantity of signs that would be installed in one labor-hour by a single individual. Alternate methods include the number of labor-hours per unit, as in the case of installing a prefabricated fireplace. Installation costs for chalkboards and tack boards can be calculated by the individual piece for boards of the same size, or by the SF area for boards of varying sizes or dimensions. This is more of a matter of preference than actual standard estimating procedure.

The work of Division 10 cannot be classified into one individual trade or crew size. Skilled labor is required for a correct installation of Division 10 work. Tasks such as installing chalkboards and tack boards, setting toilet partitions, and installing flagpoles are better executed by multi-person crews due to size, weight, and other physical attributes of these products. Many tasks, such as installing bathroom accessories or room signage, are best executed by a single individual.

Knowing the level of assembly required when a product arrives on site can often mean the difference between success and failure in predicting an accurate cost. Be sure to consider learning curve productivity for self-performed work under this section if you do not have historical cost data models for these items for reference.

Other special considerations for accurately estimating Division 10 work include the cost for unwrapping or uncrating items and disposing of shipping packaging. While this may not be a major concern for a single pre-fabricated fireplace, it does constitute a cost when estimating multi-unit dwellings, such as condominium and apartment projects. Projects that are phased often pose other challenges. For example, many manufacturers prefer to price their product with a single drop shipment versus per phase. If storage, re-handling, and distribution costs are required per phase, be sure to include them in the estimate.

Takeoff for Division 10 work can be used as a checklist against other items in separate divisions. For example, if grab bars in toilet compartments require wood blocking within framed wood or metal stud walls, you can check the quantity of wood blocking against the total number of grab bars as a way of verifying both tasks.

Conclusion

Although Division 10—Specialties does not typically amount to a large portion of the total estimated cost of a project, there are often many items included from a variety of locations. While specialties may be shown on the drawings, occasionally they are not. In this case, the specifications may be the determining factor for both quantity and quality.

Division 10 includes such an enormous quantity and variety of different types of specialties that would be impractical to attempt to provide labor-hours for installation costs within this chapter. For additional information on installation costs, consult *Means Estimating Handbook, Second Edition*.

Chapter Sixteen

Equipment, Furnishings, & Special Construction

While equipment, furnishings, special construction, and conveying systems occupy four separate divisions in CSI MasterFormat (Divisions 11-14), we have combined their coverage into one chapter because of their limited applicability to residential/light commercial construction. Much of the work is subcontracted due to its highly specialized nature. Examples include Division 11's equipment for banks, libraries, medical, or ecclesiastical applications, as well as elevators and wheelchair lifts in Division 14—Conveying Systems. Other items, such as rugs, furniture, window treatments, and artwork in Division 12—Furnishings, can be contracted separately by the owner, and only coordinated by the general contractor. Each particular scenario requires careful evaluation and acknowledgement within the estimate. The discussion of these divisions in this chapter concerns only their most common applications and estimating guidelines for the average residential/light commercial project.

Equipment

CSI Division 11—Equipment includes central vacuum cleaning systems, residential kitchen appliances, and any related specialized equipment. All buildings are initially designed with a specific function in mind, such as libraries, churches, medical or dental offices, retail spaces, or restaurants, all of which require specialized equipment to allow them to perform their individual trade or business. Occasionally, systems or equipment are contracted directly by the owner under a separate agreement from the contract with the general contractor, but more often it is the responsibility of the general contractor to provide this equipment installed, tested, and fully functional as part of the base contract. Many contracts even provide for owner training.

Some of the equipment is delivered in the final phase of the project and installed with minimum impact to the schedule, while other items are installed in various phases of construction and require the general and specialized equipment contractors to maintain close contact as the project progresses. For these types of equipment, you must calculate the costs of interfacing systems with the structure itself. Consider the cost related to leaving a portion of the structure (roof or wall) open until such time as the equipment can be loaded into the building and installed.

For example, consider bank vault doors. While the actual cost of the equipment portion of the work may be outside of the experience of the average general contractor's estimator, calculating the cost of the interface work is not. Many estimators will attempt to establish budgets based on historical cost data from previous projects. However, since most general contractors subcontract this work, detailed costs of materials, labor, and equipment may not be available. The only information may be the subcontract amount, plus any authorized change orders. This information should be used to establish budgets as "plugs" in the estimate until firm subcontractors' quotes are available. Other options include subcontractor quotes over a period of time, which can establish a unit cost for the work.

When soliciting a bid from a specialized subcontractor, it is the estimator's responsibility to carefully craft the scope of work to be priced with reference to the relevant CSI MasterFormat section of work within the project documents. This includes coordination between mechanical and electrical disciplines for work that may be needed to complete the specialized equipment package. As an example, consider the coordination required for restaurant kitchen equipment. There are gas, electrical, and plumbing requirements for virtually every piece of equipment within the kitchen. Some equipment, such as exhaust hoods over cooking lines, requires coordination with roof work, ductwork, structural reinforcement, and even the fire alarm system. Making sure that all coordinated work is included is no insignificant task. Once the subcontractor's proposal has been submitted, be sure to carefully review and qualify the work.

Most of the work of Division 11 can be found on the architectural drawings. All plan views, elevations, and schedules should be reviewed for reference notes and illustrations. On some projects where the scope of work is extensive, separate drawings in the project bid set will include specialty drawings. The architect will not always provide the graphic detail for Division 11 work that is frequently found with other items, and may rely on the language of the specifications and the expertise of the specialty contractor to fill in the missing details. Due to the highly specialized nature of the design of these systems, the architect will often refer to the manufacturers' product literature for pricing information. Review the Division 11 specification section for items not shown on the drawings. Consult other discipline drawings, such as the mechanical and electrical, to ensure pricing accuracy.

Residential appliances in Division 11 include ranges, refrigerators, dishwashers, and laundry equipment. Most vendors provide pricing on residential appliances furnished and delivered to the site only, excluding installation. Appliances can also be purchased, delivered, and set in place if specifically requested. Be sure to price appliances through a supplier that can provide up-to-date quotes—often as simple as searching the specified manufacturers' Web site and soliciting a price. The actual hook-up, or *tie-in*, labor and material costs are the responsibility of other trades, such as the plumbing and electrical contractors. Coordinate the various trades to ensure that all tie-in costs are included.

Taking off Quantities

Simple Division 11 items, such as residential appliances, are taken off and priced by the piece (EA). Other, more complicated equipment, such as athletic equipment and all of the related components—including installation, can be priced as a lump sum (LS).

Installation Labor

Estimating labor for Division 11 work follows the takeoff unit costs, by the individual piece (EA). For residential appliances, a multi-person crew is required. Labor costs are calculated by the number of labor-hours per each appliance. The work of Division 11 cannot be classified into one individual trade or crew size, as it depends on the task at hand.

Special considerations for accurately estimating this work include costs of unwrapping or uncrating items and disposing of shipping packaging. While this may not be a major concern for a single refrigerator, it does impose a financial impact when estimating multiple appliances for multi-unit dwellings, such as for apartment projects. If storage, re-handling, and distribution costs are required per phase, they must be also included in the estimate.

Furnishings

Division 12—Furnishings is frequently handled under a separate contract directly with the owner. The items most commonly included within the general contract for this division are window treatments. These include vertical or horizontal blinds, roller shades, and drapery rods. Again, this work is often estimated as furnished and installed, since it is subcontracted. Other items, especially on commercial projects, include artwork, rugs, interior plantings, and furniture.

Consult the architectural drawings in plan view and elevation to determine window opening sizes. Window schedules are also helpful. Quantities can be determined from reviewing plan views in conjunction with elevations. It is essential that you review the window treatment specification section for products and special characteristics necessary for accurate pricing. Fire-rated and non-combustible window treatments, for example, have a tremendous impact on pricing.

Taking off Quantities

Window treatments, such as blinds and shades, are taken off by the area of the opening they occupy, and are listed in the takeoff by width by height. Drapery rods are taken off by the width of opening and listed in the takeoff in LF. Most other items within Division 12 are taken off by the individual piece and are listed as EA. The takeoff should describe the item or task sufficiently to allow accurate pricing.

Labor

Estimating labor for Division 12 work can be done in a variety of ways. The most common method is to follow the takeoff units and estimate labor costs by the individual piece (EA). For example, the labor cost for installing window shades could be calculated by the quantity of shades that can be installed in one labor-hour by a single individual. The difference in labor costs between installing a 36" wide shade versus a 42" wide shade is negligible. Most estimators price installation by the piece rather than by size, although alternate methods include quantifying the number of labor-hours per unit, as for larger vertical blinds. Productivity is measured and based on the production of an individual, rather than a crew. Installation costs for other items follow the same procedure.

Special Construction

Division 13 includes a variety of unique and highly specialized work. In the residential/light commercial market, there are few applications, including swimming pools, security alarms, sauna rooms, storage tanks, and hazardous material abatement. All require specialized training—both to execute and estimate. In some circumstances, such as hazardous material remediation, licensing and compliance with federal guidelines are mandatory.

Prepare a budget estimate for comparison purposes based on your own available historical data. It is recommended that you secure quotes for complete installations. Make sure all coordinated work is included.

Conveying Systems

Elevators, wheelchair lifts, escalators, and industrial conveying systems are included in Division 14. All are highly specialized equipment that require licensing and are heavily regulated by government agencies. Accurately estimating the work requires an in-depth understanding of the various components and their assembly. As in the case of all of the work of this chapter, you should prepare a budget estimate as a plug or for use in comparing prospective bids. Any historical data can be organized into a database—useful as a reliable prediction of future costs. Even bids from subcontractors that were not used can be a source of cost information. Review the project bid documents carefully to identify and coordinate the work of other trades.

Takeoff and Labor

Due to the enormous quantity and variety of specialties included in these sections, it would be impractical to attempt to provide takeoff quantities and labor-hours for estimating installation costs for conveying systems. It is recommended that you seek additional guidance from manufacturers for installation costs.

Conclusion   While most general contractors subcontract the work of these divisions, it is recommended that you become familiar with the scope of work and establish budget costs as guidelines for reviewing subcontractors' proposals. It is also important to verify that the scope of work being priced is defined accurately and completely.

Chapter Seventeen

Mechanical Systems

D
ivision 15 includes fire protection, plumbing, and HVAC (heating, ventilating, and air conditioning) systems. The work is typically performed by trades or firms with specialized training, often with licenses and permits separate from those of the general contractor. Taking off and estimating mechanical systems requires a working knowledge of the particular trade or system and, often, specialized education and training not normally within the realm of the general contractor's estimating experience. Nevertheless, you should be able to develop sound, realistic budgets for comparison purposes and to evaluate mechanical contractors' pricing on bid day. While reviewing mechanical drawings and specifications, you will become familiar with the scope of work involved, which provides the basis for a more thorough review of subcontractor pricing.

Division 15 work is typically shown on the mechanical drawings. *(See the "Mechanical Drawings" section of Chapter 1.)* Mechanical drawings are labeled with the following prefixes: "M" for mechanical; "P" for plumbing; "FP" for fire protection; and "H" or "HVAC" for heating, ventilating, and air conditioning. Review all drawings in the bid set, including architectural and civil, for related work that may be shown on other drawings, as well as for detailed information on dimensions and measurements for room sizes, floor-to-floor heights, location of services entering the building, and coordination with other work within the particular area. Mechanical drawings with schedules are helpful in determining types and quantities of materials for takeoff. *(See the "Schedules" section of Chapter 1.)* Specialized details, such as riser diagrams showing the configuration and components of piping systems, are often included.

Consult the specification sections for the products, methods, and techniques of installation, as well as the related work of other trades that will affect pricing. A review of Division 1, "Temporary Facilities," of the specs may be necessary to determine what, if any, special requirements, such as hoisting or staging, may be included.

This chapter will cover the basic procedures and methods for takeoff and pricing, limited to the mechanical systems normally encountered in residential and light commercial construction.

Fire Protection Systems

The three main components of a fire protection system are detection, alarm, and suppression. Suppression of fire may be accomplished by fire standpipe systems, automatic sprinkler systems, or a combination of the two. There are several different classifications of automatic sprinkler systems designed for specific fire-fighting applications. For budgeting purposes, most fire protection work can be reduced to cost per square foot of the space being protected or cost per sprinkler head. Dry pipe sprinkler systems tend to be more expensive due to added equipment and appurtenances.

Fire standpipe systems require hose stations placed at various locations within the structure, according to design and local building code requirements. Most fire protection systems in residential and light commercial construction are classified into one of two groups for estimating purposes: wet pipe sprinkler and dry pipe sprinkler systems. In wet pipe systems, water is constantly under pressure in each head. These sprinklers can be used in areas that are not subject to freezing. Dry pipe sprinkler systems are used where freezing is a concern, and feature compressed air that restrains water at the supply sources until needed. Other types of fire protection systems include pre-action, deluge, halon, and fire cycle systems. Sprinkler systems may need to function in conjunction with other systems in the building, such as fire alarms. Review subcontractor proposals and ensure that all components, including those being provided by other trades, have been accounted for in the estimate.

Study the fire protection drawings for locations of sprinkler heads; sizes and materials of piping; and location of valves, fittings, appurtenances, and water sources. Special equipment, such as compressors for dry systems, backflow preventers, and alarm bells, may be shown on riser diagrams or details. Architectural floor and reflected ceiling plans will provide dimensions and ceiling heights. The specifications will detail the materials to be used, method of installation, and required compliances of the various governing agencies. Related work by other trades is also listed in this section, and includes wired connection of flow or tamper switches to the fire alarm system or power wiring for a dry pipe system compressor.

Although systems are generally similar in residential and light commercial construction, the grade and type of materials can be significantly different. In general, the delivery system for residential work is CPVC piping. CPVC is a polyvinylchloride pipe designed to work under pressure. Black iron or steel piping are most commonly used in the commercial industry. In the absence of a definitive specification, reference the applicable code or the authority having jurisdiction.

Taking off Quantities

All takeoff quantities should be listed separately according to type and classification of system. In addition to materials, special items such as shop drawings, permits and fees, and special staging or rigging equipment for the installation of larger diameter pipes and valves should be included within the estimate. Additional takeoff guidelines are as follows:

- *Riser and distribution piping material for standpipe and automatic sprinkler systems*: by the LF, separated according to type of pipe (steel, black iron, or CPVC), size (diameter), and method of connection (grooved joint or threaded).
- *Fittings*: by the piece (EA) according to type (elbow, tee, reducer, etc.), size (diameter), method of connection, and material composition (steel, black iron, CPVC, etc.).
- *Valves and special appurtenances*: by the individual piece (EA) according to type, manufacturer, model, size, use or application, and other identifying information needed for pricing. Includes gauges, couplings, flanges, water motor alarms and bells, siamese connections, backflow preventers, control panels or devices, and storage cylinders.
- *Sprinkler heads and discharge nozzles*: by the piece (EA) according to type (pendent, upright, or sidewall), temperature range, manufacturer, and model number.
- *Trim pieces/escutcheons*: by the piece (EA) according to type, finish, model, and application.

In most cases, the sprinkler contractor's work begins at the interior of the building where the fire protection water service line enters the structure. Site piping and related excavation and backfill are typically the responsibility of the site contractor, although the sprinkler contractor in some jurisdictions may do this work. Review the specifications regarding the exact scope of work.

Be sure to include costs for testing water pressure, reviewing plans with local government agencies, commissioning and testing, owner training, and the review/approval processes by insurance underwriters, if applicable.

Labor

Fabrication and installation of fire protection systems are done by pipefitters. Commercial projects in particular require special tools, licenses, and equipment, and many of the components are not available on the open market. As a means of increasing installation productivity, most grooved steel pipe or threaded black iron pipe is fabricated off-site from a "cut list" generated from shop drawings. A specialty subcontractor to the sprinkler subcontractor cuts and threads or grooves all pipe to specific lengths based on the cut list. The materials are then marked and delivered to the site for installation by the sprinkler subcontractor.

Crews consisting of multiple pipefitters assemble pre-fabricated pipe, starting from the largest diameter distribution pipes to smaller branch piping. Production is measured by the crew's output, most often in LF of pipe per day. In addition to the actual assembly of piping, installation of hangers, bracing, and seismic restraint of pipe assemblies also consumes labor-hours. As with most trades, productivity can be affected by a variety of circumstances, such as extremes in temperature. Large open floor plans proceed quicker than small confined spaces, such as attics or crawlspaces. Working from staging or lifts will reduce productivity, and may even require an additional person to hand materials up from the ground. Labor costs for the testing and commissioning of systems should also be included in the estimate. Figure 17.1 illustrates labor-hour guidelines for installing various types of piping used in fire sprinkler systems.

Plumbing

All buildings that will be occupied require some type of plumbing—from simple toilets in warehouses, to elaborate bathrooms in upscale residences, to sophisticated plumbing systems in hospitals and restaurants. As with fire protection, plumbing work requires special knowledge and training of both the estimator and the tradespeople doing the work. It requires licensed plumbers and a separate permit and inspection process.

Carefully review the plumbing drawings, as well as the architectural plans. Some plumbing plans provide riser diagrams to be used in determining piping quantities. Fixture and equipment schedules are also helpful in determining quantities and types of plumbing fixtures and equipment to be furnished and/or installed. Other drawings within the bid set, such as special equipment plans (e.g., kitchen equipment plans for restaurants), should be studied for equipment furnished by others and installed or connected under the plumbing contract. Some plumbing drawings show under-slab and above-slab piping on the same sheet. This requires graphic symbols to illustrate the difference between locations. It may be helpful to review plumbing legends so that all symbols are understood prior to starting the estimate. Figure 17.2 is an example of a plumbing plan showing a waste vent and water piping on the same plan. Figure 17.3a illustrates an example of a riser diagram for soil and vent piping for the preceding plumbing plan. Figure 17.3b is the riser diagram for the hot and cold water piping for the plan in Figure 17.2.

Special drawings with enlarged plan views and details for clarification of certain aspects of work are common, as in the example of the domestic water heater in Figure 17.4. Details or diagrams offer clarification only, and are often not drawn to scale.

Consult Division 15 of the specifications for the scope of work, product information, and acceptable methods of installation, as well as the related work in other sections. For the purpose of takeoff and pricing, plumbing work can be broken down into eight subsystems, described in the following pages.

Installation Time in Labor-Hours for Steel Pipe

Description	Labor-Hours	Unit
Steel Pipe Labor-hours to Install Black, Schedule #10, Grooved Joint or Plain End with a Mechanical Joint Coupling and Pipe Hanger Every Ten Feet		
2" Pipe Size	.186	L.F.
2-1/2" Pipe Size	.262	L.F.
3" Pipe Size	.291	L.F.
3-1/2" Pipe Size	.302	L.F.
4" Pipe Size	.327	L.F.
5" Pipe Size	.400	L.F.
6" Pipe Size	.522	L.F.
8" Pipe Size	.585	L.F.
10" Pipe Size	.706	L.F.
12" Pipe Size	.800	L.F.
Black or Galvanized Schedule #40 Grooved Joint or Plain End with a Mechanical Joint Coupling and Pipe Hanger Every Ten Feet		
3/4" Pipe Size	.113	L.F.
1" Pipe Size	.127	L.F.
1-1/4" Pipe Size	.138	L.F.
1-1/2" Pipe Size	.157	L.F.
2" Pipe Size	.200	L.F.
2-1/2" Pipe Size	.281	L.F.
3" Pipe Size	.320	L.F.
3-1/2" Pipe Size	.340	L.F.
4" Pipe Size	.356	L.F.
5" Pipe Size	.432	L.F.
6" Pipe Size	.571	L.F.
8" Pipe Size	.649	L.F.
10" Pipe Size	.774	L.F.
12" Pipe Size	.889	L.F.
Fittings for Use with Grooved Joint or Plain End Steel Pipe Elbows 90° or 45°		
3/4" Pipe Size	.160	Ea.
1" Pipe Size	.160	Ea.
1-1/4" Pipe Size	.200	Ea.
1-1/2" Pipe Size	.242	Ea.
2" Pipe Size	.320	Ea.
2-1/2" Pipe Size	.400	Ea.
3" Pipe Size	.485	Ea.
4" Pipe Size	.640	Ea.
5" Pipe Size	.800	Ea.
6" Pipe Size	.960	Ea.
8" Pipe Size	1.143	Ea.
10" Pipe Size	1.333	Ea.
12" Pipe Size	1.600	Ea.

Flanged Joint

Grooved Joint Steel Pipe

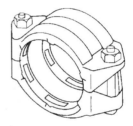

Grooved Joint Coupling

Mechanical Joint Elbow
90° –Plain End Pipe

Figure 17.1a

Description	Labor-Hours	Unit
Tees		
3/4″ Pipe Size	.211	Ea.
1″ Pipe Size	.242	Ea.
1-1/4″ Pipe Size	.296	Ea.
1-1/2″ Pipe Size	.364	Ea.
2″ Pipe Size	.471	Ea.
2-1/2″ Pipe Size	.593	Ea.
3″ Pipe Size	.727	Ea.
4″ Pipe Size	.941	Ea.
5″ Pipe Size	1.231	Ea.
6″ Pipe Size	1.412	Ea.
8″ Pipe Size	1.714	Ea.
10″ Pipe Size	2.000	Ea.
12″ Pipe Size	2.400	Ea.
Labor-hours to Install Black or Galvanized Schedule #40 Threaded with a Coupling and Pipe Hanger Every Ten Feet. The Pipe Hanger is Oversized to Allow for Insulation.		
1/2″ Pipe Size	.127	L.F.
3/4″ Pipe Size	.131	L.F.
1″ Pipe Size	.151	L.F.
1-1/4″ Pipe Size	.180	L.F.
1-1/2″ Pipe Size	.200	L.F.
2″ Pipe Size	.250	L.F.
2-1/2″ Pipe Size	.320	L.F.
3″ Pipe Size	.372	L.F.
3-1/2″ Pipe Size	.400	L.F.
4″ Pipe Size	.444	L.F.
5″ Pipe Size	.615	L.F.
6″ Pipe Size	.774	L.F.
8″ Pipe Size	.889	L.F.
10″ Pipe Size	1.043	L.F.
12″ Pipe Size	1.333	L.F.
Fittings for Use with Steel Pipe. Threaded Fittings, Cast Iron, 125 lb. or Malleable Iron Rated at 150 lb. Elbows, 90° or 45°		
1/2″ Pipe Size	.533	Ea.
3/4″ Pipe Size	.571	Ea.
1″ Pipe Size	.615	Ea.
1-1/4″ Pipe Size	.727	Ea.
1-1/2″ Pipe Size	.800	Ea.
2″ Pipe Size	.889	Ea.
2-1/2″ Pipe Size	1.143	Ea.
3″ Pipe Size	1.600	Ea.
3-1/2″ Pipe Size	2.000	Ea.
4″ Pipe Size	2.667	Ea.
5″ Pipe Size	3.200	Ea.
6″ Pipe Size	3.429	Ea.
8″ Pipe Size	4.000	Ea.

Tee – Plain End Pipe

Threaded and Coupled Steel Pipe

45° Elbow – Malleable Iron

Tee – Cast Iron

Figure 17.1b

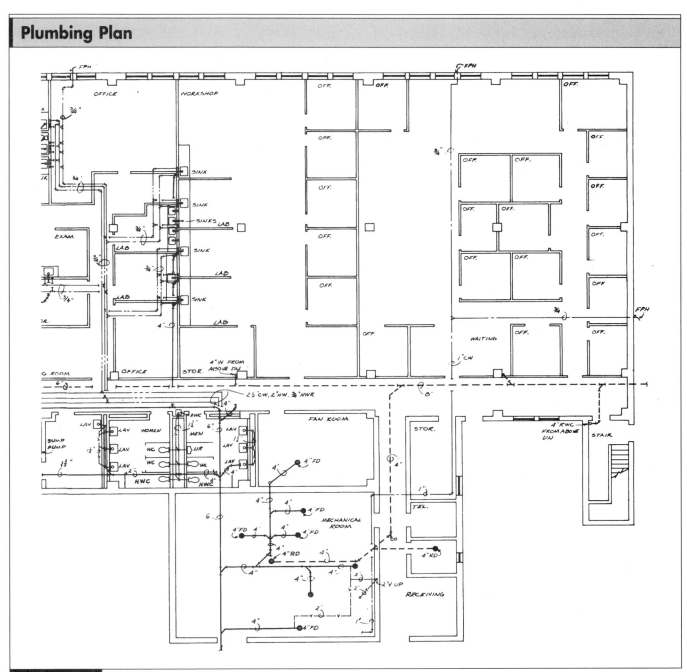

Figure 17.2

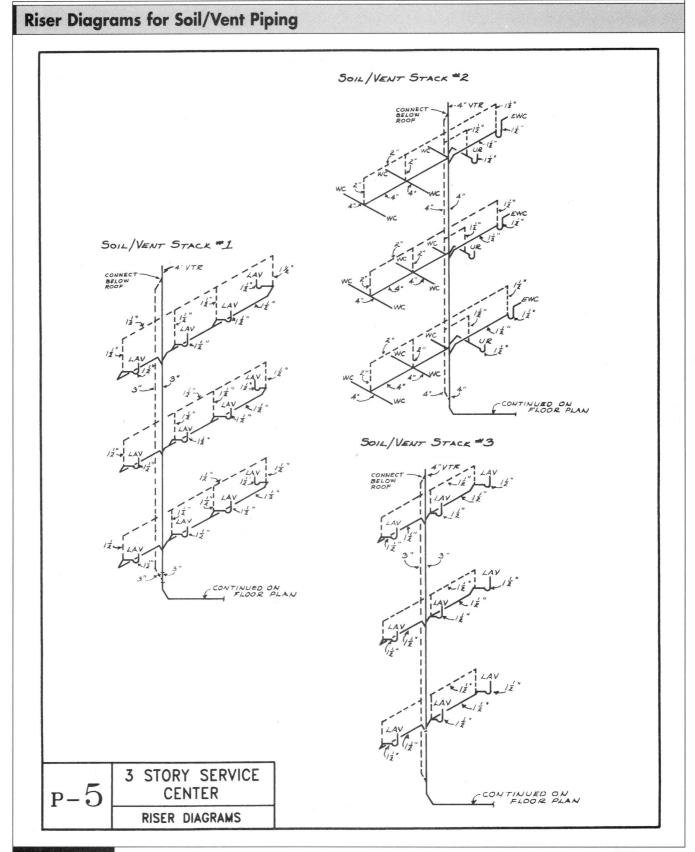

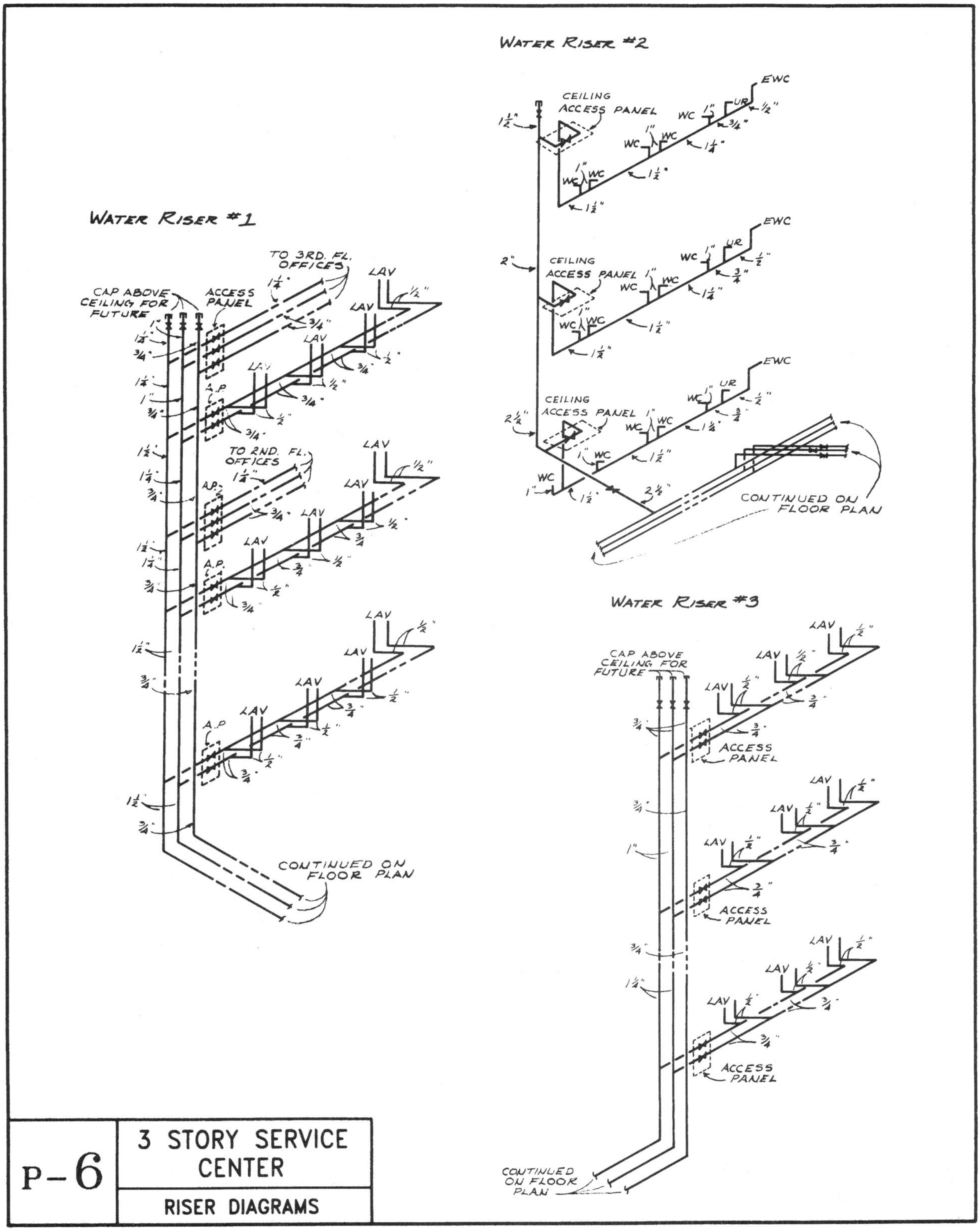

WATER RISER #1
CAP ABOVE CEILING FOR FUTURE
ACCESS PANEL
TO 3RD. FL. OFFICES
TO 2ND. FL. OFFICES
A.P.
LAV
CONTINUED ON FLOOR PLAN
WATER RISER #2
CEILING ACCESS PANEL
WC
UR
EWC
CONTINUED ON FLOOR PLAN
WATER RISER #3
CAP ABOVE CEILING FOR FUTURE
LAV
ACCESS PANEL
CONTINUED ON FLOOR PLAN
P-6
3 STORY SERVICE CENTER
RISER DIAGRAMS

Figure 17.3b

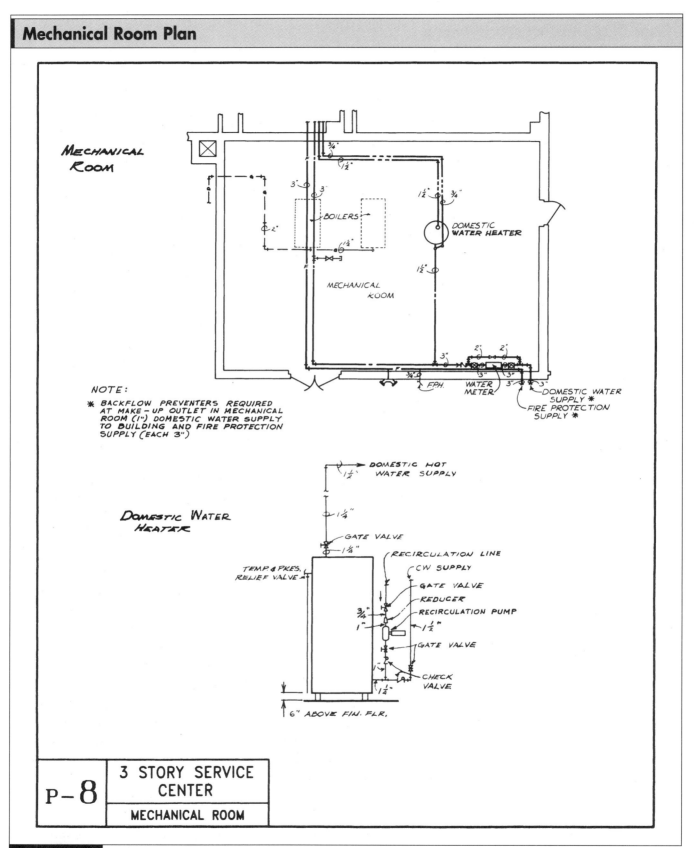

NOTE:
* BACKFLOW PREVENTERS REQUIRED AT MAKE-UP OUTLET IN MECHANICAL ROOM (1") DOMESTIC WATER SUPPLY TO BUILDING AND FIRE PROTECTION SUPPLY (EACH 3")

P-8   3 STORY SERVICE CENTER

MECHANICAL ROOM

Figure 17.4

Fixtures and Trims

Plumbing fixtures include water closets (toilets), urinals, shower stalls, tubs, and lavatories. Trims, such as valves, faucets, trip levers, and drains, are included in this portion of the estimate. Fixtures and trims are taken off and priced by counting the individual pieces and listing them as EA. Quantities of fixtures may be used in determining the quantities of trims. For example, each lavatory will require a faucet and drain, each tub will require a shower/tub valve and trip lever drain, and each water closet will require a toilet seat. Fixtures and their corresponding trims are listed according to type, manufacturer, model, color or finish, and special features, such as handicap compliance. To reduce the chance for error, the estimator may opt to separate fixture and trim quantities according to specific bathrooms or toilets, or by the floor for multi-level commercial restrooms. This will allow the takeoff to be completed for each bathroom or toilet before proceeding to the next one.

Equipment

Equipment for plumbing work includes such items as water heaters, water storage tanks, interior grease interceptors, and sump pumps. Hook-up of equipment supplied by others, such as garbage disposals, gas ranges and ovens, refrigerators with automatic ice-makers, and dishwashers, must be included. Special devices, such as washing machine outlets and venting kits for water heaters, should also be included.

Equipment is taken off and priced by counting the individual piece (EA), and listed according to type, manufacturer, model, size, and capacity. Equipment that requires only hook-up should be listed separately by the piece with the same qualifications as noted above. Special devices needed for the complete installation should be noted separately with reference to the equipment for which it is required. Some equipment provided under the plumbing contract may require the work of other trades, such as power wiring of water heaters, power wiring of draft inducers, and special flues for gas-burning appliances such as water heaters. Penetrations through roofing systems and flashing of roof vents may also be required.

Below-Grade Sanitary Waste and Vent Piping

Below-grade sanitary waste piping carries waste from the individual plumbing fixture and above-grade waste piping in the house/building to the drain and out of the building. Below-grade vent piping ties into vertical risers that vent the system to the exterior. A variety of fittings and devices is used, in addition to the piping itself, including couplings, elbows, tees, tee-wyes, clean-outs, traps, and floor drains, to mention just a few. Fittings, devices, and piping are available in a number of different materials, from PVC to cast iron. Review the specifications for the type of materials for specific applications. Plumbing plans will help determine quantities, size and type of piping, fittings, and devices that will be used in the below-grade application.

Taking off Quantities

Fittings and devices are taken off and priced by counting the individual piece (EA) and listing them separately according to type (elbow, tee, clean-out, etc.), material composition (PVC, service-weight cast-iron, extra heavy-weight cast iron, etc.), method of connection to piping (lead and oakum, hubless, neoprene joint, or PVC cement), and size (diameter). Less accurate, alternate methods include allowing a percentage of the costs of the pipe for the fittings. This approach is not recommended, except for preliminary budgeting.

Piping is taken off and priced by the LF and should be listed separately according to type, size, and method of installation. LF of individual types and sizes of pipe can be converted to actual lengths of pipe required. If cast-iron soil pipe is of the lead-joint design, it will be necessary to determine the total amount of lead, oakum (jute packing), and gas (propane) to complete the installation. This can be done after the fittings and piping takeoff has been completed so that the total number of joints is known. Cast-iron soil pipe is manufactured in 5' and 10' lengths (for lead, 5' is used). The amount of lead per joint is determined by the diameter of the pipe. Figure 17.5 lists the amount of lead (in pounds) per joint to caulk cast-iron pipe.

The following example shows how to determine quantities of lead, oakum, and gas for cast-iron soil pipe, assuming the following quantities of service-weight soil pipe and fittings have been taken off:

20 LF – 4" service-weight soil pipe

3 EA – 4-1/8" bends

1 EA – 6" x 4" wye

Lead Required to Caulk Cast Iron Soil Pipe Joints

Pipe & Fitting Diams. Inches	Lead Ring Depth Inches	Service Weight Cu. Ins.	Wt. Lbs.	Extra Heavy Weight Cu. Ins.	Wt. Lbs.
2	1	2.81	1.15	2.91	1.19
3	1	3.90	1.60	4.17	1.71
4	1	4.98	2.04	5.25	2.15
5	1	6.06	2.49	6.24	2.56
6	1	7.15	2.93	7.42	3.04
8	1.25	15.06	6.17	15.49	6.35
10	1.25	18.90	7.75	19.34	7.93
12	1.25	25.53	10.47	26.02	10.67
15	1.5	43.09	17.67	43.38	17.8

Figure 17.5

The procedure is as follows. (Note that each hub, rather than the opening, is the basis for the number of joints.)

20 LF of 4" (5' length) = four 4" joints x 2.04 lbs./joint = 8.16 lbs.
3 EA – 4-1/8" bends
3 x (1/4" joint) = 3 x 2.04 = 6.12 lbs.
1 EA – 6" x 4" wye 1 x (1 – 6" joint + 1 – 4" joint)
  = (1 x 2.93) + (1 x 2.04) = 4.97 lbs.
Total lead = 19.25 lbs.

Oakum is typically estimated at one-tenth the weight of lead. Therefore, 19.25 lbs. divided by 10 = 1.92 lbs. of oakum. Gas consumption is approximated at one (instopropane) cylinder per 200 lbs. of lead.

If cast-iron soil pipe is of the neoprene joint clamp type (hubless), or if the waste piping is PVC, count the number of joints to arrive at the quantity of clamps, gaskets, or couplings.

Below-grade sanitary waste piping may include excavation and backfill for the placement of the piping—typically the responsibility of the site or general contractor. However, this is not a foregone conclusion. Review the specifications and General Conditions to determine the exact scope of work to avoid costly duplications or omissions.

Above-Grade Sanitary Waste and Vent Piping

Above-grade sanitary waste provides piping for the flow of waste from upper floors of the building to the below-grade system where it will exit the structure. Vent piping allows the escape of gases generated by the waste through the upper level of the structure, typically the roof. The piping and fittings used below grade are similar to those used above grade and are determined by the specifications and the plans. In addition, be sure to consider hangers and supports for bracing or restraining piping.

Taking off Quantities

Procedures for takeoff and pricing follow those of the below-grade system. Fittings are counted and listed as EA according to types and sizes. Piping is taken off and priced by the LF and listed according to type, size, and method of installation. The procedures for calculating lead, oakum, gas and/or gaskets, clamps, and couplings are the same as for the below-grade system. Additional items for the support of piping are taken off and priced by the individual piece and listed as EA, according to size, application, and type. Because pipe hangers and supports are omitted from the drawings for clarity, it is necessary to complete the piping estimate for horizontal run and riser to determine the quantity of each. Refer to the specifications for the required intervals of hangers and supports to determine the number needed and any special seismic restraint.

The takeoff and estimating procedure for above-grade waste and vent piping should be altered slightly to accommodate the fact that above-grade piping is in two planes: horizontal runs and branches in the horizontal plane, and risers and drops to fixtures and equipment in the vertical plane.

Riser diagrams provide dimensions showing floor-to-floor heights. With this information, the length of risers and the approximate length of drop pieces to fixtures can be calculated. Horizontal piping and risers are taken off separately to reduce the chance for error in referencing between multiple drawings. Special staging or rigging may be required to install some of the heavier cast-iron pipe in above-grade applications and must be included in the estimate.

Below-Grade Storm System Piping

This storm drainage system, the lowest part of the piping system, receives clear water from roof leaders (on flat roof buildings), cooling or condensate water, or other clear water within the structure. It conveys the drainage to the building's storm sewer or drain.

The takeoff/pricing procedure and units are the same as those for the below-grade sanitary waste and vent piping system. Although similar, the storm system takeoff and prices should be kept separate from the sanitary system.

Above-Grade Storm System Piping

Above-grade storm system piping consists of roof drains, leaders, and horizontal offsets that will tie into the below-grade storm system at the floor level. The takeoff/pricing procedure and units are the same as those for the above-grade sanitary waste and vent piping systems. Again, although similar, keep these two systems separate in the takeoff. It is a good idea to also keep horizontal pipe offsets for above-grade storm systems (that will be above finished ceilings) separate in the takeoff, since they are normally insulated to prevent condensation.

Hot and Cold Water Piping

Hot and cold water piping is a part of virtually every plumbing job. It includes piping, fittings, valves, control devices, and all the related appurtenances for conveying water to plumbing fixtures and equipment—often referred to as *domestic water piping* (excluding piping for fire protection systems). The cold-water supply typically starts at the point where the water service enters the building and is distributed to the various fixtures and equipment within the structure. The hot-water supply starts typically at the hot water heater and is distributed to the various fixtures within the building.

Standard piping materials include types L and K copper tubing and, in limited applications, brass, galvanized steel pipe, and PVC. The most common method of joining copper pipe and fittings is by solder joint, or rolled-groove pressure fittings for copper tubing, threaded fittings for steel and brass pipe, and cement joint fittings for PVC. Fittings include elbows, tees, 45° and 22.5° bends, couplings, and reducing fittings. Control devices include a variety of valves, such as check, globe, gate, ball, and butterfly. Other special devices include such items as backflow preventers, relief valves, pressure-reducing valves, shock absorbers, vacuum breakers, and frost-proof hose bibs.

Taking off Quantities

Fittings, valves, and control devices are taken off and priced by counting the individual pieces (EA) and listing them according to type, material composition, size, and application. Water piping is taken off and priced by the LF, following a similar procedure to above-grade sanitary piping. Start by taking off mains and branches, then risers and drops. The LF quantities can be converted to individual lengths of pipe. All piping quantities should be listed according to type, grade, and size (diameter).

Pipe hangers and supports are taken off and priced by dividing the total LF of water piping in each size category by the specified intervals, as noted in the specifications or by code requirements. Solder, flux, and gas are used for joining copper water pipe. Copper pipe and fittings are joined by soft (non-lead) solder.

Solder, flux, and gas are difficult items to estimate, but by using the chart in Figure 17.6, one can arrive at a relatively accurate amount of each. The number of joints required for each size fitting and device must be counted to determine a total number of joints in each size category.

Many designs, as well as local plumbing and energy codes, require pipe insulation to retard heat loss and prevent condensation. It is available in a wide variety of sizes and compositions for different applications and is manufactured in both rigid and flexible forms, with or without fittings.

Once the water piping and fittings have been taken off, you can calculate the quantity of insulation. Insulation for individual fittings is taken off and priced by the piece (EA). It should be listed in the takeoff according to the diameter and length of the pipe to be covered and the type of insulation (fiberglass or closed cell).

Access panels installed in the finish surface of walls or ceilings may also be included as part of the plumbing work. These are taken off and priced

Estimated Pounds of Soft Solder Required to Make 100 Joints

Size	⅜"	½"	¾"	1"	1¼"	1½"	2"
Pounds	.5	.75	1.0	1.4	1.7	1.9	2.4
Size	2½"	3"	3½"	4"	5"	6"	8"
Pounds	3.2	3.9	4.5	5.5	8.0	15.0	32.0

Two oz. of flux will be required for each pound of solder. One tank of PRESTO gas will be required for every 500 joints.

Figure 17.6

according to size, type, manufacturer, model, and location and are listed by the piece (EA). Note that access panels in fire-rated walls or ceiling assemblies are required to be fire-rated as well.

Natural Gas System Piping

Piping for natural gas starts at the entrance of the gas service to the building and is distributed to the various gas-fueled appliances within the building, such as water heaters, furnaces, boilers, ranges, clothes dryers, and rooftop HVAC units. Piping materials are typically black steel pipe with malleable iron-threaded fittings. Fittings for gas piping are similar to those of other piping systems and include elbows, bends, unions, and tees. Valves for the control of the flow of gas within the pipe are called *gas cocks*, and are typically brass.

Study the mechanical plans and Division 15 specifications for the location, size, and type of pipe, and for the appliances to be connected. Architectural and mechanical roof plans can be used to calculate the horizontal runs of gas pipe required to supply the units. Flexible connectors and valves can also be determined from these drawings.

Taking off Quantities

The procedure for taking off and pricing gas piping is similar to that of above-grade sanitary waste and vent piping. Fittings and valves are taken off and priced by the individual piece (EA) and listed according to type and size (diameter). Piping is taken off and priced by the LF, according to type and size. Since gas pipe and fittings are joined by a threaded connection, lead, oakum, or solder are not required. Pipe hangers and supports follow the same procedure as for water piping.

Special devices for regulating the pressure of gas supplied to appliances may also be required (such as for ranges or commercial ovens) and must be included in the estimate. Flexible gas connectors for connecting movable appliances to a stationary gas supply may also need to be included in the estimate. Some local codes may require a separate permit for gas work. This usually constitutes an additional fee over and above the plumbing portion of the work.

Labor

Plumbing fixtures, waste and vent piping, and water piping are installed by plumbers. Crews can consist of an individual plumber or can be composed of numerous plumbers and their helpers, called *apprentices*. Productivity will vary depending on the task. Installing fixtures or hooking up equipment is typically performed by an individual plumber, while the installation of below-grade or above-grade cast iron can require a multi-person crew. Insulation of water piping or roof leaders may be done by a separate subcontractor to the plumber called an *insulator*. Installation of all types and sizes of piping is priced by the LF and based on the amount of pipe that a crew can install in a single day. As with all above-grade piping, productivity is affected by the number of fittings, direction changes in the pipe, and accessibility in the work space. Additional costs include staging or platforms to access the work, which must be included as part of the costs of performing the work.

As with fire protection costs, budget estimates for plumbing work should be done purely for comparison or conceptual purposes. Since almost all piping related to water and sewer are to service a fixture, it is not uncommon to reduce budgetary plumbing costs to a cost per plumbing fixture. For example: a water closet has costs for the fixture itself, trims, waste and vent piping (below-and above-grade), water piping, and insulation. The same components apply to a storm water piping system. Each roof drain or downspout leader has attached piping. The total cost of the storm water system piping and fittings, both above- and below-grade, can be reduced to a cost per roof drain or leader.

As a simple example, if the total cost of materials, labor, tools, and equipment for the storm water piping system is $16,000 and the building had eight roof drains, the costs could be budgeted as $2,000 per drain.

Figure 17.7 provides guidelines for labor-hours to install various applications of cast piping and fittings for plumbing systems.

Heating, Ventilating, & Air Conditioning (HVAC)

Heating, ventilating, and air conditioning systems, commonly referred to as HVAC, include the various components that provide heating, cooling, and fresh air to the occupied space of the building or residence. One of the most common methods involves gas- or oil-fired furnaces that supply warm air through a series of supply and return-air ductwork. This same system of ductwork can be used to supply cooled air in summer.

Alternate methods of heating employ gas- or oil-fired boilers that force hot water through a system of radiant baseboard installed in individual rooms. This is referred to as a *hydronic heating system.*

Study the mechanical plans for the layout, locations, and sizes of ductwork and fin tube radiation baseboard. Special mechanical plans and details that illustrate the components of boilers and rooftop HVAC units may also be included. Architectural drawings should be reviewed for dimensions and coordination with architectural features, such as ceilings. Division 15 specifications for the HVAC work also list the specific materials, manufacturer, and model of the heating and cooling units, as well as the various appurtenances required for a complete system.

For purposes of takeoff and estimating, HVAC work can be divided into two general categories: ducted systems for the distribution of heated or cooled air, and radiant heating systems for forced hot water.

Both takeoff and estimating for HVAC systems, like other Division 15 work, require a specialized knowledge of the individual systems, which is not normally within the realm of the general contractor's estimating

Installation Time in Labor-Hours for Cast Iron

Description	Labor-Hours	Unit
Cast Iron Soil Pipe Service Weight, Single Hub with Hangers Every Five Feet, Lead and Oakum Joints Every Ten Feet		
2" Pipe Size	.254	L.F.
3" Pipe Size	.267	L.F.
4" Pipe Size	.291	L.F.
5" Pipe Size	.316	L.F.
6" Pipe Size	.329	L.F.
8" Pipe Size	.542	L.F.
10" Pipe Size	.593	L.F.
12" Pipe Size	.667	L.F.
Push on Gasket Joints Every Ten Feet		
2" Pipe Size	.242	L.F.
3" Pipe Size	.254	L.F.
4" Pipe Size	.281	L.F.
5" Pipe Size	.304	L.F.
6" Pipe Size	.320	L.F.
8" Pipe Size	.516	L.F.
10" Pipe Size	.571	L.F.
12" Pipe Size	.653	L.F.
Cast Iron Soil Pipe Fittings **Hub and Spigot Service Weight** Bends or Elbows		
2" Pipe Size	1.000	Ea.
3" Pipe Size	1.140	Ea.
4" Pipe Size	1.230	Ea.
5" Pipe Size	1.330	Ea.
6" Pipe Size	1.410	Ea.
8" Pipe Size	2.910	Ea.
10" Pipe Size	3.200	Ea.
12" Pipe Size	3.560	Ea.
Tees or Wyes		
2" Pipe Size	1.600	Ea.
3" Pipe Size	1.780	Ea.
4" Pipe Size	2.000	Ea.
5" Pipe Size	2.000	Ea.
6" Pipe Size	2.180	Ea.
8" Pipe Size	4.570	Ea.
10" Pipe Size	4.870	Ea.
12" Pipe Size	5.330	Ea.

Eighth Bend

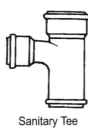

Sanitary Tee

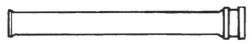

Single Hub Soil Pipe

Figure 17.7a

Installation Time in Labor-Hours for Cast Iron

Description	Labor-Hours	Unit
Push on Gasket Joints		
Bends or Elbows		
2" Pipe Size	.800	Ea.
3" Pipe Size	.941	Ea.
4" Pipe Size	1.070	Ea.
5" Pipe Size	1.140	Ea.
6" Pipe Size	1.260	Ea.
8" Pipe Size	2.670	Ea.
10" Pipe Size	2.910	Ea.
12" Pipe Size	3.200	Ea.
Tees or Wyes		
2" Pipe Size	1.330	Ea.
3" Pipe Size	1.600	Ea.
4" Pipe Size	1.780	Ea.
5" Pipe Size	1.850	Ea.
6" Pipe Size	2.180	Ea.
8" Pipe Size	4.000	Ea.
10" Pipe Size	4.870	Ea.
12" Pipe Size	5.330	Ea.
Cleanouts		
Floor Type		
2" Pipe Size	.800	Ea.
3" Pipe Size	1.000	Ea.
4" Pipe Size	1.333	Ea.
5" Pipe Size	2.000	Ea.
6" Pipe Size	2.667	Ea.
8" Pipe Size	4.000	Ea.
Cleanout Tee		
2" Pipe Size	2.000	Ea.
3" Pipe Size	2.222	Ea.
4" Pipe Size	2.424	Ea.
5" Pipe Size	2.909	Ea.
6" Pipe Size	3.200	Ea.
8" Pipe Size	6.400	Ea.
Drains		
Heelproof Floor Drain		
2" to 4" Pipe Size	1.600	Ea.
5" and 6" Pipe Size	1.778	Ea.
8" Pipe Size	2.000	Ea.
Shower Drain		
1-1/2" to 3" Pipe Size	2.000	Ea.
4" Pipe Size	2.286	Ea.
Cast Iron Service Weight Traps		
Deep Seal		
2" Pipe Size	1.143	Ea.
3" Pipe Size	1.333	Ea.
4" Pipe Size	1.455	Ea.

Cleanout, Floor Type

Cleanout Tee

Heelproof Floor Drain

Shower Drain

Deep Seal Trap

Figure 17.7b

Installation Time in Labor-Hours for Cast Iron

Description	Labor-Hours	Unit
P Trap		
2" Pipe Size	1.000	Ea.
3" Pipe Size	1.143	Ea.
4" Pipe Size	1.231	Ea.
5" Pipe Size	1.333	Ea.
6" Pipe Size	1.412	Ea.
8" Pipe Size	2.909	Ea.
10" Pipe Size	3.200	Ea.
Running Trap with Vent		
3" Pipe Size	1.143	Ea.
4" Pipe Size	1.231	Ea.
5" Pipe Size	2.182	Ea.
6" Pipe Size	3.000	Ea.
8" Pipe Size	3.200	Ea.
S Trap		
2" Pipe Size	1.067	Ea.
3" Pipe Size	1.143	Ea.
4" Pipe Size	1.231	Ea.
No Hub with Couplings Every Ten Feet OC		
1-1/2" Pipe Size	.225	L.F.
2" Pipe Size	.239	L.F.
3" Pipe Size	.250	L.F.
4" Pipe Size	.276	L.F.
5" Pipe Size	.289	L.F.
6" Pipe Size	.304	L.F.
8" Pipe Size	.464	L.F.
10" Pipe Size	.525	L.F.
No Hub Couplings*		
1-1/2" Pipe Size	.333	Ea.
2" Pipe Size	.364	Ea.
3" Pipe Size	.421	Ea.
4" Pipe Size	.485	Ea.
5" Pipe Size	.545	Ea.
6" Pipe Size	.600	Ea.
8" Pipe Size	.970	Ea.
10" Pipe Size	1.230	Ea.

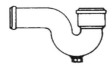

P Trap

Running Trap with Vent

S Trap

No Hub Coupling

*Note: In estimating labor for no hub fittings, all the labor is included in the no hub couplings. One coupling per joint.

Figure 17.7c

experience. The various disciplines of labor involved in the HVAC will be discussed at the end of the section.

Ducted Systems

Ducted systems include a wide variety of heating and cooling systems with metal ductwork for the supply and return of conditioned air to and from spaces within a building. The heated or cooled air can be supplied from a single self-contained unit or from separate components at various locations within or outside the structure. Ductwork and equipment shown on the project drawings will have been engineered to suit the specific application based on the design criteria. In much the same fashion as piping for water and waste systems, ductwork is installed in a series of main trunks and branches to specific areas as required. Different "fittings" or transition pieces allow ducts to change direction, circumvent obstacles, or reduce in size, as required by the particular application.

Special devices that control the flow of air within the ductwork are called *dampers*. Round or rectangular outlets that diffuse the air delivered to the space are called *diffusers*. They are typically located at the ceiling level. Similar devices that have a grille and damper for regulating air flow at the device are called registers. Louvered or perforated panels at the inlet to return-air ducts are called *grilles*.

Controls that regulate the temperature of the space—*thermostats*—signal to the furnace the need for more or less heat. Figures 17.8 illustrates gas- and oil-fired warm air ducted systems, respectively.

Taking off Quantities

Ductwork is taken off by the LF and listed according to type, size, and application (supply or return). In addition to horizontal mains, vertical risers and drops are also necessary for the distribution of air between multiple floors. Flexible ducts for short runs to diffusers are taken off and priced by the LF.

Since the supply ductwork and fittings are usually insulated, it is helpful to separate the quantities of each in the takeoff. Fittings, transition pieces, reducers, collars for the connection of flexible ducts, and dampers are taken off and priced by the individual piece (EA) and listed according to type, size, and application. Devices installed in the finished space, such as registers, grilles, thermostats, and diffusers, are taken off and priced by the individual piece (EA) and listed according to type, size, manufacturer, model, and finish.

Once the ductwork portion of the takeoff has been completed, calculate the quantity of insulation needed. To do so, the total surface area of the various-sized ducts and fittings must be determined. The easiest method

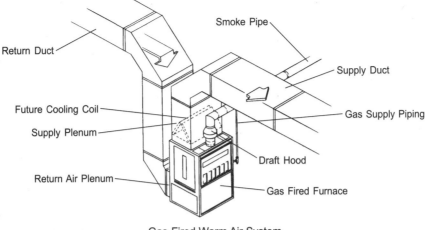

Return Duct

Smoke Pipe

Supply Duct

Future Cooling Coil

Supply Plenum

Gas Supply Piping

Draft Hood

Return Air Plenum

Gas Fired Furnace

Gas-Fired Warm Air System

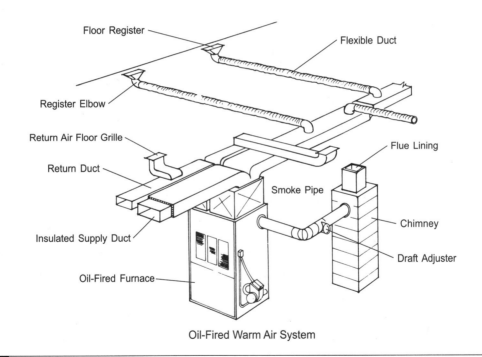

Floor Register

Flexible Duct

Register Elbow

Return Air Floor Grille

Flue Lining

Return Duct

Smoke Pipe

Chimney

Insulated Supply Duct

Draft Adjuster

Oil-Fired Furnace

Oil-Fired Warm Air System

Figure 17.8

considers the fittings as ductwork, and measures through the fittings when doing a takeoff from the plan. For example:

Assuming a takeoff quantity of 43' of 12" x 16" supply duct to be insulated:

Surface area = (12" + 16") x 2 = 4.67 SF per LF of duct
= 43 LF x 4.67 SF/LF = 200.8 SF

Sound lining in the interior of the duct is taken off and priced by the SF using the same procedure as for duct insulation.

Equipment takeoff for furnaces, air conditioning condensing units, evaporators, electric coils, and heat pumps is by the individual piece (EA) and listed according to type, size or capacity, manufacturer, model, series, and any other special identifying criteria. Components to complete the system may include flues for the furnace, control wiring for the thermostat, testing and balancing, and filters, which are taken off individually and listed as each (EA), lump sum (LS), or whatever units best represent the scope of work. Once the list of all necessary components is complete, prices should be solicited from suppliers.

Consult the mechanical drawings and specifications to determine the exact scope of HVAC work. Items such as power wiring to the furnace, installation of a condensing unit or compressor, furnishing and installation of oil tanks for oil-fired systems, and gas piping for gas-fired furnaces are not typically part of the HVAC contractor's work.

For commercial projects with rooftop equipment, hoisting or crane services are necessary. Check the specifications to verify who will provide the crane or hoisting of the equipment and note this information in the takeoff.

Testing and balancing of completed duct systems is mandatory for most commercial projects, and must be done by an independent contractor at the expense of the HVAC contractor. Reports are typically required to confirm that the design criteria have been met. Testing and balancing should be included as a separate cost in the HVAC estimate. Prices should be solicited from a qualified test and balance contractor for the most accurate pricing.

Sheet metal ductwork, fabricated from galvanized steel sheets, is often converted to weight (lbs.) for the pricing of the raw material (sheets). The calculation for this conversion takes into account the gauge (thickness) and weight per SF of the material being used. Consult Figure 17.9 to obtain the weight per LF of ductwork for various types of sheet metal.

The total weight in pounds of ductwork should be increased by 10%–15% for waste, hangers, and clips. The total weight in pounds can be priced prior to the fabrication.

Ductwork (Duct Weight in Pounds per L.F. Straight Runs)

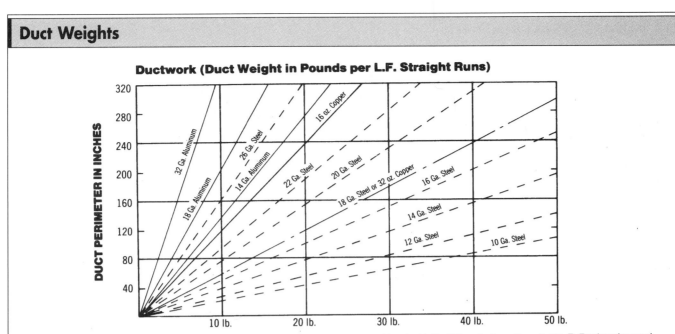

Add to the above for fittings: 90° elbow is 3 L.F.; 45° elbow is 2.5 L.F.; offset is 4 L.F.; transition offset is 6 L.F.; square-to-round

transition is 4 L.F.; 90° reducing elbow is 5 L.F. For bracing and waste, add 20% to aluminum and copper, 15% to steel.

Figure 17.9

Forced Hot Water Systems (Hydronic Heating Systems)

An alternate method of heating is oil- or gas-fired hot water (or steam) boilers, manufactured in cast-iron, steel, or copper, and are available pre-assembled (packaged) or in sections for field assembly. Figure 17.10 illustrates a forced hot-water heating system.

In addition to the boiler itself, appurtenances required to complete the system include expansion tanks, pressure-relief and pressure-regulating valves, zone valves, circulators, pipe and fittings, flow control valves, oil burners (for oil-fired systems), operating controls, and fin tube radiant baseboard.

Taking off Quantities and Material Pricing

The following takeoff quantities apply to forced hot water systems:

- *Fin tube radiant baseboard*: taken off and priced by the LF (as is cast-iron baseboard). Quantities of each should be kept separate and listed according to type, manufacturer, model or rating (BTU output), and finish of the protective enclosure.

- *Boilers*: taken off and priced by the individual unit and quantified as EA, listed according to size (BTU rating), type of fuel used, construction (steel, cast-iron), manufacturer, model or series, and level of assembly required.

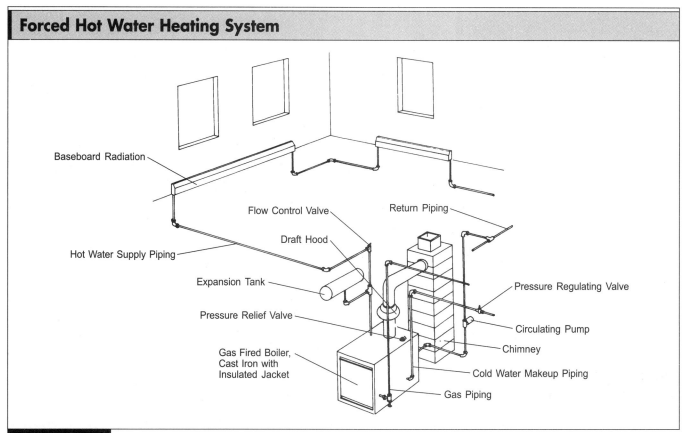

Baseboard Radiation

Flow Control Valve

Return Piping

Draft Hood

Hot Water Supply Piping

Expansion Tank

Pressure Regulating Valve

Pressure Relief Valve

Circulating Pump

Chimney

Gas Fired Boiler,
Cast Iron with
Insulated Jacket

Cold Water Makeup Piping

Gas Piping

Figure 17.10

- *Appurtenances (expansion tanks, circulators, zone valves, pressure valves, draft hoods, flues, and oil tanks)*: taken off and priced by the piece (EA) and listed according to manufacturer, model, function or type, size, and any other identifying features.
- *Piping to and from radiant baseboard*: taken off and priced by the LF and listed according to size and material (steel, copper, etc.).
- *Fittings and valves*: taken off and priced by the individual piece (EA) according to type, size, material, and method of joining. This same procedure is used for taking off looped radiant systems.

Remember that related work of other trades may be necessary for a complete system, including power wiring, gas piping, control wiring, and piping of oil tanks. Review the specifications carefully to determine the exact scope of work.

Labor

Many trades are involved in the completed HVAC system. Sheet metal workers, sometimes called *tin knockers*, cut, shape, and assemble ductwork from sheets of raw galvanized tin. They install the sound liners inside the ductwork. The ductwork is then shipped to the site, and installed or *hung* from the structure. Tin knockers install the collars into the ductwork, called *takeoffs*, and connect the ductwork to the grilles or diffusers that provide and circulate the air. Fabrication labor should be kept separate from installation labor.

Crews may consist of two sheet metal workers or many, depending on the needs of the project. Productivity is measured by actual weight or LF of hard or flexible duct installed. In addition, consider the setting of equipment, roof top units, cabinet unit heaters, VAV boxes, air handling equipment, and coils. All equipment installation costs are based on the individual piece and the condition of the installation. Frequently, hoisting equipment, such as cranes or lifts, is required to set the equipment.

Pipefitters and/or plumbers are also part of the HVAC crew and install the hydronic heating equipment, such as boilers, expansion tanks, zone valves, fin tube radiation, and circulating equipment. Again, depending on the size of the project and equipment, hoisting equipment may be needed. Costs for this portion of the labor are calculated by labor-hours per piece of equipment or per LF of fin tube radiation.

Insulators are also required to wrap ductwork and insulate piping and boiler components. Cost for pipe insulation is based on LF of insulation, and will vary with the diameter of the pipe and the number of fittings. Insulation of ductwork, water heaters, and boilers is priced by the SF per labor-hour or per crew day.

Lastly, all HVAC equipment requires some type of automatic temperature control (ATC) system to operate. Some systems are very sophisticated and require a highly specialized subcontractor to install, test, and program. Others are a simple thermostat with low-voltage wiring. Installation costs depend on the system and quantity of the devices. Labor costs can be broken down into labor-hours per device.

Conclusion

One of the main premises of quantity takeoff is that the information derived from the contract documents is accurate. For example, a footing 1' high x 2' wide x 54' long contains 4 CY of concrete regardless of who does the takeoff. In order to do an accurate takeoff, detailed plans and specifications would be required, including an individual mechanical design for plumbing, heating, and air conditioning systems. For commercial projects, this is required by law for most states, but for residential construction, it is often left to the individual plumbing or HVAC contractor to design and install a system that will perform its function in accordance with local codes and standards.

It is not essential to itemize the takeoff and estimate for mechanical systems in the same manner as for other aspects of the project, such as carpentry, painting, or roofing. Listing the basic criteria helps establish a budget estimate for the individual mechanical trades. Historical data from projects with similar criteria can then be compared with actual quotes from subcontractors to arrive at reliable costs.

Chapter Eighteen

Electrical Systems

D ivision 16 covers electricity distribution and specialized systems for fire and security alarms, communications, electric heating, technology/data wiring, and low-voltage wiring. Electrical work is performed by individuals or firms with specific training and licensing. Separate permits are also required. To take off and estimate electrical work, it is extremely beneficial to have a working knowledge of the material components of the particular systems. Actual electrical expertise is not normally within the realm of the general contractor's estimating experience. A practicing electrician can contribute greatly to your understanding of the installation portion of the estimate. Since most general contractors subcontract their electrical work, they will not need to produce a detailed estimate.

Division 16 work is typically shown on the electrical drawings labeled with the prefix "E." Be sure to review all drawings within the bid set for electrical work that may be shown on other drawings, such as site lighting, utilities plans, or hook-up of equipment provided by others. Consult mechanical drawings for related work in other sections, such as power and control wiring and detection and alarm systems for fire protection. As with mechanical drawings, electrical drawings employ their own trade-specific graphic symbols for conveying information. Review all legends and graphic symbols on the electrical drawing.

Electrical drawings often use schedules that are helpful in determining the materials for the takeoff. Typical schedules include lighting fixtures, panels, equipment, and feeders. Specialized details, such as the electrical riser diagram, illustrate the various components of the system and their configurations. Riser diagrams are for the graphic representation of information only, and are not drawn to scale.

Consult the architectural drawings for dimensions, room sizes, floor-to-floor heights, ceiling heights, location of services entering the building, and coordination with other work within the area.

Review Division 16 specifications thoroughly for the products, methods, and techniques of installation, and the related work of other trades. A careful review of Division 1—General Requirements, "Temporary Controls and Facilities," is necessary to determine what, if any, special requirements are to be included in the takeoff and estimate. Some classic examples include:

- Temporary lighting and power for the project
- Maintenance and relocation of temporary lighting and power
- Temporary connection/disconnection of special construction equipment with electrical needs (hoists, welding machines, floor sanders, etc.)
- Electrical utility company charges for services (utility pole relocation costs, engineering and design costs, etc.)

These costs should still be considered part of the electrical portion of the project, even if not specifically referenced. Figure 18.1 illustrates a simplified electrical system for a light commercial project.

This chapter covers takeoff procedures for the type of electrical systems generally encountered in light commercial and residential construction. The starting point for takeoff, however, should be determined by your own preference.

Typical Commercial Electric System

This figure shows the basic lighting and power components used for the interior of a typical commercial project.

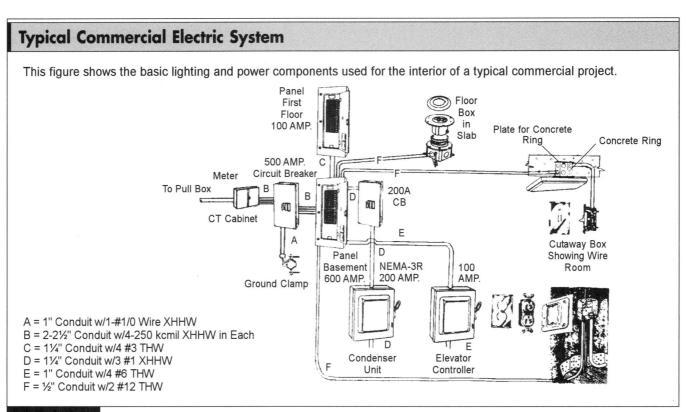

A = 1" Conduit w/1-#1/0 Wire XHHW
B = 2-2½" Conduit w/4-250 kcmil XHHW in Each
C = 1¼" Conduit w/4 #3 THW
D = 1¼" Conduit w/3 #1 XHHW
E = 1" Conduit w/4 #6 THW
F = ½" Conduit w/2 #12 THW

Figure 18.1

Raceways

Raceways are channels constructed to house and protect electrical conductors. They include conduits, wireways/cable trays, surface metal raceways, and underfloor ducts. As part of the raceway system, fittings are needed to change direction, connect, and support the various types of raceway runs. The most common type of raceway is conduit, which can be aluminum, rigid galvanized steel, steel intermediate conduit (IMC), rigid plastic-coated steel, PVC, or electrical metallic tubing (EMT). Conduit can be wall-mounted, suspended overhead, encased in concrete, or buried.

Taking off Quantities

Raceways are taken off and priced by the LF and classified according to type, size, and application. Individual fittings for wireways, underfloor ducts, surface metal raceways, and larger diameter conduits are taken off and priced by the piece (EA) and listed according to type, size, and material. In most instances, fittings are not shown on drawings for standard conduit installations. For smaller-diameter conduits, fittings can be accounted for by adding a percentage to the total conduit materials. Percentages will vary with the complexity of the run. Many of the applications of particular fittings are dictated by local electrical codes or the individual project requirements.

Divide the takeoff and pricing of conduit into three categories: power distribution, branch power, and branch lighting. *Power distribution* includes the main conductors to supply power to the various panels. *Branch power* and *branch lighting* refer to the branches of the panels that provide power and lighting to various locations. Using these categories, all conduit quantities need not be taken off at one time and can be determined system by system. Since drawings are represented graphically in only two dimensions, length and width, the third dimension, depth, is implied. Be sure to include quantities for the vertical portion of the raceway that is not shown. Raceways installed higher than 15' above the floor should be noted separately because of their reduced productivity. Also note that electrical drawings are "diagrammatic" in nature, and not necessarily exactly as the work will be built. For example, the exact location and configuration of raceways may be subject to change as a result of conditions in the field. Figure 18.2 provides labor-hours for installing conduit.

Conductors & Grounding

A conductor is a wire or metal bar with a low resistance to the flow of electricity. Grounding is accomplished by a conductor connected between electrical equipment, or between a circuit and the earth. Wire is the most common material used to conduct current from the electrical source to electrical use. Copper or aluminum wire conductors with insulating jackets are available in a variety of voltage ratings and insulating materials. Wire is installed within raceways, such as conduit or flexible metallic conduit (sometimes referred to as Greenfield or flex). Flexible metallic conduit is a single strip of aluminum or galvanized steel, spiral-wound and interlocked

Installation Time in Labor-Hours for Conduit

Conduit to 15' high, includes couplings, fittings, and support.

Description	Labor-Hours	Unit
Rigid Galvanized Steel 1/2" Diameter	.089	L.F.
1-1/2" Diameter	.145	L.F.
3" Diameter	.320	L.F.
6" Diameter	.800	L.F.
Aluminum 1/2" Diameter	.080	L.F.
1-1/2" Diameter	.123	L.F.
3" Diameter	.178	L.F.
6" Diameter	.400	L.F.
IMC 1/2" Diameter	.080	L.F.
1-1/2" Diameter	.133	L.F.
3" Diameter	.267	L.F.
4" Diameter	.320	L.F.
Plastic Coated Rigid Steel 1/2" Diameter	.100	L.F.
1-1/2" Diameter	.178	L.F.
3" Diameter	.364	L.F.
6" Diameter	.800	L.F.
EMT 1/2" Diameter	.047	L.F.
1-1/2" Diameter	.089	L.F.
3" Diameter	.160	L.F.
4" Diameter	.200	L.F.
PVC Nonmetallic 1/2" Diameter	.042	L.F.
1-1/2" Diameter	.080	L.F.
3" Diameter	.145	L.F.
6" Diameter	.267	L.F.

Rigid Steel,
Plastic Coated Coupling

PVC Conduit

PVC Elbow

Aluminum Conduit

EMT Set Screw Connector

Aluminum Elbow

EMT Connector

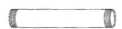

Rigid Steel, Plastic Coated Conduit

EMT to Conduit Adapter

Rigid Steel, Plastic Coated Elbow

EMT to Greenfield Adapter

Figure 18.2

348

to provide a circular cross section of high strength and flexibility for the protection of the wire within. Other products similar to flex are covered with liquid-tight plastic and used where protection from liquids or precipitation is required. Other types of conductors include armored cable (BX & MC), a fabricated assembly of cable with a metal enclosure similar in appearance to flex. Non-metallic sheathed cable (Romex) is manufactured with insulated conductors enclosed in an outer sheath of plastic or fibrous material. It is available with or without a bare ground wire made of copper or aluminum conductors.

Special wires, such as those used in low-voltage control wiring signals and telecommunications, are also available. Special connectors or terminations at the end of each wire may be required, and various fasteners such as staples, clips, and flex fittings are also necessary. Consult the specifications for the specific conductors required for each application. In the absence of a specification section to define the various conductors, defer to the electrical code having jurisdiction.

Taking off Quantities

Wire, flex, and cables are taken off and priced by the LF and divided by 100 to arrive at CLF. The total quantity of wire installed within conduits or flex is determined by multiplying the number of conductors by the LF of conduit or flex and converting to CLF. All wire and cables should be listed in the takeoff according to type, size (rating), conductor material, and application (feeders, branch power, and branch lighting).

Special fittings for connecting of wire or cables, sometimes referred to as *terminations*, are taken off and priced by the individual piece (EA) and listed according to type, size, application, and method of connection. For smaller conductors, the fittings are estimated by adding a percentage of the cost of the conductors. For connectors on larger conductors, such as those used on feeders, the individual termination devices are counted.

In addition to grounding conductors, accessory items such as ground rods, clamps, and exothermic weld metal are taken off and priced by the individual piece (EA) and listed according to type, size, and application. An allowance of 10% for waste and connections on conductor quantities is usually acceptable, but may be increased for lengths of wire or cables with numerous interruptions, such as intermediate connections or splices.

Wire should be taken off and separated according to application (feeders and service entrance, branch power, and branch lighting). Take care in the takeoff to allow for sufficient lengths for connections, especially in larger feeders where incorrect footage is costly. Review the governing codes concerning terminations to ensure that all items have been included. Figure 18.3 provides guidelines for labor-hours of various sized conductors.

Wiring Devices & Boxes

Boxes are used in electrical wiring at each junction point, outlet, or switch to provide access to electrical connections and serve as a mounting for fixtures or switches. They may also be used as pull or splice points for

Installation Time in Labor-Hours for Electrical Conductors: Wire and Cable

Description	Labor-Hours	Unit
600V Copper #14 AWG	.610	CLF
#12 AWG	.720	CLF
#10 AWG	.800	CLF
#8 AWG	1.000	CLF
#6 AWG	1.230	CLF
#4 AWG	1.510	CLF
#3 AWG	1.600	CLF
#2 AWG	1.780	CLF
#1 AWG	2.000	CLF
#1/0	2.420	CLF
#2/0	2.760	CLF
#3/0	3.200	CLF
#4/0	3.640	CLF
250 kcmil	4.000	CLF
500 kcmil	5.000	CLF
1000 kcmil	9.000	CLF

Figure 18.3

wire in long runs or conduits. A wiring device, such as a switch or receptacle, controls (but does not consume) electricity.

Boxes often require plaster rings, covers, and various fasteners for support. In addition to receptacles and switches, wiring devices include pilot lights, relays, low-voltage transformers, and a variety of specialized controls and finish wall plates.

Taking off Quantities

Outlet boxes, pull or junction boxes, receptacles, switches, wall plates, relays, and wiring devices in general are taken off and priced by the individual piece (EA). In sufficient numbers, they can be extended to 100-piece counts. Be sure to include the necessary accessories for a complete application. For example, for outlet boxes, include plaster rings and extensions (if required); for pull boxes, include covers; and for receptacles and switches, include plates. The various items should be listed according to type, size, composition, capacity or application, and color (if applicable). In general, boxes and devices have a low unit cost and warrant the inclusion of a waste factor. Depending on the size of the project, 5%–10% is usually adequate for waste.

Review the specs for the exact scope of work for control devices, such as relays and low-voltage transformers, which may affect other trades. Special devices may be provided by other trades and installed and wired under the electrical specification section. Examples include relays for heating or cooling units, flow and tamper switches for automatic sprinkler systems, smoke/heat detectors for installation within the heating system, and temperature-sensing controls for heating applications. Figure 18.4 provides installation time for various types of wiring devices.

Description	Labor-Hours	Unit
Receptacle 20A 250V	.290	Ea.
Receptacle 30A 250V	.530	Ea.
Receptacle 50A 250V	.720	Ea.
Receptacle 60A 250V	1.000	Ea.
Box, 4" Square	.400	Ea.
Box, Single Gang	.290	Ea.
Box, Cast Single Gang	.660	Ea.
Cover, Weatherproof	.120	Ea.
Cover, Raised Device	.150	Ea.
Cover, Brushed Brass	.100	Ea.

30 Amp, 125 Volt, NEMA 5

50 Amp, 125 Volt, NEMA 5

Box, Single Gang

Cover

Duplex Receptacle

Receptacle, Including Box and Cover

20 Amp, 250 Volt, NEMA 6

Receptacles

Figure 18.4

Starters, Boards, & Switches

Be sure to calculate quantities of panelboards, starters for motors, control stations, circuit breakers, safety switches and disconnects, fuses, and meter centers and sockets.

Taking off Quantities

The following takeoff guidelines apply.

- *Control stations:* by the individual unit (EA), listed according to type, manufacturer, classification, and application.
- *Circuit breakers:* by the individual piece (EA), listed according to manufacturer, type (number of poles), capacity (rating), voltage, method of installation (plug-in or bolt-on), and classification (NEMA).
- *Panelboards:* by the individual unit (EA), listed according to size (capacity in Amps), type, voltage, and manufacturer. Some standard board and breaker assemblies are available as pre-assembled units, such as load centers used in residential construction.
- *Starters:* by the individual piece (EA), listed according to size, voltage, NEMA enclosure, and type.

- *Safety switches* and *disconnects:* by the individual unit (EA), listed according to size, type (duty), number of poles, voltage, NEMA classification, and ampere rating.
- *Fuses:* by the individual piece (EA), listed according to amp, voltage, and type or class.
- *Meter centers* and *sockets:* by the individual unit (EA), listed according to size and type for meter sockets, and by bus capacity, number of meter sockets, and type of enclosure for meter centers.

Most of the electrical components in this section can vary in price dramatically with a change to the model number or NEMA classification. Any specific information in the specs that could be used to define the price more accurately should be noted in the takeoff. Most electrical estimators assemble a list of components for pricing by supply houses, similar to carpentry estimators listing materials for pricing by the lumberyard or supplier. *(Refer to Chapter 11, Wood & Plastics.)* Figures 18.5a and b provide labor-hours to install motor starters and controls.

In addition to the above-mentioned components, special fasteners or auxiliary components may be required. These include perforated support bars, threaded rods, or steel angles. Plywood sheets or concrete pads for mounting electrical equipment or anchors to attach items to concrete or masonry surfaces, must be included as part of the takeoff and estimate. Refer to the specifications to clarify the exact scope of work. Since starters for motors are frequently furnished as part of the mechanical package, verify that they are not supplied by others to avoid costly duplication or omission. One fuse should be counted for each line (or phase) to be protected.

Installation Time in Labor-Hours for Starters

Description	Labor-Hours	Unit
Starter 3-Pole 2 HP Size 00	2.290	Ea.
5 HP Size 0	3.480	Ea.
10 HP Size 1	5.000	Ea.
25 HP Size 2	7.270	Ea.
50 HP Size 3	8.890	Ea.
100 HP Size 4	13.330	Ea.
200 HP Size 5	17.780	Ea.
400 HP Size 6	20.000	Ea.
Control Station Stop/Start	1.000	Ea.
Stop/Start, Pilot Light	1.290	Ea.
Hand/Off/Automatic	1.290	Ea.
Stop/Start/Reverse	1.510	Ea.

Figure 18.5a

Description	Labor-Hours	Unit
Heavy Duty Fusible Disconnect 30 Amps	2.500	Ea.
60 Amps	3.480	Ea.
100 Amps	4.210	Ea.
200 Amps	6.150	Ea.
600 Amps	13.330	Ea.
1200 Amps	20.000	Ea.
Starter 3-pole 2 HP Size 00	2.290	Ea.
5 HP Size 0	3.480	Ea.
10 HP Size 1	5.000	Ea.
25 HP Size 2	7.270	Ea.
50 HP Size 3	8.890	Ea.
100 HP Size 4	13.330	Ea.
200 HP Size 5	17.780	Ea.
400 HP Size 6	20.000	Ea.
Control Station Stop/Start	1.000	Ea.
Stop/Start, Pilot Light	1.290	Ea.
Hand/Off/Automatic	1.290	Ea.
Stop/Start/Reverse	1.510	Ea.

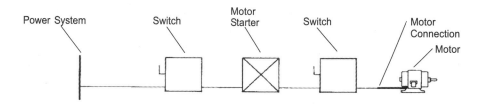

Figure 18.5b

Lighting

Lighting is a fundamental part of the electrical estimate and can represent a considerable portion of the cost. Varieties of lighting include interior and exterior, surface-mounted and recessed, emergency and exit fixtures, track lighting, and the lamps for various fixtures. An enormous variety of light fixtures are manufactured to suit every application. Lamps for fixtures include incandescent, fluorescent, mercury vapor, halogen, metal halide, and high-pressure sodium.

Taking off Quantities

Count, list, and price each fixture for the estimate by the individual unit (EA) according to the manufacturer, model, type, color or finish, location (wall, ceiling, room), and interior or exterior application. The number of lamps can be determined per fixture and listed by individual lamp (EA). The assembly for ceiling fans or chandeliers should also be noted, if applicable.

Emergency and exit lighting should be kept separate from general light fixtures and quantified and priced by the individual piece (EA).

Interior and exterior light fixtures should be taken off and priced separately. Most exterior light fixtures are either wall- or pole-mounted,

353

and very large fixtures may require cranes or boom trucks to install. Large interior fixtures, such as chandeliers, may also require some type of rigging or hoisting and structural support for attachment. As previously noted, most electrical estimators assemble light fixture types and quantities for pricing by supply houses, or if the quantity is sufficient, directly from manufacturers' representatives. This ensures current pricing, volume discounts, and accuracy. Figure 18.6 provides labor-hours for installation of various types of lighting.

Special Systems

These include fire alarms, cable and closed-circuit TV, technology and data wiring and systems, intercoms, electric heating, energy management, and security systems. Each is a separate system that functions independently of other electrical systems or in conjunction with other building systems.

Taking off Quantities

The takeoff procedure for special systems should follow that of other electrical systems. Each should be taken off and priced separately. Raceways and wiring (conductors) should be taken off and priced by the LF and listed according to identifying characteristics and application. Devices should be taken off and priced by the individual piece (EA) and listed according to type, application, manufacturer, model, and function. Be sure to include all necessary boxes, covers, plates, connectors, and equipment for a complete system.

As many specialty systems are designed to perform a specific series of functions, specifications often require testing of the completed system to prove compliance with design criteria. Testing may also be required by an independent firm at your expense. Owner training may additionally be required. Reviewing the specifications will help determine the scope and responsibility of testing and training.

For buildings already in use, tie-ins to existing systems may have to be done during off-hours (nights and weekends) to avoid disruption of normal operations. This should be noted in the takeoff for accurate pricing of the labor portion of the estimate.

Equipment Hook-ups

Appliances and equipment that cannot be simply plugged into the power supply must be "hard wired." This work is typically done by the electrical contractor. Examples include electric ranges and ovens, heating or cooling units, dishwashers, garbage disposals, and commercial equipment for specialty operations, such as restaurants or manufacturing. The equipment is typically supplied and set in place by a dealer.

Consult the specialty drawings showing the equipment and the related specifications for the exact scope of work. Occasionally, electrical power drawings show the electrical interface with various types of equipment.

Installation Time in Labor-Hours for Incandescent Lighting

Wire or cable termination of light fixtures are included in the installation time of light fixtures. Means *Electrical Cost Data* book provides a unique reference number with detailed labor task items.

Description	Labor-Hours	Unit
Ceiling, Recess Mounted Alzak Reflector		
150W	1.000	Ea.
300W	1.190	Ea.
Surface Mounted Metal Cylinder		
150W	.800	Ea.
300W	1.000	Ea.
Opal Glass Drum 10" 2-60W	1.000	Ea.
Pendant Mounted Globe 150W	1.000	Ea.
Vaportight 200W	1.290	Ea.
Chandelier 24" Diameter x 42" High		
6 Candle	1.330	Ea.
Track Light Spotlight 75W PAR Halogen	.500	Ea.
Wall Washer Quartz 250W	.500	Ea.
Exterior Wall Mounted Quartz 500W	1.510	Ea.
1500W	1.900	Ea.
Ceiling, Surface Mounted Vaportight		
100W	2.650	Ea.
150W	2.950	Ea.
175W	2.950	Ea.
250W	2.950	Ea.
400W	3.350	Ea.
1000W	4.450	Ea.

Track Lighting Spotlight

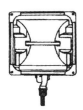

Exterior Fixture, Wall Mounted, Quartz

Round Ceiling Fixture with Concentric Louver

Round Ceiling Fixture with Reflector, No Lens

Round Ceiling Fixture, Recessed, with Alzak Reflector

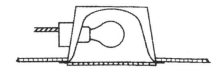

Square Ceiling Fixture, Recessed, with Glass Lens, Metal Trim

Fixtures

Figure 18.6a

Installation Time in Labor-Hours for Fluorescent Lighting

Description	Labor-Hours	Unit
Troffer with Acrylic Lens 4-40W RS 2' x 4'	1.700	Ea.
2-40W URS 2' x 2'	1.400	Ea.
Surface Mounted Acrylic Wrap-around Lens		
4-40W RS 16" x 48"	1.500	Ea.
Industrial Pendant Mounted		
4' Long, 2-40W RS	1.400	Ea.
8' Long, 2-75W SL	1.820	Ea.
2-110W HO	2.000	Ea.
2-215W VHO	2.110	Ea.
Surface Mounted Strip, 4' Long, 1-40W RS	.940	Ea.
8' Long, 1-75W SL	1.190	Ea.

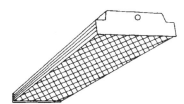

Surface or Pendant Mounted Fixture with
Wrap-around Acrylic Lens, 4 Tube

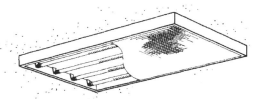

Surface Mounted Fixture with
Acrylic Lens, 4 Tube

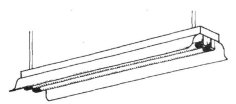

Pendant Mounted Industrial Fixture, 2 Tube

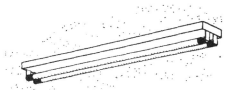

Surface Mounted Strip Fixture, 2 Tube

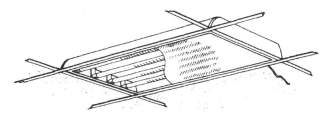

Troffer Mounted Fixture with Acrylic Lens, 4 Tube

Figure 18.6b

Taking off Quantities

Appliances and equipment that require hook-up are taken off and priced by the individual piece (EA) and listed according to type and method of installation (such as flexible-connected, piped, overhead, or in-floor), and any other special requirements.

Control devices or disconnect switches may be needed to meet governing codes and may not always be noted in the specifications. It is a good idea to become familiar with the applicable codes governing the electrical installation of the particular equipment.

Miscellaneous Electrical Work

Some items may be harder to classify and are best categorized in a miscellaneous electrical group, such as permits, utility company tie-in fees, cutting and drilling for electrical access, and temporary power and lighting.

Taking off Quantities

Each miscellaneous item should be taken off and listed separately. Permits and utility company fees are taken off and priced per occurrence, and can be listed in the estimate as a lump sum (LS). Fees for electrical permits are typically based on the individual job and paid when a permit is applied for or issued. (Utility companies typically charge a set fee to tie in service or a transformer, per occurrence.)

Cutting and drilling through wood, drywall, or other lightweight material is often considered part of the normal scope of work and therefore does not constitute a separate takeoff item. Cutting or coring through masonry or concrete, however, may involve special equipment or additional time, especially for large quantities. Take off and price the cuts or cored holes by the "piece" (EA) and list them according to size (diameter or length × width), type of material, thickness of the material, and equipment needed.

Temporary lighting and power, often necessary during the construction process, are typically defined in Division 1—General Requirements. They may also be noted in Division 16—Electrical under "Related Work." Since temporary power panels and lights are reusable, the materials portion of the cost may include only lamps and wire, and can be taken off and priced as a lump sum (LS). Installation and removal of temporary power and lighting facilities can be quantified by labor-hours. Maintenance, such as changing lamps and adding or relocating temporary lights and power, is calculated as labor-hours per week or month, depending on the specific needs of the project.

Minor excavation and backfilling for the installation conduits or direct-burial cables may also be required. Excavation and backfill are typically part of the general or site contractor's work. This is not absolute. Review the specifications for the exact scope of work concerning excavation and backfill for electrical work.

Electrical Labor

Electricians and their helpers, referred to as apprentices, are responsible for performing electrical work. Depending on the specific task, productivity can be measured by the output of the individual, as in the case of installing receptacles, switches, and their respective plates. Other tasks, such as pulling feeders and hanging raceways, clearly require multiple personnel for cost-effective installations. Labor to install light fixtures will vary depending on the size and type of fixture and the height from the floor.

Occasionally, production may be reduced by the use of staging or ladders to perform the work. It may also require that an additional individual be added to the crew for the support of personnel on the staging. This should be taken into account when establishing crew size. Simple tasks, such as installing finish devices, plates, junction or work boxes, can be estimated by the piece (EA) by calculating the quantity of devices that can be installed by one electrician in a day. The same applies for the conductors. Base the unit price on the anticipated linear footage of wire that will be pulled by the crew in a day.

Other operations, such as installing panelboards, switchgear, load centers, motor starters and the like, are based on labor-hours per individual piece. Frequently, bucket trucks or arial platforms are needed. These costs are time-sensitive and calculated by the day, week, or month.

The same basic procedure for takeoff and pricing of mechanical work is used for electrical work. Often, residential designers include the layout of lighting, switches, and receptacles on the architectural drawings, which can be used to establish the cost of the electrical portion of the work. In addition, other information on power-consuming equipment, such as furnaces, water heaters, air conditioning units, and appliances, is needed to determine the electrical budget.

Conclusion

While electrical work is clearly performed by individuals licensed and experienced in the trade, it is not uncommon for the general contractor to generate a budget estimate for the electrical scope of the work. The overview provided in this chapter will help you accurately assess the work involved and its costs.

Chapter Nineteen

Estimating by Computer

Since the mid-1980s, construction companies have increasingly relied on computers for an ever-growing number of purposes. Contractors have even managed to make computers as much a part of the job site as cranes and concrete ready-mix trucks. The introduction of this time-saving "tool" to an industry always striving for faster ways to produce was a "match made in heaven." Integration into large construction firms was almost immediate, with smaller contractors wading in one step at a time.

Contractors currently use computers to communicate with field offices via e-mail, compile labor-hours and costs through job cost systems, track inventory, plan and monitor CPM schedules, and a multitude of other equally important functions. However, nowhere in the industry has the efficiency of computers simplified and improved the construction process as much as is has for estimating. The ability to accelerate what once were slow, tedious calculations, combined with the accuracy offered by computers, has allowed estimators to perform these basic functions more efficiently and cost-effectively. Leaving number-crunching to the computer allows more time for strategizing and exploring new methods to perform the actual construction work.

The estimating and bidding process has always been rife with last-minute changes. Bids submitted late from suppliers and subcontractors to prevent "bid shopping" have always proved problematic. How can last-minute changes be made accurately? Computer estimating builds in the flexibility of making changes—even at the last minute—without having to retrace steps or redo calculations. By changing just one number, the entire estimate can be recalculated automatically. Computer estimating is also essential for performing "what-if" calculations when multiple scenarios need to be priced to determine the best approach and corresponding markup. Prior to computers, this process often took a multi-person staff, or at the very least, extra time to check the accuracy of the calculations.

This can now be done in a matter of minutes. Even the cost of performance and payment bonds can be calculated by using a computer-generated algorithm. In the past, this had always been done by hand by dividing the bid price into tiers, then applying the bond premium to each tier.

The evolution of computers in construction has not been without some minor problems, however. Remember, a computer is a tool to increase accuracy and productivity. In that respect, it is no different than an electric saw or drill and will perform only as well as the level of expertise of the individual operating it allows. In short, good tools don't make good craftspeople. The same applies to estimating. A computer will enhance your estimating ability, but cannot replace it.

Estimating Software

Computerized estimating provides the distinct advantages of flexibility, efficiency, and accuracy. These are desirable, if not necessary, attributes to succeed in winning projects. Reduced to its simplest terms, an estimating program is a series of mathematical formulas, mainly multiplication, that multiply a quantity by a price. A database may be provided as part of a software package, or you can create your own unit prices from a historical database.

Estimating software for the construction industry is as varied as the firms that use them. Selecting and purchasing the right software for your company or application can be a daunting task. Some systems are extremely complex and require compatible hardware, such as digitizers. These packages often offer "links" to other modules that will provide complete integration. For example, once you complete an estimate and the bid has been won, many packages offer the ability to "roll" the estimated costs over into a job cost reporting system for comparison. Other systems are little more than enhanced spreadsheets with built-in macros. The available software will be discussed in more detail later in this chapter.

Selecting the Right Software

It is important that the estimating software fits the intended usage. Selecting a complex system that exceeds the company's needs can prevent it from being used to its full capacity, and can be costly to you by requiring support services and training. However, purchasing software too simple for the application can relegate it to the dust heap next to the thermal paper fax machines. While these are at extreme opposite ends of the spectrum, they occur with more frequency than one would expect.

Here are some simple suggestions when shopping for estimating software:

- Evaluate the application needs to see if a simple spreadsheet program, such as Excel® or Lotus,® will suffice or whether a more complex system is required.
- Anticipate that the software should meet approximately 80% of the company's application needs. No "canned" software packages will satisfy them 100%.

- View demonstrations on as many different packages as practical. Ask if the software comes with a demonstration or trial period to ensure that it meets the company's needs.
- Request references from contractors in the same market or type of work who currently use the particular software for additional verification of its usefulness.
- The selected software should allow for some growth. Although a difficult parameter to judge, growth depends on the business cycle of the company. Companies whose sales volume is expanding at an exponential rate may be unable to satisfy this requirement, as they will outgrow software products rapidly as a result of constantly changing needs.
- Make sure the software fits the budget and is cost-effective.
- Train personnel who will use the software.
- Investigate non-trade-specific software first that may suit your needs before looking into programs designed specifically for a trade, such as electrical, plumbing, or site contractors.
- Assess whether systems can be integrated with other departments, such as job cost reporting, general ledger accounting, or payroll.

While much of the above appears to be common sense, it sometimes gets overlooked in the search for ways to increase productivity. Remember, estimating software is not a panacea. It cannot cure bad estimating practices. Regardless of the advertising claims, it will not instantly increase the volume of work. It may, however, eventually allow the estimator to bid more, thereby increasing opportunities.

Types of Software
Computerized Spreadsheets

Estimating spreadsheets come in a variety of generic applications, such as Microsoft Excel® or Lotus.® This software requires a basic understanding of both the estimating process and the particular application. It is important to note, however, that the takeoff will still be performed by hand. The spreadsheet can be modeled after a Cost Analysis form, Figure 19.1, in a columnar format. Use the following headings as titles for each column, starting from left to right:

- Number of task
- Description of task
- Quantity of task
- Units being priced
- Unit cost for material component
- Total cost for material component
- Unit cost for labor component
- Total cost for labor component
- Unit cost for equipment or subcontractor component
- Total cost for equipment or subcontractor component
- Summary of totals for material, labor, equipment, and subcontractors

Cost Analysis Form

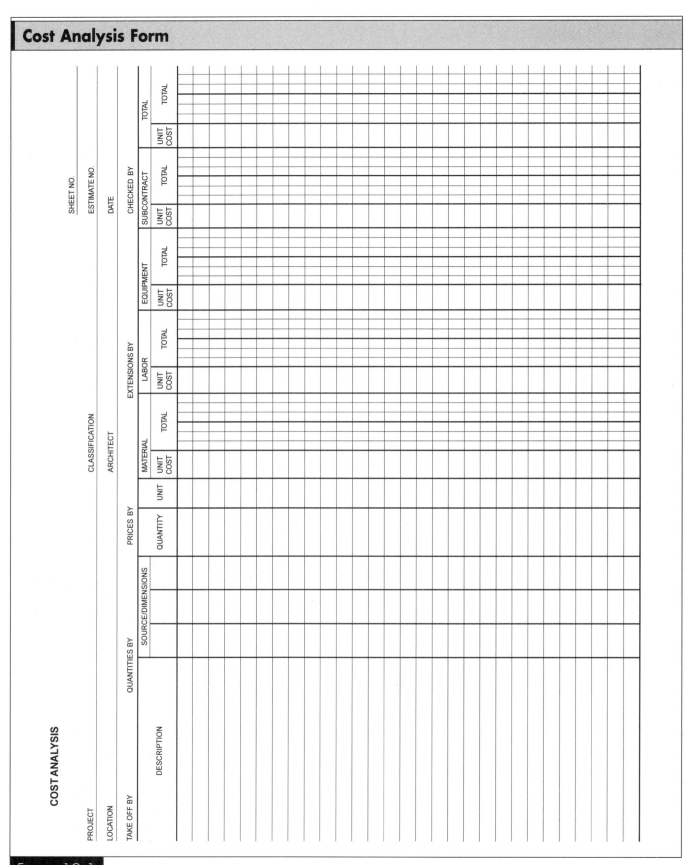

Figure 19.1

Figure 19.2 illustrates the format for a simple estimating spreadsheet built from Microsoft Excel.®

Packaged Databases

Construction cost databases may be helpful in meeting your estimating needs. They can offer material, labor, tools, and equipment costs, most often in a unit price format, often according to CSI MasterFormat divisions. Databases can be used as a standard for determining the costs of various tasks or activities. Packaged databases and combined estimating software programs are based on average costs, and may require adjustments for a specific location. Note that not all contractors require a packaged database to efficiently estimate by computer. Many contractors and subcontractors whose projects are of a limited scope, or who perform repetitive types of work, have no need for a full 16 division MasterFormat database.

Comprehensive as they may be, remember that databases may not represent the costs incurred by *your* firm. Some packages allow you to adjust unit prices and make refinements based on your company's own historical performance of a task or localized pricing of products. Work can be broken down into the CSI MasterFormat system, by division and section number. The cost for each section can be summarized and linked to a recapitulation or *recap sheet*, which summarizes each section number within the estimate.

Figure 19.3 illustrates a recap sheet used for summarizing costs contained within the actual cost analysis sheets.

Historical Database

The most accurate costs can be achieved by documenting your own expenditures on the projects your company builds and reconfiguring them to be used as a database. This is referred to as a *historical database*, and is always preferable to packaged software. If historical costs are collected accurately and unit prices are derived correctly, there is no better source of costs than this true representation. A historical database is a collection of "snapshots" of costs along the schedule of a project that has been completed. The costs for work are actual, not presumed, and relate to performance and techniques of one particular crew or individual.

One of the by-products of tracking costs by computer is the ability to track labor-hours. While the importance of historical costs of materials should not be diminished, the real value is the historical cost of labor and its derivative, productivity. Since the majority of production employees are paid by the hour, there is a direct correlation between dollars and time. Although wages change, productivity in performing the same task usually does not fluctuate. This allows you to factor in wage increases by using the hours recorded in the database to predict future costs. The following scenario illustrates this fact.

A carpenter was documented over time to be able to hang an average of 1,200 SF of 1/2" GWB per 8-hour day, under specific conditions. When

Sample Estimating Spreadsheet

SECTION	DESCRIPTION	QUANTITY	UNIT	----MATERIAL----		----LABOR----		----EQUIPMENT----		----TOTAL----
				UNIT COST	TOTAL	UNIT COST	TOTAL	UNIT COST	TOTAL	TOTAL
09250	**Gypsum Drywall Systems**									
1.01	Partition Type 1	756	SF	$1.54	1,164.24	$1.90	1,436.40	$0.12	90.72	$2,691.36
1.02	Partition Type 2	900	SF	$1.90	1,710.00	$2.20	1,980.00	$0.11	99.00	$3,789.00
1.03	Partition Type 3	860	SF	$2.23	1,917.80	$2.21	1,900.60	$0.90	774.00	$4,592.40
1.04	Partition Type 3A	182	SF	$3.21	584.22	$3.00	546.00	$1.10	200.20	$1,330.42
1.05	Partition Type 4	200	SF	$2.10	420.00	$2.00	400.00	$0.12	24.00	$844.00
1.06	Partition Type 5	451	SF	$2.20	992.20	$2.30	1,037.30	$0.00	0.00	$2,029.50
1.07	Partition Type 6	80	SF	$1.55	124.00	$1.10	88.00	$0.00	0.00	$212.00
	Gypsum Drywall Systems Totals				$ 6,912.46		$ 7,388.30		$ 1,187.92	$ 15,488.68

Figure 19.2

364

Estimate Summary Sheet (Recapitulation)

Bid Date: July 30, 2003
Time: 2:00PM

New and Renovated Office Building
Boston, MA

BASE BID
Addenda #1, #2

Sect.	Description	Materials	Labor	Equipment	Sub	Totals	Remarks
1000	Project Overhead Summary Sheet				$ 405,726	405,726	
2050	Selective Demolition				52,200	52,200	Acme Demolition Company
2110	Site Clearing				769,200	769,200	Super Site work Contractors, Inc.
2112	Pavement Cutting				-		Included in Section 2110
2200	Earthwork				-		Included in Section 2110
2205	Protection of Existing Facilities				-		Included in Section 2110
2229	Pavement Subgrade				-		Included in Section 2110
2513	Bituminous Concrete Paving				-		Included in Section 2110
2527	Bituminous Concrete Curb				-		Included in Section 2110
2576	Pavement Patching				-		Included in Section 2110
2584	Pavement Markings				-		Included in Section 2110
2600	Sanitary Sewer System				-		Included in Section 2110
2722	Site Storm Sewerage Systems				-		Included in Section 2110
2820	Chain Link Fencing				5,500	5,500	All State Fence Co, Inc.
2900	Landscaping				26,975	26,975	Green Landscaping Co.
3300	Cast-in Place Concrete (Redi-mix)	26,554				26,554	Tri-County Concrete
3300	Cast-in Place Concrete (Foundations)			3,600	108,000	111,600	Cape Pumping Co./Smith Foundations, Inc.
3300	Cast-in Place Concrete (Flatwork)			7,169	26,350	33,519	Jones Concrete Finishing Co.
3300	Cast-in Place Concrete (Sidewalks)			1,277	5,785	7,062	Jones Concrete Finishing Co.
3300	Reinforcing Steel/WWF	17,557				17,557	Rusty's Steel Company, Inc. deliv. bar/WWF
4200	Masonry				276,500	276,500	ABC Masonry Contractors
5120	Structural Steel				156,200	156,200	State Iron Works, Inc.
5200	Steel Joists				-		State Iron Works, Inc.
5300	Metal Decking				-		State Iron Works, Inc.
5500	Metal Fabrications				80,735	80,735	Columbus Metal Fabricators
6100	Rough Carpentry	7,973	13,248			21,221	Self-performed work
6200	Finish Carpentry	16,785	53,486			70,271	Self-performed work
7100	Caulking and Dampproofing				17,600	17,600	All Weather Caulking, Inc.
7210	Building Insulation	1,841			24,190	26,031	Self-performed work
7500	Elastomeric Roofing/Flashings				126,780	126,780	Sky Roofers, Inc.
8100	Metal Doors and Frames	31,025	8,694			39,719	Megga-Hardware/Self-performed work
8400	Aluminum Doors and Frames				17,584	17,584	Cape Storefronts, Inc.
8500	Aluminum Windows				156,000	156,000	Modern Aluminum Window, Inc.
8700	Finish Hardware	37,000	19,668			56,668	Megga-Hardware/Self-performed work
8800	Glass and Glazing				5,500	5,500	Able Glass Co.
9250	Gypsum Drywall Systems				113,910	113,910	Eastern Drywall Systems Co.
9300	Ceramic Tile				32,000	32,000	Western Ceramic Tile
9500	Acoustical Ceilings				83,670	83,670	Capital Ceiling Systems
9650	Resilient Flooring and Base				79,800	79,800	Top-Notch Floors
9680	Carpet				112,000	112,000	Top-Notch Floors
9900	Painting & Coatings				99,780	99,780	Commercial Painters, Inc.

Figure 19.3a

Estimate Summary Sheet (Recapitulation)

Sect.	Description	Materials	Labor	Equipment	Sub	Totals	Remarks
10100	Visual Display Boards				13,500	13,500	Office Interior Contractors
10150	Toilet Compartments				12,500	12,500	Office Interior Contractors
10400	Identification Devices				3,500	3,500	Office Interior Contractors
10520	Fire Protection Specialties		540		2,000	2,540	Office Interior Contractors
10810	Toilet Accessories		3,542		3,500	7,042	Office Interior Contractors
11480	Kitchen Equipment				123,490	123,490	The Kitchen Suppliers Co.
12300	Manufactured Casework				29,750	29,750	New England Casework
12490	Window Treatments				4,214	4,214	Clear-Vue Window Decor, Inc.
13280	Hazardous Materials Remediation				6,950	6,950	ACM Abaters, Inc.
14240	Hydraulic Elevators				155,456	155,456	Uptown Elevators, Inc.
14420	Wheelchair Lifts				16,883	16,883	Uptown Elevators, Inc.
15300	Fire Protection				65,000	65,000	Safety Fire Protection Contracting Co.
15400	Plumbing				138,900	138,900	Best Plumbing Co.
15500	HVAC				890,990	890,990	New England Pipe HVAC Co., Inc.
16000	Electrical				192,300	192,300	Sparky's Electrical
	Sub Total	138,735	99,178	12,046	4,440,918	4,690,877	
	All Risk Insurance					15,949	
	General Liability					37,527	
	Sub Total					4,744,353	
	Main Office Overhead					317,872	
	Sub Total					5,062,225	
	Profit					404,978	
	Sub Total					5,467,203	
	Performance and Payment Bonds					56,697	
	BID					**5,523,900**	

Figure 19.3b

estimating a second project with similar conditions but a higher wage rate, it could be predicted that the same carpenter will produce the same average. The increase in wages could be adjusted in the unit price for the labor.

The following is a simple example of how a wage increase will affect unit price.

Project 1 – Cost for carpenter per day: 8 hours x $32.50 per hour = $260 per day/1,200 SF per day = $0.22 per SF labor cost.

Project 2 – Cost for carpenter per day with increased wage rate: 8 hours x $35.00 per hour = $280 per day/1,200 SF per day = $0.24 per SF labor cost.

This same example can be used for increases in other labor-related costs, such as insurance rates, benefits, or tax increases. Using a simple spreadsheet application, such as Microsoft Excel,® a file can be created to adjust unit prices as labor costs change, or productivity rises or falls with the change in difficulty of the task.

Materials are somewhat easier to price. The graphic representation of a task on the drawings is finite. In other words, you can quantify the material by measuring from the drawings. Requesting a proposal for materials from local suppliers is usually sufficient to capture the costs of the total materials needed for the estimate. The ambiguous portion of the material cost is waste. A well-documented database can provide sufficient detail for the comparison between the net and gross quantities of purchased materials. Over multiple projects, you can adjust the factor for waste based on the actual conditions.

Estimating Templates for Reuse

Most contractors and subcontractors create similar estimates over and over. Estimating by computer allows you to build a template for a particular type of estimate. Each time a new project is to be bid, you can copy the template for that type of estimate and make the necessary adjustments for the individual projects. This is a common time-saving feature in construction estimating programs, even those created from generic spreadsheet software. Figure 19.4 illustrates a template estimate.

For example, consider a drywall and metal stud subcontractor who is bidding interior drywall partitions for an office building. The unit price for each type of partition could be built into a template by the SF or LF, so all that is required is performing the takeoff, entering quantities of the various types of partitions, and making adjustments for specific project conditions, including overhead and profit. By perfecting this template, the contractor could bid more work, thereby increasing the chances for winning work.

Project Overhead Summary Sheets

Computerized project overhead summary sheets allow you to view different project overhead costs based on different schedules. All projects have two components for overhead: direct and indirect costs. Indirect overhead is usually applied as a percentage of the total overhead of the main office. Direct overhead are those non-production costs that are unique to each project. They include such items as supervision, temporary facilities, building permits and fees, and dumpsters. Some of these costs are fixed, such as for a building permit, but many are time-sensitive and will vary with the amount of exposure on the project. Figure 19.5 illustrates a Project Overhead Summary Sheet.

Conclusion

In summary, computers have a tremendous value in construction applications. Estimating by computer provides flexibility, accuracy, and speed in producing bids. Its value is limited only by the construction and estimating knowledge—as well as computer skills—of its users. Those looking to purchase computer estimating programs should do so only after careful review and understanding of the company's needs.

Estimating Template

PROJECT NAME: New Office Building
LOCATION: Boston, MA
ARCHITECT: ABC Architects
SCOPE OF ESTIMATE: Section 09250 Gypsum Drywall

TOTAL COST:
SQUARE FOOT: SF
COST PER SF: PER SF

Pages   2
Estimate   #1
Date: 07/01/04
Estimator   WJD

ADDENDA: #1 and #2

BID DATE: July 6, 2004

DESCRIPTION	QUANTITY	UNIT	MATERIAL UNIT COST	MATERIAL TOTAL	LABOR UNIT COST	LABOR TOTAL	EQUIPMENT/SUB UNIT COST	EQUIPMENT/SUB TOTAL	TOTAL
DIVISION 9 - FINISHES									
9250.00 **Gypsum Board Systems**									
9.01 Partition Type 1	18732	SF	$1.25	23,415.00	$2.00	37,464.00	$0.20	3,746.40	$64,625.40
9.02 Partition Type 2	15162	SF	$2.10	31,840.20	$2.20	33,356.40	$0.00	0.00	$65,196.60
9.03 Partition Type 3	3752	SF	$3.00	11,256.00	$2.70	10,130.40	$0.10	375.20	$21,761.60
9.04 Partition Type 4	4774	SF	$2.47	11,791.78	$4.10	19,573.40	$0.03	143.22	$31,508.40
9.05 Partition Type 5	13496	SF	$1.10	14,845.60	$2.40	32,390.40	$0.00	0.00	$47,236.00
9.06 Partition Type 6	45360	SF	$1.09	49,442.40	$2.44	110,678.40	$0.00	0.00	$160,120.80
9.07 Partition Type 7	18528	SF	$2.34	43,355.52	$1.85	34,276.80	$0.00	0.00	$77,632.32
9.08 Partition Type 8	14496	SF	$2.10	30,441.60	$1.99	28,847.04	$0.00	0.00	$59,288.64
9.09 Partition Type 9	5472	SF	$2.33	12,749.76	$2.19	11,983.68	$0.09	492.48	$25,225.92
9.10 Partition Type 10	4416	SF	$3.10	13,689.60	$4.00	17,664.00	$0.00	0.00	$31,353.60
9.11 Partition Type 11	1584	SF	$0.78	1,235.52	$1.10	1,742.40	$1.10	1,742.40	$4,720.32
9.12 Partition Type 12	1296	SF	$1.15	1,490.40	$1.55	2,008.80	$0.00	0.00	$3,499.20
9.13 Not Used	1	EA	$0.00	0.00	$0.00	0.00	$0.00	0.00	$0.00
Gypsum Board Systems Totals				245,553.38		340,115.72		6,499.70	**592,168.80**
Sales Tax on Materials	5%								$ 12,277.67
Subtotals									$ 604,446.47
Main Office Overhead	10%								$ 60,444.65
Subtotals									$ 664,891.12
Profit	10%								$ 66,489.11
Subtotals									$ 731,380.23
Bond	1.2%								$ 8,776.56
Total									$ 740,156.79
								BID	740,157.00

Figure 19.4

Project Overhead Summary Sheet

Project: New & Renovated Office Building

Architect: ABC Architects, Inc.

Duration: 18 months (78 weeks)

Liquidated Damages: N/A

Sect	Description	Quantity	Unit	Cost	Total	Remarks
1.01	Office trailer - G.C.	18	mons	345.00	6,210.00	12' x 40' trailer
	a.) Furnishings	1	LS	800.00	800.00	
	b.) Setup and delivery	1	EA	340.00	340.00	
	c.) Breakdown and return	1	LS	340.00	340.00	
	d.) Trailer cleaning	18	mons	45.00	810.00	
1.02	Storage Trailers	14	mons	120.00	1,680.00	
	a.) Delivery and pickup	1	LS	240.00	240.00	
1.03	Office trailer - clerk or arch.				-	See spec Section 1500- C.2
	a.) Furnishings	1	LS	530.00	530.00	See list in Section 01500;C.2
	b.)Fax machine	1	EA	450.00	450.00	
	c.) Copy machine	1	EA	800.00	800.00	
	d.) Answering machine	1	EA	75.00	75.00	
	e.) Desk phone	1	EA	20.00	20.00	
	f.) Computer/printer					
	g.) Supplies	1	LS	500.00	500.00	
	h.) Toilet hookup and dismantle		LS	600.00	-	
	I.) Software		LS	600.00	-	
1.04	Telephone service				-	
	a.) Install and removal	3	LINES	125.00	375.00	See Section 01500-Temp Facilities
	b.) Monthly serv.- GC	36	mons	175.00	6,300.00	
	c.) Monthly serv.- Clerk	18	mons	150.00	2,700.00	
1.05	Temporary electric				-	
	a.) Office trailers hookup	3	EA	500.00	1,500.00	
	b.) Trailer consumption	18	mons	175.00	3,150.00	
	c.) Project consumption	18	mons	150.00	2,700.00	
1.06	Water cooler/ consumption	18	mons	30.00	540.00	
1.07	Thermometer	1	EA	20.00	20.00	
1.08	Temporary toilets	36	mons	85.00	3,060.00	
1.09	Temp. construction fence	985	LF	4.00	3,940.00	
1.10	Staging					
	a.) Set up/dismantle	1	LS	2,000.00	2,000.00	
	b.) Monthly rental	18	mons	200.00	3,600.00	
1.10a	Ramps to trailers		LS	-	-	
1.11	Manlifts				-	
	a.) Delivery and pickup				-	
	b.) Monthly rental			-	-	None required
1.12	Small tools and equipment	1	LS	2,000.00	2,000.00	
1.13	Temporary water				-	
	a.) Hook up/dismantle	1	LS	200.00	200.00	Hook up and dismantle by Plumber
	b.) Consumption	18	mons	50.00	900.00	
	c.) Fees	1	EA	250.00	250.00	Meter rental from Municipality
1.14	Temp. heat				-	
	a.) Trailers				-	In Section 1.05 above
	b.) Project	5	mons	700.00	3,500.00	
1.15	Temporary protection	6	mons	300.00	1,800.00	
1.16	Winter protection					
	a.) Plowing		mons			
	b.) Enclosures	1	LS	8,000.00	8,000.00	Enclose & remove staging for masonry
	c.) Heat			-	-	
1.17	Fork lift or lull				-	
1.18	Crane	4	days	1,100.00	4,400.00	Hoist for roofer
1.19	Project photos	1	LS	200.00	200.00	

Figure 19.5a

Project Overhead Summary Sheet

Sect.	Description	Quantity	Unit	Cost	Total	Remarks
1.20	Tree protection				-	Carried in site work proposal
1.21	General cleaning - ongoing	20	wks	1,439.00	28,780.00	25% of the schedule
1.22	Final cleaning	15000	SF	0.20	3,000.00	
1.23	Materials handling & distribution	40	LH	36.00	1,440.00	Receiving and handling material
1.24	Project sign	1	EA	750.00	750.00	Included in sub bid from Acme Signs
1.25	First aid kits	2	EA	75.00	150.00	
1.26	Temporary fire protection	1	LS	150.00	150.00	
1.27	Dumpsters- 30 CY	45	EA	620.00	27,900.00	1 dumpster per 2000 S.F floor space.
1.28	Pest control		LS	500.00	-	
1.29	Cutting and patching					All cut and patch over 6" dia by GC
	a.) Labor to core holes	120	LH	36.00	4,320.00	Direct labor by employees
	b.) Purchase coring machine/bits	1	LS	2,000.00	2,000.00	
1.30	Permits				-	
	a.) Building permit	1	LS	8,500.00	8,500.00	Based on budget value
	b.) Occupancy permit				-	
	c.) Miscellaneous fees				-	
1.31	Police details	2	days	248.00	496.00	At street opening and patch
1.32	Layout				-	
	a.) Registered	7	days	1,080.00	7,560.00	Control provided by Surveyor
	b.) Own forces				-	By Superintendent
1.33	Testing				-	
	a.) Soil testing			-	-	By Owner
	b.) Concrete testing			-	-	By Owner
1.34	Miscellaneous hardware	18	mons	120.00	2,160.00	
1.35	Pickup trucks		mons	-	-	
	a.) Gasoline usage	78	wks	50.00	3,900.00	
1.36	CPM schedule-initial devel.		LS			By Project Manager
	a.) Update CPM	17	mons	100.00	1,700.00	By Project Manager
1.37	Dewatering				-	
	a.) Localized dewatering				-	By Site Contractor
1.38	Special safety equipment	1	LS	400.00	400.00	Rebar caps 300
1.39	Attorneys fees				-	
1.40	Interior barricades	4	mons	300.00	1,200.00	Restrict access between reno /new
1.41	As-builts				-	
	a.) Microfilm				-	
	b.) Printing /reproduction				-	
	c.) Mylars	1	LS	3,000.00	3,000.00	Complete set
1.42	Project closeout	2	Phases			By Project Manager
1.43	Site security					
	a.) Watchman					
	b.) Custodial overtime					
1.44	Utility company charges					
	a.) Electric					
	b.) Water taps					
	c.) Sewer					
	d.) Gas					
	e.) Cable /tel.					
	f.) Assessments					
1.45	Special requirements					
1.46	Insurance					
	a.) Builders risk	1	LS	-	-	Included in Estimate Summary Sheet
	b.) 3YR extended comp opps	1	LS	-	-	Included in Estimate Summary Sheet
	c.) 10M add umbrella	1	LS	-	-	Included in Estimate Summary Sheet
1.47	Punchlist	10	wks	1,623.00	16,230.00	
1.48	Personnel				-	
	a.) Superintendent	78	wks	1,920.00	149,760.00	100% of schedule
	b.) Asst. superintendent		wks			
	c.) Project manager	28	wks	2,000.00	56,000.00	35% attention
	d.) Administrative staff	28	wks	800.00	22,400.00	35% attention
	TOTAL				405,726.00	

Figure 19.5b

Chapter Twenty

Profit & Contingencies

Two crucial, but difficult to calculate costs must be added to the estimate in the recapitulation, or *recap*, phase of estimating, just prior to submitting the bid. These are profit and contingency. These topics are rarely addressed in even the best estimating texts on the market today. The most reasonable explanation for this lack of information is that determining the appropriate profit and/or contingency is a process that relies more on experience or judgment rather than calculating a quantity and pricing it, such as the cost of concrete. If ten different estimators were queried, they would most likely say that profit is assigned as a percentage of the cost of the work. However, the actual decision-making process that led to that particular percentage would be different from one estimator to the next. The same applies to contingencies.

This chapter will introduce specific considerations to review before determining an appropriate profit and contingency (if applicable) on a project-by-project basis. Although profit is the *last* number to be added to an estimate (with the exception of a performance and payment bond premium) before the bid is submitted, we will discuss profit before contingency, since not all projects warrant a contingency.

Profit

One of the main yardsticks for measuring the success of a construction project is profit. Without it, the project would be considered a failure. Profit can be loosely defined as the amount of money left after all of the bills have been paid. It is the necessary component to make a business viable, fiscally healthy, and able to grow. Profit is the basis for our business economy. Predicting the correct amount of profit that a project can support is one of the most difficult tasks for the construction professional. Too small a profit, and the return does not warrant the risk taken. Too large a profit, and the bid can be lost to greed. Ideally, the amount of profit to be added should be the maximum the project can support, but just slightly less than the next bidder's.

It is generally acknowledged among construction estimating professionals that the cost of materials, labor, and equipment calculated by the professional contractor's estimator will be roughly the same for most contractors bidding the same project. Some items will be higher, and some will be lower. However, in the end, all costs should be about equal. This also applies to subcontractors. On bid day, subcontractors submit quotes to the majority of general contractors bidding a project. Some subcontractors may have been solicited by a particular general contractor, while others just "cover all the bases" by submitting bids to all of the bidders. If the statement that "cost is cost" is true, then it could be inferred that adding overhead and profit to the estimate can be the deciding factor in winning or losing a bid.

In some companies, determining profit is the responsibility of the estimator, while other contractors consider it to be the domain of senior management or principals only. Irrespective of the party assigned this duty, it is clear that by the end of the estimate preparation, the person with the best understanding of the risk involved and the uniqueness of the project is the estimator. As a result, the estimator is the most likely candidate to contribute to the decision making process in determining the profit.

Many texts recommend 10% as the appropriate profit percentage to be added, regardless of the project. Others vary between 8% and 15% of the cost of the work. While acknowledging that both may be acceptable for *some* projects and *some* contractors, it is clearly not a one-size-fits-all process.

How to Determine Profit

The actual mechanical process of assigning profit to a project can be done two different ways:

- As a percentage of the cost of the work, or
- As a fixed fee based on time.

Regardless of the selected method, many factors affect the determination of profit. Some are tangible, and some less so. As with all portions of the estimate, careful consideration should be given to the reasons behind each decision. While acknowledging that there are no clear answers or step-by-step procedures for arriving at the correct profit for a project, there are a series of considerations that should be reviewed when determining the appropriate amount to apply. The following sections show the thought process that must take place before the bid is finalized, and should provide guidance for properly assigning the right amount of profit. These guidelines are not presented in any specifc order; their order of importance will vary depending on the individual project.

Risk vs. Reward

All construction projects entail a certain degree of risk, which can manifest itself in many forms. As a means of off-setting the risk, specific management techniques are used to "share" it. For example, a general contractor might secure a performance and payment bond from a subcontractor who has a large share of the work in order to assign some of the risk to another party. However, from a business standpoint, a project with a high degree of risk requires more management time, resources, and generally creates more of a strain on a company's infrastructure. As a result, the company should be compensated for the risk endured. In other words, risk must be rewarded, which, in the construction business, is defined as profit. Profit is the reward for risk assumed, managed, and triumphed over. The reward should match the risk, supported by the general theory that the more risk involved, the higher the profit should be. There is no magic formula to calculate profit as a function of risk, yet almost all reasoning for applying a specific profit to a project can be traced back to the risk involved. One must carefully evaluate the risk that the project will impose on the company, and define or quantify it in terms that can be used to determine a profit.

Reputation in the Marketplace

All completed projects will have an impact on your company's standing in the marketplace. Many larger construction firms with marketing departments actively pursue projects that will enhance the chances of future work, or that have high visibility in their sphere of influence. While it does not take a marketing genius to figure out that a high-profile project will receive more attention, this may not always be a good thing. Projects that are "built in the newspaper" or under the watchful eye of the public can be a management nightmare. Along with the normal management team, damage control specialists may be needed to help keep public opinion and rumors in check, as these types of projects have a momentum and dynamic all their own. They can have a tremendous impact on a firm's reputation and on future business opportunities. Be sure to consider what the successful completion of the project will mean for the company and its reputation in the marketplace. Conversely, it is always wise to also speculate on how a failure would affect the firm's reputation.

Scheduling Impacts

A project's schedule greatly affects the amount of profit that should be added to the estimate. Projects with durations in excess of a year will affect the company's balance sheet for multiple years and will need to carry enough profit for the firm beyond the current year. Losses will affect more than the current year's balance sheet as well. It is a recognized fact that projects extending beyond one year in duration are more difficult to manage because of potential changes in the marketplace that cannot be accurately predicted at bid time. Wage increases, inflated material costs, availability of resources, and the economy in general are some of the variable factors.

Carefully review project durations that appear to be too short. Those with unrealistic schedules often require infusions of capital and extra management to be completed on time. While these costs can be accounted for in the estimate, you also need to consider the fact that you may not be able to perform other work at the same time, which means lost business opportunities.

By the time the estimate has been completed and you are ready to add profit, a construction schedule should have been developed—and refined. This is neccesary to determine project duration for time-sensitive costs. *(See Chapter 6, General Requirements.)* The schedule should enable the estimator to support or reject the owner's timeline under the contract provisions.

Contract Documents and Team Relationships

The level of design development in the bid documents also has an impact on profit. The more complete the design, the less risk to the contractor. While the level of design development affects the amount of justifiable profit, it also may necessitate adding a contingency. (This will be addressed from another perspective later in this chapter under the topic "Contingencies.") A contractor's prior history and working relationship with the architects and engineers for the project is also critical. Successful relationships with architects, engineers, and even owners play a significant role in assigning profit. If the contractor is viewed as part of the "team," rather than as an adversary, this has a direct impact on the profit line. The contractor's expertise is seen as critical to a successful project and must be rewarded by allowing reasonable profit. Contractors involved with architects, engineers, or owners who have a reputation for taking a "hard-line" approach often add greater profit margins to their estimates to compensate for these adversarial relationships.

Contract Clauses

Many contractors/estimators interpret the tone of the contract (included in the project manual) as a precursor to the way the project will be administered. Are the general and supplemental conditions peppered with unfavorable contract clauses or punitive language toward the contractor? Does the contract have liquidated damages or penalties of any kind? If so, are they reasonable? Is there exculpatory language that absolves the owner and architect from responsibility for delay to the project? While the owner will often downplay the use of penalties clauses, they are there for a reason. Should the relationship deteriorate, the owner has the right to exercise his or her contractual rights. Review the contract clauses carefully, and if necessary, seek legal advice on specific language that may be a concern. If the final decision results in bidding the project, make sure that adequate profit is included to compensate for the risk.

Impact on the Company's Resources

When determining profit, be sure to address the following questions as they pertain to your company's needs and resources.

- Does the company have access to capable subcontractors and suppliers to perform the work? Are a majority of subcontractors being carried in the bid unknown and untested?
- Does the company have enough of its own labor resources to self-perform work or augment underachieving subcontractors?
- Does the management staff have the skill sets necessary to administer the project?
- Will the firm have to hire new individuals to supervise or manage the project? If so, would this be considered additional risk as a result of the unknown factors involved?
- Does the company have the working capital to finance the work between owner payments? Not having adequate finances to capitalize a project puts tremendous tension on relationships with subs and suppliers who are key to a successful project.
- If the project can be administered by the current personnel and infrastructure, what effect will it have on company morale?
- Will the project tax the company to the extent that no other projects will get their fair share of attention or management, or worse—that the company will not be able to handle other projects?

All of the above are necessary considerations to determine the impact on the company's resources, a key factor in assigning profit.

Repeat Business

Many estimators consider the potential for repeat business when applying profit. This is a very real and important consideration. Estimators and management teams often reduce their profit in the hopes that the owner will reward this behavior with repeat business. This is a common and sound business practice for many sectors of the construction industry. Bear in mind, however, that too small of a profit may not make future projects with a particular owner attractive for your company. For the contractor who does frequent business with a client, remember that "a contractor is only as good as his last job." Reducing profit in hopes of repeat business can often have a negative effect because projects with insufficient or marginal profit lines are frequently relegated to the "back burner" in favor of more lucrative ones. This can end the repeat business cycle that you were hoping to develop.

Project Location

Many desirable projects may be outside your company's normal sphere of influence. While this does not necessarily mean you should not bid the project, you must acknowledge that there are inherent problems that come with working outside the typical business area. These include travel time and related costs, subcontractors' and suppliers' abilities to service the location, and general unknowns of doing business with new building departments and inspectional services, as well as public utilities.

Bidding Strategies

Many estimators employ a bidding strategy for winning work, which encompasses a wide range of techniques meant to provide an advantage, such as tracking the workload of the competition to determine potential threats. Most contractors strive to create a market niche for themselves. The theory is that as you do repetitive work, the learning curve disappears, and, as a result, the firm becomes more financially successful. In doing so, the company fits into a niche that is shared by competitors. Contractors who competively bid projects will find themselves frequently competing against the same firms. The ability to track who is busy and who is "hungry" is helpful, since the hungry contractor is more of a threat than the busy one. Other bidding strategies include unique means and methods, such as prefabrication, or assembly off site, which often helps the bidder be more competitive. A successful bidding strategy provides an edge over the competition.

Specialization

One-of-a-kind projects with no comparison model warrant an increased profit. While there are very few projects in the residential/light commercial sector of the construction industry that have never been done before, unique projects often involve highly-specialized contractors, thereby limiting competition. The fewer the competitors, the bigger the profit that can be expected.

Workload

Frequently, the profit margin is determined by how much work your company is currently involved in. Contractors with sufficient work add larger profit margins, using the logic that if more work is going to be added, it will have to be highly profitable as it taxes the company's infrastructure. Contractors with minimal work under contract are prone to taking projects with little or no profit, as any cash flow is preferable to a negative profit and loss statement. While this is true, accepting low-profit work can be an extremely dangerous practice and is not advocated in any situation other than the most dire of circumstances.

Demographics

By virtue of their locations (and the requirements of the market), certain projects warrant a larger profit margin. For example, assuming that all other (construction) costs are equal, a residential project in an area with higher real estate values will typically be assigned a larger profit percentage than a similar residence built in a lower-priced area.

Contingencies

Contingencies, or adding money to address an unknown condition, are the most misunderstood line items in an estimate. The estimator should try to anticipate any costs that are not capable of being recovered if discovered. There are two schools of thought on contingencies:

Approach 1: Always Adding a Contingency

Contingencies should be added for costs that cannot otherwise be recovered. Justifications for contingencies include call-backs that are not the contractor's responsibility, but are sometimes done to further a firm's reputation. Consider the residential developer/contractor who repairs damage caused by an unidentifiable party. Repairing the damage is a good business move and keeps the client happy. It also portrays the contractor as a reputable businessperson who stands behind his work even when there is a question of who is responsible.

Other scenarios include adding contingencies for "weak" or incomplete documents. It is not uncommon for architectural services to be kept to a minimum in the design stage of a residence. The homeowner's logic is often that if an architect's services can be kept to designing only the essentials, a "good" contractor can flush out the details and make the design "work." Even the most conscientious estimator cannot anticipate every condition, unforseen or otherwise. Again, adding a contingency to help the homeowner or client over some unexpected costs goes a long way toward future business. However, it is important to know when enough is enough.

Approach 2: Never Adding a Contingency

Some people feel that adding any money to an estimate that is not applied to a tangible, defined cost or scope of work is a sign of a weak estimate. It is the purpose of an estimate to accurately anticipate *all* costs to be incurred in a project. The contract documents, plans, and specifications act as the basis for the estimate. The drawings represent the quantity, and the specifications represent the quality. If an item or scope of work in question is not shown on the drawings or called out in the specifications, it is extra to the contract. Adding money to the estimate for work that is not defined at bid time is often considered irresponsible, and can dramatically affect hard competitive bids.

How to Decide if Contingencies Are Necessary

Other more general questions arise as a result of the adding contingencies. For example:

- What if the amount of the contingency is insufficient and does not cover the cost of the work?
- What if the amount is too much and reduces the competitiveness of the bid?
- Does performing work at no cost to the owner under the guise of a contingency create a dangerous precedent for future uncovered problems?
- Should the owner be aware of the contingency and its amount?
- If the contingency is not spent, is it returned to the owner?

Conclusion

It is clear from the discussion in this chapter that there are no hard and fast rules for assigning profit or contingencies to an estimate, but merely considerations that must be carefully reviewed for each and every project. Ample thought beforehand, paired with increased experience, will help estimators arrive at the appropriate profit margin for the individual company and project.

Estimating Resources

Many contracting companies start out as a one-person shop, requiring the owner to perform many tasks in order for the company to run smoothly. The owner must act as the company's administrator, as well as its bookkeeper, site supervisor, skilled laborer, salesperson, and the one person that any contracting company cannot do without—the estimator.

Estimating construction costs can be performed in any number of methods. Experience will often allow construction companies/estimators to begin developing estimates based on jobs that have already been completed, referred to as *conceptual estimating*. *Square foot estimates* are often quoted by contractors who have gone through the process of dividing a completed project's total cost by the number of constructed or renovated square feet. Occasionally, a contractor will be able to quote costs for floor, wall, and roof systems. This is called *assemblies estimating*.

Unit Cost Estimating

While each of the above methods has its advantages, the most common and accurate method of estimating is by individual unit costs for the various tasks in a construction project. *Unit cost* estimating assigns a price that reflects the material and labor cost of a specific component based on a commonly used unit of measure. It also allows the owner of the company the flexibility to delegate the estimating tasks to a person with less field experience, who can calculate the quantity of each material necessary for the particular job. Once completed, the material quantities can be multiplied by unit costs, which are derived from the owner's experience or the company's historical records.

If, due to a number of possible reasons, the owner's experience and historical records are not available or well-established, estimators may have to rely on construction cost databases, such as those provided by RSMeans. These databases—available in print and electronic formats—are easy to use and provide quick access to accurate costs once the estimator learns the format and proper use of the information.

Using Cost Databases & *Means* Contractor's Pricing Guides

A successful project is built on the foundation of an accurate and dependable estimate. Means *Contractor's Pricing Guide: Residential Detailed Costs* is a powerful construction tool that enables you to construct such an estimate. It covers every aspect of construction pricing, with over 8,000 items. All the cost data is organized according to the 16 MasterFormat divisions of the Construction Specifications Institute (CSI), similar to the organization of this book. Unit prices are organized by their specific classification and number for easy reference. This system allows for thorough organization into the "divisions" of work involved in a construction project, such as concrete, wood and plastics, and finishes. These natural breaks make double-checking costs easier, and help with organizing quotes from subcontractors.

For the casual user, Means *Contractor's Pricing Guide: Residential Detailed Costs* is designed to be quickly and easily understood, so you can get right to your estimate. For the regular user, it's a handy desk reference for current construction costs and productivity rates. Its intended use is by contractors and estimators involved primarily in residential construction costing less than $750,000. This includes building homes, as well as condominiums, row houses, townhouses, and apartments. With reasonable exercise of judgment, however, costs may be applicable to any building work.

Location Factors

Costs vary depending on your regional economy. You can adjust the national average costs in the book to your precise location by using the over 930 location factors for major cities throughout the U.S. and Canada.

How to Use Line Items

Each "line item" is assigned a specific twelve digit line item number, which identifies the division, subdivision, and major classification that the line item falls into. For example, please refer to Figure 1.

If the cost of a 28' span roof truss is required to frame the roof of a garage, using the book, you could quickly locate the correct line item in the table of contents or key word index. Then it is a simple matter of scanning the descriptions to find what is needed.

The descriptions are arranged in a hierarchical format. If an item is indented further to the right than any item above it, some portion of the above description applies. In this example, the description found on line item 06170-980-5200 reads "28' span." You can see it is indented further to the right than line numbers 06170-980-5010 – 5000 and 0010. Some part of each of those lines makes up the complete description for the roof truss. By reading the descriptions and using common sense, the proper placement of portions of the descriptions can be completed in your head to arrive at the appropriate complete description:

Roof trusses, common wood, 2" x 4" metal plate connected, 24" OC, 4/12 slope, 1' overhang, 28' span

06100 | Rough Carpentry

06170 | Prefabricated Structural Wood

			CREW	DAILY OUTPUT	LABOR-HOURS	UNIT	2004 BARE COSTS				TOTAL INCL O&P	
							MAT.	LABOR	EQUIP.	TOTAL		
600	1800	70' span	F-3	9,250	.004	SF Flr.	2.27	.09	.07	2.43	2.72	600
	1900	85 psf live load, 26' span	↓	2,300	.017	↓	2.11	.36	.27	2.74	3.22	
980	0010	**ROOF TRUSSES**										980
	0020	For timber connectors, see div. 06090-800										
	5000	Common wood, 2" x 4" metal plate connected, 24" O.C., 4/12 slope										
	5010	1' overhang, 12' span	F-5	55	.582	Ea.	24	11.65		35.65	46	
	5050	20' span	F-6	62	.645		39	13.40	9.85	62.25	76.50	
	5100	24' span [R06170 -100]		60	.667		46.50	13.85	10.20	70.55	85.50	
	5150	26' span		57	.702		65	14.60	10.75	90.35	108	
	5200	28' span		53	.755		56.50	15.70	11.55	83.75	101	
	5240	30' span		51	.784		76	16.30	12	104.30	124	
	5250	32' span		50	.800		79.50	16.65	12.25	108.40	128	
	5280	34' span		48	.833		97	17.35	12.75	127.10	150	
	5350	8/12 pitch, 1' overhang, 20' span		57	.702		60	14.60	10.75	85.35	102	
	5400	24' span		55	.727		71	15.15	11.15	97.30	116	
	5450	26' span		52	.769		77	16	11.75	104.75	124	
	5500	28' span		49	.816		83	17	12.50	112.50	133	
	5550	32' span		45	.889		97.50	18.50	13.60	129.60	153	
	5600	36' span		41	.976		116	20.50	14.95	151.45	177	
	5650	38' span		40	1		126	21	15.30	162.30	190	
	5700	40' span	↓	40	1	↓	143	21	15.30	179.30	210	

06180 | Glued-Laminated Construction

			CREW	DAILY OUTPUT	LABOR-HOURS	UNIT	MAT.	LABOR	EQUIP.	TOTAL	TOTAL INCL O&P	
400	0010	**LAMINATED FRAMING** Not including decking										400
	0020	30 lb., short term live load, 15 lb. dead load										
	0200	Straight roof beams, 20' clear span, beams 8' O.C.	F-3	2,560	.016	SF Flr.	1.58	.33	.24	2.15	2.55	
	0300	Beams 16' O.C.		3,200	.013		1.14	.26	.19	1.59	1.90	
	0500	40' clear span, beams 8' O.C.		3,200	.013		3.03	.26	.19	3.48	3.98	
	0600	Beams 16' O.C.	↓	3,840	.010		2.47	.22	.16	2.85	3.26	
	0800	60' clear span, beams 8' O.C.	F-4	2,880	.014		5.20	.29	.32	5.81	6.55	
	0900	Beams 16' O.C.	"	3,840	.010		3.87	.22	.24	4.33	4.88	
	1100	Tudor arches, 30' to 40' clear span, frames 8' O.C.	F-3	1,680	.024		6.80	.50	.36	7.66	8.70	
	1200	Frames 16' O.C.	"	2,240	.018		5.30	.37	.27	5.94	6.80	
	1400	50' to 60' clear span, frames 8' O.C.	F-4	2,200	.018		7.30	.38	.41	8.09	9.15	
	1500	Frames 16' O.C.		2,640	.015		6.20	.32	.35	6.87	7.75	
	1700	Radial arches, 60' clear span, frames 8' O.C.		1,920	.021		6.85	.43	.47	7.75	8.75	
	1800	Frames 16' O.C.		2,880	.014		5.25	.29	.32	5.86	6.65	
	2000	100' clear span, frames 8' O.C.		1,600	.025		7.10	.52	.57	8.19	9.30	
	2100	Frames 16' O.C.		2,400	.017		6.20	.35	.38	6.93	7.85	
	2300	120' clear span, frames 8' O.C.		1,440	.028		9.40	.58	.63	10.61	12	
	2400	Frames 16' O.C.	↓	1,920	.021		8.60	.43	.47	9.50	10.70	
	2600	Bowstring trusses, 20' O.C., 40' clear span	F-3	2,400	.017		4.24	.35	.26	4.85	5.50	
	2700	60' clear span	F-4	3,600	.011		3.81	.23	.25	4.29	4.86	
	2800	100' clear span		4,000	.010		5.40	.21	.23	5.84	6.55	
	2900	120' clear span	↓	3,600	.011		5.80	.23	.25	6.28	7	
	3100	For premium appearance, add to S.F. prices					5%					
	3300	For industrial type, deduct					15%					
	3500	For stain and varnish, add					5%					
	3900	For 3/4" laminations, add to straight					25%					
	4100	Add to curved				↓	15%					
	4300	Alternate pricing method: (use nominal footage of										
	4310	components). Straight beams, camber less than 6"	F-3	3.50	11.429	M.B.F.	2,350	238	175	2,763	3,175	
	4400	Columns, including hardware		2	20		2,525	415	305	3,245	3,800	
	4600	Curved members, radius over 32'		2.50	16		2,575	335	245	3,155	3,675	
	4700	Radius 10' to 32'	↓	3	13.333	↓	2,550	277	204	3,031	3,525	

Figure 1

The complete description provides information that helps you understand what is included in the unit cost. If the quantity of roof trusses has already been determined, then the simple method of using the cost data is to multiply the quantity by the cost shown in the column entitled "Total Incl. O&P."

For example: 50 Trusses x $101 = $5,050

If you are "building an estimate," then simply find the line items in the cost data that describe the material or task whose quantities are developed, and multiply the quantity by the unit cost. If you were starting with trusses, this estimate might move on to sheathing, drip edge, felt paper, asphalt shingles, ridge vent, and cap shingles next.

However, occasionally you may need more information or may want to modify the published information. All the components necessary to alter or modify a cost are available in the columns to the right of the description. In order to develop a unit cost, certain pieces of information are necessary, including who is going to do the work and what equipment is needed, how much work can be done in a set time period, and how much the crew, equipment, and materials will cost.

Simply put, a unit cost is developed like this:

A carpenter gets paid $200 dollars per 8-hour day. That carpenter can install 200 LF of wood trim in an 8-hour day. The wood trim costs $1.00 per LF. The unit cost for this wood trim would be:

$200 per day divided by 200 LF per day equals $1.00 per LF, plus: $1.00 per LF for the material, or $2.00 per LF to supply and install the wood trim.

This formula is the basis for all unit price line items published by RSMeans. Using the truss example again, you can find all the information required to develop the cost in the columns of information provided. The "Crew" column tells us who is going to do the work and what equipment (if any) is required. The "Daily Output" column tells us how much work the crew can do in an 8-hour day. The "Labor-Hours" states how long it takes to install one unit of work (one truss or one linear foot of wood trim, or one SF of roofing). The "Unit" column provides the unit of measure everything found in that particular line item is based on. Finally, the "Material," "Labor," and "Equipment" columns list the costs involved.

Material costs are based on RSMeans' research, as are the labor costs. Labor is derived by dividing the cost per day for the crew by the daily output. Each of the Trades are categorized by individual tradespeople, such as carpenters (abbreviated "Carp"), or as crews (such as "F-6," made up of multiple carpenters, laborers, and equipment operators). The daily costs for each of the trades can be found in the reference section of the book. Equipment costs, also derived by dividing the cost for the equipment by the daily output, are also found in the reference section.

The "Total" column is the mathematical sum of the material, labor and equipment columns. The "Total Incl. O&P" column is the "Total" unit price with overhead and profit added in. An amount equal to 10% is added to the material and equipment costs. Depending on the trades involved, an amount of up to 101.3% is added to the labor costs for Workers' Compensation insurance, taxes and insurance, home office overhead, and profit.

All this information will allow the user of RSMeans data to make any alterations or modifications required. For example, if a quote for roof trusses exceeds the price of materials that RSMeans research indicates, then simply replace the RSMeans price with the quote and recalculate the unit cost.

Conclusion

Professional cost data resources are a reliable way to verify estimates quickly—for both novices and experts. Time and experience will allow you to move faster through the data, find the items you need, and include them within your estimate. As with any tool, the data found in RSMeans may not do everything that you need to complete your estimate, but, used in combination with all the estimating tools at your disposal, the data from RSMeans is an indispensable part of your estimating toolbox.

Index

Notes